KB087280

THIS IS
GRAMMAR

THIS IS GRAMMAR 중급 1

지은이 넥서스영어교육연구소
펴낸이 임상진
펴낸곳 (주)넥서스

출판신고 1992년 4월 3일 제311-2002-2호 2-28
10880 경기도 파주시 지목로 5
Tel (02)330-5500 Fax (02)330-5555

ISBN 979-11-5752-365-8 54740
979-11-5752-362-7 (SET)

가격은 뒤표지에 있습니다.
잘못 만들어진 책은 구입처에서 바꾸어 드립니다.

www.nexusEDU.kr

넥서스영어교육연구소 지음

NEXUS Edu

Preface

To Teachers and Students,

This brand new edition of *This Is Grammar* contains a wide range of engaging exercises designed to improve students' English grammar skills in the areas of speaking and writing. In Korea, middle and high school students have traditionally learned English grammar through rote memorization. We believe, however, that grammar learning is more effectively realized when explicit explanation is paired with practice. *This Is Grammar*(Updated version) provides Korean students with opportunities to practice using English while learning more about the world around them.

The exercises in the workbooks have been specially redesigned to give students more practice producing the target structures in a wide range of natural contexts. The teacher's guide includes additional grammar explanations and notes, comments on usage, and classroom presentation tips.

In sum, *This Is Grammar* provides teachers in Korea with a comprehensive set of materials to help them teach their students English grammar more effectively and with greater ease. It will help beginner to advanced level students improve their English skills in the areas of speaking and writing. We trust you will enjoy using *This Is Grammar* as a classroom textbook or by itself as a self-study aid.

- Christopher Douloff

This Is Grammar 최신개정판은 무조건 외우면서 학습하던 과거의 방법과는 달리, 현실에서 많이 쓰이는 진정성 있는 문장들을 토대로 핵심 문법을 체계적으로 설명하고 있다. 또한, 자연스러운 문맥 안에서 영어의 문장 구조가 습득될 수 있도록 단계별 연습문제와 활동들을 제공하고 있어 초급부터 고급까지의 학습자들이 문법 지식을 바탕으로 말하기와 쓰기 등의 영어 실력을 향상시키는 데 큰 도움을 줄 수 있으리라 기대한다. *This Is Grammar*(최신개정판)가 강의용뿐만 아니라 자습서로서도 훌륭히 그 역할을 해 낼 수 있으리라 믿으며, 학습자들의 영어 실력 향상에 큰 다리 역할을 할 수 있기를 기대한다.

- 집필진 Christopher Douloff, McKathy, Rachel S. L., Jenicia H., Jackie Kim

Series of features
시리즈의 특징

초급
1, 2

기초 문법 강화 + 내신 대비

영어의 기본 구조인 형태(form)와 의미(meaning), 용법(usage) 등을 설명하여 기초적인 문법 지식을 강화할 수 있도록 하였습니다. 다양한 유형의 연습문제를 단계별로 구성하였습니다. 또한, 시험에 자주 등장하는 문법 문제를 Review 및 Review Plus에서 다루고 있어 기본 실력을 강화하고 내신에 대비할 수 있도록 구성하였습니다.

중급
1, 2

문법 요약(Key Point) + 체계적인 문법 설명

Key Point 부분에 도식화 · 도표화하여 한눈에 보기 쉽게 문법을 요약해 놓았습니다. Key Point에는 문법의 기본적인 내용을, FOCUS에는 문법의 상세한 설명을 수록해 놓았습니다. 이를 통해 기초 문법부터 심화 문법까지 체계적으로 습득할 수 있습니다. 또한, 문법 오류 확인 문제부터 문장 완성하기와 문장 바꿔 쓰기 등의 다양한 유형의 연습문제들로 문법 지식을 확실히 다질 수 있도록 구성하였습니다.

고급
1, 2

핵심 문법 설명 + 각종 수험 대비

중 · 고급 영어 학습자들을 대상으로 수능, 텝스, 토플, 토익 등 각종 시험을 완벽하게 대비할 수 있도록 핵심적인 문법 포인트를 분석, 정리하였습니다. 다양하고 진정성 있는 지문들을 통해 풍부한 배경지식을 함께 쌓을 수 있도록 하였습니다. 고급 1권으로는 일목요연하게 정리된 문법으로 수험 완벽 대비를 할 수 있도록 하였고, 그리고 고급 2권으로는 문장 쓰기에서 에세이 쓰기까지의 영작 연습을 통해 기본적인 작문 실력을 향상시킬 수 있도록 구성하였습니다.

Workbook

초급 1, 2, 중급 1, 2, 고급 1 총 5권

별책으로 구성된 Workbook은 원어민이 직접 집필하여 생생한 실생활 영어 표현으로 문장을 구성 하였으며, Unit별 2페이지씩 연습문제를 수록하여 학습한 내용을 다시 한 번 점검하고 확실한 본인의 실력을 쌓을 수 있도록 구성 하였습니다.

Composition and Features
구성과 특징

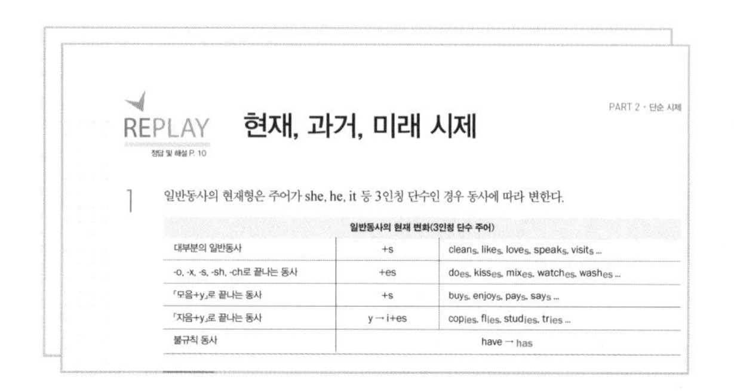

REPLAY 현재, 과거, 미래 시제

PART 2 · 단순 시제

정답 및 해설 P. 10

1 일반동사의 현재형은 주어가 she, he, it 등 3인칭 단수인 경우 동사에 따라 변한다.

일반동사의 현재 변화(3인칭 단수 주어)		
대부분의 일반동사	+s	cleans, likes, loves, speaks, visits ...
-o, -x, -s, -sh, -ch로 끝나는 동사	+es	does, kisses, mixes, watches, washes ...
「모음+y」로 끝나는 동사	+s	buys, enjoys, pays, says ...
「자음+y」로 끝나는 동사	y → i+es	copies, flies, studies, tries ...
불규칙 동사	have → has	

• **REPLAY** 문법의 기본 형태와 의미, 그리고 쓰임을 간단히 요약하였으며 Check-up을 통해 기초 문법을 다질 수 있습니다.

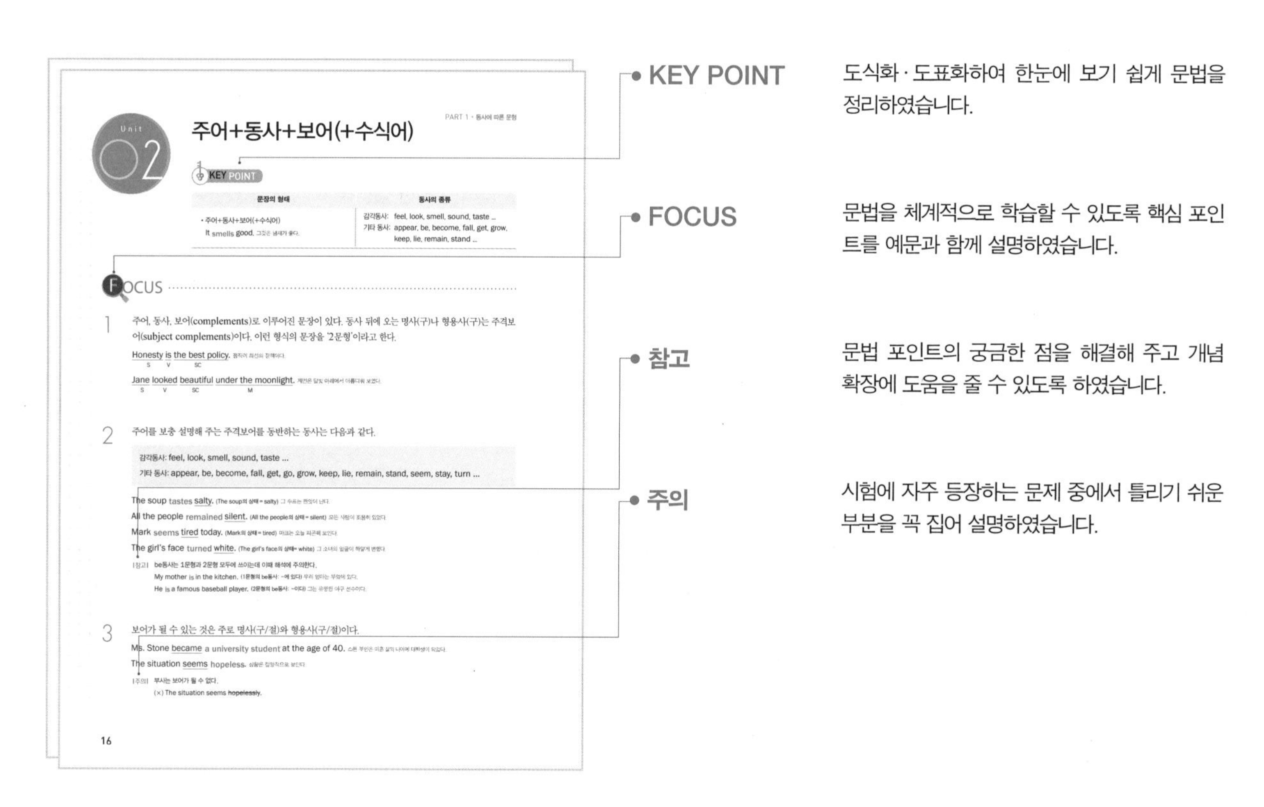

Unit 02 주어+동사+보어(+수식어)

PART 1 · 동사에 따른 문형

KEY POINT

문장의 형태	동사의 종류
• 주어+동사+보어(+수식어) It smells good.	감각동사: feel, look, smell, sound, taste ... 기타 동사: appear, be, become, fall, get, grow, keep, lie, remain, stand ...

FOCUS

1 주어, 동사, 보어(complements)로 이루어진 문장이 있다. 동사 뒤에 오는 명사(구)나 형용사(구)는 주격보어(subject complements)이다. 이런 형식의 문장을 '2문형'이라고 한다.

Honesty is the best policy.

Jane looked beautiful under the moonlight.

2 주어를 보충 설명해 주는 주격보어를 동반하는 동사는 다음과 같다.

감각동사: feel, look, smell, sound, taste ...
기타 동사: appear, be, become, fall, get, go, grow, keep, lie, remain, stand, seem, stay, turn ...

The soup tastes salty.
All the people remained silent.
Mark seems tired today.
The girl's face turned white.

|참고| be동사는 1문형과 2문형 모두에 쓰이는데 이때 해석에 주의한다.
My mother is in the kitchen.
He is a famous baseball player.

3 보어가 될 수 있는 것은 주로 명사(구/절)와 형용사(구/절)이다.

Ms. Stone became a university student at the age of 40.
The situation seems hopeless.

|주의| 부사는 보어가 될 수 없다.
(×) The situation seems hopelessly.

16

• **KEY POINT** 도식화·도표화하여 한눈에 보기 쉽게 문법을 정리하였습니다.

• **FOCUS** 문법을 체계적으로 학습할 수 있도록 핵심 포인트를 예문과 함께 설명하였습니다.

• **참고** 문법 포인트의 궁금한 점을 해결해 주고 개념 확장에 도움을 줄 수 있도록 하였습니다.

• **주의** 시험에 자주 등장하는 문제 중에서 틀리기 쉬운 부분을 꼭 집어 설명하였습니다.

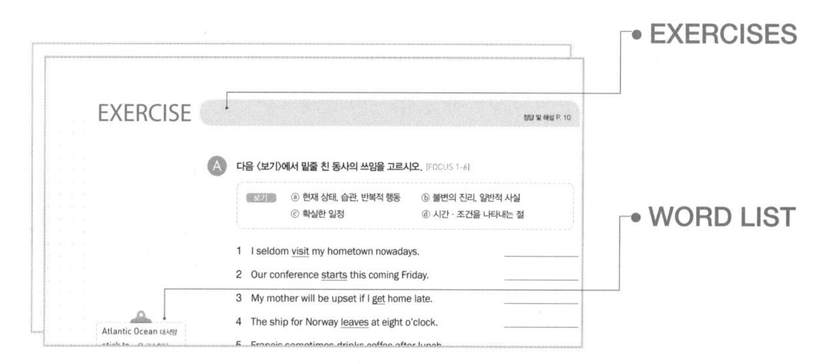

EXERCISE

정답 및 해설 P. 10

A 다음 〈보기〉에서 밑줄 친 동사의 쓰임을 고르시오. [FOCUS 1-6]

보기 ⓐ 현재 상태, 습관, 반복적 행동 ⓑ 불변의 진리, 일반적 사실 ⓒ 확실한 일정 ⓓ 시간·조건을 나타내는 절

1 I seldom visit my hometown nowadays.
2 Our conference starts this coming Friday.
3 My mother will be upset if I get home late.
4 The ship for Norway leaves at eight o'clock.

Atlantic Ocean 대서양

• **EXERCISES** 고르기, 빈칸 채우기, 문장 쓰기, 영작하기 등 다양한 유형의 연습문제들로 체계적인 학습을 할 수 있습니다.

• **WORD LIST** 문제에 나오는 단어들을 뜻과 함께 정리하여 제공함으로써 문법 학습에 집중할 수 있도록 도움을 줍니다.

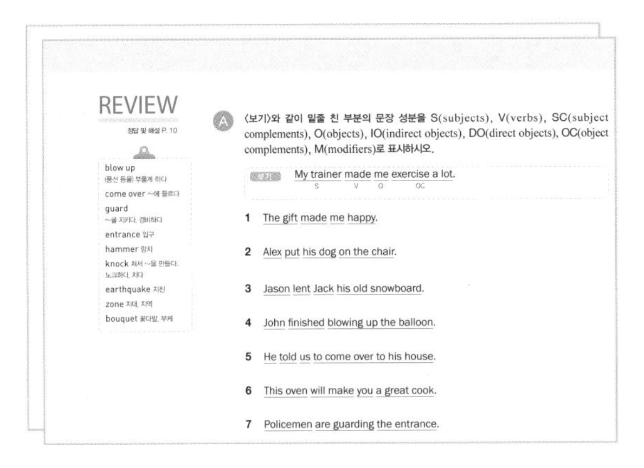

REVIEW

정답 및 해설 P. 10

blow up (풍선 등을) 부풀게 하다
come over ~에 들르다
guard ~을 지키다, 경비하다
entrance 입구
hammer 망치
knock 쳐서 ~을 만들다; 노크하다, 치다
earthquake 지진
zone 지대, 지역
bouquet 꽃다발, 부케

A 〈보기〉와 같이 밑줄 친 부분의 문장 성분을 S(subjects), V(verbs), SC(subject complements), O(objects), IO(indirect objects), DO(direct objects), OC(object complements), M(modifiers)로 표시하시오.

보기 My trainer made me exercise a lot.
S V O OC

1 The gift made me happy.
2 Alex put his dog on the chair.
3 Jason lent Jack his old snowboard.
4 John finished blowing up the balloon.
5 He told us to come over to his house.
6 This oven will make you a great cook.
7 Policemen are guarding the entrance.

• REVIEW

문장 완성하기, 문장 고쳐 쓰기, 문장 배열하기 등 PART에서 배운 문법을 통합하여 학습할 수 있습니다.

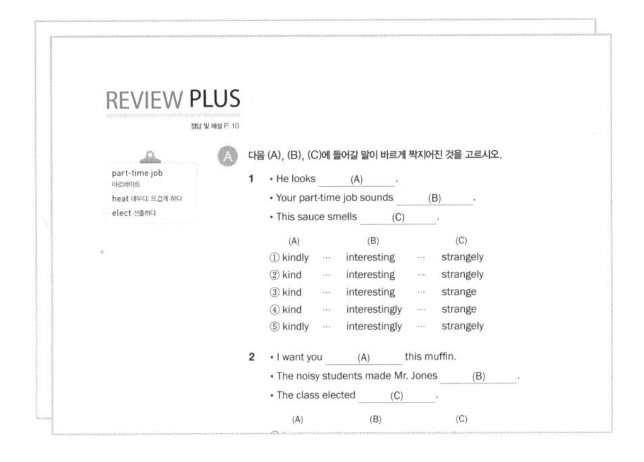

REVIEW PLUS

정답 및 해설 P. 10

part-time job 아르바이트
heat 데우다; 뜨겁게 하다
elect 선출하다

A 다음 (A), (B), (C)에 들어갈 말이 바르게 짝지어진 것을 고르시오.

1 • He looks ___(A)___.
• Your part-time job sounds ___(B)___.
• This sauce smells ___(C)___.

	(A)		(B)		(C)
①	kindly	…	interesting	…	strangely
②	kind	…	interesting	…	strangely
③	kind	…	interesting	…	strange
④	kind	…	interestingly	…	strange
⑤	kindly	…	interestingly	…	strangely

2 • I want you ___(A)___ this muffin.
• The noisy students made Mr. Jones ___(B)___.
• The class elected ___(C)___.

(A) (B) (C)

• REVIEW PLUS

어법상 올바른 문장 고르기, 어색한 대화 찾기, 지문에서 문법 오류 찾아 고치기 등의 활동으로 학습한 문법을 적용하여 응용력을 키울 수 있습니다.

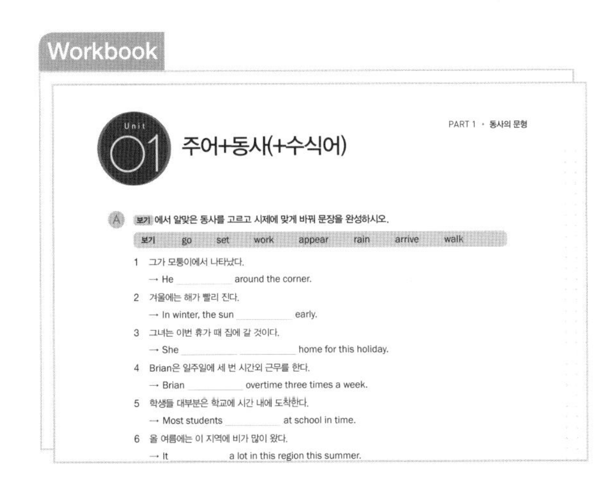

Workbook

Unit 01 주어+동사(+수식어)

PART 1 • 동사의 문형

A 보기 에서 알맞은 동사를 고르고 시제에 맞게 바꿔 문장을 완성하시오.

보기 go set work appear rain arrive walk

1 그가 모퉁이에서 나타났다.
→ He ________ around the corner.
2 겨울에는 해가 빨리 진다.
→ In winter, the sun ________ early.
3 그녀는 이번 휴가 때 집에 갈 것이다.
→ She ________ ________ home for this holiday.
4 Brian은 일주일에 세 번 시간외 근무를 한다.
→ Brian ________ overtime three times a week.
5 학생들 대부분은 학교에 시간 내에 도착한다.
→ Most students ________ at school in time.
6 올 여름에는 이 지역에 비가 많이 왔다.
→ It ________ a lot in this region this summer.

• UNIT EXERCISES

UNIT별로 2페이지에 걸쳐 문장, 대화, 지문 등 다양한 유형의 연습문제를 수록하였습니다. 공부한 내용을 제대로 이해하였는지 Workbook을 통해 확인할 수 있습니다.

Contents 차례

중급 1

Contents 차례

중급 2

PREP PART

문장의 구성
Sentence Structures

품사

품사	예시
Noun 명사	people, animals, things, happiness ...
Pronoun 대명사	I, my, me, mine, myself ...
Adjective 형용사	good, bad, fast, slow, many, much ...
Adverb 부사	very, well, patiently, fast, slowly ...
Verb 동사	bite, plant, wait, eat, exercise ...
Preposition 전치사	in, on, at, from, in front of, to, for ...
Conjunction 접속사	and, but, or, when, because, if ...
Interjection 감탄사	wow, oops, oh no, ouch ...

1 품사(parts of speech)란 문장을 구성하는 각 단어를 기능과 의미에 따라 모아 놓은 것이다. 영어에는 명사, 대명사, 형용사, 부사, 동사, 전치사, 접속사, 감탄사의 8품사가 있다.

Wow!	He	made	very	delicious	cookies	and	pies	in	the	kitchen.
감탄사	대명사	동사	부사	형용사	명사	접속사	명사	전치사	정관사	명사

Wow! He made very delicious cookies and pies in the kitchen.
와! 그가 부엌에서 아주 맛있는 쿠키와 파이를 만들었어.

2 명사(nouns)는 생물이나 무생물의 이름 또는 추상적인 개념 등을 나타내는 말이다.

I think **love** is the greatest **power** known to **man.** 나는 사랑이 인류에게 알려진 가장 강력한 힘이라고 생각한다.

You should visit the **information center** in **Seattle.** 시애틀에 있는 정보 센터를 방문해 보세요.

Jason usually takes his **dog** to the **park** near his **house.** 제이슨은 보통 자신의 개를 집 근처의 공원으로 데리고 간다.

Aerobic **exercise** is good for your **heart** and **lungs.** 유산소 운동은 심장과 폐에 좋다.

3 대명사(pronouns)는 명사를 대신하여 쓰는 말로, 인칭, 소유, 재귀, 지시, 부정대명사 등이 있다.

I lent **my** robot to **my** friend, Greg, and **he** lent **it** to **another one** of **our** friends, Gary.
나는 로봇을 내 친구 그레그에게 빌려주었고, 그는 그것을 우리의 또 다른 친구 게리에게 빌려주었다.

Sharon stood in front of a row of dresses, and **she** picked the priciest **one** among **them.**
샤론은 일렬로 늘어선 옷 앞에 섰고 그중에서 가장 값비싼 것을 골랐다.

Matthew studied Spanish by **himself**, but **he** can speak **it** fluently.
매튜는 스페인어를 독학했지만 아주 유창하게 말할 수 있다.

4 형용사(adjectives)는 명사나 대명사의 성질, 상태, 모양을 설명하는 말이다.

English is an **international** language. 영어는 국제적인 언어이다.

Many people considered Rachel one of the **finest** figure skaters.
많은 사람들은 레이첼을 최고의 피겨 스케이팅 선수 중 한 명이라고 생각했다.

5 부사(adverbs)는 때, 장소, 방법 등을 나타내는 말로, 형용사나 동사, 다른 부사, 문장 전체를 수식한다.

Our team won the game **easily**. 우리 팀이 그 경기를 쉽게 이겼다.

He answered all the questions **very honestly**. 그는 모든 질문에 매우 솔직하게 대답했다.

Frankly, I don't like seafood. 솔직히 나는 해산물을 좋아하지 않는다.

6 동사(verbs)는 주어의 동작이나 상태를 나타내는 말이다.

Jonathan **is** the tallest boy in the class. 조나단은 반에서 가장 키가 큰 소년이다.

Mike **grew** up to be an Olympic weightlifter. 마이크는 자라서 올림픽 역도 선수가 되었다.

You **should finish** your homework before you **go out** and **play**. 너는 밖에 나가 놀기 전에 숙제를 끝마쳐야 한다.

7 전치사(prepositions)는 주로 명사나 대명사 앞에 와서 그 어구에 의미를 더해준다.

Please show me a postcard **from** New York. 뉴욕에서 온 엽서를 제게 보여 주세요.

The flight **to** Cairo departs **at** 12:30. 카이로행 비행기는 12시 30분에 출발한다.

The bus stop is right **in front of** the post office. 버스 정류장은 우체국 바로 앞에 있다.

8 접속사(conjunctions)는 단어와 단어, 구와 구, 절과 절을 연결하는 말이다.

The knives **and** forks are in the drawer. (단어 - 단어) 칼과 포크는 서랍 안에 있다.

I like taking pictures **and** listening to music. (구 - 구) 나는 사진 찍는 것과 음악 듣는 것을 좋아한다.

I really enjoyed the class, **but** I couldn't quite understand some parts of it. (절 - 절)
그 수업은 정말 재미있었지만, 어떤 부분은 잘 이해할 수 없었다.

9 감탄사(interjections)는 말하는 사람의 감정이나 느낌, 놀람 등을 표현하는 말로 주로 구어체에서 쓴다.

Oh dear! Does it hurt? 맙소사! 아프니?

Well, what did he say? 음, 그가 뭐라고 말했어?

Oops, sorry about that. 이런, 미안해요.

구와 절

단어	〈	구	〈	절
meal		a delicious meal		Paul cooked us a delicious meal last night. (Paul: S, cooked: V)
식사		맛있는 식사		어젯밤에 폴이 우리에게 맛있는 음식을 요리해 줬다.

FOCUS

1 두 개 이상의 단어가 모여 명사, 형용사, 부사 등 하나의 품사 역할을 하는 것을 구(phrases)라고 한다. 이때 구는 주어와 동사를 포함하지 않는다.

to get up early 일찍 일어나는 것

the Dalmatian **on the sofa** 소파 위에 있는 달마티안 개

for two hours 두 시간 동안

2 명사구는 명사처럼 주어, 목적어, 보어의 역할을 한다.

Playing a musical instrument is not easy. (주어) 악기를 연주하는 것은 쉽지 않다.

I've just finished **writing my final report.** (목적어) 나는 기말 보고서 작성을 막 끝마쳤다.

To see is **to believe.** (보어) 보는 것이 믿는 것이다.

3 형용사구는 형용사처럼 명사를 수식하는 역할을 한다.

The girl **standing at the door** is my little sister. 문 앞에 서 있는 소녀는 내 여동생이다.

4 부사구는 부사처럼 형용사, 동사, 다른 부사, 문장 전체를 수식하는 역할을 하며, 시간, 장소, 이유, 방법, 목적, 결과, 정도, 양보 등을 나타낸다.

I'll meet you **in an hour.** 한 시간 후에 보자.

The resort is located **on the coast.** 그 리조트는 해안가에 있다.

5 절(clauses)은 주어와 동사를 포함하고 하나의 품사 역할을 하며, 명사절, 형용사절, 부사절 등이 있다.

That(s) is(v) / **what I(s′) wanted(v′) to say.** (명사절_보어) 그게 내가 말하고 싶었던 거야.

Heaven(s) helps(v) those / **who(s′) help(v′) themselves.** (형용사절_those 수식) 하늘은 스스로 돕는 자를 돕는다.

Our flight to New York(s) was canceled(v) / **because the weather(s′) was(v′) so awful.** (부사절_이유)
우리의 뉴욕행 비행기는 날씨가 너무 나빠서 취소되었다.

문장 성분

The teacher thought his students brilliant.
S V O OC
그 선생님은 생각했다 자신의 학생들을 명석하다고
→ 그 선생님은 자신의 학생들이 명석하다고 생각했다.

FOCUS

1 주어(subjects)는 '~은/는, ~이/가'로 해석되는 문장의 주체로 주로 문장 앞에 온다.

Whales are mammals. (명사_주어) 고래는 포유류이다.

They resemble each other. (대명사_주어) 그들은 서로 닮았다.

Memorizing Chinese characters is not easy. (명사구_주어) 한자 암기는 쉽지 않다.

That the woman is a genius is true. (명사절_주어) 그 여자가 천재라는 것은 사실이다.

2 동사(verbs)는 주어의 동작이나 상태 등을 나타내는 말로, be동사, 일반동사, 조동사가 있다.

Ally is very sensitive to cold weather. (be동사) 엘리는 추운 날씨에 매우 민감하다.

I decided to start exercising. (일반동사) 나는 운동을 시작하기로 결심했다.

May I use your mobile phone? (조동사) 당신의 휴대 전화를 사용해도 될까요?

3 목적어(objects)는 동사가 나타내는 행위의 대상이 되는 말이다.

I like cake. (명사_목적어) 나는 케이크를 좋아한다.

Chris loves you. (대명사_목적어) 크리스는 너를 사랑한다.

She expected to visit Turkey last summer. (명사구_목적어) 그녀는 지난여름에 터키에 갈 거라 기대했었다.

They didn't believe that she was innocent. (명사절_목적어) 그들은 그녀가 결백하다는 것을 믿지 않았다.

4 보어(complements)는 주어나 목적어의 성질, 상태를 보충 설명해 주는 말로, 주격보어와 목적격보어가 있다.

The food smelled strange, but it tasted good. (주격보어) 그 음식은 냄새는 이상해도 맛은 좋았다.
S SC S SC

The teacher told Kate to study hard. (목적격보어) 선생님께서 케이트에게 열심히 공부하라고 말씀하셨다.
O OC

5 문장을 구성하는 기본 4대 요소는 앞서 설명한 주어, 동사, 목적어, 보어이고, 그 외에 문장을 구성하는 요소에는 부가적인 정보를 제공해 주는 역할을 하는 수식어(modifiers)가 있다. 명사와 대명사를 수식하는 형용사(구)와 동사, 형용사, 다른 부사, 문장 전체를 수식하는 부사(구)가 이에 해당한다.

The book on your desk was very interesting. (명사 수식_형용사구) 네 책상 위에 있는 그 책은 정말 재미있었다.

Sarah met Justin at the subway station. (장소 부사구) 사라는 지하철역에서 저스틴을 만났다.

PART 1

동사에 따른 문형
Sentence Patterns

주어+동사(+수식어)

문장의 형태	동사의 종류
• 주어+동사(+수식어) Tim runs (quickly). 팀은 (빨리) 달린다.	appear, arrive, come, go, rain, rise, run, walk ...
• 주어+be동사+수식어 He is in the gym. 그는 체육관에 있다.	be동사

1

주어(subjects)와 동사(verbs)만으로 의미가 통하는 경우가 있다. 이때 수식어(modifiers)가 문장의 앞이나 뒤에 나오기도 한다. 이런 형식의 문장을 '1문형'이라고 한다.

The sun (S) is shining (V). 태양이 빛나고 있다.

In a few minutes (M), my sister (S) will come (V). 몇 분 후에 내 여동생이 올 것이다.

In a few minutes (M), my sister (S) will come (V) with her friend (M). 몇 분 후에 내 여동생이 친구와 함께 올 것이다.

2

동사 뒤에 반드시 장소나 시간 등의 수식어가 와야 의미가 통하는 경우가 있다.

My classroom (S) is (be동사) in the next building (M). 우리 교실은 옆 건물에 있다.

The sunglasses (S) were (be동사) on the table (M). 선글라스는 탁자 위에 있었다.

|참고| There나 Here가 문장 앞에 쓰여 '~이 있다'라는 뜻의 1문형을 만든다. 이때 주어는 be동사 뒤에 나오므로 주어와 동사의 수 일치에 주의한다.

「There/Here+be동사+주어(+수식어)」 ~이 있다/여기에 ~이 있다

There is a restroom over there. 저쪽에 화장실이 있습니다.

There are many people in the shopping mall. 쇼핑몰에 많은 사람이 있다.

3

「주어+동사(+수식어)」의 형태로 쓸 경우, 해석에 유의해야 하는 동사들이 있다.

count 중요하다	do 충분하다	last 지속되다
matter 중요하다, 문제가 되다	pay 수지가 맞다, 이익이 되다	work 작동하다, 효과가 있다

First impressions of people **count**. 사람들의 첫인상이 중요하다.

A glass of cold water will **do**. 찬물 한 잔이면 충분할 것이다.

This bad weather won't **last**. 이 궂은 날씨는 오래가지 않을 것이다.

It doesn't **matter**. 그것은 문제가 되지 않는다.

Crime doesn't **pay**. 범죄는 이익이 되지 않는다.

This copy machine doesn't **work**. 이 복사기는 작동하지 않는다.

EXERCISES

정답 및 해설 P. 1

〈보기〉와 같이 밑줄 친 부분의 문장 성분을 S(subjects), V(verbs), M(modifiers)으로 표시하시오.

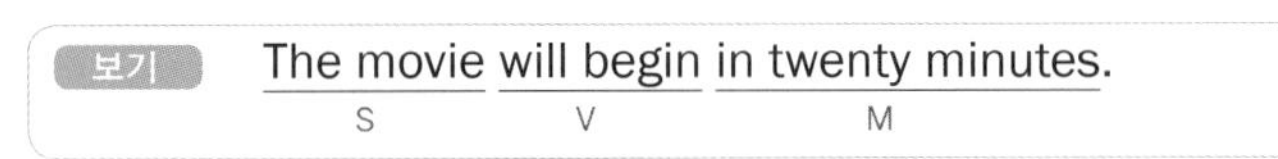

1 My friends are in the library.

2 The pharmacy is across from the hospital.

3 In ten minutes, the cell phone shop will be closed.

4 The swimming pool is on the fifth floor of the hotel.

5 The plants are growing nicely in the new greenhouse.

6 My mother exercises in the park Monday through Friday.

7 The rehearsal will be in the gymnasium tomorrow afternoon.

pharmacy 약국
greenhouse 온실
rehearsal 리허설, 시연
gymnasium 체육관

B 밑줄 친 수식어 중 문장 성립에 필수적인 것을 고르시오.

1 ① I was in the library.
② They come from Spain.
③ My cousins will arrive soon.
④ The moon rises at 7:30 p.m.

2 ① It will rain in Seoul.
② The cat is on my desk.
③ They are walking in the park.
④ He went to the supermarket.

come from ~ 출신이다
rise (해 등이) 뜨다, 일어나다

C 〈보기〉에서 알맞은 동사를 골라 빈칸에 써넣으시오.

보기 matter do pay work lasted counts

1 Every minute ________.

2 The movie ________ nearly three hours.

3 Kindness sometimes does not ________.

4 This room won't ________ for three people.

5 The metal detector didn't ________ properly.

6 You can go or stay. It doesn't ________ to me.

matter 중요하다, 문제가 되다
do 충분하다
pay 보답을 받다; 이익이 되다, 수지가 맞다
work 작동하다
last 지속되다
count 중요하다
nearly 거의
kindness 친절
metal detector 금속 탐지기
properly 제대로; 적당히

주어+동사+주격보어(+수식어)

문장의 형태	동사의 종류
• 주어+동사+보어(+수식어) It **smells** good. 그것은 냄새가 좋다.	감각동사: feel, look, smell, sound, taste ... 기타 동사: appear, be, become, fall, get, grow, keep, lie, remain, stand ...

1

주어, 동사, 보어(complements)로 이루어진 문장이 있다. 동사 뒤에 오는 명사(구)나 형용사(구)는 주격보어(subject complements)이다. 이런 형식의 문장을 '2문형'이라고 한다.

Honesty(S) is(V) the best policy(SC). 정직이 최선의 정책이다.

Jane(S) looked(V) beautiful(SC) under the moonlight(M). 제인은 달빛 아래에서 아름다워 보였다.

2

주어를 보충 설명해 주는 주격보어를 동반하는 동사는 다음과 같다.

감각동사: feel, look, smell, sound, taste ...
기타 동사: appear, be, become, fall, get, go, grow, keep, lie, remain, stand, seem, stay, turn ...

The soup **tastes** salty. (The soup의 상태 = salty) 그 수프는 짠맛이 난다.

All the people **remained** silent. (All the people의 상태 = silent) 모든 사람이 조용히 있었다.

Mark **seems** tired today. (Mark의 상태 = tired) 마크는 오늘 피곤해 보인다.

The girl's face **turned** white. (The girl's face의 상태= white) 그 소녀의 얼굴이 하얗게 변했다.

|참고| be동사는 1문형과 2문형 모두에 쓰이는데 이때 해석에 주의한다.
My mother **is** in the kitchen. (1문형의 be동사: ~에 있다) 우리 엄마는 부엌에 있다.
He **is** a famous baseball player. (2문형의 be동사: ~이다) 그는 유명한 야구 선수이다.

3

보어가 될 수 있는 것은 주로 명사(구/절)와 형용사(구)이다.

Ms. Stone became **a university student** at the age of 40. 스톤 부인은 마흔 살의 나이에 대학생이 되었다.

The situation seems **hopeless.** 상황은 절망적으로 보인다.

|주의| 부사는 보어가 될 수 없다.
(×) The situation seems ~~hopelessly~~.

4 smell, look, feel, taste, sound 등의 감각동사 뒤에는 형용사 보어가 온다.

Skunks smell **terrible.** 스컹크는 냄새가 지독하다.

She looks **beautiful** in that black dress. 그녀는 그 검정 드레스를 입으니 아름다워 보인다.

I feel **sick** today. 나는 오늘 아프다.

The cake in this bakery tastes **good.** 이 빵집의 케이크는 맛있다.

Your opinion sounds **fun.** 네 의견은 재미있게 들린다.

|주의| 1. 감각동사 뒤에는 바로 명사 보어가 오지 않는다.

(×) Skunks smell ~~terribleness~~.
(×) She looks ~~beauty~~ in that black dress.

2. 감각동사는 「감각동사+형용사」, 「감각동사 like+명사」의 형태로 쓰인다.

He **looked** angry all day. 그는 온종일 화나 보였다.
It **looks like** magic. 그것은 마술처럼 보인다.
It **smells** sweet. 그것은 달콤한 냄새가 난다.
It **smells like** honey. 그것은 꿀 향기가 난다.

5 동사와 형용사 주격보어를 함께 쓰는 관용 표현에 주의한다.

come true 실현되다
go bad (음식 등이) 상하다
grow old 나이가 들어가다
run short 부족하다
fall asleep 잠이 들다
go wrong 잘못되다
keep silent 침묵하다, 입 다물고 있다
turn pale 창백해지다

Your dreams will **come true** someday. 언젠가 너의 꿈이 실현될 것이다.

The baby **fell asleep** just now. 그 아기가 이제 막 잠들었다.

Don't drink the milk. It has **gone bad.** 그 우유를 마시지 마. 상했어.

Everything **went wrong.** 모든 것이 잘못되었다.

As you **grow old**, you get wiser. 나이가 들어감에 따라 더욱 현명해진다.

He asked me to **keep silent** about it. 그는 내게 그것에 대해 이야기하지 말아달라고 부탁했다.

We're **running short** of gas. 우리는 연료가 떨어져가고 있어.

They **turned pale** at the news. 그들은 그 소식을 듣고 창백해졌다.

EXERCISES

정답 및 해설 P. 1

local 지방의, 지역적인
keep silent 침묵하다
as a result 결과적으로
remain ~으로 남아 있다
unsolved 해결되지 않은
freely 자유롭게, 방해받지 않고
elected 선출된
midterm test 중간고사

〈보기〉와 같이 밑줄 친 부분의 문장 성분을 S(subjects), V(verbs), SC(subject complements), M(modifiers)으로 표시하시오.

She is a teacher at the local middle school.
S V SC M

1 The boys kept silent.

2 The gentleman looked happy after the meal.

3 She became the CEO of the company in 2014.

4 As a result, their problems remained unsolved.

5 The man became the first freely elected president of the country.

6 Diana didn't seem happy with the results of the midterm test.

calm 침착한
grow ~이 되다; 기르다; 자라다
fashionable 유행을 따르는, 유행하는
professional 본업으로 하는; 전문직의
fridge 냉장고
sour 신맛이 나는

B ( ) 안에서 가장 알맞은 것을 고르시오.

1 They remained (calm / calmly).

2 It is growing (dark / darkly) outside.

3 Christine looks (beautiful / beautifully).

4 She seems very (fashionable / fashionably).

5 The girl became (professionally / a professional writer).

6 The milk in the fridge tastes (sour / sourly), so don't drink it.

7 It's getting (dark / darkly), so we need to go home right now.

cheerful 명랑한
herbal medicine 한약
bitter 쓴

( ) 안에서 가장 알맞은 것을 고르시오.

1 You look like (handsome / your father).

2 The cheese smells (strange / strangeness).

3 Her voice sounded (cheerful / cheerfulness).

4 I felt (sad / sadness) after watching the movie.

5 He looked (angry / anger) when I told him the truth.

6 This Korean herbal medicine tastes (bitter / bitterness).

D 〈보기〉에서 알맞은 것을 골라 빈칸에 써넣으시오.

보기			
fall asleep	grow old	come true	go bad
ran short	kept silent	went wrong	turn pale

1 We ________________ of office supplies.

2 You will gain lots of experience as you ________________.

3 I just ________________ because I didn't know what to say.

4 I hope I am able to ________________ as soon as the plane takes off.

5 If you keep pursuing your dream, it will ________________.

6 I could never be a doctor because I ________________ at the sight of blood.

7 All of a sudden, everything ________________, and the space shuttle exploded.

8 Let's not buy so many vegetables. They'll ________________ if we don't eat them all.

office supply 사무용품
take off 이륙하다
at the sight of ~을 보고
all of a sudden 갑자기
space shuttle 우주 왕복선
explode 폭발하다

E 밑줄 친 부분이 맞지 않다면 바르게 고치시오.

1 The kids kept quiet.

2 She felt very coldly.

3 Her voice was sharp.

4 The baby seems sadly.

5 He rarely remains calmly.

6 She appeared very tiredly.

7 The pizza smelled so well.

8 The soldiers stood straightly.

9 He will become a great doctor.

10 His motive remained a mystery.

11 The kids are growing impatiently.

12 The meatball spaghetti went badly.

13 The food at that restaurant always tastes a bit salt.

14 My mother looked happiness when we gave her the gift.

rarely 거의 ~않다
straightly 똑바로
motive 진의; 동기
impatiently 초조하게

주어+동사+목적어(+수식어)

문장의 형태	동사의 종류
• 주어+동사+목적어(+수식어) I like jazz music very much. 나는 재즈 음악을 무척 좋아한다.	answer, discuss, enter, explain, marry, mention, like, reach ...
• 주어+동사+목적어+수식어 She put it on the shelf. 그녀는 그것을 선반에 놓았다.	lay, provide, put ...

1

주어, 동사, 목적어(objects)로 이루어진 문장이 있다. 이런 형식의 문장을 '3문형'이라고 한다.

Yumi(S) loves(V) chocolate(O). 유미는 초콜릿을 좋아한다.

A bad workman(S) blames(V) his tools(O). 서투른 일꾼이 연장만 나무란다.

|참고| 목적어를 수반하는 동사를 '타동사'라 하고, 목적어를 수반하지 않는 동사를 '자동사'라 한다.

2

주어, 동사, 목적어, 수식어로 이루어진 문장이 있다.

Her father(S) laid(V) his hand(O) on her shoulder(M). 그녀의 아버지는 그녀의 어깨에 손을 올려놓았다.

The teacher(S) put(V) the students' reports(O) on the table(M). 선생님은 학생들의 보고서를 테이블 위에 놓았다.

3

명사, 명사구, 명사절 등은 목적어가 될 수 있다.

I really need **a break.** (명사_목적어) 나는 정말로 휴식이 필요해요.

He wanted **to hold her hand.** (명사구_목적어) 그는 그녀의 손을 잡기를 원했다.

They believed **that he didn't tell a lie.** (명사절_목적어) 그들은 그가 거짓말을 하지 않았다고 믿었다.

4

목적어는 주로 '~을/를'이라고 해석하지만, '~을/를'로 해석하지 않더라도 다음과 같은 경우 전치사를 넣지 않도록 주의해야 한다.

Alex **married** Cindy in 2014. (marry ~~with~~) 알렉스는 2014년에 신디와 결혼했다.

I **explained** the situation. (explain ~~about~~) 나는 그 상황에 대해 설명했다.

The students **answered** the questions. (answer ~~to~~) 학생들은 그 질문에 답했다.

The twins **resemble** their mother. (resemble ~~with~~) 쌍둥이는 자신들의 어머니와 닮았다.

They **entered** the classroom. (enter ~~into~~) 그들은 교실에 들어갔다.

We **discussed** the economic crisis. (discuss ~~about~~) 우리는 경제 위기에 대해 토론했다.

We **attend** middle school. (attend ~~to~~) 우리는 중학교에 다닌다.

He **mentioned** her many times. (mention ~~about~~) 그는 그녀에 대해 여러 번 언급했다.

EXERCISES

정답 및 해설 P. 2

〈보기〉와 같이 밑줄 친 부분의 문장 성분을 S(subjects), V(verbs), O(objects), SC(subject complements), M(modifiers)로 표시하시오.

1 I met Nick in the library yesterday.

2 She didn't mention him all evening.

3 John suddenly appeared in the doorway.

4 Ben looked cute in his Halloween costume.

5 I had a very strange dream about you last night.

6 Your feet smell terrible! You had better wash them.

7 Your brother's old leather jacket fits you perfectly.

8 They conducted a survey to learn about consumer needs.

9 I know that he will accept my offer in the end.

10 You look exhausted! So, did you finish the work completely?

doorway 현관, 출입구
costume 의상, 복장
fit ~에 어울리다; ~에 적합하다
conduct a survey 설문조사를 하다
need 요구; 필요
exhausted 지친

B 문장을 읽고, 어색한 부분을 바르게 고치시오.

1 People often tell me that I resemble with my mother.

2 I answered to the phone quickly, but they had already hung up.

3 My brother Paul married with Jiyoung three years ago in Korea.

4 I'm very interested in your idea. Let's discuss about it over dinner.

5 The teacher explained about the rules of the game to the children.

6 Before you enter into the country, you must have a valid passport.

7 Over forty thousand people attended to the funeral of Cardinal Kim.

hang up 전화를 끊다
be interested in ~에 관심이 있다
valid 유효한
funeral 장례식
cardinal 추기경

주어+동사+간접목적어+직접목적어

문장의 형태	
주어+수여동사(주다/해주다)+간접목적어+직접목적어	
• S+V+IO+DO → S+V+DO+ to +IO give, send, show, teach ...	I **gave** my classmates some cookies. → I **gave** some cookies **to** my classmates. 나는 학급 친구들에게 약간의 쿠키를 주었다.
• S+V+IO+DO → S+V+DO+ for +IO build, buy, cook, get, make ...	He **built** his mother a house. → He **built** a house for his mother. 그는 어머니에게 집을 지어 주었다.
• S+V+IO+DO → S+V+DO+ of +IO ask	They **asked** my family some questions. → They **asked** some questions **of** my family. 그들은 나의 가족에게 몇 가지 질문을 했다.

FOCUS

1 주어, 동사, 간접목적어(indirect objects)와 직접목적어(direct objects)로 이루어진 문장이 있다. 이런 형식의 문장을 '4문형'이라고 한다.

My father(S) gave(V) me(IO) a new calendar(DO). 우리 아버지가 나에게 새 달력을 주었다.

She(S) bought(V) her daughter(IO) a pair of inline skates(DO). 그녀는 딸에게 인라인 스케이트를 사 주었다.

They(S) asked(V) me(IO) the way to the subway station(DO). 그들은 나에게 지하철역으로 가는 길을 물어보았다.

|참고| 간접목적어와 직접목적어를 필요로 하는 동사를 '수여동사'라고 한다.

2 수여동사가 있는 문장에서 간접목적어는 '~에게', 직접목적어는 '~을/를'로 해석한다. 간접목적어와 직접목적어의 자리를 바꿔 4문형을 3문형으로 만들 수 있는데 이때는 목적어 사이에 전치사(to/for/of)를 넣는다.

My grandmother lent me her shawl. (S+V+IO+DO) 우리 할머니가 나에게 숄을 빌려주었다.

→ My grandmother lent **her shawl** to **me**. (S+V+O+M)

I bought my sister a beautiful skirt. (S+V+IO+DO) 나는 여동생에게 아름다운 치마를 사 주었다.

→ I bought **a beautiful skirt** for **my sister**. (S+V+O+M)

He asked me a difficult question. (S+V+IO+DO) 그는 나에게 어려운 질문을 했다.

→ He asked **a difficult question** of **me**. (S+V+O+M)

3 문장 전환 시 전치사 to를 쓰는 수여동사는 bring, give, send, show, teach, tell, write, hand 등이다.

That accident **brought** us some luck. 그 사고는 우리에게 약간의 행운을 가져다주었다.

→ That accident **brought** some luck **to** us.

A kind woman **gave** me the book. 어떤 친절한 여자가 나에게 그 책을 주었다.

→ A kind woman **gave** the book **to** me.

| 참고 | 동사마다 to 또는 for가 절대적으로 정해져 있는 것은 아니다. 예를 들어 bring 같은 동사는 '~을 위해서(많은 노력이나 수고를 포함)'라는 의미가 강할 경우 to 대신에 for를 쓸 수 있다. to 또는 for 전치사와 함께 쓰는 동사를 알려준 것은 대부분의 경우에 제시한 동사와 함께 쓰는 것이 가장 자연스럽기 때문이다.

I'll **bring** a glass of water **to** you. 내가 너에게 물 한 잔 가져다줄게.

In case you are bored, I will **bring** a book **for** you. 네가 지루할 경우에 대비해서, 내가 너를 위해 책을 한 권 가져올게.

4 문장 전환 시 전치사 for를 쓰는 수여동사는 build, buy, cook, get, make 등이다.

Rita **built** the girls a model airplane. 리타는 그 소녀들에게 모형 비행기를 만들어 주었다.

→ Rita **built** a model airplane **for** the girls.

He **cooked** us Chinese food. 그는 우리에게 중국 음식을 요리해 주었다.

→ He **cooked** Chinese food **for** us.

5 문장 전환 시 전치사 of를 쓰는 수여동사는 ask 등이다.

You should not **ask** someone personal questions. 너는 누군가에게 개인적인 질문을 하면 안 된다.

→ You should not **ask** personal questions **of** someone.

| 참고 | 수여동사로 착각하기 쉬운 타동사에 주의한다.

explain, describe, prove, announce, suggest, introduce, propose, confess

He explained me his new strategy. (X)

He explained his new strategy to me. (O) 그는 내게 자신의 새로운 전략에 대해 설명했다.

| 주의 | 간접목적어가 전치사 뒤에 오는 경우, 「전치사+간접목적어」는 목적어가 아니라 수식어가 된다.

S+V+IO+DO: 4문형

S+V+DO+전치사+IO: 3문형
(전치사+IO: 수식어)

EXERCISES

정답 및 해설 P. 2

spill ~을 엎지르다, 흘리다
list 목록
award 수여하다, 주다
scholarship 장학금
regret 후회하다
coworker 동료
depressed 우울한
financial crisis 재정위기
manage on ~로 꾸려나가다
salary 봉급

〈보기〉와 같이 밑줄 친 부분의 문장 성분을 S(subjects), V(verbs), SC(subject complements), O(objects), IO(indirect objects), DO(direct objects), M(modifiers)로 표시하시오.

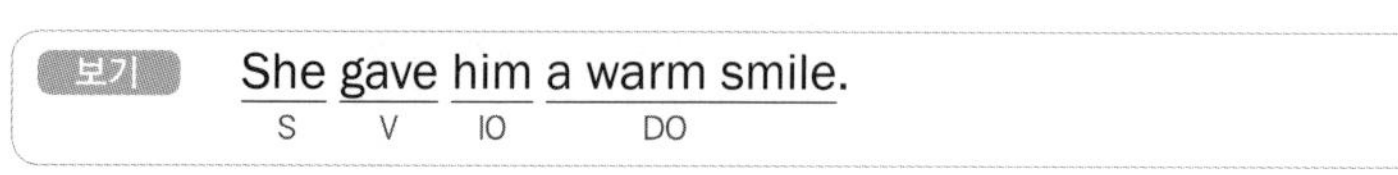

1 Everyone looks tired.

2 She handed me the bill.

3 He built a nice house for his parents.

4 I had to walk home alone late at night.

5 Brandon showed me his family photos.

6 I have spilt something on my new pants.

7 I have emailed the list of addresses to you.

8 Would you send a postcard to me in Europe?

9 My friend sent me a Christmas card last week.

10 I would like to pour you some more grapefruit juice.

11 The university has awarded her a $500 scholarship.

12 You won't regret it. This machine will save you a lot of money.

13 Frank and his coworker James look really depressed today.

14 My parents promised me a new notebook computer for Christmas.

15 During the financial crisis, the family had to manage on just my father's salary.

B 〈보기〉와 같이 알맞은 전치사를 이용하여 문장을 바꿔 쓰시오.

보기	Ms. Lim teaches us English.
	→ Ms. Lim teaches English to us.

1 She will tell you the secret.

→ ______________________________

2 I brought them some blankets.

→ ______________________________

3 The boy wrote Jennifer a fan letter.

→ ______________________________

4 She will get me the concert tickets.

→ ______________________________

5 Julia sometimes buys her son robots.

→ ______________________________

6 The teacher asked him a few questions.

→ ______________________________

7 He will build her a beautiful tree house.

→ ______________________________

8 My father cooked me a delicious meal.

→ ______________________________

9 I bought my grandmother a birthday cake.

→ ______________________________

10 The tour guide showed us many attractions.

→ ______________________________

11 Junsu made his girlfriend a wooden bookshelf.

→ ______________________________

12 The boy showed us his new toy.

→ ______________________________

13 The computer brought us a comfortable life.

→ ______________________________

주어+동사+목적어+목적격보어

문장의 형태	
주어 + 동사 + 목적어 + 목적격보어	
목적격보어로 〈명사〉를 취하는 동사: call, elect, name ...	She **calls** him "Mr. Perfect." 그녀는 그를 '퍼펙트 씨(완벽한 남자)'라고 부른다.
목적격보어로 〈형용사〉를 취하는 동사: find, keep, make ...	He **makes** her happy. 그는 그녀를 행복하게 해준다.
목적격보어로 〈to부정사〉를 취하는 동사: allow, ask, get, tell, want ...	My mom **wants** me to set the table. 엄마는 내가 상 차리기를 바란다.
목적격보어로 〈동사원형〉을 취하는 동사: 사역동사: have, let, make 지각동사: hear, see, feel, watch ...	They **let** the dog eat their bread. 그들은 개에게 빵을 먹게 했다.

FOCUS

1 주어, 동사, 목적어, 목적격보어(object complements)로 이루어진 문장이 있다. 이러한 형식의 문장을 '5문형'이라고 한다.

My parents (S) call (V) my little sister (O) "Princess." (OC) 부모님은 여동생을 '공주님'이라고 부른다.

We (S) saw (V) the girls (O) play soccer. (OC) 우리는 소녀들이 축구를 하는 것을 보았다.

2 목적격보어가 명사인 경우, 목적어와 목적격보어는 같은 것을 가리킨다. 명사를 목적격보어로 취하는 동사에는 call, choose, name, elect, appoint 등이 있다.

My name is Catherine, but my friends **call** me **Cathy.** (me = Cathy)
내 이름은 캐서린이지만, 친구들은 나를 '캐시'라고 부른다.

The students **elected** him **class leader.** (him = class leader)
학생들은 그를 학교 대표로 뽑았다.

3

목적격보어가 형용사인 경우, 목적격보어는 목적어의 상태를 보충 설명해 준다. 형용사를 목적격보어로 취하는 동사에는 keep, make, find, turn, drive 등이 있다.

This blanket will **keep** you **warm.** (you의 상태 = warm)
이 담요는 당신을 따뜻하게 해줄 거예요.

He **found** Jennifer **attractive.** (Jennifer의 상태 = attractive)
그는 제니퍼가 매력적이라는 것을 깨달았다.

|주의| 목적격보어 자리에 부사를 쓰지 않도록 주의한다.
(×) This blanket will keep you ~~warmly~~.

4

목적격보어가 to부정사인 경우, 목적어와 목적격보어 사이에 주어와 서술어 관계가 성립한다. to부정사를 목적격보어로 취하는 동사에는 allow, ask, tell, want 등이 있다.

My parents won't **allow** me **to go** to the party.
우리 부모님은 내가 그 파티에 가는 것을 허락하지 않으실 것이다.

He **asked** her **to come** to the concert.
그는 그녀에게 연주회에 와 달라고 요청했다.

I **want** you **to leave** now.
나는 당신이 지금 떠나 주길 바라요.

5

동사원형을 목적격보어로 취하는 동사에는 사역동사(have, make, let)와 지각동사(hear, see, feel, watch 등)가 있다.

My mother **had** me **throw away** the garbage.
우리 어머니는 나에게 쓰레기를 버리게 했다.

The news **made** him **feel** awkward.
그 소식은 그를 곤란하게 만들었다.

I **saw** Jason **play** the piano.
나는 제이슨이 피아노 치는 것을 보았다.

|참고| 1. 목적격보어로 〈현재분사〉를 취하는 경우가 있다. 이때는 목적어와 목적격보어가 능동, 진행의 관계이다.
I **found** him **dozing off** in the back of the classroom. (그가 졸고 있는 진행의 상태)
나는 그가 교실 맨 뒤에서 졸고 있는 것을 보았다.

2. 목적격보어로 〈과거분사〉를 취하는 경우가 있다. 이때는 목적어와 목적보어가 수동의 관계이다.
I need to **get** it **done** by tomorrow morning. (그것이 완료되는 수동의 개념)
나는 그것을 내일 아침까지 끝내야 한다.

3. get은 '~로 하여금 …하게 하다'라는 사역의 의미를 지니지만 목적격보어로 동사원형이 오지 않는다.
목적어와 목적격보어의 관계에 따라, to부정사, 현재분사, 과거분사가 온다. 의미에 맞춰 목적격보어를 잘 선택해야 한다.
I'll **get** Sujin **to give** you a call. 수진이한테 너에게 전화하라고 할게.

4. help는 to부정사와 동사원형을 목적격보어로 취한다.
I **helped** him **to find** his keys.
I **helped** him **find** his keys. 나는 그가 열쇠 찾는 것을 도와주었다.

EXERCISES

정답 및 해설 P. 3

luggage 짐
awkward 불편한; 어색한
rub ~을 문지르다
advertise ~을 광고하다

〈보기〉와 같이 밑줄 친 부분을 S(subjects), V(verbs), SC(subject complements), O(objects), OC(object complements)로 표시하시오.

보기	His mother	made	him	clean his room.
	S	V	O	OC

1 She heard Harry go out.

2 Sally allowed me to use her cell phone.

3 He asked his mom to make galbi for dinner.

4 My luggage is large, heavy, and awkward to carry.

5 Suzy rubbed the blackboard clean for the teacher.

6 Nowadays, companies advertise their services on the Internet.

lawyer 변호사
fireplace 벽난로
customer 고객

(　　) 안에서 가장 알맞은 것을 고르시오.

1 She kept us (busy / busily) all day.

2 My mom wants me (be / to be) a lawyer.

3 I didn't see him (talk / to talk) to her today.

4 The fire in the fireplace made us (warm / warmly).

5 She couldn't get them (finish / to finish) the project.

6 We heard the baby (cry / to cry) in the early morning.

7 The movie I saw yesterday made me (feel / to feel) sad.

8 His father had him (wash / to wash) the new family car.

9 Her parents let her (watch / to watch) TV until 10 o'clock.

10 The doctor told me (take / to take) the medicine three times a day.

11 We asked the customers not (smoke / to smoke) in the restaurant.

12 I found the questions (difficult / difficultly), but I answered all of them.

13 I said I saw Walter (enter / to enter) the room with a camera.

C 〈보기〉에서 알맞은 것을 골라 문장을 완성하시오.

보기			
	asked / to buy	found / more serious	helped / finish
	named / Sarah	made / angry	elected / president

1 They ______________ their daughter ______________.

2 The students ______________ me ______________ of our class.

3 Some disrespectful students ______________ Mr. Jones ______________.

4 I ______________ the situation ______________ than I expected.

5 My mother ______________ me ______________ some milk on my way home.

6 Her father ______________ her ______________ her homework before she went out to play.

elect 선출하다
disrespectful 무례한
situation 상황
on one's way
~로 가는 길[도중]에

D 우리말과 같은 뜻이 되도록 주어진 단어를 배열하시오.

1 네가 이 머핀을 데워줬으면 해. (this muffin, you, heat, want, to)
→ I ____.

2 김 선생님이 사무실로 돌아오시면 알려 드릴게요. (I'll, know, you, let)
→ ______________________________ when Mr. Kim is back in the office.

3 그들은 그를 이사회 회장으로 선출했다. (president of the board, him, elected)
→ They ____.

4 균형 잡힌 식사와 규칙적인 운동은 당신을 건강하게 해줄 것입니다. (you, healthy, keep)
→ Balanced diet and regular workouts will ______________________.

5 내 여동생은 멀리서 누군가 자기의 이름을 부르는 것을 들었다.
(her name, heard, call, somebody)
→ My sister ______________________________ in the distance.

6 우리 형은 내가 대학 전공을 선택하는 데 도움을 주었다.
(choose, helped, me, my college major)
→ My brother ____.

7 존슨 씨는 마침내 그 회사가 계약서에 서명을 하도록 만들었다.
(the contract, the company, sign, got, to)
→ Mr. Johnson finally ______________________________________.

8 그는 내가 어려운 임무에 도전할 수 있도록 격려해 주었다.
(me, a difficult task, to, encouraged, try)
→ He ____.

board 이사회
workout 운동
in the distance
멀리서, 먼 곳에서
major 전공; 주요한
contract
계약서, 계약, 계약하다
task 임무, 과제

REVIEW

정답 및 해설 P. 4

blow up (풍선 등을) 부풀게 하다
come over ~에 들르다
guard ~을 지키다, 경비하다
entrance 입구
hammer 망치
knock 쳐서 ~을 만들다; 노크하다, 치다
earthquake 지진
zone 지대, 지역
bouquet 꽃다발, 부케

A 〈보기〉와 같이 밑줄 친 부분을 S(subjects), V(verbs), SC(subject complements), O(objects), IO(indirect objects), DO(direct objects), OC(object complements), M(modifiers)로 표시하시오.

보기 My trainer made me exercise a lot.
(S: My trainer / V: made / O: me / OC: exercise a lot)

1 The gift made me happy.

2 Alex put his dog on the chair.

3 Jason lent Jack his old snowboard.

4 John finished blowing up the balloon.

5 He told us to come over to his house.

6 This oven will make you a great cook.

7 Policemen are guarding the entrance.

8 The leaves are red, yellow, and orange.

9 The train from Paris arrived four hours late.

10 She took a hammer and knocked a hole in the wall.

11 After the earthquake, the city resembled a war zone.

12 I sent my mother a bouquet of flowers on her birthday.

stern 엄격한
warning 경고

B 문장을 읽고, 어색한 부분을 찾아 바르게 고쳐 쓰시오.

1 He is not going to let her to go.

2 I make sandwiches of my parents.

3 Some students find grammar easily.

4 Jerry's new cell phone is small and lightly.

5 My father bought my sister for a new car for her birthday.

6 The teacher gave his students to a stern warning.

C 우리말과 같은 뜻이 되도록 주어진 단어를 배열하시오.

1 그 연극은 매우 좋았다. (very good, was, the play)

→ ______________________________

2 나는 그 퍼즐이 어렵다는 것을 알았다. (found, I, difficult, the puzzle)

→ ______________________________

3 그는 자신의 방을 부드러운 색조의 푸른색으로 칠했다.
(a soft shade of blue, painted, he, his room)

→ ______________________________

4 그들은 내가 그 방을 떠나는 것을 허락하지 않았다.
(me, didn't allow, leave, to, the room, they)

→ ______________________________

5 그는 어제 수업 중에 나를 '바보'라고 불렀다.
(called, me, he, in class yesterday, a fool)

→ ______________________________

6 나는 책상에서 자고 있는 제레미를 보았다.
(Jeremy, at his desk, I, saw, sleeping)

→ ______________________________

7 윌리엄 부인의 아이들은 서로 다투고 있었다.
(arguing, Ms. William's children, were, with each other)

→ ______________________________

8 그 야구 선수는 담장 너머로 공을 쳤다.
(the baseball player, over the fence, the ball, hit)

→ ______________________________

9 나는 그에게 뮤지컬 「캣츠」 표 두 장을 보냈다.
(sent, two tickets, I've, him, for the musical *Cats*)

→ ______________________________

10 우리 언니는 결국 작년에 의사가 되었다.
(finally became, my sister, last year, a doctor)

→ ______________________________

11 우리 어머니는 근처의 미장원에서 파마를 했다.
(at the nearby beauty shop, had, my mother, permed, her hair)

→ ______________________________

12 우리 아버지는 어머니 생일날 어머니를 위해 아침을 요리했다.
(for Mom, breakfast, my father, on her birthday, cooked)

→ ______________________________

REVIEW PLUS

정답 및 해설 P. 5

part-time job 아르바이트
heat 데우다; 뜨겁게 하다
elect 선출하다

A 다음 (A), (B), (C)에 들어갈 말이 바르게 짝지어진 것을 고르시오.

1
- He looks ______(A)______.
- Your part-time job sounds ______(B)______.
- This sauce smells ______(C)______.

	(A)		(B)		(C)
①	kindly	…	interesting	…	strangely
②	kind	…	interesting	…	strangely
③	kind	…	interesting	…	strange
④	kind	…	interestingly	…	strange
⑤	kindly	…	interestingly	…	strangely

2
- I want you ______(A)______ this muffin.
- The noisy students made Mr. Jones ______(B)______.
- The class elected ______(C)______.

	(A)		(B)		(C)
①	heat	…	angry	…	leader me
②	heat	…	angrily	…	leader me
③	to heat	…	angrily	…	me leader
④	to heat	…	angry	…	leader me
⑤	to heat	…	angry	…	me leader

count 중요하다
fire (총 등을) 쏘다; 불
by mistake 실수로
takeout food 포장음식

B 다음 중 문형이 다른 하나를 고르시오.

1
① He is my father.
② Chanwoo came late.
③ Cheetahs run very fast.
④ Your opinion doesn't count.
⑤ The bus arrived earlier today.

2
① The car was repaired.
② The cook added salt to the soup.
③ The hunter fired his gun at the deer.
④ Jenny broke the dish by mistake.
⑤ James ordered takeout food for lunch.

PART 2

단순 시제
The Simple Tenses

현재, 과거, 미래 시제

정답 및 해설 P. 6

1

일반동사의 현재형은 주어가 she, he, it 등 3인칭 단수인 경우 동사에 따라 변한다.

일반동사의 현재 변화(3인칭 단수 주어)		
대부분의 일반동사	+s	cleans, likes, loves, speaks, visits ...
-o, -x, -s, -sh, -ch로 끝나는 동사	+es	does, kisses, mixes, watches, washes ...
「모음+y」로 끝나는 동사	+s	buys, enjoys, pays, says ...
「자음+y」로 끝나는 동사	y → i+es	copies, flies, studies, tries ...
불규칙 동사	have → has	

CHECK-UP

주어진 동사를 사용하여 현재 시제로 문장을 완성하시오.

1 Minji ____________ (love) turtles.

2 She ____________ (be) not here now.

3 He ____________ (watch) Japanese dramas.

4 Jim ____________ (carry) his cell phone to school every day.

2

일반동사의 과거 변화는 다음과 같다.

일반동사의 과거 변화		
대부분의 일반동사	+(e)d	called, changed, lived, talked ...
「자음+y」로 끝나는 동사	y → i+ed	cried, dried, hurried, studied, tried, worried ...
• 1음절로 「단모음+자음」인 동사 • 2음절로 뒤에 강세가 있는 동사	끝자음 하나 더 +ed	stopped, dropped, planned, hugged, occurred, preferred, slipped, skipped ...
불규칙 동사	cost → cost, cut → cut, know → knew, send → sent ...	

CHECK-UP

주어진 동사의 과거형을 쓰시오.

1 eat ____________

2 carry ____________

3 find ____________

4 leave ____________

5 sing ____________

6 begin ____________

7 know ____________

8 wear ____________

9 think ____________

10 run ____________

11 write ____________

12 spend ____________

3 일반동사 현재형의 긍정문, 부정문, 의문문은 다음과 같다.

	현재 시제	
긍정문	She lives in Seoul.	They live in Seoul.
부정문	She doesn't live in Seoul.	They don't live in Seoul.
의문문	Does she live in Seoul?	Do they live in Seoul?

일반동사 과거형의 긍정문, 부정문, 의문문은 다음과 같다.

	과거 시제	
긍정문	He watched TV last night.	They watched TV last night.
부정문	He didn't watch TV last night.	They didn't watch TV last night.
의문문	Did he watch TV last night?	Did they watch TV last night?

미래를 나타내는 will과 be going to의 긍정문, 부정문, 의문문은 다음과 같다.

미래 시제	will + 동사원형	be going to + 동사원형
긍정문	She will stay in the office.	We are going to stay in the office.
부정문	She won't stay in the office.	We aren't going to stay in the office.
의문문	Will she stay in the office?	Are we going to stay in the office?

CHECK-UP

주어진 동사를 문맥에 맞게 현재, 과거, 미래(will)로 바꿔 쓰시오.

1 Mina ______________ (arrive) soon.

2 She ______________ (study) very hard last night.

3 They ______________ (meet) Christine a few days ago.

4 Amy ______________ (not, take) a piano lesson yesterday.

5 It ______________ (not, be) snowy this coming Saturday.

6 He ______________ (volunteer) at the local library every day this year.

7 A: ___________ you ___________ (send) the file to me?
B: Yes, I ______________ (send) it tomorrow.

8 A: ___________ you often ___________ (help) your mother?
B: Yes, I do. I usually ______________ (clean) the house every weekend.

현재 시제

쓰임	예문
변하지 않는 진리나 일반적인 사실	The moon **goes** around the earth. 달은 지구 주위를 돈다.
반복적인 행동이나 습관	I **drink** a glass of water in the morning. 나는 아침에 물을 한 잔 마신다.
빈도수	My brother **goes** swimming three times a week. 내 남동생은 일주일에 세 번 수영한다.
시간표 등에 의해 확정된 미래의 일	The flight to London **departs** at 9:30. 런던행 비행기는 9시 30분에 출발한다.
시간·조건의 부사절	I'll send you a postcard when I **arrive** in New York. 내가 뉴욕에 도착하면 너에게 엽서를 보낼게.

FOCUS

1 변하지 않는 진리나 일반적 사실을 나타낼 때 현재 시제(simple present)를 쓴다.

Your heart **beats** over 100,000 times a day. 당신의 심장은 하루에 십만 번 이상을 뛴다.

A baseball **has** exactly 108 stitches. 야구공은 정확히 백팔 개의 바늘땀을 가지고 있다.

A house fly **lives** at least 14 days. 집파리는 최소한 14일을 산다.

| 참고 | 속담은 주로 현재형을 사용한다.

Actions **speak** louder than words. 말보다 행동이 중요하다.

2 반복적인 행동이나 습관, 현재의 상태 등을 나타낼 때 현재 시제를 쓴다.

I usually **leave** for school in the morning with my brother. We **walk** to school together.
나는 아침에 대개 남동생과 함께 학교로 향한다. 우리는 함께 걸어서 학교에 간다.

My sister **volunteers** at the shelter five hours a week. She **is** generous with her time.
우리 언니는 일주일에 다섯 시간씩 보호 시설에서 자원봉사를 한다. 그녀는 자신의 시간을 아끼지 않는다.

Jihye **is** in the second grade at Sinwha High School.
지혜는 신화 고등학교 2학년이다.

3 현재 상태의 빈도수(frequency)를 이야기할 때 현재 시제를 쓴다.

I **brush** and **floss** my teeth every night. 나는 매일 밤 이를 닦고 치실로 이 사이를 깨끗이 한다.

Julia never **drinks** coffee at night. 줄리아는 밤에 절대로 커피를 마시지 않는다.

My uncle occasionally **goes** fishing with my father on Sundays. 삼촌은 때때로 일요일마다 우리 아버지와 낚시를 간다.

| 참고 | 현재 시제는 흔히 빈도부사 always, usually, sometimes 등과 함께 쓴다. 빈도부사는 be동사나 조동사 뒤, 일반동사 앞에 위치한다.

4 대중교통, 영화, 회의 등의 일정과 같이 이미 확정된 미래의 일에 현재 시제를 사용한다.

The meeting **starts** in an hour.
회의가 한 시간 후에 시작한다.

The next bus to Chicago **departs** at 9 p.m.
시카고행 다음 버스는 밤 아홉 시에 출발한다.

The movie **starts** at 8:40, so let's leave in about thirty minutes.
영화가 여덟 시 사십 분에 시작하니 삼십 분쯤 후에 출발하자.

|참고| go, come, leave, arrive, start, end 등의 동사는 주로 현재형으로 미래를 나타낸다.

5 when(~할 때), until(~할 때까지), after(~ 후에), before(~ 전에) 등이 이끄는 시간의 부사절에서 미래 시제 대신 현재 시제를 사용한다.

I'll wait here until you **finish**. Then we'll go together.
네가 끝날 때까지 여기서 기다릴게. 그러고 나서 함께 가자.

Before Soyeon **leaves** Europe, she will buy her mother a souvenir.
소연이는 유럽을 떠나기 전에 어머니를 위한 기념품을 살 것이다.

Alex and Kevin are going to travel across America after they **finish** their final exams.
알렉스와 케빈은 기말고사가 끝나고 나서 미국 횡단 여행을 할 것이다.

6 if(만약 ~한다면), unless(만약 ~하지 않는다면)가 이끄는 조건의 부사절에서 미래 시제 대신 현재 시제를 사용한다.

If you **come** with me, I will treat you to a hamburger.
네가 나와 함께 가면 햄버거를 사줄게.

Unless you **apologize**, Hyerim will not forgive you.
네가 사과하지 않으면, 혜림이가 너를 용서하지 않을 거야.

We will all be late unless you **hurry** up.
네가 서두르지 않으면 우리 모두 늦을 거야.

|참고| if가 조건(만약 ~라면)의 뜻이 아닌 '~인지 아닌지(를)'의 뜻으로 쓰일 때는 미래 시제 will을 사용할 수 있다.

I don't know **if** Jeff will join our soccer club. (*NOT* joins)
나는 제프가 우리 축구 클럽에 참여할 것인지 아닌지 모른다.

We're not sure **if** David will come to the party tomorrow. (*NOT* comes)
우리는 데이비드가 내일 파티에 올지 안 올지 확신하지 못한다.

EXERCISES

정답 및 해설 P. 6

conference 회의
reach ~에 이르다, 닿다
height 높이
keep on ~을 계속 켠 채로 있다
work out 운동하다
belong to ~에 속하다
punish 처벌하다

A 〈보기〉에서 밑줄 친 동사의 쓰임을 고르시오.

보기
ⓐ 현재 상태, 습관, 반복적 행동　ⓑ 불변의 진리, 일반적 사실
ⓒ 확실한 일정　ⓓ 시간 · 조건을 나타내는 절

1 I seldom visit my hometown nowadays. ______
2 Our conference starts this coming Friday. ______
3 My mother will be upset if I get home late. ______
4 The ship for Norway leaves at eight o'clock. ______
5 Francis sometimes drinks coffee after lunch. ______
6 Mount Everest reaches a height of 8,848 meters. ______
7 When I get there, I'll call you. Keep your phone on. ______
8 Do you regularly work out at the gym on Mondays? ______
9 Whales and dolphins belong to marine mammals. ______
10 Unless you hand in your homework today, you will be punished. ______

vacuum 진공청소기로 청소하다
stick to ~을 고수하다
low-fat diet 저지방식 식사
argue with ~와 논쟁하다
be in trouble 곤경에 빠지다
travel 이동하다; 여행하다
selfie 셀프 카메라

B 주어진 동사를 이용하여 현재 시제로 문장을 완성하시오.

1 Sara ______ (practice) yoga every morning.
2 My brother ______ (vacuum) the house every night.
3 My friend Jeremy ______ (not, go) anywhere on foot.
4 The next bus into the city ______ (come) in 20 minutes.
5 You'll lose weight if you ______ (stick to) this low-fat diet.
6 Peter's grandparents often ______ (spend) winters in the USA.
7 You must finish eating your dinner before you ______ (watch) TV.
8 Don't argue with him unless you ______ (want) to be in big trouble.
9 ______ the festival ______ (begin) tomorrow at eight o'clock?
10 The earth ______ (travel) around the sun once every 365 days.
11 The play ______ (end) at 8 p.m., and you can take selfies with the actors.
12 She always ______ (listen) to the radio when she prepares breakfast.

C 〈보기〉에서 알맞은 동사를 골라 현재 시제로 문장을 완성하시오.

보기					
	return	harm	be	start	go
	do	come	arrive	connect	need

1 The railway ___________ Seoul and Daegu.

2 Second-hand smoke ___________ nonsmokers.

3 Does your music recital ___________ at 8:00 or 8:30?

4 I'll call you when John ___________ at Incheon Airport.

5 Greg ___________ jogging every morning to keep healthy.

6 I'll let you know when Mr. Park ___________ back to his office.

7 Ron seldom ___________ his homework without somebody's help.

8 If you ___________ not interested in this item, how about that one?

9 You ___________ to arrive at the airport two hours before the flight.

10 When the team ___________ next week, the city will give them a parade.

harm ~에게 해를 끼치다
second-hand smoke 비흡연자가 마시게 되는 남의 담배 연기
cf. second-hand smoking 간접흡연
recital 독주회

D 우리말과 같은 의미가 되도록 주어진 단어를 배열하시오.

1 다음 학기는 9월에 시작한다. (starts, in September, the next semester)
→ ___________________________________

2 내 여동생은 홍차보다 허브차를 좋아한다. (prefers, to black tea, my sister, herbal tea)
→ ___________________________________

3 너는 항상 늦으면서 결코 사과하지 않는다. (are, always late, and never apologize, you)
→ ___________________________________

4 뮌헨행 기차는 플랫폼B에서 5분 후에 떠난다. (leaves, in five minutes, the train to Munich)
→ ___________________________________ on platform B.

5 평화 회의는 4년마다 열린다. (takes places, the Peace Conference, every four years)
→ ___________________________________

6 캐나다에서는 '사이다'라는 말은 무알콜 사과 주스를 가리킨다.
(refers to, the term 'cider', non-alcoholic apple juice)
→ In Canada, ___________________________________.

7 고급 식당에서는 수석 웨이터가 고객을 테이블로 안내해 준다.
(assigns, to tables, customers)
→ A head waiter at expensive restaurants ___________________________________.

prefer A to B B보다 A를 선호하다
apologize 사과하다
Munich 뮌헨(독일의 도시)
Peace Conference 평화 회의
take place 개최되다; 일어나다
refer to ~을 가리키다
term 용어
cider 사과 주스
non-alcoholic (음료가) 알코올을 함유하지 않은
assign ~을 배정하다; ~를 임명하다
head waiter 수석 웨이터, 급사장

과거 시제

쓰임	예문
과거에 이미 끝난 동작이나 상태, 습관	I often **played** soccer after school. 나는 종종 방과 후에 축구를 했다.
과거 시제와 함께 쓰이는 특정 어구	I **went** to bed late last night, so I'm very tired now. 나는 어젯밤에 늦게 잠자리에 들어서 오늘은 매우 피곤하다.
과거에 있었던 역사적 사실	Leonardo da Vinci **painted** *the Mona Lisa*. 레오나르도 다 빈치는 모나리자를 그렸다.

1 과거에 일어난 일, 즉 과거에 이미 끝난 동작이나 상태, 습관 등은 과거 시제(simple past)를 쓴다.

When I **was** young, I **played** soccer for my school team.
나는 어렸을 때 우리 학교 팀에서 축구를 했다.

Amy **made** me a yogurt smoothie this morning.
에이미가 오늘 아침에 나에게 요구르트 스무디를 만들어 주었다

Greg **visited** his grandmother yesterday.
그레그는 어제 할머니를 방문했다.

2 과거 시제는 주로 특정한 과거 시점을 나타내는 어구(~ ago, yesterday, last ~, in+과거년도)와 함께 쓴다.

I **lived** on Jejudo five years ago, but now I live in Seoul.
나는 5년 전에 제주도에 살았지만, 지금은 서울에 산다.

Emily walks to school every day, but she **took** the subway yesterday.
에밀리는 매일 걸어서 학교에 가지만, 어제는 지하철을 탔다.

Korea's soccer team **made** it to the semifinals in the 2002 World Cup.
한국 축구팀이 2002년 월드컵에서 준결승전에 진출했다.

3 역사적 사실은 과거 시제로 쓴다.

Sumerians **invented** writing in the 4th century B.C.
수메르인이 기원전 4세기에 문자를 발명했다.

In 1443, Sejong the Great **invented** the Korean writing system, *Hunminjeongeum*.
세종대왕이 1443년에 한글 표기법인 훈민정음을 창제했다.

The first Korean astronaut, Yi Soyeon, **headed** for space on April 8th, 2008.
한국의 첫 번째 우주인인 이소연이 2008년 4월 8일에 우주로 향했다.

|참고| 「used to+동사원형」은 '~하곤 했다'라는 의미로, 과거의 습관적인 행동이나 상태를 나타낸다.
I **used to ride** a bike on weekends. 나는 주말에 자전거를 타곤 했다.

EXERCISES

정답 및 해설 P. 7

A 주어진 동사를 이용하여 과거 시제로 문장을 완성하시오.

1 Mary ________ (worry) too much about her grade last week.

2 I never ________ (imagine) that I would travel around the world.

3 Michael ________ (brag) about his play after the game was over.

4 I ________ (wait) for her, but she never ____________ (show up).

5 I ________ (forget) to take my key before I ________ (leave) home.

6 Jacob ________ (watch) the people walking by when he was in the café.

7 The Korean War ____________ (break out) in 1950 and ________ (cease) in 1953.

8 Ms. Smith ________ (supply) her students with brushes before they ________ (start) to paint.

brag 허풍 떨다, 자랑하다
show up 나타나다
break out (전쟁, 질병 등이) 발발하다
cease 중단되다
supply ~을 주다, 공급하다

B 주어진 동사를 문맥에 맞게 현재 또는 과거로 바꿔 쓰시오.

1 My brother's birthday ________ (be) this coming Thursday.

2 Millions of years ago, dinosaurs ________ (inhabit) the earth.

3 George Washington ________ (be) the first president of the USA.

4 Brian hardly visited his grandma, but now he ________ (live) with her.

5 Amy ________ (hurt) her leg 2 days ago, so she couldn't go to the party.

6 My mom ________ (arrange) the flowers carefully in the vase yesterday.

7 Columbus ________ (reach) America in 1492, but now some people ________ (say) he wasn't the first.

8 Mary ________ (skim) through the newspaper on her way to work this morning. So she ____________ (not, need) it anymore now.

inhabit ~에 살다, 서식하다
arrange ~을 정돈하다; 배열하다
skim through ~을 대충 읽다

C 글을 읽고, 밑줄 친 부분을 바르게 고치시오.

Neil Armstrong ① lands on the surface of the Moon on July 20, 1969. However, he ② isn't alone. He ③ is accompanied by Buzz Aldrin. Armstrong and Aldrin ④ spend a day on the surface of the Moon before returning to the Earth. Armstrong ⑤ announces to the world, "That's one small step for a man; one giant leap for mankind."

land ~에 착륙하다; 육지
surface 표면
be accompanied by ~을 동반하다
announce 알리다, 발표하다; 공고하다
leap 뜀, 도약; 껑충 뛰다
mankind 인류; 인간

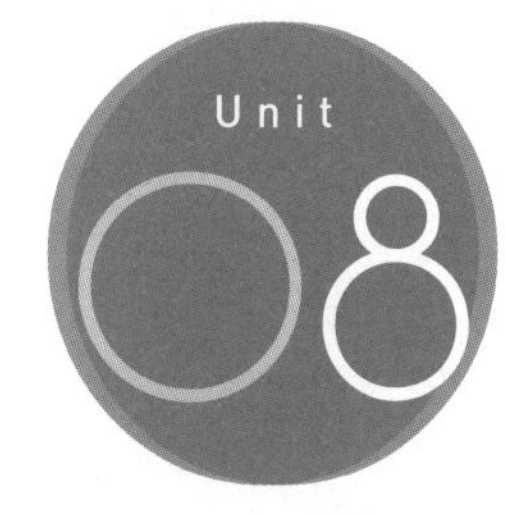

미래 시제

	will + 동사원형	be going to + 동사원형
의미	• 단순 미래 • 미래의 일을 추측 • 화자의 의지나 고집에 의한 순간적 결정	• 단순 미래 • 미래의 일을 추측 • 근거가 있거나 미리 계획된 일정
예문	It **will be** sunny today. 오늘은 화창할 것이다. If I finish early, I'**ll drop** by tonight. 내가 일찍 끝나면 오늘 잠깐 들를게.	I'**m going to move** to Tokyo next year. 나는 내년에 도쿄로 이사 갈 것이다. My dad **is going to pick** me up at the airport. 우리 아빠가 공항으로 나를 데리러 올 것이다.

FOCUS

1 미래 시제(simple future)는 아직 일어나지 않은 미래의 일을 예측할 때 쓰며, 보통 「will+동사원형」 또는 「be going to+동사원형」으로 나타낸다.

If you are not careful, you'**ll break** the vase.

→ If you are not careful, you'**re going to break** the vase.
조심하지 않으면, 꽃병을 깰 것이다.

According to the weather forecast, it'**ll snow** tomorrow.

→ According to the weather forecast, it'**s going to snow** tomorrow.
일기 예보에 따르면 내일 눈이 올 거야.

2 말하는 사람의 의지 또는 말하는 그 순간에 결정된 일을 표현할 때 주로 조동사 will을 쓴다.

A: I'm so tired. 나 너무 피곤해.

B: I'**ll get** you some coffee. 내가 커피를 좀 갖다줄게.

A: Chris! Someone is knocking at the door. 크리스! 누가 문을 두드리고 있어.

B: Don't worry. I'**ll get** it. 걱정하지 마. 내가 갈게.

3 근거가 있거나 미리 계획된 일정을 나타낼 때 주로 be going to를 쓴다.

A: Oh, no! Look at those black clouds! 오, 안 돼! 저 먹구름 좀 봐!

B: It'**s** probably **going to rain.** (근거 있는 추측) 비가 올 것 같아.

A: What **are** you **going to do** this weekend? 이번 주말에 무엇을 할 거니?

B: I'**m going to see** a musical with Minhee. (미리 계획된 일정) 나는 민희와 뮤지컬을 볼 거야.

4 대중교통, 영화, 회의 등의 일정과 같이 이미 정해진 일은 현재 시제를 미래의 의미로 사용하기도 한다. 대표적인 동사로는 go, come, leave, arrive, start, depart, end 등이 있다.

My flight to Sydney **departs** tomorrow at 9:00 a.m. 시드니행 비행기가 내일 오전 9시에 출발한다.

Does the performance **start** at 7:30 or 8:00? 공연이 7시 반에 시작하니, 아니면 8시에 시작하니?

|참고| 이런 종류의 동사는 주로 '가다', '오다', '출발하다', '도착하다' 등의 의미를 담고 있어서 '왕래발착(往來發着)' 동사라고 부른다.

5 사람의 계획된 일정은 현재진행형(be+-ing)을 사용한다. 이때는 현재진행 중인 동작과 구별하기 위해 주로 미래를 나타내는 어구(next, tomorrow 등)와 함께 사용한다.

Brenda **is entering** a speech contest next week. 브렌다는 다음 주에 말하기 대회에 참가할 것이다.

→ Brenda **is going to enter** a speech contest next week.

Are you **seeing** Thomas this weekend? 너는 이번 주말에 토머스를 만날 거니?

→ **Are** you **going to see** Thomas this weekend?

|참고| 1. 미래 vs. 현재진행

He **is taking** a picture of my family next week. (미래) 그는 다음 주에 우리 가족의 사진을 찍을 것이다.

He **is taking** a picture of my family now. (현재진행) 그는 지금 우리 가족의 사진을 찍고 있다.

2. 「be about to+동사원형」은 '막 ~하려고 하다'라는 뜻으로, 대개 짧은 시간 이내에 일어날 미래의 일을 나타낸다.

Shhh! Brandon **is about to fall** asleep. 쉿! 브랜든이 막 잠들려고 해.

3. 「be to+동사원형」은 '~할 예정이다'라는 뜻으로, 공식적인 일정, 행사와 같이 격식을 갖추어야 하는 경우에 사용한다.

The G-8 leaders **are to have** a summit meeting in Tokyo. G-8 지도자들은 도쿄에서 정상 회담을 개최할 예정이다.

EXERCISES

정답 및 해설 P. 7

have a party
파티를 열다
sleep over
~의 집에서 잠을 자다
concentrate on
~에 집중하다
snore 코를 골다

A 밑줄 친 동사가 현재진행인지 미래인지 밝히시오.

1 John is playing hockey tonight. ________

2 What are you doing this Friday? ________

3 Please be quiet. I am studying for the test. ________

4 The music is very loud. Are they having a party? ________

5 Caroline is sleeping over at her friend's next weekend. ________

6 I can't concentrate on my study. My brother is snoring so loudly. ________

special today
(식당 등의) 오늘의 특별 요리
lasagna 라자냐
(파스타, 치즈, 고기, 토마토 소스 등으로 만든 이탈리아 요리)
grilled 구운
salmon 연어
garlic bread 마늘빵
soy milk 두유
instead
그 대신에; 그보다도

B will과 be going to 중 가장 적절한 것을 고르고, 주어진 단어를 이용하여 대화를 완성하시오.

1 A: It's beautiful outside today. Let's go for a quick bike ride.
B: I'm sorry. I have a prior plan. I ____________ (go) mountain climbing with my father.

2 A: It's getting late. I think I ____________ (take) a taxi home.
B: Really? It's a beautiful night, so I think I ____________ (walk).
A: OK. See you tomorrow.

3 A: What do you have on special today?
B: We have lasagna and grilled salmon on special.
A: Then, I ____________ (have) the lasagna with garlic bread.

4 A: Remember to buy a newspaper when you're out.
B: Don't worry, I ____________ (not, forget).
A: And ________ you ________ (buy) some bread for me on the way home, too? Thanks!

5 A: Karen and I ____________ (see) a movie tomorrow night. Do you want to join us?
B: Sure. I don't have any other plans.
A: Great! We ____________ (meet) you in front of Movie World at 6:30 then.

6 A: Mom! Jason drank the last of the juice.
B: Sorry, dear. I ____________ (buy) some more this afternoon when I go out shopping. Have some of the soy milk instead.
A: Soy milk? No thanks!

C 주어진 단어를 이용하여 현재진행으로 문장을 완성하시오.

1 A: __________ the kids __________ (go) to school tomorrow?
B: No, they're not. It's the school's anniversary.

2 A: Jane's not here right now.
B: What __________ she __________ (do)?
A: She ____________________ (babysit) the neighbor's kids.

3 A: How about going out for a bite?
B: I can't. I ____________________ (meet) Gunwoo for lunch in a few minutes.

4 A: You must ____________________ (get) excited about your trip to the East Sea now.
B: Yup! I've already booked my ticket. I ____________________ (leave) next Thursday.

5 A: Why is she absent from class?
B: She ____________________ (participate) in a swimming contest next Monday. So she is practicing now.

school anniversary 개교기념일
bite 한입; 간단한 식사; 물다
book 예약하다; 책
be absent from ~에 결석하다
participate 참가하다

D 〈보기〉에서 알맞은 동사를 골라 will 또는 be going to를 이용하여 대화를 완성하시오.

보기	go	change	come	close	make

1 A: I think I ____________________ the window. I'm a bit chilly.
B: No problem. Shall I get you a blanket?

2 A: I've decided to redecorate my dorm room.
B: Oh, really? What __________ you ____________________?

3 A: Will you please turn down the TV? I'm trying to read.
B: Sorry. I ____________________ and watch TV in the other room then.

4 A: Why did you buy so many bananas?
B: I ____________________ banana pancakes for breakfast tomorrow.

5 A: Why is it so hot in here?
B: The air conditioning system is down again. I called the service center already. The repairman ____________________ and fix it tomorrow.

chilly 추운, 쌀쌀한
redecorate ~을 새로 장식하다
dorm 기숙사
turn down ~의 소리를 줄이다
down (기계 등이) 고장 난; 아래로
repairman 수리공

REVIEW

정답 및 해설 P. 8

liquid 액체
be off 떠나다, 출발하다
economics 경제학
offer 제안하다; 제공하다
take 받아들이다; 가지고 가다
banknote 지폐
be made of ~으로 만들어지다
last 지속되다
paper bill 종이 지폐
have an argument 언쟁하다
homesick 향수병의

A ( ) 안에서 가장 알맞은 것을 고르시오.

1 Sound (travels / is traveling) faster in liquids than in air.

2 Becky (works / is working) right now. She (be / will be) off on her Caribbean holiday next week.

3 After she (finishes / will finish) high school next year, she (goes / will go) to college to study economics.

4 Jenny (is / was) offered a teaching job last week. But, strangely, she (decides / decided) not to take it.

5 Nowadays, Australian banknotes (are / were) made of plastic. They (last / are lasting) much longer than paper bills.

6 My parents (have / had) an argument last night. Now, they (aren't speaking / aren't going to speak) to each other.

7 Suhee (calls / called) me from Vancouver yesterday. She's homesick, so she (came / is coming) back to Korea next month.

8 My sister (go / is going) abroad to study next week for two months. My brother will go abroad to study when she (comes / will come) back.

be up 깨어 있다
for a while 잠깐, 잠시 동안
what are friends for? 친구 좋다는 게 뭐야.

B 주어진 동사를 현재, 과거, 미래(will)로 바꿔 대화를 완성하시오.

1 A: How often ________ you ________ (go) to the movies?
B: I go to the movies once a month.

2 A: Are you going to be up for a while?
B: No. After I ________ (send) this email to John, I'm going to bed.

3 A: Why ________ you ________ (not, call) me last night?
B: Sorry. I ________ (be) too tired, so I ________ (go) to bed early.

4 A: I'm getting sleepy. Let's take a break.
B: That sounds great. I ________ (get) some coffee for you.

5 A: I don't want to have dinner alone. ________ you ________ (join) me?
B: Sure, why not? After all, what are friends for?

6 A: ________ you ________ (meet) Jennifer last Saturday?
B: Yes, I ________ (do). We ________ (go) to see a movie, but we ________ (not, enjoy) it at all.

C 〈보기〉에서 알맞은 동사를 골라 어법과 문맥에 맞게 현재, 과거, 미래(will)로 바꿔 문장을 완성하시오.

[1-5] 보기 rain cost graduate want raise

1 Those shoes are really nice, but they ____________ too much.

2 I'll translate that document for you if you ____________ me to.

3 Our charity ____________ $20,000 to help the needy last year.

4 I really don't enjoy living in Seattle because it ____________ so often.

5 Kelly ____________ with honors next year if she can keep her grades up.

[6-10] 보기 drop by look be start join

6 I didn't learn to dance when I ____________ a child.

7 I'm going out for dinner. Will you ____________ me?

8 I'll probably ____________ Mike's house on my way home from school.

9 I met an old friend from school this morning, and she ____________ really happy.

10 The course doesn't ____________ until September, but you'll need to register early.

graduate 졸업하다
translate ~을 번역하다
document 문서, 서류
charity 자선기금; 자선 단체; 자선
raise 모으다; 올리다; 기르다
needy (매우) 가난한
with honors 우수한 성적으로
keep up 유지하다, ~을 계속하다
drop by (~에) 잠깐 들르다
register 등록하다

D 주어진 동사를 어법과 문맥에 맞게 바꿔 글을 완성하시오.

1 Jane often meets new and unfamiliar words when she ______________ (read) English books. But she never ______________ (get) discouraged or ______________ (give up). Instead, she ______________ (try) to guess what the word means and ______________ (look) it up in her dictionary.

2 Millions of years ago, enormous dinosaurs ______________ (roam) the earth. A 41-foot monster called Giganotosaurus ______________ (be) the biggest of these predators. However, a few months ago, scientists in Patagonia ______________ (uncover) an even larger dinosaur.

3 Next week is my birthday. To celebrate, I ______________ (do) something really exciting: bungee jumping! My friend James and I ______________ (go) bungee jumping.

unfamiliar 친숙하지 않은, 낯선, 잘 모르는
discouraged 낙담한
look up (사전 등으로) 찾아보다
enormous 거대한
roam 돌아다니다
predator 육식 동물
uncover 폭로하다, 드러내다
celebrate 축하하다

REVIEW PLUS

정답 및 해설 P. 9

lifetime 일생
flag 기, 깃발
display
나타내다, 전시하다

문장을 읽고, (A), (B), (C)에서 가장 알맞은 것을 고르시오.

- Mozart (A) (writes / wrote) more than 600 pieces of music in his lifetime.
- It (B) (takes / is taking) me over an hour to get to school every morning by subway.
- The US flag (C) (displays / will display) thirteen stripes, one for each of the original thirteen states.

shrink
(천 등이) 오그라들다, 줄어들다
cash 현금으로 바꾸다; 현금
traveler's check
여행자 수표
promptly
시간을 지키는; 즉석의

대화를 읽고, (A), (B), (C)에서 가장 알맞은 것을 고르시오.

- A: That sweater won't fit him if he (A) (washes / will wash) it in hot water.
  B: That's right. Wool shrinks in hot water.
- A: I need to cash a traveler's check. What time do the banks open?
  B: Most banks (B) (open / is opening) promptly at 9:30 a.m.
- A: That's a beautiful dress. Where are you going to wear it?
  B: I think I (C) (wear / will wear) it to David and Emma's wedding next Sunday.

calorie 칼로리(열량의 단위)
contain
~이 들어있다, ~을 포함하다
include ~을 포함하다
reduce 줄이다, 감소시키다
scrap
쓰레기로 버리다; 한 조각

다음을 읽고, (A), (B), (C)에 들어갈 말이 바르게 짝지어진 것을 고르시오.

Most fast foods ____(A)____ high in calories. For example, the Triple Whoppers with Cheese contain 1,250 calories. And that includes 69 grams of fat! You can reduce the total number of calories by simply scraping off all of the mayonnaise, cheese, and bacon. And if you ____(B)____ the French fries and order a Diet Coke, you ____(C)____ the total number of calories even more.

	(A)		(B)		(C)
①	are	···	skip	···	reduce
②	are	···	skip	···	will reduce
③	are	···	will skip	···	reduce
④	were	···	will skip	···	will reduce
⑤	were	···	will skip	···	reduce

PART 3

진행 시제
The Progressive Tenses

현재진행, 과거진행 시제

정답 및 해설 P. 10

1 -ing형은 「동사원형+ing」가 기본형이다.

동사	규칙	예시
대부분의 동사	+ing	flying, watching ...
-e로 끝나는 동사	e 빼고+ing	giving, living ...
「단모음+자음」으로 끝나는 동사	+자음 하나 더+ing	setting, swimming ...
-ie로 끝나는 동사	ie → y+ing	lying, dying ...

CHECK-UP

주어진 동사의 -ing형을 쓰시오.

1 eat ______________

2 come ______________

3 cut ______________

4 die ______________

5 ride ______________

6 lie ______________

7 stop ______________

8 plan ______________

9 cry ______________

10 hurry ______________

11 set ______________

12 give ______________

13 live ______________

14 see ______________

2 현재진행형의 기본 형태는 「am/are/is+-ing」이다.

현재진행 시제		
긍정문	She is watching TV now.	They are watching TV now.
부정문	She isn't watching TV now.	They aren't watching TV now.
의문문	Is she watching TV now?	Are they watching TV now?

CHECK-UP

주어진 동사를 현재진행으로 바꿔 문장을 완성하시오.

1 You ______________ (walk) too fast.

2 He ______________ (chat) with his friend.

3 My mother ______________ (prepare) dinner.

4 ______________ it ______________ (snow) outside?

5 I ______________ (not, listen) to the radio at this moment.

3 과거진행형의 기본 형태는 「was/were+-ing」이다.

과거진행 시제

긍정문	He was sleeping at that time.	You were sleeping at that time.
부정문	He wasn't sleeping at that time.	You weren't sleeping at that time.
의문문	Was he sleeping at that time?	Were you sleeping at that time?

CHECK-UP

A 대화를 읽고, ( ) 안에서 가장 알맞은 것을 고르시오.

1 A: Did you finish washing your dad's car?
B: No, I (am doing / was doing) it now.

2 A: Why didn't you answer the phone last night?
B: I (am sleeping / was sleeping) then.

3 A: What was John doing when you arrived?
B: He (is reading / was reading) a book.

4 A: What was the weather like this morning?
B: It (is raining / was raining) when I came to school.

5 A: Did you call me at 11 p.m. last night?
B: No, I didn't. I (am taking / was taking) a shower then.

B 〈보기〉에서 알맞은 동사를 골라 지시대로 바꿔 쓰시오.

보기 walk wait play cry

1 (현재) Jinwoo ________________ the flute.
(현재진행) Jinwoo ________________ the flute.

2 (현재) Andrew ________________ to school.
(현재진행) Andrew ________________ to school.

3 (과거) The baby ________________ last night.
(과거진행) The baby ________________ last night.

4 (과거) Daniel ________________ for his mother to pick him up.
(과거진행) Daniel ________________ for his mother to pick him up.

현재진행

쓰임	예문
말하는 시점에 진행 중인 동작	Sophia **is making** a birthday cake for Mike now. 소피아는 지금 마이크를 위해 생일 케이크를 만들고 있다.
현재를 포함하여 일정 기간 계속되는 일	My friend and I **are taking** Japanese classes this semester. 내 친구와 나는 이번 학기에 일본어 수업을 듣고 있다.
이미 확정된 가까운 미래	Alex and Amy **are performing** at the party tomorrow. 알렉스와 에이미는 내일 파티에서 연주를 할 것이다.

FOCUS

1 현재진행(present progressive)은 어떤 동작이나 상태가 말하는 시점에서 진행되고 있음을 나타낸다.

Linda is in the classroom. She **is studying** biology.
린다는 교실에 있다. 그녀는 생물학을 공부하고 있다.

He **is talking** too loudly on the phone. It'**s bothering** me.
그가 너무 큰 소리로 통화하고 있다. 그것이 나를 신경 쓰이게 한다.

Be quiet, please. The baby **is sleeping**.
조용히 좀 해주세요. 아기가 자고 있어요.

2 현재진행은 these days, this week, this month, this semester 등의 시간 표현과 함께 쓰여 어떤 동작이나 상태가 최근 일정 기간 동안 계속되는 것을 나타낸다.

I **am reading** a play by Shakespeare these days. 나는 요즘 셰익스피어의 희곡을 읽고 있다.

Your grades **are getting** better this semester. 이번 학기에 너의 점수가 점점 더 좋아지고 있다.

She **is living** with her sister in New York this year. 올해 그녀는 뉴욕에서 동생과 함께 살고 있다.

3 현재진행은 가까운 미래를 나타내는 시간 표현과 함께 쓰여 이미 확정된 일정을 나타낸다.

A: I'**m taking** my first skydiving lesson tomorrow. 나는 내일 처음으로 스카이다이빙 수업을 들을 거야.
B: Wow! Be careful. 와! 조심해.

A: **Are** you really **learning** paragliding next month? 너 정말 다음 달에 패러글라이딩을 배울 거니?
B: Yes, I am. I'm so excited! 응. 나 매우 설레!

A: I'**m meeting** David for lunch this afternoon. 나는 오늘 오후에 데이비드와 점심 먹으러 만날 거야.
B: Say "Hello" to him for me. 그에게 안부 전해 줘.

4 현재 시제와 현재진행 시제를 사용하는 경우, 다음과 같은 차이점이 있다.

The Rhine **runs** into the North Sea. (일반적 사실)
라인 강은 북해로 흘러 들어간다.

I have a cold. My nose **is running**. (진행 중인 동작이나 상태)
나는 감기에 걸렸다. 콧물이 흐른다.

Alison usually **drives** her son to school in the morning. (현재의 상태 및 습관, 반복적 일상)
엘리슨은 아침에 대개 아들을 학교까지 차로 태워 준다.

Brian **is driving** a lot more these days. (일정 기간의 동작, 상태, 변화)
브라이언은 요즈음 운전을 훨씬 더 많이 한다.

|참고| 1. usually, always 등의 빈도부사는 주로 현재의 상태 및 습관, 반복적 일상을 나타내는 현재 시제와 사용한다.
I **always** get the first train. 나는 늘 첫 기차를 탄다.
2. always가 현재진행 시제와 함께 쓰이면 불평의 의미를 포함한다.
He's **always** borrowing my cell phone. 그는 항상 내 휴대 전화를 빌린다.

5 일반적으로 감정, 소유, 지각, 인지 등의 상태를 나타내는 동사는 진행형으로 쓰지 않는다.

감정동사	appreciate 감사하다 envy 부러워하다 like 좋아하다 prefer 더 좋아하다	care 돌보다 fear 두려워하다 love 사랑하다 please 기쁘게 하다	dislike 싫어하다 hate 미워하다, 증오하다 mind 꺼리다 surprise 놀라게 하다
소유동사	belong ~에게 속하다 possess 가지다, 소유하다	have 가지고 있다	own 소유하다
지각동사	feel (신체적으로) 느끼다 see ~이 보이다 taste ~한 맛이 나다	hear ~이 들리다 smell ~한 냄새가 나다	look ~하게 보이다 sound ~하게 들리다
인지동사	believe ~라고 믿다 forget 잊다 recognize 인식하다 think ~라고 생각하다	doubt 의심하다 know 알다 realize 깨닫다 understand 이해하다	feel (정신적으로) 느끼다 need 필요하다 suppose 가정하다 wish 바라다
기타 동사	appear ~인 것 같이 보이다 contain 포함하다 resemble 닮다	be ~이다 cost 비용이 들다 seem ~인 것 같다	consist 구성하다 exist 존재하다 weigh 무게가 나가다

I **hear** you loud and clear. (*NOT* I am hearing ~.)
나는 네 말이 크고 분명하게 들려.

I **prefer** to eat at another restaurant. (*NOT* I am preferring ~.)
나는 다른 식당에서 먹는 게 더 좋아.

Who **owns** the car with license plate number NY1248? (*NOT* Who is owning ~?)
누가 NY1248이라는 번호판을 단 차의 주인인가요?

6 위의 몇몇 동사들은 동작을 나타낼 때 진행형을 사용할 수 있다.

	상태 (진행형 불가)	동작 (진행형 가능)
cost	(돈·시간 따위가) 들다	~의 비용이 들고 있다
have	~을 가지고 있다	(시간을) 보내다, ~을 먹다
look	~하게 보이다	~을 보다(+at), ~을 찾다(+for)
smell	~한 냄새가 나다	~의 냄새를 맡다
taste	~한 맛이 나다	~을 맛보다
think	~라고 생각하다	~에 대해 생각하다
weigh	~의 무게가 나가다	~의 무게를 재다

Richard **has** two laptop computers. (상태)
리차드는 두 대의 노트북 컴퓨터를 가지고 있다.

They **are having** a great time at the concert. (동작)
그들은 콘서트에서 즐거운 시간을 보내고 있다.

The kids **are having** peanut butter and jelly sandwiches for lunch. (동작)
아이들은 점심으로 땅콩버터와 젤리가 들어간 샌드위치를 먹고 있다.

This stew **tastes** a bit salty. (상태) 이 스튜는 약간 맛이 짜다.

The cook **is tasting** the stew. (동작) 요리사가 스튜를 맛보고 있다.

I **think** Kevin is right. (상태) 나는 케빈이 옳다고 생각한다.

I **am thinking** of you. (동작) 나는 너에 대해 생각하고 있다.

|참고| 1. [be+being+형용사]는 평소와는 다른 일시적인 행동을 묘사할 때 쓴다.
He is usually diligent, but he **is being lazy** these days. 그는 보통 부지런한데, 요새 게으름을 피운다.
He always gets up at 10. He **is** very **lazy**. 그는 항상 10시에 일어난다. 그는 매우 게으르다.

2. 현재 '~해 보인다', '~하게 느낀다'라는 의미로 쓰일 때 look/feel은 현재 시제와 현재진행 두 가지 형태로 모두 쓸 수 있다.
You **look** tired today. = You **are looking** tired today. 너 오늘 피곤해 보인다.
I **feel** excited now. = I **am feeling** excited now. 나는 지금 신이 난다.

EXCERCISES

정답 및 해설 P. 10

A 밑줄 친 현재진행의 의미를 〈보기〉에서 골라 그 기호를 쓰시오.

보기
ⓐ 말하는 시점에 진행 중인 행동
ⓑ 현재를 포함하여 일정 기간 계속되는 일
ⓒ 가까운 미래의 확정적인 일

1 We are having hamburgers now. Do you want one? ________

2 My husband is rarely doing the house chores nowadays. ________

3 I am staying at my friend's apartment in the city this week. ________

4 Everything is settled. They are leaving on the ten o'clock train. ________

5 I'm making tuna casserole tonight. Will you stay for dinner? ________

6 Excuse me, I'm looking for an anniversary present for my wife. ________

house chore 집안일
settle 결정하다; (움직이지 않도록) 놓다
casserole 캐서롤(찜 냄비 요리)
look for ~을 찾다
anniversary 기념일

B 주어진 동사를 현재나 현재진행으로 바꿔 문장을 완성하시오.

1 Most Korean students ________ (study) even after school.

2 Every morning, Mr. Kim ________ (drive) his children to school.

3 Jean ________ (help) out in her mom's shop once or twice a week.

4 ________ your brother ________ (clean up) the garage right now?

5 Many Canadians ________ ________ (spend) their winter holidays in Mexico this year.

6 At the moment, I ________ ________ (prepare) lunch. So, I don't have time to talk now.

7 Look! It ________ ________ (rain) outside. I don't have an umbrella, so I need to borrow one.

8 The photographer ________ ________ (change) the camera's battery. Please be patient!

9 ________ you usually ________ (feed) the ducks bread? You know, that isn't very healthy for them.

10 Tracy ________ ________ (volunteer) in Africa this month, and she ________ ________ (fly) to the Philippines next month.

11 I ________ ________ (try) to lose weight before summer, so I ________ ________ (exercise) at the fitness center these days.

even ~조차
garage 차고; (자동차) 수리 공장
photographer 사진작가
patient 참을성 있는
feed 먹이를 주다
fitness center 헬스클럽

cost 비용이 들다; 가격
cheaper 값이 더 싼
contain ~이 들어 있다

( ) 안에서 가장 적절한 것을 고르시오.

1 The chef (tastes / is tasting) the soup in the kitchen now.

2 These flowers (smell / are smelling) so good. Let's buy some for Mom.

3 (Do you have / Are you having) coffee now? It smells fantastic!

4 Mike (looks for / is looking for) you now. Send him a text message.

5 The baker (tastes / is tasting) the chocolate cake. It looks delicious.

6 These shoes (cost / are costing) too much. Help me find a cheaper pair.

7 Tommy (has / is having) two laptop computers, but they are not working.

8 I (don't like / am not liking) living in London because it always rains so much.

9 It is good to have food which (contains / is containing) lots of vitamins and minerals.

10 My mother (makes / is making) me wash my hands as soon as I'm back from school.

11 It's still snowing! I (think / am thinking) we're going to have a white Christmas this year.

local 지방의, 지역적인
flea market 벼룩시장
correctly 정확히, 바르게
fridge (=refrigerator) 냉장고

D 〈보기〉에서 알맞은 동사를 골라 현재나 현재진행으로 바꿔 문장을 완성하시오.

보기				
	study	make	answer	go
	visit	do	act	read

1 Every Sunday, we ________________ the local flea market.

2 My mother usually ________________ newspapers at 7 a.m.

3 Your friend ________________ foolishly. Please tell him to stop.

4 She always ________________ the teacher's questions correctly.

5 We ________________ for tomorrow's world history exam right now.

6 I ________________ a shopping list now. Open the fridge and tell me what we need.

7 The children are making too much noise in the restaurant. But their parents ________________ nothing.

8 Jake ________________ to church every Sunday, and after church he plays basketball with his friends.

E 우리말과 같은 뜻이 되도록 주어진 단어를 이용하여 문장을 완성하시오.

clerk 직원
sniff 냄새를 맡다
refresh (원기, 에너지를) 되찾게 하다

1 그녀는 내가 그에 대해 모든 것을 알고 있다고 믿고 있다. (believe, know)

→ She ______________ that I ______________ everything about him.

2 점원이 내가 고른 사과들의 무게를 재고 있었다. (weigh)

→ The clerk ______________ the apples I picked.

3 아버지는 차고에 있다. 그는 차를 고치고 있다. (fix)

→ My father is in the garage. He ______________ his car.

4 개가 내 운동화에 대고 냄새를 맡고 있었다. (sniff at)

→ A dog ______________________ my sneakers.

5 마리아는 피아노를 연주하고 있다. 그리고 우리는 그녀의 연주를 듣고 있다. (play, listen to)

→ Maria ______________ the piano, and we ______________ her.

6 나는 요새 집에서 요가를 하고 있다. 그것은 나의 기운을 북돋아준다. (do, make)

→ I ______________ yoga at home these days. It ______________ me feel refreshed.

7 너는 휴가 때 이탈리아에 갈 거니? 얼마나 머무를 거니? (go, stay)

→ ___________ you ___________ to Italy for the holidays? How long ___________ you ___________?

F 우리말과 같은 뜻이 되도록 주어진 단어를 배열하시오.

schoolyard 운동장
appreciate 감사하게 생각하다
semester 학기
aquarium 수족관

1 Tina는 식당에서 점심을 먹고 있다. (lunch, having, at the cafeteria, is)

→ Tina ____.

2 그들은 다음 달에 결혼을 할 것이다. (married, next month, getting, are)

→ They ____.

3 지금 학생 몇 명이 운동장에서 축구 하고 있다. (soccer, are, the schoolyard, playing, in)

→ Some students ______________________________________ now.

4 제게 기회를 한 번 더 주셔서 감사합니다. (a chance, that, me, appreciate, I, you, gave)

→ ____ again.

5 우리 아버지는 아침을 먹으면서 신문을 읽고 있다. (the newspaper, my father, reading, is)

→ ______________________________________, having breakfast.

6 그녀는 이번 학기에 학교에서 발레를 가르치고 있다. (teaching, in a school, is, ballet)

→ She ______________________________________ this semester.

7 돌고래는 수족관에서 수영을 하고 있고 사람들은 그들을 보고 있다.
(watching, swimming, are, in the aquarium, are, them)

→ Dolphins ____________________, and people ____________________.

과거진행

쓰임	예문
과거 어느 한 시점에서 진행되고 있는 행동	Allen was swimming in the pool an hour ago. 앨런은 한 시간 전에 수영장에서 수영하고 있었다.
과거진행 vs. 과거	When Emily was watching TV, Sarah came to see her. 과거진행(1st action) 과거(2nd action) 에밀리가 TV를 보고 있을 때 사라가 그녀를 보러 왔다.

FOCUS

1 과거진행(past progressive) 시제는 어떠한 일이나 행동이 과거의 어느 특정한 시점에서 진행되고 있었음을 의미한다.

A: What were you doing yesterday afternoon? 너는 어제 오후에 무엇을 하고 있었니?

B: I was playing tennis with my friend. 내 친구랑 테니스를 치고 있었어.

A: What was Sally doing when Brandon came home? 브랜든이 집에 왔을 때 샐리는 무엇을 하고 있었니?

B: She was watching a movie with her friends. 그녀는 친구들과 영화를 보고 있었어.

2 과거의 비슷한 시점에 일어난 두 가지 일을 나타낼 때, 먼저 시작된 일은 과거진행 시제를 사용하고 나중에 일어난 일은 과거 시제를 사용한다.

I was talking to Emma. (1st action) 나는 엠마와 말하는 중이었다.

Rachel called me. (2nd action) 레이첼이 나를 불렀다.

→ While I was talking to Emma, Rachel called me.
내가 엠마와 말하는 동안 레이첼이 나를 불렀다.

Darren was having dinner. (1st action) 대런은 저녁을 먹고 있었다.

Darren's parents came home. (2nd action) 대런의 부모님이 집에 오셨다.

→ While Darren was having dinner, his parents came home.
대런이 저녁을 먹고 있을 때, 그의 부모님이 집에 오셨다.

I was walking in the park. (1st action) 나는 공원에서 걷고 있었다.

It began to pour. (2nd action) 비가 억수같이 퍼붓기 시작했다.

→ When I was walking in the park, it began to pour.
내가 공원에서 걷고 있을 때 비가 억수같이 퍼붓기 시작했다.

|참고| 주절과 부사절 모두에 과거진행이 사용될 경우, 어떤 일이 동시에 진행되는 것을 의미한다.
While I was studying upstairs, my brother was sleeping downstairs.
내가 위층에서 공부하는 동안, 우리 형은 아래층에서 잠을 자고 있었다.

EXERCISES

정답 및 해설 P. 11

A 주어진 동사를 과거 또는 과거진행으로 바꿔 대화를 완성하시오.

storm in (화내며 난폭하게) 들어오다
get in trouble 곤경에 빠지다
stop in (~에) 잠깐 들르다
assignment 숙제; 할당
get angry with ~에게 화내다
blare (텔레비전의 소리가) 크게 울리다

1 A: What's wrong, Mom? You look upset.
B: Dad ____________ (hurt) himself while he ____________ ____________ (work) today.

2 A: I ____________ ____________ (make) the whole class laugh when Mr. Park ____________ ____________ (storm in).
B: Then what happened? Did you get in a lot of trouble?

3 A: What were you doing right after school? I ____________ ____________ ____________ (wait for) you.
B: I stopped in to see Mr. Nicholas. I ____________ (have) a question about the history assignment.

4 A: Why did you get so angry with Michelle this afternoon?
B: While she ____________ ____________ (wash) her hair in the bathroom, the TV ____________ ____________ (blare) in the living room.

5 A: Bill and I had a small party last night. We ____________ (want) to invite you, but you ____________ ____________ (not, answer) the phone.
B: Oh, I ____________ ____________ (sleep) when you ____________ (call).

B 주어진 동사를 먼저 시작된 일(1st action)은 과거진행으로, 나중에 일어난 일(2nd action)은 과거로 바꿔 문장을 완성하시오.

run into ~와 우연히 만나다
giggle 낄낄 웃다

1 When I ________________ (walk) home today, I ________________ (run into) my old English teacher.

2 While we ________________ (have) a great time, we ________________ (hear) the sad news on the radio.

3 I did not hear any bell ringing. I ________________ (listen) to music when you ________________ (call) me.

4 When we ________________ (study) history to prepare for the final exam, my father ________________ (bring) us some cookies.

5 Amy ________________ (see) Jennifer at the mall yesterday. She ________________________________ (laugh and giggle) with her new boyfriend, Steve.

미래진행

쓰임	예문
미래의 특정 시점에서 진행 중인 상황	They **will be playing** soccer this time tomorrow afternoon. 그들은 내일 오후 이 시간에 축구를 하고 있을 것이다.
이미 계획된 미래의 행동이나 사건	Julia **will be participating** in the speech contest on Friday. 줄리아는 금요일에 말하기 대회에 참가할 것이다.

FOCUS

1

미래진행(future progressive)은 미래의 어느 특정한 시점에서 진행 중일 일이나 사건에 대해 이야기할 때 사용한다. 미래진행의 형태는 「will be+-ing」와 「be going to be+-ing」가 있다.

We will explore the island from 2 p.m. to 5 p.m. Natalie will join us at 3 p.m.
우리는 두 시부터 다섯 시까지 그 섬을 탐험할 것이다. 나탈리는 세 시에 우리와 합류할 것이다.

→ We **will be exploring** the island when Natalie joins us.
나탈리가 우리와 합류할 때 우리는 그 섬을 탐험하고 있을 것이다.

Tomorrow at nine, I **will be taking** my last exam of this year.
내일 아홉 시에 나는 올해의 마지막 시험을 보고 있을 것이다.

She **is going to be studying** the traditional dances of Korea this summer.
그녀는 이번 여름에 한국 전통무용을 공부할 것이다.

The government **will be announcing** more tax cuts in the spring.
정부는 봄에 더 많은 세금 인하를 발표할 것이다.

2

이미 계획된 미래의 일을 이야기할 때 흔히 미래진행 또는 현재진행을 사용한다.

We **will be leaving** for New Zealand at eight in the evening.

→ We **are leaving** for New Zealand at eight in the evening.
우리는 저녁 여덟 시에 뉴질랜드로 떠날 거야.

Professor Cooper **will be giving** the first presentation at the conference.

→ Professor Cooper **is giving** the first presentation at the conference.
쿠퍼 교수님이 회의에서 첫 번째로 발표할 거야.

EXERCISES

정답 및 해설 P. 11

A 주어진 동사와 will을 이용하여 미래진행(will)으로 바꿔 쓰시오.

1 This time next week I ______________ (sit) on a beach.

2 Stop by at 2 p.m. I ______________ (wait for) you in my office.

3 He ______________ (watch) his favorite TV drama *CSI* at nine.

4 This plane ______________ (land) in approximately ten minutes.

5 I ______________ (sleep) at midnight, so please call me earlier.

6 ________ you ____________ (bring) your best friend to the party?

7 Take a warm jacket with you. It ______________ (freeze) tonight.

8 Our grandparents ______________ (visit) us tomorrow. We'll pick them up at the airport.

stop by 방문하다
land ~에 착륙하다; 육지
approximately 거의, 대략
midnight 한밤중; 암흑
bring 데려오다; 가져오다
freeze 얼 정도로 춥다; 얼음이 얼다

B 〈보기〉에서 알맞은 동사를 골라 미래진행(will)으로 바꿔 대화를 완성하시오.

보기 | work | see | play | eat | go | cook | study

1 A: ________ you ____________ Mike later today?
B: Yes, I will. Shall I have him call you?

2 A: I ______________ to the supermarket later today.
B: Please get some ham for my lunch.

3 A: ________ you ____________ dinner at 6 o'clock?
B: No. I will be done by then. Drop by anytime after 6.

4 A: ________ you ____________ supper from now on, Dad?
B: Yes. And Mom will continue to cook breakfast and lunch.

5 A: Do you want to come over and watch a movie on Saturday night?
B: I'd love to, but I ______________ then. I have several tests next week.

6 A: My band ______________ at the Centennial Music Hall this weekend. Will you come?
B: Sure! What time will you guys be going on?

7 A: Will you go to New York on business next week?
B: No. I ______________ in my office then. The business trip has been delayed.

supper 저녁식사
come over (집에) 들르다
centennial 100주년; 100년마다의
go on 무대에 나타나다; 계속하다
delay 연기하다, 미루다

REVIEW

정답 및 해설 P. 12

tool 연장, 도구
fix 수리하다; 고정시키다
UFO(=Unidentified Flying Object) 미확인 비행 물체
alien 외계인
pack (짐 등을) 꾸리다
own 소유하다
wheel 바퀴
fall off 떨어져 나오다
awful 지독한, 끔찍한
air (방을) 환기하다
direction 지시 사항

A ( ) 안에서 가장 적절한 것을 고르시오.

1 I (prefer / am preferring) to eat at home.

2 Mr. Park (is getting / was getting) married next month.

3 Kevin (needs / is needing) some tools to fix his bicycle.

4 (Do you believe / Are you believing) in UFOs or aliens?

5 Why (does she look / is she looking) for Jessica now?

6 While I was packing, my lazy brother (is sleeping / was sleeping).

7 Who (owns / is owing) the mountain bike in front of my garage?

8 I didn't learn much Italian when I (am / was) in Italy two years ago.

9 Mike was riding his bike down the road when the wheel (falls off / fell off).

10 You (don't seem / won't seem) very happy these days. What's the matter?

11 The room (smells / is smelling) awful! How about opening the window and airing it out?

12 (Do you understand / Are you understanding) these directions?

contain ~이 들어있다; ~을 포함하다
mammal 포유동물
amusement park 놀이공원
finals 기말고사
cram 벼락공부를 하다
float 뜨다
lie 눕다 (lie–lay–lain)
weird 이상한
from scratch 무(無)에서, 처음부터
hold (회의 등을) 열다; 잡고 있다
press conference 기자 회견

B 밑줄 친 부분을 바르게 고치시오.

1 This bottle is containing two liters of water.

2 Dolphins are not fish; they are being mammals.

3 We have a good time in the amusement park now.

4 My cousins usually are going to church on Sundays.

5 My finals start next week. I will cramming all weekend long.

6 Oil and water are not mixing and oil is floating on the water.

7 When he lies on the bed, he heard a weird sound from outside.

8 This pie is tasting amazing! Did you really make it from scratch?

9 I am resembling my father, and my sister is resembling my mother.

10 The President was holding a press conference tomorrow morning.

C 〈보기〉에서 알맞은 동사를 골라 시제에 맞게 대화를 완성하시오.

보기 change learn take speak wait attend

1 A: She can't talk to you right now. She __________ __________ a nap.
B: Okay. Please let me know when she wakes up.

2 A: I __________ __________ __________ for you in my office at 7.
B: Okay. I will call you when I leave home.

3 A: What language __________ they __________ now? It sounds familiar.
B: I'm not sure, but I think it's French.

4 A: You look great in that suit. What's the occasion?
B: I __________ __________ my aunt's wedding today.

5 A: I changed my mind. Let's meet at the library.
B: Oh, you __________ constantly __________ your mind!

6 A: I __________ __________ __________ __________ to play the guitar this summer.
B: Really? Can I join you?

take a nap 낮잠을 자다
familiar 익숙한, 친숙한
suit 정장, 옷
occasion 행사; 경우
constantly 끊임없이

D 우리말과 같은 뜻이 되도록 주어진 단어와 진행 시제를 이용하여 문장을 완성하시오.

1 집 앞에서 너를 기다리고 있을게. (wait)
→ I __________ __________ __________ for you in front of the house.

2 나는 다음 주에 운전 수업을 들을 예정이다. (have, week)
→ I __________ __________ my driving lesson __________ __________.

3 우리는 내일 저녁 8시에 도서관에서 공부하고 있을 것이다. (study)
→ We __________ __________ __________ in the library at 8 p.m. tomorrow.

4 나는 다른 방향을 보고 있었기 때문에 너를 보지 못했어. (see, face)
→ I __________ __________ you because I __________ __________ the other way.

5 너 청소할 때 제임스를 보았니? (clean, see)
→ When you __________ __________ the classroom, __________ you __________ James?

6 내가 운동장에서 놀고 있을 때, 비가 오기 시작했다. (play, start, rain)
→ When I __________ __________ in the schoolyard, it __________ __________ __________.

face ~의 쪽을 향하다

REVIEW PLUS

정답 및 해설 P. 13

earthquake 지진
strike 강타하다, 치다
chop (도끼 등으로) 패다; (야채 등을) 잘게 썰다
pain 고통
chest 가슴; 흉부
somewhere 어딘가
unhealthy 건강에 해로운

A 다음 (A), (B), (C)에 들어갈 말이 바르게 짝지어진 것을 고르시오.

- They were having a picnic in the park when the earthquake ___(A)___.
- My father ___(B)___ wood when he felt a sharp pain in his chest.
- I ___(C)___ anything after 10 p.m. I read somewhere that it is unhealthy.

	(A)		(B)		(C)
①	strikes	···	is chopping	···	eat never
②	strikes	···	was chopping	···	eat never
③	struck	···	was chopping	···	eat never
④	struck	···	was chopping	···	never eat
⑤	struck	···	is chopping	···	never eat

chore 늘 하는 일, 집안일
take out ~을 꺼내다, 들어내다
trash 쓰레기
whisper 귓속말을 하다, 소곤거리다

B 다음 대화를 읽고, 빈칸에 가장 적절한 것을 고르시오.

1 A: Wow! You guys finished all of your chores so quickly.
B: While Jack ________ the living room, I washed the dishes and took out the trash.

① is cleaning ② will clean ③ clean
④ was cleaning ⑤ cleans

2 A: Why is that girl looking at me and ________ to Mary?
B: I don't know. Maybe she's interested in you.

① whispering ② will whisper ③ whispers
④ whispered ⑤ whisper

witness 목격하다
squeeze in 비집고 들어가다
get stuck 꼼짝 못하게 되다
a couple of 두 사람의
wedge 좁은 틈 사이로 물건을 끼워서 열다

C 다음을 읽고, (   ) 안에서 가장 알맞은 것을 고르시오.

Michelle ① (witnesses / witnessed) a terrible accident on the subway this evening. Just as the doors ② (are closing / were closing) at City Hall station, an old woman tried to squeeze in between them. But she got stuck. Luckily, a couple of strong teenage boys ③ (are standing / were standing) next to the door when it happened. They were able to wedge the door open and pull her to safety.

PART 4

완료 시제
The Perfect Tenses

현재완료

정답 및 해설 P. 14

1 동사의 과거분사(past participles)는 일반적으로 동사원형에 '(e)d'를 붙여서 만든다.

과거분사의 형태		
대부분의 일반동사	+(e)d	invited, listened, looked, waved ...
「자음+y」로 끝나는 동사	y → i+ed	studied, dried, tried, cried, worried ...
1음절로 「단모음+자음」인 동사 2음절로 뒤에 강세가 있는 동사	끝자음 하나 더 +ed	stopped, dropped, planned, slipped, occurred, preferred ...
불규칙 동사	begin → **begun**, drive → **driven**, find → **found** ...	

CHECK-UP

주어진 동사의 과거분사를 쓰시오.

1 break ____________

2 bring ____________

3 build ____________

4 buy ____________

5 catch ____________

6 choose ____________

7 come ____________

8 cost ____________

9 cut ____________

10 draw ____________

11 drink ____________

12 feed ____________

13 fall ____________

14 fight ____________

15 fly ____________

16 send ____________

17 write ____________

18 begin ____________

19 grow ____________

20 hit ____________

21 hold ____________

22 hurt ____________

23 keep ____________

24 lend ____________

25 lose ____________

26 mean ____________

27 pay ____________

28 put ____________

29 read ____________

30 set ____________

31 sit ____________

32 steal ____________

33 wear ____________

34 go ____________

35 drive ____________

36 lay ____________

2 현재완료(present perfect)의 기본 형태는 「have/has+과거분사(p.p.)」이다.

현재완료		
긍정문	She has been to New York.	They have cleaned the bathroom.
부정문	She hasn't been to New York.	They haven't cleaned the bathroom.
의문문	Has she been to New York?	Have they cleaned the bathroom?

CHECK-UP

〈보기〉와 같이 현재완료 문장을 완성하시오.

> 보기
> (긍정문) Leo __has worked__ (work) at the bank since 2007.
> (부정문) Jessica __hasn't eaten__ (not, eat) anything all day long.
> (의문문) __Have__ you __watched__ (watch) the DVD several times?

1 (의문문) ________ we ________ (meet) before?

2 (부정문) I ________________ (never, be) to Russia.

3 (긍정문) Alice ________________ (live) in Tokyo since 2010.

4 (긍정문) We ________________ (be) friends since last winter.

5 (긍정문) He ________________ (lose) his wallet several times.

6 (긍정문) He ________________ (work) at the bank since 2007.

7 (부정문) I ________________ (not, decide) what to do next.

8 (의문문) ________ you ________ (visit) many parts of Korea?

9 (의문문) ________ you ________ (see) the movie before?

10 (부정문) Sam and David ________________ (never, try) sushi before.

11 (부정문) Hyesu ________________ (not, attend) class since last Monday.

12 (긍정문) I ________________ (watch) the musical at the theater seven times.

13 (의문문) ________ Carla ________ (be) interested in working with children?

14 (부정문) Sandra ________________ (never, win) the lottery in her whole life.

현재완료

현재완료(have/has+p.p.)
: 과거 어느 시점부터 지금까지

past — now — future

	예문	주로 함께 쓰는 부사
경험	I've never been to Egypt. 나는 한 번도 이집트에 가본 적이 없다.	before, ever, never, once, twice ...
완료	I've just finished my homework. 나는 방금 숙제를 끝마쳤다.	already, just, yet ...
계속	I've waited for him since two o'clock. 나는 두 시부터 그를 기다렸다.	since, for ...

FOCUS

1

현재완료(present perfect)는 어느 특정한 과거 시점에서 시작된 동작이나 상태가 현재까지 영향을 미칠 때 쓴다.

Evan lost his key, and he still doesn't have it. 에반은 열쇠를 잃어버렸고, 아직도 그것을 가지고 있지 않다.

→ Evan **has lost** his key. 에반은 열쇠를 잃어버렸다.

I forgot Doris's last name, and I can't remember it now. 나는 도리스의 성(姓)을 잊어버렸고, 지금도 그것을 기억할 수가 없다.

→ I**'ve forgotten** Doris's last name. 나는 도리스의 성(姓)을 잊어버렸다.

My mother went out, and she is not here now. 우리 어머니는 밖에 나가셨고, 지금 여기 안 계신다.

→ My mother **has gone** out. 우리 어머니는 밖에 나가셨다.

|주의| have gone은 '가버리고 없다'라는 뜻으로 1인칭이나 2인칭을 주어로 사용할 수 없다.

2

현재완료는 ever, never, before, once, twice, three times 등과 함께 쓰여 경험의 뜻을 나타낸다.

A: **Have** you ever **tried** snails? I used to eat them when I was young.
너는 달팽이를 먹어 본 적이 있니? 나는 어렸을 때 그것을 먹곤 했어.

B: No, I**'ve** never **tried** them. But I**'ve tried** oysters a couple of times.
나는 달팽이를 먹어 본 적이 없어. 하지만 굴은 두세 번 먹어 봤어.

|주의| have gone to vs. have been to

have gone to는 '~로 가버렸다 (그래서 현재 이곳에 없다)'는 의미이고, have been to는 '~에 가본 적이 있다(경험)'는 의미이다.

He **has gone to** the USA to study music. 그는 음악을 공부하기 위해 미국으로 갔다. (그래서 현재는 여기 없다는 뜻)

I **have been to** many countries, and I love Italy best. 나는 많은 나라에 가봤지만 이탈리아가 가장 좋다.

3 현재완료는 just, already, yet 등과 함께 쓰여 완료의 뜻을 나타낸다. yet은 주로 부정문이나 의문문에 사용된다.

A: Are you hungry? 너 배고프니?

B: No, I've just had dinner. 아니, 방금 저녁을 먹었어.

A: Don't forget to mail the postcards. 엽서 부치는 것을 잊지 마.

B: I've already mailed them. 벌써 부쳤어.

A: Has it stopped raining yet? 이제 비 오는 거 멈췄니?

B: No, it hasn't. 아니, 안 멈췄어.

A: Have you opened your gifts? 너는 선물을 열어 봤니?

B: No, I haven't opened them yet. 아니, 아직 안 열어 봤어.

4 현재완료는 since, for 등과 함께 쓰여 계속의 뜻을 나타낸다. since 뒤에는 정확한 시각이나 연도 등이 나오고, for 뒤에는 기간이 나온다.

since	+	nine o'clock / 2008 / December 28th / yesterday / Friday / I was born ...
for	+	three hours / two days / four weeks / a month / ten years / ages / a long time ...

Subin has studied in China since 2007. 수빈이는 2007년부터 중국에서 공부하고 있다.

Everything is going well. We haven't had any problems so far. 모든 일이 잘되어 가고 있어. 우리는 지금까지는 별문제 없어.

A: Have you seen Jordan recently? 최근에 조던을 본 적 있니?

B: I haven't seen Jordan for about a month. 나는 약 한 달 동안 조던을 본 적이 없어.

5 현재완료는 어떤 일이 일어난 정확한 시간이 중요하지 않을 때 주로 사용한다. 특정한 시간이 언급되고, 현재까지 연결되는 동작이나 상태가 없다면 과거 시제를 사용한다.

I didn't play ice hockey last winter. 나는 지난겨울에 아이스하키를 하지 않았다.

I have never played ice hockey in my life. 나는 평생 아이스하키를 해본 적이 없다.

Stephen Hawking wrote the book *A Brief History of Time* in 1988.
스티븐 호킹은 1988년에 '시간의 역사'라는 책을 썼다.

William Gibson has written many sci-fi books, including *Neuromancer* and *Count Zero*.
윌리엄 깁슨은 '뉴로맨서'와 '카운트 제로'를 포함하여 많은 공상 과학 책을 써왔다.

Pablo Picasso was born in 1881. 파블로 피카소는 1881년에 태어났다.

Have you ever been to Pablo Picasso's exhibition? 파블로 피카소의 전시회에 가 본 적이 있니?

EXERCISES

정답 및 해설 P. 14

hold (회의 등을) 열다, 잡고 있다
send in ~을 제출하다
application 지원(서)
reach (전화 등으로) 연락하다

A 주어진 동사를 현재완료로 바꿔 문장을 완성하시오.

1 The TV was off. Now, the TV is on.
→ Someone ______________ (turn on) the TV.

2 Mom called Pizza House. A pizza is on its way.
→ Mom ______________ (order) a pizza.

3 Anne just left for the library with Gilbert. They are out now.
→ Anne and Gilbert ______________ (go) out.

4 My school is holding an English speech contest. I sent in my application.
→ I ______________ (enter) the English speech contest.

5 Jasper is trying to reach Sarah. He called at 9 a.m., 11 a.m., and 4 p.m.
→ Jasper ______________ (call) Sarah three times today.

6 Anika came to Korea in early September. She is still in Korea, and now it is late November.
→ Anika ______________ (be) in Korea for almost three months.

remind 생각나게 하다, 상기시키다
shovel ~을 삽으로 파다; 삽
walk 인도; 걷다
report card 성적표
do well 성적이 좋다; 잘하다; 성공하다

B 주어진 단어와 현재완료를 사용하여 대화를 완성하시오.

1 A: Are you hungry? I can make you something to eat.
B: No, thanks. I ______________ a snack. (have, just)

2 A: Don't forget to call your sister and remind her about the party.
B: I ______________ her. (call, already)

3 A: ________ it ________ snowing ________? (stop, yet)
B: No, it hasn't. I think we should wait a while before shoveling the walk.

4 A: ________ you ________ your parents your report card ________? (show, yet)
B: No, I haven't. I'm not too worried, though. I did well in math and English.

5 A: Bella ______________. (leave, already) You just missed her by a few minutes.
B: That's too bad. Will you give her a message for me?

6 A: Somebody ______________ (steal) my wallet! I can't find it anywhere.
B: Have you checked your desk and locker?

C since와 for 중 알맞은 것을 골라 빈칸에 써넣으시오.

1 I haven't had a decent meal __________ I arrived.

2 I haven't eaten anything __________ this morning.

3 I've known Tom and Cindy __________ about two years now.

4 They have never traveled abroad __________ they got married.

5 My father has worked for the same company __________ 15 years.

6 Mr. Thompson has read the same newspaper __________ 10 years.

7 The underground in London has been in operation __________ 1933.

8 Pam hasn't attended yoga class __________ she moved to a new city.

9 Dad is always busy. So he hasn't had a vacation __________ five years.

10 My father has owned this old record player __________ he was a child.

11 I haven't seen your sister __________ ages. She's really growing up quickly!

12 My sister has played on the basketball team __________ months.

decent 적당한, 알맞은
get married 결혼하다
underground (英) 지하철 cf. subway (美) 지하철
in operation 운행 중, 활동 중
for ages 오랫동안
for months 오랫동안

D 주어진 동사를 과거와 현재완료 중 가장 알맞은 것으로 바꿔 문장을 완성하시오.

1 The price of oil ______________ (go up) recently.

2 What time __________ the rehearsal __________ (finish) yesterday?

3 Jodie lives in Vancouver. She ______________ (live) there all her life.

4 I ______________ (be) to Busan three times since I moved to Korea.

5 Sam ______________ (marry) his girlfriend in Las Vegas last weekend.

6 My parents ______________ (be) happily married for over thirty years.

7 Emily ______________ (treat) sick people in Africa for over twenty years.

8 The Maple Leaf ______________ (be) Canada's official flag since 1965.

9 We ______________ (not, have) a vacation for years. It's time for a break.

10 Amy lives in Jamaica. She ______________ (never, see) snow in her life.

11 Last night, I ______________ (hear) a strange noise coming from the next apartment.

12 Emma has a beautiful garden. She ______________ (plant) roses and tulips last week.

maple 단풍나무
official flag 국기
plant (씨를) 뿌리다, (식물을) 심다

현재완료진행

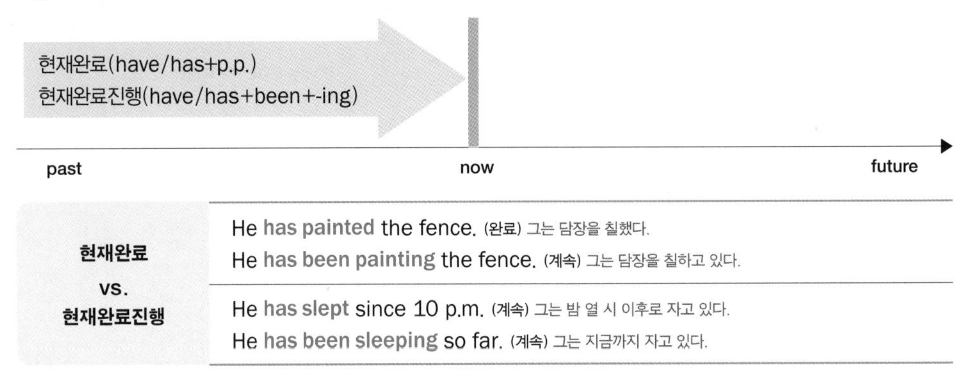

현재완료 vs. 현재완료진행	He **has painted** the fence. (완료) 그는 담장을 칠했다. He **has been painting** the fence. (계속) 그는 담장을 칠하고 있다.
	He **has slept** since 10 p.m. (계속) 그는 밤 열 시 이후로 자고 있다. He **has been sleeping** so far. (계속) 그는 지금까지 자고 있다.

FOCUS

1 현재완료진행(present perfect progressive)은 특정한 과거 시점에 시작한 행동이 현재에도 진행 중임을 나타낼 때 사용한다. 현재완료진행의 기본 형태는 「have/has+been+-ing」이다.

Bill's eyes are red. He **has been playing** the video game for six hours.
빌의 눈이 충혈되었다. 그는 여섯 시간째 비디오 게임을 하고 있다.

A: Why are your clothes wet? What **have** you **been doing**? 네 옷이 왜 젖었니? 뭐 하고 있었어?

B: I **have been washing** my father's car. 아버지의 차를 세차하고 있는 중이었어.

A: Where have you been? I**'ve been waiting** for you for over an hour! 너 어디 있었니? 나는 한 시간도 넘게 너를 기다리고 있었어!

B: I'm sorry. I got lost. 미안. 길을 잃었었어.

2 의문사 how long은 현재완료나 현재완료진행과 함께 사용하는 반면, 의문사 when은 주로 정확한 때를 나타내는 단순 시제와 함께 사용한다.

A: How long **have** you **been sitting** here? 얼마나 오랫동안 여기에 앉아 있었니?

B: I **have been sitting** here since this morning. 오늘 아침부터 여기에 앉아 있었어.

A: How long **have** you **lived** here? 얼마나 오랫동안 여기 살았니?

B: I **have lived** here for almost ten years. 나는 거의 10년 동안 여기에 살았어.

A: When **did** you **start** studying Japanese? 너는 언제 일본어 공부를 시작했니?

B: I **started** studying Japanese two years ago. 나는 2년 전에 일본어 공부를 시작했어.

3

「How long ~?」은 행동이나 상태가 얼마나 계속되고 있는가를 묻는 것이므로 현재완료 또는 현재완료진행으로 쓸 수 있다. 「How many ~?」, 「How much ~?」는 계속의 개념보다는 완료의 개념이 강하므로 현재완료진행보다는 현재완료로 쓴다.

It is snowing now. It began snowing two hours ago. 지금 눈이 오고 있다. 두 시간 전에 눈이 오기 시작했다.

A: How long **has** it **been snowing**? 얼마나 오랫동안 눈이 오는 거니?

B: It **has been snowing** for two hours. 두 시간째 눈이 오는 거야.

A: How long **have** you **been reading** that book? 얼마나 오랫동안 그 책을 읽었니?

B: I **have been reading** it for two hours. 두 시간 동안 읽고 있어.

A: How many pages of that book **have** you **read**? 그 책을 몇 페이지나 읽었니?

B: I **have read** almost 100 pages. 거의 100쪽을 읽었어.

A: How much money **have** you **got**? 돈을 얼마나 가지고 있니?

B: I **have got** 100 dollars. 백 달러 있어.

4

동작이 완료되었음에 중점을 둘 때는 현재완료를, 동작이 계속됨에 중점을 둘 때는 현재완료진행을 쓴다.

Somebody **has eaten** all my chocolate cake! The box is totally empty. (완료)
누군가 내 초콜릿 케이크를 먹어 버렸어! 상자가 완전히 비었어.

Wendy **has been eating** my chocolate chip cookies. She's going to eat them all. (계속)
웬디가 내 초콜릿 칩 쿠키를 먹고 있어. 그녀가 그것을 모두 먹어 치울 거야.

Where's the DVD I gave you? What **have** you **done** with it? (완료)
내가 너에게 준 DVD는 어디에 있니? 그것을 어떻게 한 거니?

It's nice to see you again. What **have** you **been doing** since we met last? (계속)
다시 만나서 반가워요. 지난번에 우리가 만난 이후로 무엇을 하며 지냈어요?

| 참고 | 현재완료진행과 계속을 나타내는 현재완료는 의미상 차이가 거의 없다. 대표적인 동사로는 work, live, study, teach, lie, sleep 등이 있다.

I **have been working** for this company for twenty years. 나는 이십 년 동안 이 회사에서 일하고 있다.

I **have worked** for this company for twenty years. 나는 이십 년 동안 이 회사에서 일하고 있다.

EXERCISES

정답 및 해설 P. 15

hang up ~을 걸다, 매달다
wet 젖은
laundry 세탁물
go well 잘 되어가다
wait in line 줄을 서서 기다리다
vacuum 진공청소기로 청소하다
dust (물건 등의) 먼지를 털다; 먼지
be absent from ~에 결근[결석]하다

A 주어진 동사를 현재완료진행으로 바꿔 문장을 완성하시오.

1 What ____________ you ____________________ (do) this week?

2 Vincent ______________________ (hang up) the wet laundry.

3 Everything ______________________ (go) well at school lately.

4 Who ______________________ (eat) my popcorn? Half the bag is gone!

5 They ______________________ (wait) in line for a half hour to get the tickets.

6 Your brother ______________________ (vacuum) the carpet. Please dust the furniture.

7 You ______________________ (play) that computer game for over three hours. Go outside and get some exercise.

8 We ______________________ (wait) for you here since seven o'clock.

take care of ~을 돌보다
collection 소장품, 수집
anniversary 기념일

B (A)와 (B)에서 알맞은 것을 하나씩 골라 문장을 완성하시오.

(A)	(B)
how much money	have you spent
how long	have you invited
how many people	have you listened
how many times	have you been babysitting

1 Your friend is taking care of his neighbor's children. Ask him.
→ ______________________________ your neighbor's children?

2 Your friend collects old books. She has a large collection. Ask her.
→ ______________________________ collecting all of these old books?

3 Your brother just bought the new Great Boys CD. He keeps listening to it. Ask him.
→ ______________________________ to that new Great Boys CD?

4 Your sister is planning a 25th wedding anniversary party for your parents. Ask her.
→ ______________________________ to Mom and Dad's 25th wedding anniversary party?

C 주어진 동사를 현재완료진행이나 과거 중 가장 알맞은 것으로 바꿔 질문을 완성하시오.

date ~와 데이트하다
lie 누워 있다; 거짓말하다
sunbed 일광욕용 침대

1 (date) ① When ________ he ________________ Susie?
② How long ________ he ________________ Susie?

2 (teach) ① When ________ you ________________ English?
② How long ________ you ________________ English?

3 (ring) ① When ________ my cell phone ________________?
② How long ________ my cell phone ________________?

4 (talk) ① When ________ Aaron ________________ to Yunhee?
② How long ________ Aaron ________________ to Yunhee?

5 (lie) ① When ________ Marco ________________ on the sunbed?
② How long ________ Marco ________________ on the sunbed?

6 (work) ① When ________ Jinwoo ________________ at Everworld?
② How long ________ Jinwoo ________________ at Everworld?

7 (wear) ① When ________ Jimin ________________ contact lenses?
② How long ________ Jimin ________________ contact lenses?

D 주어진 상황에 맞게 가장 알맞은 것을 골라 연결하시오.

go backpacking 배낭여행을 하다
enthusiastic 열광적인, 열렬한
post 게시하다
manual 설명서; 수동의

1 Nancy went backpacking around South America. She began her trip last month. She has been to Chile, Brazil, and Columbia.
① She ______ to three countries so far. • ⓐ has traveled
② She ______ for one month. • ⓑ has been traveling

2 Jasmine is an enthusiastic blogger. She plans to post more than ten messages this week. She just finished posting three messages.
① Jasmine ______ messages to her blog all week. • ⓐ has been posting
② Jasmine ______ three messages so far. • ⓑ has posted

3 Mr. Brown started watching movies this morning. Now, it is 3 p.m. He is still watching movies, and now he just started the fifth movie.
① He ______ movies since this morning. • ⓐ has watched
② He ______ four movies so far. • ⓑ has been watching

4 Michael started reading his new cell phone manual about two hours ago. He is still reading it, and now he just finished reading page 120.
① He ______ the manual for over two hours. • ⓐ has read
② He ______ 120 pages so far. • ⓑ has been reading

과거완료와 과거완료진행

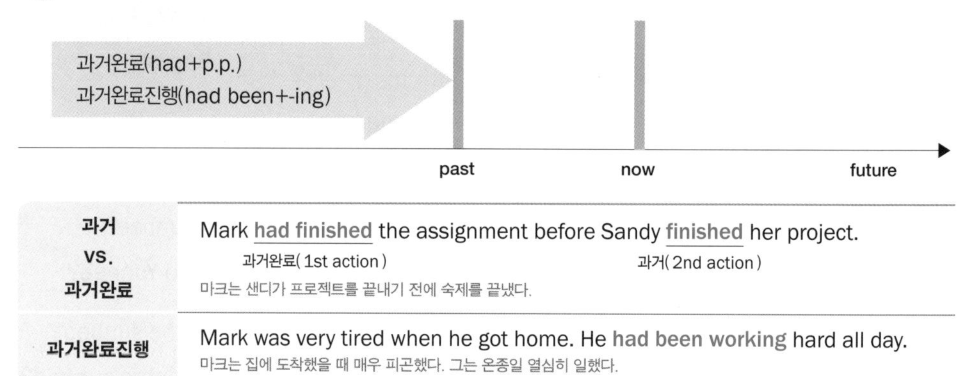

과거 vs. 과거완료	Mark **had finished** the assignment before Sandy **finished** her project. 과거완료(1st action) 과거(2nd action) 마크는 샌디가 프로젝트를 끝내기 전에 숙제를 끝냈다.
과거완료진행	Mark was very tired when he got home. He **had been working** hard all day. 마크는 집에 도착했을 때 매우 피곤했다. 그는 온종일 열심히 일했다.

FOCUS

1

과거완료(past perfect)는 특정한 과거 시점 이전부터 그 과거 시점까지의 경험, 계속, 완료 등을 나타내며, 형태는 「had+p.p.」이다.

Karen didn't want to go to the restaurant because she **had** already **eaten** dinner.
카렌은 레스토랑에 가고 싶지 않았다. 왜냐하면, 벌써 저녁을 먹었기 때문이다.

When I got home last night, I found that somebody **had broken** into my apartment.
내가 어젯밤에 집에 갔을 때 누군가가 내 아파트에 침입한 것을 알게 되었다.

Before I moved to Hawaii, I **had been** there three times.
나는 하와이로 이주하기 전에 하와이에 세 번 방문했었다.

|참고| 현재완료는 과거의 일이 현재까지 영향을 주는 것을, 과거완료는 어떤 과거 시점 이전(대과거)의 일이 그 과거 시점까지 영향을 주는 것을 의미한다.
I'm full. I**'ve just had** dinner. 나는 배가 부르다. 나는 막 저녁을 먹었다.
I **was** full. I **had just had** dinner then. 나는 배가 불렀다. 나는 그때 막 저녁을 먹었었다.

2

과거완료는 과거에 일어난 일의 순서를 나타내는 데 사용된다.

By the time Sheila **got** back, Chris **had gone**. (크리스가 먼저 떠나고, 쉴라가 도착함)
쉴라가 돌아왔을 때 크리스는 가버리고 없었다.

Before Sandra **moved** to Korea, she **had lived** in India for 20 years. (샌드라가 인도에 살다가 한국으로 이사함)
샌드라는 한국으로 이사하기 전에 이십 년 동안 인도에 살았다.

|참고| before나 after와 같이 시간 관계가 명확한 접속사와 함께 쓰는 경우, 과거완료가 아닌 과거로 써도 된다.
After the wedding **ended[had ended]**, we went to the coffee shop together.
결혼식이 끝난 뒤 우리는 함께 커피숍에 갔다.

3

과거완료진행은 「had been+-ing」로 표현한다.

He was out of breath. He **had been running**. 그는 숨이 찼었다. 그는 계속 달려왔었다.

At last, the bus came. I **had been waiting** for twenty minutes. 마침내 버스가 왔다. 나는 20분 동안 기다렸었다.

|참고| 그 밖에도 완료 시제에는 미래완료 「will have+p.p.」와 미래완료진행 「will have been+-ing」가 있다.

EXERCISES

정답 및 해설 P. 16

A 주어진 동사를 과거완료로 바꿔 문장을 완성하시오.

insist 주장하다
actual 실제의

1 She insisted that she ______________ (never, meet) him.

2 The actual size was larger than we ______________ (expect).

3 She was very happy after she ______________ (hear) the news.

4 Mom ______________ (already, finish) cooking dinner when I got home.

5 I didn't know him because I ______________ (never, see) him before.

6 When I visited Jackie, she ______________ (go out) with her mother.

B 주어진 동사를 과거(2nd action)나 과거완료(1st action)로 바꿔 문장을 완성하시오.

admit 자백하다; 인정하다
trash bin 쓰레기통

1 I ______________ (remember) that I ______________ (forget) my keys.

2 He ______________ (miss) the party because no one ______________ (tell) him about it.

3 David ______________ (eat) Thai food before, so he ______________ (know) what to order.

4 When Kerry ______________ (come) to school, Sally wasn't there. She ______________ (go) home.

5 Tony ______________ (admit) that he ______________ (hit) the other car but said that he hadn't damaged it seriously.

6 I ______________ (lose) my dog this morning, but I ______________ (find) him later in my neighbor's trash bin.

C 주어진 동사를 과거완료진행으로 바꿔 문장을 완성하시오.

wet 젖은
dining table 식탁
mess 엉망진창인 상태
nap 낮잠 자다

1 Pete was sitting alone. His eyes were red and wet.
→ He ______________________ (cry).

2 Mark's holiday pictures were all grouped together on the dining table.
→ He ______________________ (organize) them on the dining table.

3 When Rick looked at himself in the mirror, his hair was a mess and his eyes were half closed.
→ Rick ______________________ (nap) on the couch.

REVIEW

정답 및 해설 P. 16

far apart 멀리 떨어져
be ready for ~에 대한 준비가 되다
the previous day 전날
reach (전화 등으로) 연락하다
get worried 걱정이 되다
biology 생물학
tough 힘든, 질긴
semester 학기
major 중요한; 전공과목
due 기한
warn 경고하다
government 정부
negative 부정적인
effect 영향, 결과, 효과
global warming 지구 온난화

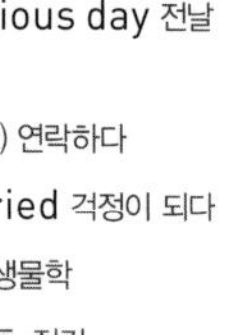

A ( ) 안에서 가장 알맞은 것을 고르시오.

1 Frank and I live far apart. We (haven't seen / hadn't seen) each other for several years.

2 I was ready for the speech. I (have prepared / had prepared) very hard the previous day.

3 I (haven't been / hadn't been) able to reach Sue all morning. I'm getting a little bit worried.

4 Angela studies biology. She (has studied / had studied) biology since she entered college.

5 When Ruth finally got to the theater, her boyfriend wasn't there. He (has gone / had gone) home.

6 This has been a really tough semester. We (have already had / had already had) five major projects due.

7 This morning, I found trash scattered all over the kitchen floor. My dog (has been trying / had been trying) to find food in the trash can.

8 Scientists (have been warning / had been warning) governments about the negative effects of global warming since the late 1970s.

celebrate 축하하다
PDA(personal digital assistant) 휴대 정보 단말기
knock over (밥상, 그릇 등을) 뒤집어엎다
splash over (물, 흙탕 등이) ~에 튀기다
call out 소리쳐 부르다
wave to ~을 향해 손을 흔들다
weight 무게
donate 기부하다
world-famous 세계적으로 유명한
philanthropist 자선가; 박애주의자

B 밑줄 친 부분을 바르게 고쳐 쓰시오.

1 The newspaper was just here. What had you done with it?

2 Our school has won the award last weekend. Now, we are celebrating.

3 Do you see my cell phone? It's not where I left it. Help me look for it, please.

4 When I knocked over the mug, coffee has splashed all over my new shoes.

5 Have you ever been to Mexico? I have been there last year with my family on vacation.

6 I called out to Nick when I have seen him from the window. He waved to me and shouted, "Hello!"

7 Sylvia had lost a lot of weight since she stopped eating junk food. She has more energy and clearer skin, too.

8 Bill Gates has donated much of his money to Africa's poor. He and his wife become world-famous philanthropists.

 ( ) 안에서 가장 알맞은 것을 고르시오.

1 I've written to Danny (last week / recently).

2 Have you eaten Italian food (before / still)?

3 What have you been doing (today / yesterday)?

4 I've been living here (in / since) the end of last year.

5 Actually, I had dinner with Amy (last night / next time).

6 I can't remember (how long / when) I've had this watch.

7 I haven't seen Jerry (for / since) a long time. How is he?

8 Terry hasn't been to London (since / when) we went there together.

9 I've been trying to get in touch with David (for ages / for the last time).

10 Look! Somebody (is breaking / broken) into that apartment. Call the police quickly.

get in touch with ~와 연락하다, 접촉하다
for ages 오랫동안
break into (건물에) 침입하다

 대화를 읽고, 밑줄 친 부분을 바르게 고치시오.

1 A: Had you ever traveled in a bendy bus before?
B: No, I don't think I have. This will be my first time.

2 A: How long are you studying here at UCLA?
B: I've been studying here since 2014.

3 A: What are you doing with those eggs now?
B: I've been separating the whites from the yolks. The yolks contain all the fat.

4 A: How long has your father worked for Great Bank?
B: My father worked there as a financial analyst for over fifteen years.

5 A: I have been trying to contact Jason for over an hour. Do you know where he is?
B: I didn't have seen him since last night.

6 A: William has been sick for quite some time. Had you visited him lately?
B: I stopped by to see him last night, but he had already gone to bed.

7 A: I took my students to the zoo today. Surprisingly, some of them had never seen a giraffe before.
B: That's not surprising. I had never seen a giraffe before, either.

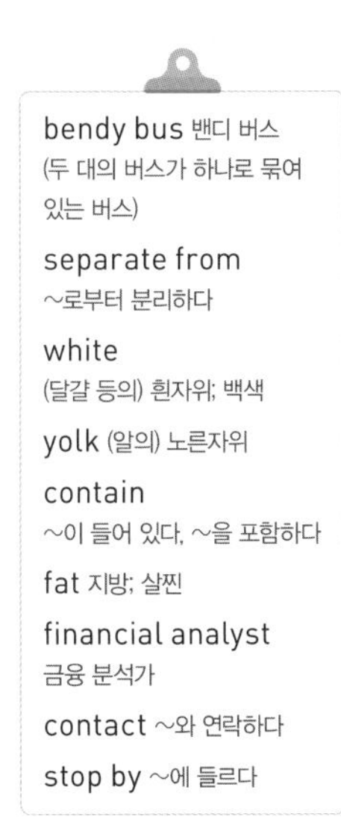

REVIEW PLUS

정답 및 해설 P. 18

investigate
수사하다, 조사하다
scene (사건의) 현장; 장면
save
남겨두다; 저축하다; 구하다
honestly 솔직히
figure out
이해하다; ~을 계산하다

다음 〈보기〉에서 알맞은 것을 골라 대화를 완성하시오.

보기			
	have started	has been crying	had already left
	have often dreamed	haven't been	has eaten

1 A: Were the police still investigating the accident when you arrived?
B: No, they ______________ the scene.

2 A: Who ______________ my ice cream? I was saving it for the movie!
B: Sorry, Jaemin. I had no idea you were going to eat it.

3 A: I ______________ taking flying lessons. I just cannot believe how exciting it is!
B: Is that right? I ______________ of learning to fly myself. Let me know how it goes.

4 A: Jisoo ______________ in her room for over half an hour now. What's wrong with her?
B: I knocked, but she won't open the door.
Honestly, I ______________ able to figure it out.

in the past year
지난 1년 동안
for instance 예를 들어
indoor 실내의
must-do 꼭 해야 할 일
bull running 황소몰이
in total 통틀어, 전체로서

다음 밑줄 친 부분이 어법상 바르지 않은 것을 고르시오.

Sam and his friend James are true adventure travelers, and together the boys ① have done and seen some amazing things in the past year. Three months ago, for instance, they traveled to Dubai and tried snowboarding for the first time at Ski Dubai, the first indoor ski resort in the Middle East. After that, they ② went deep sea scuba diving in Australia on the Great Barrier Reef. Neither ③ has ever seen such beautiful beaches before. And while they were in Australia, Sam learned about another must-do activity: bull running. This was just the kind of exciting activity the two ④ had been looking for! So last month, they flew to Pamplona, Spain to run with the bulls at the festival of San Fermin. In total, they ⑤ have been traveling for ten months now.

List of Irregular Verbs

Simple Form	Simple Past	Past Participle
arise 일어나다	arose	arisen
awake (잠에서) 깨우다, 깨다	awoke	awoken
be ~이다, 있다	was/were	been
bear 낳다	bore	born/borne
beat 때리다	beat	beaten
become 되다	became	become
begin 시작하다	began	begun
bend 구부리다	bent	bent
bet (돈을) 걸다	bet(ted)	bet(ted)
bid 값을 매기다, 입찰하다	bid	bid
bind ~을 묶다, 감다	bound	bound
bite 물다	bit	bitten
bleed 피를 흘리다	bled	bled
blow (바람이) 불다	blew	blown
break 부수다	broke	broken
breed (새끼를) 낳다	bred	bred
bring 가져오다	brought	brought
broadcast 방송하다	broadcast	broadcast
build 세우다, 짓다	built	built
burn (불)타다, 태우다	burned/burnt	burned/burnt
burst 터뜨리다	burst	burst
buy 사다	bought	bought
cast 던지다	cast	cast
catch 붙잡다	caught	caught
choose 고르다, 선택하다	chose	chosen
cling 달라붙다, 집착하다	clung	clung
come 오다	came	come
cost (비용이) 들다	cost	cost
creep 기다	crept	crept
cut 자르다	cut	cut
deal 다루다, 취급하다	dealt	dealt
dig (땅을) 파다	dug	dug
dive (물속으로) 뛰어들다	dived/dove	dived
do 하다	did	done
draw 끌어당기다	drew	drawn
dream 꿈꾸다	dreamed/dreamt	dreamed/dreamt
drink 마시다	drank	drunk
drive 운전하다	drove	driven
dwell 살다, 거주하다	dwelled/dwelt	dwelled/dwelt
eat 먹다	ate	eaten
fall 떨어지다, 넘어지다	fell	fallen
feed ~에게 먹이를 주다	fed	fed
feel 느끼다	felt	felt
fight 싸우다	fought	fought
find 발견하다	found	found
fit ~에 꼭 맞다	fit(ted)	fit(ted)
flee 도망치다	fled	fled
fling 내던지다	flung	flung
fly 날다, 날리다	flew	flown
forbid 금지하다	forbade	forbidden
forecast 예고하다	forecast	forecast
forget 잊다	forgot	forgotten
forgive 용서하다	forgave	forgiven
freeze 얼다, 얼리다	froze	frozen
get 받다, 얻다	got	gotten/got
give 주다	gave	given
go 가다	went	gone
grind 갈다	ground	ground
grow 자라다	grew	grown
hang 매달다, 매달려 있다;	hung	hung
교수형에 처하다	hanged	hanged
have 가지다	had	had
hear 듣다	heard	heard
hide 숨기다	hid	hidden/hid
hit 때리다	hit	hit
hold 붙잡고 있다	held	held
hurt 상처 입히다, 아프다	hurt	hurt
keep 유지하다	kept	kept
kneel 무릎을 꿇다	kneeled/knelt	kneeled/knelt
knit 뜨다, 짜다	knitted/knit	knitted/knit
know 알다	knew	known
lay ~을 …에 두다	laid	laid
lead (앞장서서) 이끌다	led	led
lean 기대다, 기대서다	leaned/leant	leaned/leant
leap 껑충 뛰다	leaped/leapt	leaped/leapt
learn 배우다	learned/learnt	learned/learnt
leave 떠나다	left	left
lend 빌려주다	lent	lent
let ~에게 …시키다	let	let
lie 눕다	lay	lain
light 불을 붙이다	lighted/lit	lighted/lit
lose 잃다	lost	lost
make 만들다	made	made
mean 의미하다	meant	meant
meet 만나다	met	met
mistake 오해하다, 착각하다	mistook	mistaken
pay 지불하다	paid	paid
put ~을 …에 놓다	put	put
quit ~을 그만두다	quit(ted)	quit(ted)
read 읽다	read	read

List of Irregular Verbs

Simple Form	Simple Past	Past Participle
ride (탈것에) 타다	rode	ridden
ring (벨이) 울리다	rang	rung
rise (해, 달이) 뜨다	rose	risen
run 뛰다	ran	run
say 말하다	said	said
see 보다	saw	seen
seek 찾다, 추구하다	sought	sought
sell 팔다	sold	sold
send 보내다	sent	sent
set 놓다	set	set
sew 바느질하다	sewed	sewed/sewn
shake 흔들다	shook	shaken
shed (눈물, 피)를 흘리다	shed	shed
shine 빛나다	shone	shone
shoot 쏘다	shot	shot
show 보여 주다	showed	showed/shown
shrink (천이) 줄다	shrank	shrunk
shut 닫다	shut	shut
sing 노래하다	sang	sung
sink 가라앉다	sank	sunk
sit 앉다	sat	sat
sleep 자다	slept	slept
slide 미끄러지다	slid	slid
sling ~을 내던지다	slung	slung
smell 냄새 맡다	smelled/smelt	smelled/smelt
sow 씨를 뿌리다	sowed	sowed/sown
speak 말하다	spoke	spoken
speed 급속하게 진행하다	speeded/sped	speeded/sped
spell 철자하다	spelled/spelt	spelled/spelt
spend (돈, 시간 등을) 쓰다	spent	spent
spill 엎지르다, 흘뜨리다	spilled/spilt	spilled/spilt
spin 돌리다, (실을) 잣다	spun	spun
spit (침을) 뱉다	spit/spat	spat
split 쪼개다	split	split
spoil 망쳐 놓다	spoiled/spoilt	spoiled/spoilt
spread 펼치다, 뿌리다	spread	spread
spring 튀다, 뛰어오르다	sprung/sprang	sprung
stand 서다, 참다	stood	stood
steal 훔치다	stole	stolen
stick 찌르다, 붙이다	stuck	stuck
sting 찌르다, 쏘다	stung	stung
stride 큰 걸음으로 걷다	strode	stridden
strike 때리다, 치다	struck	struck
string 실을 꿰다	strung	strung
strive 노력하다, 힘쓰다	strove	striven

Simple Form	Simple Past	Past Participle
swear 맹세하다	swore	sworn
sweep 쓸다, 청소하다	swept	swept
swell 부풀다, 증가시키다	swelled	swelled/swollen
swim 수영하다	swam	swum
swing 흔들다	swung	swung
take 잡다, 데리고 가다	took	taken
teach 가르치다	taught	taught
tear 찢다	tore	torn
tell 말하다	told	told
think 생각하다	thought	thought
throw 던지다	threw	thrown
thrust 밀어붙이다	thrust	thrust
tread 밟다, 짓밟다	trod	trod/trodden
understand 이해하다	understood	understood
undertake (책임을) 맡다, 착수하다	undertook	undertaken
upset 전복시키다	upset	upset
wake (잠에서) 깨다	waked/woke	waked/woken
wear 입다	wore	worn
weave (천을) 짜다	wove	woven
weep 울다	wept	wept
win 이기다, 받다	won	won
wind 굽이치다, 휘감다	wound	wound
withdraw 물러나다	withdrew	withdrawn
write 쓰다	wrote	written

PART 5

명사
Nouns

명사

정답 및 해설 P. 18

1

명사(nouns)는 생물이나 무생물의 이름 또는 추상적인 개념 등을 나타낸다.

종류	쓰임	예문
보통명사	일반적인 사물에 두루 쓰이는 이름	A student reads a book at the library.
집합명사	같은 종류의 것이 여럿 모여 전체를 나타내는 명사	My family has always been very close.
물질명사	나누어 셀 수 없는 물질을 나타내는 명사	I want some pepper and salt for my soup.
추상명사	추상적인 개념을 나타내는 명사	I think love has the greatest power.
고유명사	특정한 사람, 사물에 쓰이는 이름	Amy and Emily are going to London in July.

CHECK-UP

제시된 개수대로 명사를 골라 밑줄을 그으시오.

1 (3개) My uncle has a cute kitten and two small puppies.

2 (4개) My classmate Linda went to Canada with her family.

3 (5개) I saw Peter at the bakery last Saturday. He was buying some bread and a cake.

2

보통명사와 집합명사는 셀 수 있는 명사(countable nouns)로 단수형과 복수형이 있다.

셀 수 있는 명사의 복수형 규칙		예시		
대부분의 명사	명사+s	a book → books a school → schools	a cat → cats a sister → sisters	
-s, -sh, -ch, -x로 끝나는 명사	명사+es	a brush → brushes a fox → foxes	a class → classes a watch → watches	
자음+o로 끝나는 명사	명사+es	a hero → heroes *예외: a memo → memos, a photo → photos	a potato → potatoes	
모음+o로 끝나는 명사	명사+s	a radio → radios	a kangaroo → kangaroos	
자음+y 로 끝나는 명사	y → i+es	a baby → babies	a candy → candies	
-f(e)로 끝나는 명사	f(e) → v+es	a knife → knives a life → lives	a leaf → leaves a thief → thieves	
불규칙		a deer → deer a tooth → teeth	a fish → fish a child → children	a sheep → sheep

CHECK-UP

주어진 명사의 복수형을 쓰시오.

1 deer ____________

2 bench ____________

3 tomato ____________

4 box ____________

5 city ____________

6 child ____________

7 photo ____________

8 wolf ____________

3 셀 수 없는 명사(uncountable nouns)는 항상 단수 취급하며, a/an을 붙이거나 복수형으로 쓸 수 없다.

셀 수 없는 명사	예문
고유명사	The **Tower Bridge** crosses the **Thames**.
추상명사	I think I'm in **love**.
물질명사	Do you put **sugar** in your **tea**?

CHECK-UP

A 셀 수 있는 명사 앞에는 C(countable nouns), 셀 수 없는 명사 앞에는 UC(uncountable nouns)라고 쓰시오.

1 ______ eraser
2 ______ letter
3 ______ furniture
4 ______ child
5 ______ chair
6 ______ homework
7 ______ sugar
8 ______ water
9 ______ mail
10 ______ dollar
11 ______ money
12 ______ truth
13 ______ Seoul
14 ______ information
15 ______ luggage

B (　) 안에서 가장 알맞은 것을 고르시오.

1 Can I borrow five (dollar / dollars)?
2 We need to buy some (furniture / furnitures).
3 I can't go out tonight. I have lots of (homework / homeworks) to do.
4 I'd like to get some (information / informations) about next semester.
5 You should brush your (tooth / teeth) before going to bed.

4 명사는 한 문장 내에서 주격, 목적격, 소유격의 역할을 한다.

명사의 역할	주격 ~은/는/이/가	**Harry** is in class.
	목적격 ~을/를	She loves **chocolate**.
	소유격 ~의	This is **Lucy's** notebook.

CHECK-UP

밑줄 친 명사를 주격, 목적격, 소유격으로 분류하시오.

1 Eagles can fly very high. ______________
2 This is Rachel's new jacket. ______________
3 My mom usually bakes bread. ______________
4 Matthew was feeding his friend's cats. ______________
5 Tony wore his brother's new black jeans. ______________

셀 수 있는 명사

단수형과 복수형이 같은 명사	a deer → deer　a fish → fish　a salmon → salmon a series → series　a sheep → sheep　a species → species
주로 복수로 쓰는 명사	pajamas　boots　scissors　pants shorts　mittens　glasses　socks
항상 단수 취급하는 명사 (학과명)	mathematics　politics　economics ethics　statistics　physics
주어-동사의 수 일치	The price of oil and cars has gone up very fast. (The price: 단수 주어 / has gone up: 단수 동사) 기름과 자동차의 가격이 매우 빠르게 상승했다. The books in Professor Kim's office are very old and rare. (The books: 복수 주어 / are: 복수 동사) 김 교수님의 사무실에 있는 책들은 매우 오래되고 희귀한 것들이다.

FOCUS

1 명사에는 셀 수 있는 명사(countable nouns)와 셀 수 없는 명사(uncountable nouns)가 있다.

A **child** needs **love** and **attention.** 아이는 사랑과 보살핌이 필요하다.

People who have **hope** have the **future.** 희망을 품은 사람은 미래가 있다.

2 셀 수 있는 명사는 주로 -(e)s를 붙여 복수를 만들지만, 규칙을 따르지 않는 명사는 복수형을 외워야 한다.

a tooth → **teeth**	a foot → **feet**	a goose → **geese**
a man → **men**	a woman → **women**	a person → **people**
a mouse → **mice**	a child → **children**	an ox → **oxen**
a crisis → **crises**	an oasis → **oases**	a basis → **bases**
an analysis → **analyses**	a medium → **media**	a bacterium → **bacteria**
a phenomenon → **phenomena**		

I had my wisdom **tooth** pulled out. 나는 사랑니를 뽑았다.

My sister has a small gap between her front **teeth.** 내 동생은 앞니 사이가 벌어져 있다.

You're acting like **a child!** 너는 어린아이처럼 행동하는구나!

She's got four **children**, all under the age of five. 그녀에게는 다섯 살 미만의 아이들이 네 명 있다.

3 단수형과 복수형이 같은 명사가 있다.

a deer → **deer** a sheep → **sheep** a salmon → **salmon**
a fish → **fish** a series → **series**

They have only one **deer**, but we have a lot of **deer**.
그들은 겨우 한 마리의 사슴을 소유하고 있지만 우리는 많은 사슴을 소유하고 있다.

My brother caught several **fish**, but I only caught one **fish**.
우리 형은 여러 마리의 물고기를 잡았지만 나는 겨우 한 마리의 물고기를 잡았다.

4 한 쌍(雙)으로 된 것은 항상 복수로 쓰고, 복수 취급한다.

pajama**s**, binocular**s**, scissor**s**, pant**s**, short**s**, mitten**s**, glass**es**, trouser**s**, sock**s**, boot**s**

Binoculars are used to look at things far away. 쌍안경은 멀리 있는 것들을 보는 데 사용된다.

Pajamas are soft clothes that you wear to bed. 파자마는 잠잘 때 입는 편한 옷이다.

|참고| 쌍(雙)으로 된 것이라도 한 짝을 말할 때는 단수로 쓸 수 있다.
I lost my left mitten. 나는 왼쪽 손모아장갑을 잃어버렸다.

5 학과명은 항상 단수 취급한다.

mathematics 수학, politics 정치학, economics 경제학, ethics 윤리학, statistics 통계학, physics 물리학

Physics is a challenging subject for many students. 물리학은 많은 학생들에게 힘든 과목이다.

Mathematics makes my head hurt. 수학은 내 머리를 아프게 만든다.

6 주어와 동사가 삽입된 구나 절에 의해 떨어져 있더라도 주어의 단·복수를 잘 파악하여 동사를 써야 한다.

Most **people** in Seoul live in apartments. 서울에서는 대부분의 사람들이 아파트에 살고 있다.

Where are my **glasses**? Have you seen them anywhere? 내 안경이 어디 있지? 내 안경을 본 적이 있니?

More **men** than women are left-handed. 여자들보다 남자들이 왼손잡이가 많다.

EXERCISES

정답 및 해설 P. 18

match 성냥; 경기; 어울리다
light 불을 붙이다; 빛
collection (물건 등의) 더미; 수집품
pour out 연달아 나가다
chimney 굴뚝
household chore 집안일
document 문서, 서류
wait in line 줄을 서서 기다리다

A 주어진 명사를 복수로 바꿔 문장을 완성하시오.

1 I always carry ___________ (match) to light the candles.

2 You have quite a collection of ___________ (necktie) here!

3 Black smoke was pouring out of the ___________ (chimney).

4 You can watch TV after you've finished your household ___________ (chore).

5 The ___________ (thief) broke into the office and stole important documents.

6 She lost her two front ___________ (tooth). When she smiles, she looks cute.

7 There are a lot of ___________ (child) waiting in line in front of the museum.

8 I noticed something strange about Mark. He wasn't wearing shoes on his ___________ (foot).

stadium 경기장
mosquito 모기
transmit ~을 옮기다, 전염시키다
ferry 페리[여객선]
mainland 본토; 본토의
every hour on the hour (매)정시에
allow 허락하다, 허용하다
plow 쟁기; 경작하다
Chinese Zodiac 중국의 12궁도, 12지신, 12지 동물(쥐, 소, 호랑이, 토끼, 용, 뱀, 말, 양, 원숭이, 닭, 개, 돼지)
suffer from ~으로 괴로워하다
nightmare 악몽

B 주어진 단어를 단수 또는 복수로 바꿔 문장을 완성하시오.

1 (block) I live a ___________ from the stadium.
The museum is over six ___________ away.

2 (woman) She's a really nice ___________.
Many more ___________ study engineering now.

3 (mosquito) There is a ___________ in the tent.
Some types of ___________ transmit malaria to humans.

4 (ferry) ___________ to the mainland leave every hour on the hour.
Our ___________ was two hours late because of the weather.

5 (sandbox) When I was a child, my father built me a ___________.
The park has several ___________ for children to play in.

6 (wife) In some countries, men are allowed to have several ___________.
I met his ___________ for the first time yesterday. She was kind.

7 (ox) ___________ were once commonly used to pull plows on farms.
According to the Chinese Zodiac, 2021 will be the year of the ___________.

8 (year) There are 365 days, or twelve months, in a ___________.
James suffered from nightmares for many ___________ after the accident.

C 〈보기〉에서 알맞은 것을 골라 단수 또는 복수로 바꿔 문장을 완성하시오.

보기			
series	short	glass	phenomenon
country	salmon	tooth	person

1 The writer described a variety of social __________ of his time.

2 I couldn't take notes in class because I left my __________ at home.

3 A __________ that causes ongoing pain may be a sign of a serious problem.

4 There are many different ways to cook __________, but the best way is to grill them.

5 She wore an old pair of __________ and a T-shirt to the neighborhood pool party.

6 I missed the second episode of the __________, so I don't know what's going on now.

7 Hundreds of __________ became instant millionaires after the lottery results were announced.

8 According to the statistics, Koreans work longer hours than people in most other industrialized __________.

phenomenon 현상
salmon 연어
describe 묘사하다; 서술하다
social 사회의, 사회적인
take notes 메모하다, 필기하다
cause ~을 야기하다, ~의 원인이 되다
ongoing 진행 중인, 계속되는
sign 징후; 신호; 표지판
episode 1회분의 이야기
instant 즉각적인
millionaire 백만장자
lottery 복권
statistic 통계
industrialize 산업화하다

D ( ) 안에서 가장 알맞은 것을 고르시오.

1 The mayor and his brothers (is / are) going to jail.

2 Illustrated comic books (is / are) what I like to read.

3 Ice on the roads (is / are) what caused the ten-car pileup.

4 Visits to our website (has / have) increased a lot this month.

5 I can't understand people who (don't / doesn't) like vegetables.

6 Advanced physics (is / are) only offered in the second semester.

7 The film that we saw yesterday (was / were) made by an Italian director.

8 My new sunglasses (was / were) crushed under the weight of my suitcase.

9 Economics (is / are) the study of how trade and money are managed.

10 Headphones (allows / allow) you to listen to music without disturbing others.

11 Statistics (is / are) a very difficult subject, but I think it is worth studying.

12 Children don't usually enjoy eating vegetables, but my son Aaron (loves / love) broccoli.

mayor 시장(市長)
jail 교도소에 가다; 교도소
illustrated 그림(사진 등)이 있는
pileup 연쇄 충돌
advanced physics 고급 물리학
director 감독
crush 눌러 부수다; 충돌하다
economics 경제학
trade 무역, 거래
disturb 방해하다

셀 수 있는 명사와 셀 수 없는 명사

셀 수 있는 명사	셀 수 없는 명사
Laura is singing **a song**. 로라가 노래를 부르고 있다.	Kathy is listening to **music**. 캐시는 음악을 듣고 있다.
They don't have enough **chairs**. 그들에게는 충분한 의자가 없다.	He doesn't have any **furniture** in his room. 그의 방에는 가구가 하나도 없다.
I'd like to have **a cup** of coffee. 나는 커피 한 잔을 마시고 싶다.	I love **coffee** in the morning. 나는 아침에 커피 마시는 것을 좋아한다.

1 셀 수 없는 명사에는 다음과 같은 것들이 있다.

액체로 된 것 water, oil, orange juice, coffee, tea, cocoa, milk ...

Would you like some **water** with your meal? 식사하시면서 물 좀 드시겠어요?

A cup of **cocoa** at bedtime might help you sleep. 코코아 한 잔은 잠드는 데 도움이 될 수도 있다.

기체로 된 것 air, gas, oxygen, steam, smoke ...

The clown let the **air** out of the balloon. 그 광대는 풍선으로부터 공기를 뺐다.

The **smoke** in the room made me feel a little dizzy. 방에서 나는 연기가 나를 약간 어지럽게 했다.

작은 입자로 된 것 sugar, pepper, salt, flour, rice, sand, corn, hair ...

Shall I grind a little **pepper** over your spaghetti? 스파게티 위에 후추를 약간 갈아 드릴까요?

Thicken the sauce with a little **flour**. 약간의 밀가루를 넣어 소스를 걸쭉하게 만드세요.

물건의 재료가 되는 것 gold, ice, glass, bread, cheese, meat, silver, iron, paper ...

Banks hold large reserves of **gold**. 은행은 많은 금을 보유하고 있다.

There's nothing better than fresh **bread** straight from the oven. 오븐에서 갓 꺼낸 신선한 빵보다 더 좋은 것은 없다.

추상적 개념 happiness, peace, truth, space, courage, pride, knowledge, information ...

You should take more **pride** in your work. 당신의 일에 더 많은 자부심을 가져야 합니다.

There is plenty of storage **space** in my new apartment. 나의 새 아파트에는 수납공간이 많이 있다.

과목과 언어 physics, mathematics, grammar, English, Japanese ...

English is rich in vocabulary. 영어는 어휘가 풍부하다.

Japanese is taught at our school in grade 3. 우리 학교에서는 3학년 때 일본어를 배운다.

유사한 품목으로 구성된 집합체 baggage, clothing, fruit, equipment, furniture, mail ...

She carried her **baggage** through customs at the airport. 그녀는 공항에서 자신의 짐을 가지고 세관을 통과했다.

Can I borrow some **money**? 돈 좀 빌릴 수 있을까?

자연현상 heat, snow, fog, hail, weather, light, gravity, sunshine, wind ...

We have nice **sunshine** today. Why don't we go for a walk? 오늘 햇빛이 좋다. 산책하러 가는 게 어때?

2 셀 수 없는 명사가 셀 수 있는 명사로 쓰일 때에는 그 의미가 달라진다.

hair 머리털 → a hair 머리카락 한 가닥 | paper 종이 → a paper 신문 | glass 유리 → a glass 유리컵
time 시간 → a time 한정된 시간, 기간 | room 공간 → a room 방 | coffee 커피 → a coffee 한 잔의 커피
iron 철 → an iron 다리미 | light 햇빛 → a light 전등(불빛) | business 사업 → a business 기업

She has very short **hair** like her sister. (*NOT* hairs) 그녀는 자기 언니처럼 머리가 아주 짧다.

There is **a hair** in my food. 내 음식에 머리카락 한 가닥이 있다.

|참고| 1. 단수와 복수의 뜻이 서로 다른 경우가 있다.

an arm 팔 – arms 무기 | earning 획득 – earnings 소득 | saving 절약 – savings 저축
pain 고통 – pains 수고 | good 이익, 선 – goods 상품 | damage 손해 – damages 배상금

2. 형용사에 -(e)s를 붙이면 뜻이 달라진다.

rich 부유한 – riches 재물 | valuable 귀중한 – valuables 귀중품 | surrounding 주변의 – surroundings 주변 환경

3 집합을 나타내는 명사는 셀 수 없지만, 그것을 구성하는 것은 셀 수 있다.

Fruit	a banana, a pear, an orange, a melon ...
Mail	a letter, a text message, a package, an email ...
Money	a dollar, a bill, a penny, a cent, a dime ...
Furniture	a chair, a sofa, a wardrobe, a bed ...
Clothing	a jacket, a skirt, a dress, a coat ...

Fruit is a good source of natural fiber. (*NOT* A fruit) 과일은 천연 섬유질의 훌륭한 공급원이다.

I only had **a pear** for lunch. 나는 점심으로 겨우 배 하나를 먹었다.

4 셀 수 없는 명사는 담는 용기나 계량 단위를 사용하여 수량을 표현한다.

a piece of paper / cake / advice | **a glass of** milk / juice / water | **a bowl of** rice
a slice of ham / cheese / pizza | **a pound of** meat / flour | **a loaf of** bread
a bar of soap / chocolate | **a spoonful of** sugar | **a carton of** milk

I baked **a loaf of** French bread. 나는 바게트 한 덩어리를 구웠다.

We need to buy **two loaves of** bread. 빵 두 덩어리를 사야 해.

EXERCISES

정답 및 해설 P. 19

- tie with ~로 묶다
- string 끈, 줄
- fine (입자가) 고운, 미세한; 좋은
- hourglass 모래시계, 물시계
- steam 증기
- simmer (약한 불에) 부글부글 끓다
- impressive 인상적인; 장엄한
- economics 경제학
- patience 인내심, 참을성
- run out 다 떨어지다[되다]

주어진 단어를 이용하여 현재 시제로 문장을 완성하시오.

1 I think this cheese ___________ (smell) a bit strange.

2 These packages ___________ (be) tied with blue strings.

3 Very fine sand ___________ (be) used to fill hourglasses.

4 Steam ___________ (be) rising from the simmering stew.

5 Those pants he bought ________________ (not, suit) him.

6 Usually, gold ___________ (be) a lot more expensive than silver.

7 Her knowledge of English grammar ___________ (be) impressive.

8 Economics ___________ (be) my least favorite subject. It's so boring.

9 Ms. Kim's patience ___________ (be) beginning to run out. Let's take our seats quickly!

10 All the lights in the office ___________ (be) turned off. Everyone must have left the office.

- wrinkled 주름이 접힌
- smooth out ~의 주름을 펴다
- iron 다리미, 철분
- wrap 포장하다
- run out of ~을 다 써버리다
- make of ~로 만들다
- pane 판유리; 한 구획
- unfortunately 불행하게도, 유감스럽게도
- come from ~에서 생산되다; ~ 출신이다
- import-export 수출입
- be forced to ~하지 않을 수 없다; ~하도록 강요받다
- due to ~때문에
- recession 불경기, 후퇴

(　　) 안에서 가장 알맞은 것을 고르시오.

1 ① His wrinkled shirt was smoothed out with (an iron / iron).
② The doctor said she needed more (an iron / iron) in her diet.

2 ① The photo was on the front page of all the (paper / papers).
② I wanted to wrap your gift, but I ran out of (a paper / paper).

3 ① Get yourself (a glass / glass) and I'll pour you a drink.
② The whole window is made of a single pane of (a glass / glass).

4 ① There isn't any (room / rooms) left, please take the next elevator.
② My brother and I used to share (a room / room) when we were kids.

5 ① Somebody must be home. There is (a light / light) on inside.
② Unfortunately, this room doesn't get enough (light / lights) in the morning.

6 ① I'm going out to get (a coffee /coffee). Would you like one?
② Some of the best (coffee / coffees) in the world comes from Indonesia.

7 ① My father is in the import-export (business / businesses).
② Several (business / businesses) have been forced to close due to the recession.

C 주어진 단어를 단수 또는 복수로 바꿔 대화를 완성하시오.

1 <at the supermarket>

Jack: Pasta, lettuce, ___________ (tomato), steak ... We have enough ___________ (food) for dinner. Let's go to the checkout counter.

Amy: Oh, no! Do you have any ___________ (money)? I don't have any cash with me.

Jack: Let me see. I have twenty ___________ (dollar). Do you think it'll be enough?

Amy: I doubt it. Let's return some of this ___________ (meat). It's a bit expensive anyway.

2 <at the airport>

Alex: I can't believe the airline lost my ___________ (luggage). I don't have any extra ___________ (cloth) to wear.

John: Don't worry. They'll return it to you at the hotel in a few days.

Alex: But what am I supposed to wear to the conference tomorrow? I cannot go there wearing these old ___________ (jean) and this ___________ (sweater).

John: We're about the same size, so I can lend you some of mine. I brought a few extra ___________ (shirt) and ___________ (pant) just in case.

lettuce 상추
checkout counter 계산대; (호텔의) 퇴숙 절차
doubt 확신하지 못하다; 의심하다
extra 여분의
be supposed to ~하기로 되어 있다
conference 회의, 학회
just in case 만약을 위해서

D 〈보기〉에서 알맞은 것을 골라 단수 또는 복수로 바꿔 문장을 완성하시오.

보기: loaf chocolate carton bottle meat advice slice spoonful

1 I would like a _____________ of cheese in my sandwich.

2 Mix some butter and a _____________ of sugar together.

3 The thief made off with twelve _____________ of rare wine.

4 She gave me a piece of _____________ that I will never forget.

5 I left two bars of _____________ in my bag, and now it has melted all over my books.

6 We need some bread. Will you buy a couple of _____________ when you're out shopping?

7 Can you buy me a _____________ of milk and a pound of _____________ on your way home today?

make off with ~을 가지고 달아나다
melt 녹다; 차차 없어지다

수량 표현

수량 표현	셀 수 있는 명사	셀 수 없는 명사
one, two, three ... every each (a) few many a number of the number of	one cup, two cups every person each person (a) few people many books a number of books the number of children	–
(a) little much a great deal of a large amount of	–	(a) little rice much oil a great deal of oil a large amount of money
some any a lot of, lots of plenty of	some oranges any oranges a lot of [lots of] pictures plenty of pictures	some water any water a lot of [lots of] sugar plenty of sugar

1

few, a few, many, a number of, the number of와 two 이상의 숫자 등은 셀 수 있는 명사의 복수형과 함께 쓴다.

There are only **a few** streetlights on outside.
밖에는 몇 개의 가로등만이 켜져 있다.

Very **few** people live in that part of the town.
그 마을의 저 지역에 사는 사람은 거의 없다.

I have **three** LED screen TVs, but Bill, my neighbor, has one.
나는 LED TV를 세 대 가지고 있지만, 나의 이웃인 빌은 한 대 가지고 있다.

|주의| 「a number of+복수 명사+복수 동사」 vs. 「the number of+복수 명사+단수 동사」

A number of students are going to private institutes after school.
많은 학생들이 방과 후에 학원에 간다.

The number of high school students has increased a lot during the past three years.
지난 3년 동안 고등학생들의 수가 많이 증가했다.

2

each, every 등은 셀 수 있는 명사의 단수형과 함께 쓴다.

Each ticket admits two people to the festival.
각각의 표로 두 명이 축제에 입장할 수 있다.

Every student has his or her own learning style.
모든 학생은 자신만의 학습 방법을 가지고 있다.

3 little, a little, much, a great deal of, a large amount of 등은 셀 수 없는 명사와 함께 쓴다.

I can't go now. I have **a little** work to do. 나는 지금 갈 수 없어. 할 일이 조금 있어.

We had very **little** rain this summer. 이번 여름에는 비가 거의 안 왔다.

How **much** money do I owe you? I can't remember. 내가 너에게 얼마나 많은 돈을 빚졌지? 기억이 나지 않아.

We spent **a great deal of** time finishing our homework. 우리는 숙제를 끝내는 데 많은 시간을 썼다.

4 some, any, a lot of, lots of, plenty of 등은 셀 수 있는 명사와 셀 수 없는 명사 모두에 쓴다.

Mary is brewing **some** coffee for us. I hope she offers us **some** cookies, too.
메리는 우리를 위해 커피를 만들고 있다. 나는 그녀가 우리에게 쿠키도 좀 주었으면 좋겠다.

The family doesn't have **any** money to buy food.
그 가족은 음식을 살 돈이 없다.

Are there **any** hamburgers left?
남은 햄버거 있나요?

There is **a lot of [lots of / plenty of]** flour leftover. Let's bake **some** banana bread.
남은 밀가루가 많이 있어. 바나나 빵을 굽자.

There are **a lot of [lots of / plenty of]** cars parked here. We may not find a spot.
여기에 주차된 차가 많구나. 주차할 곳을 찾지 못할지도 몰라.

| 참고 | 1. 명사와 함께 쓰는 수량을 나타내는 표현은 이외에도 all of, most of, none of 등이 있다.

All (of) my friends live in Korea. 내 친구들 모두는 한국에 산다.

Most (of) my friends live in Seoul. 내 친구들의 대부분은 서울에 산다.

None of my friends lives in Canada. 내 친구 누구도 캐나다에 살지 않는다.

2. 부정문, 의문문, 조건문에서는 any를 쓴다.
하지만 의문문도 긍정의 대답을 기대하는 요청이나 제안의 뜻일 경우 some을 쓴다.

Do you have **any** special plans for Christmas? 크리스마스에 특별한 계획이라도 있니?

Can I have **some** more coffee, please? 커피 좀 더 주실래요?

| 주의 | 1. hundred, thousand가 '수백'이나 '수천'처럼 막연한 숫자를 나타낼 때에는 복수 형태를 사용한다.

hundreds of times 수백 번

thousands of years 수천 년

There were **six hundred** people at the seminar. 세미나에는 600명의 사람들이 있었다.

There were **hundreds of** people at the performance. 공연장에는 수백 명의 사람들이 있었다.

2. 「숫자+명사+형용사」가 하나의 형용사 역할을 할 때, 그 형용사 안의 명사는 항상 단수를 사용한다.

He is a **fifteen-year-old** boy. 그는 열다섯 살 소년이다.

My brother is **fifteen years old.** 내 동생은 열다섯 살이다.

The 63 building is a **249-meter-tall** building. 63빌딩은 249미터 건물이다.

The 63 building is **249 meters tall.** 63빌딩은 249미터이다.

EXERCISES

정답 및 해설 P. 20

liquid 액체; 액체의
hold ~을 담다; 붙들다; 개최하다
flat 평지, 습지
attract 유인하다; (주의 등을) 끌다
migratory bird 철새
hugely 엄청나게
donate 기부하다
charity 자선단체; 자선기금; 자선
sauce (요리의) 소스
shaker (소금·설탕 등을 담아 뿌리는) 용기

( ) 안에서 가장 알맞은 것을 고르시오.

1 How (many / much) liquid does this bottle hold?

2 The mud flats attract (many / much) migratory birds.

3 He is hugely popular. He has very (few / little) enemies.

4 Each (member / members) of the group has a unique style.

5 Mr. Black has been a teacher here for (many / much) years.

6 Ten cents is donated to charity for every (bottle / bottles) sold.

7 I've been having (a few / a little) problems with this new computer.

8 This sauce needs (a few / a little) salt. Can you pass me the shaker?

planet 세상; 행성
key chain 열쇠고리

B 주어진 명사와 much 또는 many를 사용하여 문장을 완성하시오.

1 How ______________________ (person) live on the planet?

2 How ______________________ (water) do you drink a day?

3 How ______________________ (sleep) did you get last night?

4 How ______________________ (key) do you have on your key chain?

5 How ______________________ (sugar) does Sally take in her coffee?

6 How ______________________ (time) do you spend on your hobbies?

run out of ~이 떨어지다
clear 맑게 하다; 선명한
encouragement 격려, 장려
end ~을 끝내다
midterm test 중간고사
cover 다루다; 포함시키다; 덮다

〈보기〉에서 알맞은 것을 모두 골라 대화를 완성하시오. [중복 사용 가능]

보기	a little	a few	some	any

1 A: Have we run out of tuna?
B: No, there are ______________ cans left.

2 A: I need to get ______________ fresh air to clear my head.
B: Why? What's the matter?

3 A: Do you have ______________ idea how we can get to the subway?
B: None at all. Let me go and ask that police officer over there.

4 A: How is Rebecca doing this year in school?
B: Fine, but with ______________ encouragement she could do even better.

5 A: If you don't have ______________ questions, I'll end the class for today.
B: Excuse me, sir. How many chapters is the midterm test going to cover?

D 주어진 단어를 알맞게 바꿔 문장을 완성하시오. [현재 시제로 쓸 것]

1 Very few people ____________ (be) against the idea.

2 Each page of these books ____________ (have) three columns of text.

3 A little ____________ (effort) will help you to find important information.

4 There ____________ (be) just a little milk left in the refrigerator.

5 A number of chances ____________ (be) waiting for you. So don't give up.

6 The number of students who ____________ (want) to study abroad ____________ (be) increasing.

against ~에 반대하는
column 문서의 단; 기둥
effort 노력
refrigerator 냉장고
give up 포기하다
increase 증가하다

E 주어진 명사와 a number of 또는 the number of를 사용하여 문장을 완성하시오.

1 He refused my offer for ______________________ (reason).

2 ______________________ (newborn baby) is decreasing every year.

3 ______________________ (people) who keep pets is increasing these days.

4 I received ______________________ (question) after the presentation.

5 ______________________ (participant) exceeded 100, so we need more seats.

6 ______________________ (fan) from foreign countries are coming to Seoul to see Korean pop stars.

refuse ~을 거절하다
offer 제안; 제안하다
reason 이유
newborn baby 신생아
decrease 감소하다
keep (가축 등을) 기르다, ~을 유지하다
participant 참가자
exceed 초과하다

F 〈보기〉에서 알맞은 것을 골라 대화를 완성하시오.

보기	few	a little	many	much	none of	any

1 A: Do we have ____________ orange juice?
B: Yes, we have ____________. Do you want some?

2 A: I don't think there is ____________ difference between the two paintings.
B: Neither do I. In fact, they look almost the same.

3 A: I'm worried about our trip. ____________ us can speak English.
B: Don't worry. We can communicate through body language.

4 A: Look! ____________ people are waiting in line at the mall!
B: A famous singer will be signing for the fans today.

5 A: There were very ____________ seats available in the lecture hall.
B: The lecture must have been very popular.

painting 작품, 그림
be worried about ~에 대해 걱정하다
communicate 의사소통하다
wait in line 줄을 서서 기다리다
available 이용할 수 있는
lecture 강의, 강연

명사의 소유격

생물	단수	단수 명사+'s	fox's fur	puppy's toy
	복수	s로 끝나는 복수 명사+'	foxes' fur	puppies' toys
		s로 끝나지 않는 복수 명사 + 's	oxen's tail	children's toys
무생물	단·복수	A of B B의 A	the title of the book 책의 제목 the end of the movie 영화의 결말	
시간, 기간	today's newspaper	this week's meeting	two months' vacation	

1 소유격은 소유관계를 나타내는 말로 '~의'라고 해석한다. 생물의 소유격은 단수 또는 복수 명사에 's를 붙이고, s로 끝나는 복수 명사에는 '(apostrophe)만 붙인다.

the girl's uniform　　the girls' school　　(×) the girls's school
the lion's roar　　the lions' roar　　(×) the lions's roar

My sister's room is neat and orderly compared to mine.
내 여동생의 방은 내 방에 비해 깔끔하고 정리가 잘 되어 있다.

A wide selection of children's books is on sale during the holidays.
다양한 종류의 어린이 책이 연휴 동안 할인 판매됩니다.

|참고| s로 끝나는 사람 이름에는 's를 붙이거나 '만 붙이고 의미가 분명한 경우 명사의 반복을 피하기 위해 's 뒤의 명사를 생략할 수 있다.
Chris's book = Chris' book
This is not my cell phone. It's Brian's (cell phone). 이건 내 휴대 전화가 아니야. 브라이언의 것이야.

2 무생물의 소유격은 「A of B」의 형태이며, 'B의 A'라고 해석한다.

The name of the book is *To Kill a Mockingbird*. 그 책의 제목은 '앵무새 죽이기'이다.

The legs of the table are wobbly. 탁자의 다리가 흔들거린다.

|참고| the top, the bottom, the beginning, the end 등이 주로 A of B의 형태로 표현된다.
The beginning of the story was boring. 그 이야기의 시작은 지루했다.

3 시간이나 기간을 나타내는 표현인 today, yesterday, Sunday, a week, three hours 등에도 's 또는 '를 붙여 소유격을 만든다.

That scandal was in yesterday's newspaper. 그 추문은 어제 신문에 났었다.

Monday's meeting has been moved to Wednesday. 월요일의 회의가 수요일로 옮겨졌다.

Students in Canada get two months' vacation in the summer. 캐나다의 학생들은 여름에 두 달의 방학을 한다.

EXERCISES

정답 및 해설 P. 21

A 주어진 단어를 소유격('s, of)을 이용하여 소유관계를 의미하는 구로 바꿔 쓰시오.

1 computer / Jerry → ______________________

2 the edge / the box → ______________________

3 the title / the movie → ______________________

4 coats / his sisters → ______________________

5 wallet / Charles → ______________________

6 the curtain / the changing room → ______________________

edge 가장자리
title 제목
changing room 탈의실

B 주어진 명사를 소유격('s, of)을 이용하여 연결하시오.

1 ______________________ is next month.
(birthday, my father)

2 ______________________ nearly scared me to death.
(the beginning, the movie)

3 ______________________ is quite cheap nowadays.
(the cost, traveling overseas)

4 ______________________ is my old friend from college.
(the owner, the restaurant)

5 ______________________ opened up recently downtown.
(center, the new children)

6 I won't be able to attend ______________________.
(graduation ceremony, James)

overseas 해외의
open up (가게 등을) 열다
graduation ceremony 졸업식

C 밑줄 친 시간 표현의 소유격을 이용하여 문장을 완성하시오.

1 I have an exam tomorrow. So I am studying for it.
→ I am studying for ____________ exam.

2 I took a rest this afternoon. It lasted thirty minutes.
→ I took ____________ rest this afternoon.

3 The campers were running out of food. It could last only one day.
→ The campers had only ____________ supply of food left.

4 The performance is in the evening. It will be delayed.
→ We are sorry to announce that this ____________ performance will be delayed.

run out of ~을 다 써버리다
supply 공급량, 공급; 공급하다
announce 알리다, 발표하다

REVIEW

정답 및 해설 P. 21

be equal to
~와 동일하다
cardboard 판지, 마분지
relative 친척; 상대적인
citrus 감귤류
comfortable
편안한, 안락한
wreck
(부서진 배·자동차의) 잔해
end up
마침내는 (~이) 되다

( ) 안에서 가장 알맞은 것을 고르시오.

1 (A dime / Dime) is equal to ten cents.

2 Have (a wonderful time / wonderful time)!

3 I bought (apple / apples) at Victoria Market.

4 I found (a paper / paper) to read on the subway.

5 We don't have any (time / times) to wait for him.

6 I need some cardboard (paper / papers) for art class.

7 I received (a package / package) from a relative of mine.

8 Vitamin C is found in (orange / oranges) and other citrus fruits.

9 Wear comfortable (clothing / clothings) to your exercise class.

10 My sister needs some (furniture / furnitures) for her new house.

11 Broken (glass / glasses) from the car wreck was all over the street.

12 Over eleven million empty plastic water (bottle / bottles) end up in the trash every year.

trouser 바지
toothpaste 치약
fridge 냉장고
carbon monoxide
일산화탄소
odorless 냄새가 없는
tip 기울이다; 뒤집히다
fall down 넘어지다

B 주어진 명사를 단수 또는 복수로 바꿔 문장을 완성하시오.

1 We have to eat a lot of fresh ________________ (vegetable).

2 These ________________ (trouser) are on sale this week.

3 I uploaded several ________________ (photo) to my blog.

4 ________________ (fur coat) have come back into fashion.

5 I finally found my sweater under my ________________ (bed).

6 We need to buy a few ________________ (tube) of toothpaste.

7 Sally sent me several ________________ (text message) today.

8 Don't forget to put the ________________ (milk) back in the fridge.

9 Carbon monoxide is a colorless, odorless ________________ (gas).

10 I need to change Korean won into US ________________ (dollar).

11 I spent the morning reading and answering my ________________ (mail).

12 Some students tipped their ________________ (chair) back and fell down.

C 〈보기〉에서 알맞은 것을 골라 단수 또는 복수로 바꿔 문장을 완성하시오.

보기	man	handkerchief	glass	money
	hair	information	carton	room

handkerchief 손수건
spill 엎지르다
take out 꺼내다
blow (코를) 풀다; (바람이) 불다
crowded 붐비는, 복잡한
room 공간; 방
arrest 체포하다
robbery 강도질
eyesight 시력
agent 대리인
further 그 이상의; 더 멀리
brush off 털다

1 How much ____________ have you got on you?

2 I spilled a ____________ of orange juice all over the floor.

3 Jason took out a ____________ and blew his nose loudly.

4 It is too crowded here. Would you make ____________ for us to pass?

5 A woman and two ____________ were arrested the day after the robbery.

6 She has poor eyesight. She has worn ____________ since she was a child.

7 When you arrive in Madrid, Spain, please contact one of our agents for further ____________.

8 After cutting my hair, the hairdresser brushed off the ____________ on my face with a sponge.

D 밑줄 친 부분을 바르게 고치시오.

chalk 분필
modern 현대의
remarkable 주목할 만한
chew up ~을 엉망으로 부수다
appoint 임명하다; 정하다
crack ~에 금이 가게 하다
exchange 교환하다
prove 입증하다, 증명하다
bridesmaid 신부 들러리

1 Could you bring me two piece of chalks?

2 Do you know the way to St. Michaels' Church?

3 Mr. Smith sat on and broke his new reading glass.

4 There are three empty rooms on the second floors.

5 We finally found Mark's puppy at the church of the back.

6 He eats breads and a cup of coffee as soon as he gets up.

7 The modern design of these buildings are quite remarkable.

8 When I opened the mail box, I found letter from a stranger.

9 Mom! The neighbor' dog is chewing up your rose garden again.

10 The President has appointed a new team of economic adviser.

11 The bottle's bottom is cracked. I'd better exchange it for another one.

12 The police believed those men were thiefs, but they couldn't prove it.

13 Let's get half a dozen watermelon, cut them in half and use them as bowls.

14 This apartment has three bedroom: a master bedroom and two smaller ones.

15 The bride threw a bouquet of flower to her bridesmaids at the end of the wedding.

REVIEW PLUS

정답 및 해설 P. 23

stick 붙다; 나뭇가지

다음 중 어법상 올바른 문장을 고르시오.

① I don't have any waters.
② We don't have much cups left.
③ Time fly when you're having fun.
④ I have piece of gum stuck to my shoe.
⑤ Mary and John shared a bottle of wine over dinner.

skid
(브레이크를 건 채) 미끄러지다
crash into ~와 충돌하다
weigh 무게를 달다
auction
경매; 경매에서 팔다

다음 (A), (B), (C)에 들어갈 말이 바르게 짝지어진 것을 고르시오.

- I skidded on the ____(A)____ and crashed into another car.
- Take your fruit and ____(B)____ to be weighed over there.
- Several items of ____(C)____ were sold at the auction.

	(A)		(B)		(C)
①	ices	···	vegetable	···	clothing
②	ice	···	vegetables	···	clothing
③	ice	···	vegetables	···	clothings
④	ices	···	vegetables	···	clothing
⑤	ices	···	vegetable	···	clothings

be similar to
~와 비슷하다
one another 서로
advertisement 광고
certainly
확실히; 틀림없이
influence
~에(게) 영향을 끼치다

다음 (A), (B), (C)에서 알맞은 것을 고르시오.

A woman stands in front of lots of (A) (box / boxes) of shampoo. She chooses one brand. Is it much better than the others? Probably not. These days, (B) (a number of / a great deal of) products are very similar to one another in their quality and price. If the products are almost the same, what makes customers buy one brand instead of another? You may feel that advertisements on TV certainly (C) (influence / influences) you.

	(A)		(B)		(C)
①	box	···	a number of	···	influence
②	box	···	a great deal of	···	influences
③	boxes	···	a number of	···	influences
④	boxes	···	a great deal of	···	influences
⑤	boxes	···	a number of	···	influence

PART 6

관사
Articles

부정관사 a/an

쓰임	예문
막연한 하나(one)	Sam bought **a comic book** to read on the plane. 샘은 비행기에서 읽을 만화책을 한 권 샀다.
~마다, ~당(per)	Jerry buys the *Economist* once **a month**. 제리는 한 달에 한 번 이코노미스트 잡지를 산다.
대표 명사(all)	**An octopus** is a strange-looking sea creature. 문어는 이상하게 생긴 바다 생물이다.

FOCUS

1 관사(articles)에는 부정관사(indefinite articles)와 정관사(definite article)가 있다. 부정관사인 a(n)은 셀 수 있는 명사의 단수와 쓰며, 정관사 the는 셀 수 있는 명사와 셀 수 없는 명사 모두와 쓴다.

I had **a cheeseburger** and **a Diet Coke** for lunch.
나는 점심으로 치즈버거 한 개와 다이어트 콜라 한 잔을 먹었다.

But **the cheeseburger** was undercooked and **the Coke** was flat.
하지만, 치즈버거는 덜 익었고, 콜라는 김이 빠져 있었다.

Can you pass me **the salt** on **the table**, please?
탁자 위에 있는 소금 좀 건네줄래?

|주의| 셀 수 있는 명사의 단수는 관사 없이 쓸 수 없다.
I ate **an apple**. (*NOT* I ate apple.) 나는 사과를 먹었다.

|참고| 어떠한 명사를 처음 화제에 올릴 때는 부정관사를 쓰고, 앞서 언급한 명사를 다시 말할 때는 정관사를 쓴다.
Once upon a time, there lived **a king** and his daughter. **The king** loved her very much.
옛날에 왕과 그의 딸이 살았습니다. 왕은 딸을 무척 사랑했습니다.

2 「a(n)+단수 명사」, 「무관사+복수 명사」, 「무관사+셀 수 없는 명사」는 특정한 명사 전체를 대표할 때 쓰인다.

A tiger is a fierce animal. (All tigers are fierce animals.) 호랑이는 사나운 동물이다.

An ostrich is an aggressive animal. (All ostriches are aggressive animals.) 타조는 공격적인 동물이다.

Dogs are faithful animals. 개는 충성스러운 동물이다.

Silver is a light gray metal. 은(銀)은 밝은 회색 금속이다.

|참고| 「the+단수 명사」는 특정한 명사 전체를 대표하기도 하지만, 「the+복수 명사」는 그 특정한 명사의 일부만을 지칭한다.
The ostrich is an aggressive animal. 타조는 공격적인 동물이다.
The ostriches are my uncle's. 그 타조들은 우리 삼촌의 것이다.

3 a(n)은 '막연한 하나(one)' 또는 '~마다, ~당(per)'을 의미한다.

막연한 하나 (one)

Can I have **a** bottle of water, please?
물 한 병 주시겠어요?

This morning, I bought **a** sketchpad and **a** box of color pencils for my art class.
오늘 아침 나는 미술 수업 때문에 스케치북 한 개와 색연필 한 상자를 샀다.

~마다, ~당 (per)

My brother and I visit an orphanage once **a** month.
우리 오빠와 나는 한 달에 한 번 보육원을 방문한다.

A: "How often do you go to concerts?" "너는 얼마나 자주 콘서트에 가니?"

B: "About twice **a** year." "일 년에 두 번쯤 가."

|참고| 1. 발음이 자음으로 시작되는 경우 a를, 모음으로 시작되는 경우 an을 붙인다.

a piano　　a university [jùːnəvə́ːrsəti]　　a European [jùərəpíːən]
an octopus　　an hour [áuər]　　an MP3 player [empiθriː pléiər]

2. 원래 사람 이름(고유명사) 앞에는 어떠한 관사도 붙이지 않지만, 사람 이름 앞에 a(n)가 붙으면 (1) 어떤 ~라는 사람/~와 같은 사람 (2) ~의 작품 등의 의미가 있다.

There's **a Dr. Kenneth** on the phone. Do you want to talk to him?
케네스 박사님이라는 분이 전화하셨어요. 통화하시겠어요?

I want to be **an Einstein** when I grow up.
나는 커서 아인슈타인 같은 사람이 되고 싶다.

He likes classical paintings. He owns **a Picasso**.
그는 고전 미술 작품을 좋아한다. 그는 피카소 작품 하나를 갖고 있다.

4 다음 표현은 어순에 주의해야 하므로 순서를 잘 암기해 두자.

such+a(n)+형용사+명사

Jenny always helps poor people. She is **such a generous person**.
제니는 항상 가난한 사람들을 돕는다. 그녀는 아주 관대한 사람이다.

quite+a(n)+형용사+명사

Park Jisung plays soccer very well. He is **quite a good soccer player**.
박지성은 축구를 매우 잘한다. 그는 꽤 훌륭한 축구 선수이다.

so+형용사+a(n)+명사

They accomplished the project in **so short a time**.
그들은 상당히 짧은 시간 안에 그 프로젝트를 완수했다.

EXERCISES

정답 및 해설 P. 24

counter 계산대
zoo-keeper (동물원의) 사육사
be in danger of ~할 위험이 있다
extinct (생명이) 멸종된; (불 등이) 꺼진
protect 보호하다
keen 대단한
perfume 향수
anniversary 기념일

A 빈칸에 a(n)과 × 중 알맞은 것을 써넣으시오. [×는 필요 없는 경우]

1 ________ orange is fruit.

2 Are ________ tomatoes vegetables?

3 ________ human being needs water to survive.

4 Alex is going to buy ________ SUV next year.

5 I have three chapters to read for ________ homework.

6 The man at the counter was reading ________ newspaper.

7 The zoo-keeper gave the monkeys ________ bunch of bananas.

8 Jacob and his family go out to dinner at least twice ________ month.

9 My brother has been playing ________ computer game since this morning.

10 ________ whales are in danger of becoming extinct. We must protect them.

11 My friend Sue is ________ chef. She works at ________ French restaurant.

12 Did you read the books I gave you? You are certainly ________ keen reader!

13 Julia is going to buy ________ car. She needs it to get to her new job outside the city.

14 Christmas only comes once ________ year, so let's make the most of it and enjoy ourselves.

15 Mr. Jones gave his wife ________ expensive bottle of perfume on their wedding anniversary.

be made of ~로 만들어지다
capital 수도; 대문자
diligent 근면한, 성실한

B 밑줄 친 부분을 바르게 고쳐 쓰시오.

1 This necklace is made of a gold.

2 My parents and I go hiking twice a months.

3 Everyone in the room believed that he was a honest man.

4 I can't believe that she made so a terrible mistake.

5 What a lovely sunshine! Why don't we have a picnic?

6 Latvia is an European country, and its capital city is Riga.

7 She is always early at school. She is such diligent student.

C 주어진 단어를 알맞게 배열하여 문장을 완성하시오.

1 Everybody fell asleep. It was ______________________.
(such, boring, speech, a)

2 He is ______________________. He also acts politely.
(such, handsome, man, a)

3 Thank you for inviting me. It was ______________________.
(quite, interesting, party, a(n))

4 He is ______________________ that I can't take my eyes off him.
(such, cute, boy, a)

5 The scenery is beautiful. I've never seen ______________________.
(so, beautiful, scene, a)

6 The performance didn't start on time. We had to wait ______________
______________. (quite, long, time, a)

7 She made ______________________ on her teacher on the first day of school. (quite, good, impression, a(n))

fall asleep 잠들다
scenery 경치, 풍경
scene 경치; 장면
on time 제 시간에
take A's eyes off B
B에서 A의 눈을 떼다
impression 인상

D 우리말과 같은 뜻이 되도록 주어진 단어와 관사를 이용하여 문장을 완성하시오.

1 그는 아시아에서 꽤 인기 있는 가수이다. (popular, singer)
→ He is ________ ________ ________ ________ in Asia.

2 Smith라는 분이 20분 전에 당신에게 전화했었어요. (Smith)
→ ________ ________ called you 20 minutes ago.

3 치즈는 소나 염소의 우유로부터 만들어진다. (be made from)
→ ________ ________ ________ ________ cows' or goats' milk.

4 우리 언니는 내년에 대학에 입학한다. (be going to)
→ My sister ________ ________ ________ ________ next year.

5 휴대 전화는 중요한 통신 도구이다. (be)
→ ________ ________ ________ ________ an important communication tool.

6 학생들은 일 년에 네 번 시험을 봐야 한다. (year)
→ Students have to take tests ________ ________ ________
________.

7 나무 좀 봐. 이렇게 큰 나무는 처음 봐. (tree, such, big)
→ Look at ________ ________! I have never seen ________
________ ________ ________.

make from ~로 만들다
communication
통신; 의사소통
tool 도구, 연장

정관사 the

쓰임	예문
이미 언급되었거나 서로 아는 것	Can you give **the comic book** back to me? 그 만화책을 나에게 돌려줄 수 있겠니?
세상에 하나밖에 없는 것	**The sun** rises in the east and sets in the west. 태양은 동쪽에서 떠서 서쪽으로 진다.
수식어구로 한정될 때	**The comic book** on the table is mine. 탁자에 있는 만화책은 내 거야.
최상급, 서수사, only, first 등으로 한정될 때	We are **the only** people in the dormitory now. 우리가 지금 기숙사에 있는 유일한 사람들이다.
the+형용사	**The young** should have dreams. 젊은이들은 꿈을 가져야 한다.
악기, 해양, 강, 산맥, 공공건물, 신문, 잡지 이름 등의 앞	Can you play **the guitar**? 너 기타 칠 줄 아니?

FOCUS

1 정관사 the는 이미 언급되었던 대상을 다시 이야기할 때 쓴다.

I saw a cute kitten on my way home. **The kitten** looked very hungry.
나는 집에 오는 길에 귀여운 고양이를 보았다. 그 고양이는 매우 배고파 보였다.

She bought a new umbrella yesterday. But she lost **the umbrella** this morning.
그녀는 어제 새 우산을 샀다. 그러나 그녀는 오늘 아침에 그 우산을 잃어버렸다.

2 정관사 the는 서로 아는 대상에 대해 이야기할 때 쓴다.

This soup is too bland. Pass me **the salt**, please. 이 수프는 너무 싱거워요. 소금 좀 건네주세요.

You should hand your homework to **the teacher** by tomorrow. 너는 내일까지 선생님께 숙제를 제출해야 한다.

3 정관사 the는 세상에 하나밖에 없는 것을 말할 때 쓴다.

The 63 Building in Seoul is easily recognizable. 서울에 있는 63빌딩은 쉽게 알아볼 수 있다.

The Great Barrier Reef is the largest coral reef system in the world. 그레이트 배리어 리프는 세계에서 가장 큰 산호초 조직이다.

|참고| the는 우리 주변의 환경과 그 안에서 하나뿐인 것을 나타내는 말에도 사용된다.
the sun　the moon　the earth　the sky　the world　the universe

4 정관사 the는 수식어구로 한정되어 가리키는 명사가 분명할 때 쓴다.

The man on the corner is trying to hail a taxi. 모퉁이에 있는 남자가 택시를 불러 세우려 하고 있다.

The box on the shelf was a gift from my grandmother. 선반에 있는 상자는 할머니에게서 받은 선물이었다.

5 최상급, 서수사, most, last, same, only, very, next 등이 붙은 말 앞에 the를 쓴다.

I think **the most important thing** is to understand different cultures.
나는 가장 중요한 것은 다른 문화를 이해하는 것이라 생각한다.

I've read only **the first chapter**.
나는 고작 첫 챕터를 읽었다.

6 「the+형용사」는 '~한 사람들'이라는 의미로, 「형용사+people」로 바꿔 쓸 수 있다.

The young always feel most free when they're having fun. (The young = Young people)
젊은 사람들은 재미있게 놀 때 가장 자유롭다고 느낀다.

The unemployed are queuing up, looking for jobs. (The unemployed = Unemployed people)
실업자들이 일자리를 구하려고 줄을 서 있다.

7 악기, 발명품, 해양, 강, 산맥, 공공건물, 신문, 잡지, 복수로 된 나라 이름 등의 앞에 주로 the를 쓴다.

Michael plays **the drums** in an amateur jazz quartet. 마이클은 아마추어 재즈 4중주단에서 드럼을 친다.

Life would be quieter without **the telephone**. 전화가 없다면 삶은 더 조용해질 텐데.

The Pacific Ocean is bigger than **the Atlantic Ocean**. 태평양은 대서양보다 더 크다.

I'd like to travel to **the Philippines**. 나는 필리핀을 여행하고 싶다.

| 참고 | 나라, 도시 등의 이름 앞에는 일반적으로 관사를 붙이지 않는다.
Seoul is very crowded. (*NOT* The Seoul) 서울은 매우 혼잡하다.

8 그 밖에 the를 붙이는 경우는 다음과 같다.

방향을 나타내는 말 앞　**the east**　**the west**　**the south**　**the north**

단위를 나타내는 말 앞　by **the** kilo　by **the** year　by **the** gram

the+사람 이름(고유명사) : 모든 사람이 알고 있는 그 사람

Do they mean **the Abraham Lincoln**, or someone else? 그 에이브러햄 링컨을 말하는 거예요, 아니면 다른 사람을 말하는 거예요?

the+사람 이름(복수) : 그 사람의 가족 전체

The Robinsons are away from home this weekend. 로빈슨 씨 가족은 이번 주말에 집에 없다.

기타

Let's go to **the movies** tonight. 오늘 밤에 영화 보러 가자.

I like listening to **the radio** while I'm jogging. 나는 조깅하면서 라디오를 듣는 것을 좋아한다.

I'll wash **the dishes**. 내가 설거지할게.

EXERCISES

정답 및 해설 P. 24

discussion 토론, 논의
cloning (생물) 클로닝, 생물 복제
exist on (음식 등에 의하여) 살아가다
steady 한결같은; 확고한
mercury ((화학)) 수은
liquid 액체의, 액체
element 요소
thermometer 온도계
valley 계곡, 골짜기

A ( ) 안에서 가장 알맞은 것을 고르시오. [×는 필요 없는 경우]

1 The shirt on (a / the / ×) sofa is mine.

2 (The / ×) main topic of discussion today is "cloning."

3 I found (a / ×) ten-dollar bill on my way home today.

4 (A / The / ×) poor need our help now more than ever.

5 He used to play (a / the) guitar in his high school band.

6 (A / The) Bank of Montreal is one of Canada's largest banks.

7 My children seem to exist on a steady diet of (a / the / ×) burgers and chips.

8 Taehee goes to aerobics class with her friends once (a / the / ×) week.

9 (A / ×) mercury is a liquid metal element that is used in thermometers.

10 A valley is an area of lower land between two lines of (a / the / ×) hills or (a / the / ×) mountains.

Statue of Liberty 자유의 여신상
endearing 사람의 마음을 끄는
monument 기념비
donate 기부하다
charity 자선 단체; 자선기금; 자선
to one's surprise 놀랍게도
clown 광대
costume 복장, 의상
section (신문의) 난, 부분
reverse 반전; 거꾸로의

B 빈칸에 a(n), the, × 중 알맞은 것을 써넣으시오. [×는 필요 없는 경우]

1 ________ Statue of Liberty is ________ endearing monument to freedom.

2 This is Daniel, ________ teacher from the UK I told you about earlier.

3 Sarah is ________ only person who will be able to solve this difficult puzzle.

4 My younger sister is ________ only person who I can share my secret with.

5 ________ bag of clothes in the box behind the chair was donated to charity.

6 Much to everyone's surprise, he was wearing ________ clown costume.

7 Hand me ________ sports section of ________ newspaper you're reading, please.

8 I used to live in ________ New York, which is one of ________ busiest cities in the world.

9 The seasons in ________ Australia are the reverse of those in ________ USA and Europe.

10 John is one of ________ smartest people I know. He has ________ talent for just about everything.

C 주어진 단어와 관사를 이용하여 문장을 완성하시오.

1 Cherries are sold by ________ (gram).

2 Teddy enjoys playing ________ (guitar) when he has free time.

3 Will you vacuum the living room while I wash ________ (dishes)?

4 ________ (young) need to face challenges and learn from experience.

5 On ____________ (last day) of our trip, we exchanged our email address.

6 Would you return ____________ (laptop computer) which I lent you last week?

7 I found ________ (wallet) yesterday. Surprisingly, the wallet was ________ (same) as mine.

vacuum 진공청소기로 청소하다
face 직면하다; 얼굴
challenge 어려움, 시련
experience 경험
exchange 교환하다

D 우리말과 같은 뜻이 되도록 주어진 단어를 이용하여 문장을 완성하시오.

1 교회에서 너를 보지 못했어. (see, at)
→ I didn't ______ ______ ______ ______.

2 Bradley 가족은 우리 집에서 두 블록 떨어진 곳에 산다. (Bradley)
→ ______ ______ live two blocks away from my house.

3 지구가 점점 더 더워지고 있다. (earth, be)
→ ______ ______ ______ getting warmer and warmer.

4 그들은 이번 여름에 미국을 여행하기로 했다. (travel to, United States, summer)
→ They decided to ______ ______ ______ ______ ______ ______ ______.

5 그 일을 끝낼 수 있는 유일한 방법은 계획을 세우는 것이다. (only way, finish, work)
→ ______ ______ ______ to ______ ______ ______ is to make plans.

6 이 강은 북쪽에서 남쪽으로 흐른다. (north, south)
→ This river flows ______ ______ ______ ______ ______ ______.

7 노약자석은 장애인이나 노인들을 위한 것이다. (physically challenged, elderly)
→ Courtesy seats are for ______ ______ ______ or ______ ______.

flow 흐르다, 흐름
courtesy seat 노약자석
physically challenged 장애를 겪고 있는

관사의 생략

쓰임	예문
일반적인 복수 명사, 셀 수 없는 명사	Different countries have different types of weather. 다른 나라들은 각기 다른 형태의 기후를 가진다.
식사, 학과목, 운동 경기 앞	What did you have for breakfast? 아침으로 무엇을 먹었니?
by+교통·통신 수단	I sent my application by fax. 나는 지원서를 팩스로 보냈다.
본래 목적으로 사용된 건물	We usually go to school at seven. 우리는 늘 일곱 시에 학교에 간다.
소유격, 지시 • 수량 형용사가 붙은 명사	The photo album belongs to my grandfather. 그 사진첩은 우리 할아버지의 것이다.

1 일반적이거나 막연한 것을 의미하는 복수 명사와 셀 수 없는 명사 앞에는 관사를 붙이지 않는다.

Men fear **death**.
사람은 죽음을 두려워한다.

Air consists chiefly of **nitrogen**.
공기는 주로 질소로 구성되어 있다.

People in **shorts** will not be allowed into the temple.
반바지를 입은 사람은 사원에 들어가는 것이 허용되지 않을 것입니다.

2 식사, 학과목, 운동 경기, 언어 앞에는 관사를 붙이지 않는다.

My family went out to eat **dinner** at Pasta Express last Sunday.
우리 가족은 지난 일요일에 파스타 익스프레스에서 저녁 외식을 했다.

Alex is planning to take **Economics 301** this semester at Brown University.
알렉스는 브라운 대학교에서 이번 학기에 경제학 301을 들을 계획이다.

Mr. and Ms. Smith play **tennis** together every Sunday.
스미스 씨 부부는 매주 일요일에 함께 테니스를 친다.

My sister speaks two languages. One is **Korean**, and the other is **Japanese**.
우리 언니는 2개 국어를 한다. 하나는 한국어이고 다른 하나는 일본어이다.

|참고| 형용사의 수식을 받는 식사 이름 앞에는 관사를 쓴다.
I had **an excellent dinner** tonight. 나는 오늘 저녁 훌륭한 저녁 식사를 했다.

3 「by+교통 · 통신 수단」으로 by와 교통 · 통신 수단 사이에는 관사를 붙이지 않는다.

My father often goes to work **by subway** these days.
우리 아버지는 요즘 종종 지하철을 타고 일하러 가신다.

Sandra went to her grandfather's farm **by bus** last weekend.
샌드라는 지난 주말에 버스를 타고 할아버지네 농장에 갔다.

My friend lives in Germany, so I sent a birthday present to her **by airmail**.
내 친구가 독일에 살고 있어서, 나는 그녀에게 생일 선물을 항공 우편으로 보냈다.

4 건물이나 장소가 본래의 목적으로 쓰인 경우, 관사를 붙이지 않는다.

Tammy **goes to bed** before midnight most days of the week.
태미는 일주일의 대부분 12시 전에 잠자리에 든다.

I **go to church** every Sunday morning with my mother.
나는 매주 일요일 아침 어머니와 함께 교회에 간다.

My brother **goes to college** in San Francisco.
우리 형은 샌프란시스코에 있는 대학에 다닌다.

| 주의 | 건물이나 장소가 본래의 목적으로 쓰이지 않은 경우에는 the가 붙는다.

My mom told me that my gym bag was under **the bed**. (*NOT* under bed)
엄마가 내 운동 가방이 침대 밑에 있다고 말해 주었다.

I went to **the church** to see the stained glass. (*NOT* went to church)
나는 스테인드글라스를 보려고 그 교회에 갔다.

| 참고 | 관사를 붙이지 않는 표현 정리

go to bed 잠자리에 가다
go to prison (죄를 지어) 교도소에 가다, 투옥되다
go to college, go to university 대학에 다니다
go to sea 선원이 되다
go to church (예배 보러) 교회에 가다
go to court 소송을 제기하다
go to school 학교에 다니다

5 소유격, 지시형용사, 수량형용사가 붙은 명사 앞에는 관사를 붙이지 않는다.

My sweater is pretty old. I'd better buy a new one. (*NOT* The my sweater)
내 스웨터는 꽤 낡았다. 새것을 하나 사는 것이 좋겠다.

I'd love to buy **this jacket**. How much is it? (*NOT* a this jacket)
이 재킷을 사고 싶어요. 얼마예요?

Some children were playing in the park. (*NOT* The some children)
몇 명의 아이들이 공원에서 놀고 있었다.

| 참고 | 그 외 관사를 붙이지 않는 경우는 다음과 같다.

He has watched **TV** all day. (*NOT* the TV) 그는 온종일 TV를 봤다.

Dad! I want to hear the end of the story. (*NOT* The dad) 아빠! 그 이야기의 결말을 듣고 싶어요.

EXERCISES

정답 및 해설 P. 25

fall in love with
~에게 반하다
prison 교도소, 감옥
under the circumstances
그 상황에서는
experienced
경험이 있는, 노련한

A (　) 안에서 가장 알맞은 것을 고르시오. [×는 필요 없는 경우]

1 Are you still learning how to play (a / the) flute?

2 He fell in love with his wife (a / the / ×) first time he saw her.

3 Whenever I travel by (a / the / ×) train, I always travel first class.

4 Lucky for him, he was able to avoid going to (a / the / ×) prison.

5 It was (a / the / ×) only thing I could do under the circumstances.

6 (A / The / X) experienced always have an easier time finding work.

7 I didn't know you played (a / the / ×) hockey. What position do you play?

stuffy
(공기 등이) 탁한; 숨막히는
White House 백악관
graduate 졸업하다
physics 물리학

B 빈칸에 a(n), the, × 중 가장 알맞은 것을 써넣으시오. [×는 필요 없는 경우]

1 Could you open ________ window, please? It's too stuffy here.

2 ________ big hotels all over the world are very much the same.

3 I met ________ girl on the way to school. She is Jane's twin sister.

4 A few lucky children were chosen to have ________ lunch with Kim Yuna.

5 I want to see ________ White House when I visit Washington next month.

6 We ate ________ breakfast together today for ________ first time in years.

7 I can graduate this year only if I successfully complete ________ Physics 101.

definitely 확실히; 명확히
nervous
초조해 하는, 불안해 하는
torture 고문; 고문하다

C (　) 안에서 가장 알맞은 것을 고르시오. [×는 필요 없는 경우]

1 A: Who's (a / the / ×) most popular teacher at school this year?
B: Ms. Choi is definitely the most popular teacher.

2 A: I'm always nervous for (a / the / ×) first few minutes of an exam.
B: I know what you mean. Those first few minutes are torture.

3 A: Do you speak any other languages besides (a / the / ×) Korean?
B: Yes, I do. I speak Spanish because I was born and raised in Spain.

4 A: Did you take (an / the / ×) umbrella with you (a / the / ×) this morning?
B: No. I bought one on my way to work.

5 A: Do you like (a / the / ×) Western food? What is (a / the / ×) your favorite dish?
B: Actually, I don't like Western food. My favorite is Chinese food.

D 문장을 읽고, 관사가 어색한 곳을 찾아 밑줄을 긋고 바르게 고쳐 쓰시오.

public 공공의; 대중
official language 공용어

1 The English is the most popular language in the world.

2 My cousin from an India taught me how to play cricket.

3 Lisa is going to her grandmother's by the train next weekend.

4 There's a public library about the two blocks away from here.

5 The two official languages of Canada are the French and the English.

6 My friends and I are going to play the basketball this Sunday morning.

7 Robert had ham and cheese sandwich, two apples, and a small carton of milk for lunch.

E 우리말과 같은 뜻이 되도록 주어진 단어와 필요한 경우 관사를 이용하여 문장을 완성하시오.

dead 다 닳은

1 내 고양이가 침대 밑에 장난감을 숨겨 놓았다. (bed)
→ My cat has hidden his toy ______ ______ ______.

2 내 휴대폰 배터리가 다 닳아서 네게 전화를 못했어. (cell phone battery)
→ ______ ______ ______ ______ was dead, so I couldn't call you.

3 우리 가족과 나는 대개 오전 7시에 아침을 먹고, 오후 6시에 저녁을 먹는다. (have, breakfast, dinner)
→ My family and I usually ______ ______ at 7 a.m., and ______ at 6 p.m.

4 나는 친구와 맛있는 점심을 먹고 함께 쇼핑을 갔다. (nice)
→ I had ______ ______ ______ with my friend, and we went shopping together.

5 나는 5시에 교회 앞에서 친구들을 만날 것이다. (church)
→ I will be meeting my friends ______ ______ ______ ______ ______ at 5.

6 대개 아빠는 차로 출근을 하는데 오늘은 버스를 탔다. (car, bus)
→ My father usually goes to work ______ ______, but today he went ______ ______.

7 나의 첫째 아들은 대학에 다니고, 막내아들은 중학교에 다닌다. (go, college, go, middle school)
→ My eldest son ______ ______ ______, and my youngest son ______ ______ ______ ______.

REVIEW

정답 및 해설 P. 26

motorcade 자동차 행렬
deliver a speech 연설하다
congress 국회, 의회
fall into ~에 빠지다
pond 연못
beaver (동물) 비버
startled 깜짝 놀란
architecture 건축물
hold (시합 등을) 열다; 잡다
athlete 운동선수
participate in ~에 참가하다
competitor 경쟁자
compete in (경기에) 참가하다

A ( ) 안에서 가장 알맞은 것을 고르시오. [×는 필요 없는 경우]

1 The President will be arriving at 10:00 a.m. by (a / the / ×) motorcade. He will be delivering a speech in front of Congress in the afternoon.

2 Suddenly, the child who had just fallen into the pond shouted, "Look! I see (a / the / ×) beaver!" Of course (a / the / ×) beaver was startled, too.

3 We visited the Taj Mahal while we were touring (a / the / ×) India. It is (a / the / ×) finest example of Mughal architecture in (a / the / ×) world.

4 We study hard in (a / the / ×) high school in order to enter (a / the / ×) good college. Ivy League schools such as Harvard, Princeton, and Yale are (a / the / ×) most popular ones.

5 (A / The) summer Olympic games are held every four years. (A / The / ×) athletes who participate in the games are called (a / the / ×) competitors. In the 2008 Beijing Olympics, a total of 10,500 athletes competed in 302 events in 28 sports.

destroy 파괴하다
minor 보다 작은, 대수롭지 않은
injury 부상, 상처
instrument 도구, 기구
wristwatch 손목시계
in addition to ~에 더하여, 게다가, ~뿐만 아니라
modern 현대의
display (정보를) 보여주다; 전시하다
tropical 열대의
category 범주
official language 공용어

B 빈칸에 a(n), the, × 중 가장 알맞은 것을 써넣으시오. [×는 필요 없는 경우]

1 My mother is usually __________ careful driver, but yesterday she had __________ worst accident of her life. __________ car she was driving was destroyed, but she survived with only minor injuries.

2 __________ instrument that most people use to tell the time is __________ wristwatch. In addition to __________ time, modern watches often display the day, date, month, and year.

3 I was given lots of __________ advice about buying new furniture. I decided to buy __________ sofa and __________ two chairs. __________ sofa was on sale, but I had to pay full price for __________ chairs.

4 __________ hurricane is __________ tropical storm with winds that reach speeds of 74 miles __________ hour or more. __________ strongest hurricane recorded was the Florida Keys Storm of 1935. A total of 500 people were killed during this Category 5 storm.

5 Canada is __________ second largest country by area in the world. The two official languages of Canada are __________ French and __________ English. __________ ice hockey and __________ lacrosse are very popular sports in Canada.

C ( ) 안에서 가장 알맞은 것을 고르시오. [×는 필요 없는 경우]

1 A: It's getting dark. Why don't you turn on (a / the / ×) light?
B: Where's (a / the / ×) switch? I can't find it.
A: It's on the wall, next to (a / the / ×) fridge.

2 A: I need (a / the / ×) sugar for (a / the / X) my coffee. Do you have any sugar?
B: Yes, here it is.
A: Thank you, but where are the spoons?

3 A: Can you help me? (A / The / ×) lid of the rice cooker won't close.
B: Well, it's broken. We'll have to go to the store and buy (a / the / ×) new one.
A: What a shame! It lasted for such (a / the / ×) long time.

4 A: That was (a / the / ×) very interesting tour. I learned a lot about (a / the / ×) city.
B: Me, too. I had no idea that (a / the / ×) New York City was originally named "New Amsterdam."
A: Also, it was the Dutch who founded (a / the / ×) city.

fridge 냉장고
lid 뚜껑
originally 원래, 본래
the Dutch 네덜란드인

D 빈칸에 a(n), the, × 중 가장 알맞은 것을 써넣으시오. [×는 필요 없는 경우]

1 A: I can't believe I failed ________ yesterday's test! I'm so embarrassed.
B: Don't worry. I'm sure you'll do better on ________ next one.

2 A: I've run out of ________ money. Is there ________ ATM nearby?
B: I think I saw ________ bank back there about ________ block down the street.

3 A: Sorry, but I broke ________ glass while I was washing ________ dishes.
B: Oh, that's all right. You weren't hurt, were you?

4 A: I don't know what this word means. Do you have ________ dictionary?
B: Sorry, but I don't. Why don't you ask ________ teacher? Raise your hand and get her attention.

5 A: Excuse me, can you tell me how to get to ________ National Gallery from here?
B: Actually, I am ________ tourist here myself. Why don't you ask ________ taxi driver over there?

embarrassed 당황스러운
run out of ~을 다 써버리다
ATM(=Automated Teller Machine) 현금 자동 입출금기
nearby 근처에, 가까이에
attention 주의, 주목

REVIEW PLUS

정답 및 해설 P. 27

unpleasant 불쾌한
communicate 말하다, 의사소통하다
up and down 아래 위로

다음 대화 중 어법상 바른 것을 고르시오.

① A: I had a unpleasant experience at the mall today.
B: You can complain to the store manager.

② A: What languages do you speak at home?
B: My brother and I communicate in the English.

③ A: Have you ever seen kangaroo?
B: Yes. I've seen one once at the circus.

④ A: Is there an elevator in your building?
B: No, there isn't. I have to walk up and down the stairs every day.

⑤ A: We're running a bit late, so maybe we should take taxi.
B: Taxi? But the traffic will be terrible now. Let's take the subway instead.

be born in ~에서 태어나다
be known for ~로 알려져 있다
theory 이론
physics 물리학
relativity 상대성; 관련성

B 다음 (A), (B), (C)에 들어갈 말이 바르게 짝지어진 것을 고르시오.

Einstein was born in Germany in 1879. He won the Nobel Prize in ___(A)___ in 1921. Einstein left his country and lived in ___(B)___ until he died in 1955. Einstein is known for his theory of ___(C)___.

	(A)		(B)		(C)
①	the physics	…	USA	…	relativity
②	the physics	…	the USA	…	relativity
③	physics	…	the USA	…	a relativity
④	physics	…	the USA	…	relativity
⑤	physics	…	USA	…	a relativity

armchair 안락의자
silverware 은식기류

다음 밑줄 친 부분이 어법상 바르지 않은 것을 고르시오.

A: Let's go to the shopping mall and look for ① some furniture for Mike. He'll need some when he goes ② to the college in the fall.
B: What type of furniture does he need?
A: Well, he already has ③ a bed and a desk. So perhaps we can look for a comfortable armchair and a desk lamp. He'll need a few plates, cups, and some silverware, too.
B: Good. And if the store is having ④ a sale, maybe we'll find him ⑤ a cheap sofa.

PART 7

대명사
Pronouns

대명사

정답 및 해설 P. 27

1 대명사(pronouns)는 명사를 대신하여 쓰는 말이다.

Turn down **the radio**, please. **It**'s bothering me.

Do you see **the man** over there? **He** is my English teacher.

2 인칭대명사에는 주격, 소유격, 목적격, 소유대명사와 재귀대명사가 있다.

단 · 복수	인칭	주격	소유격	목적격	소유대명사	재귀대명사
단수	1	I	my	me	mine	myself
	2	you	your	you	yours	yourself
	3	she	her	her	hers	herself
		he	his	him	his	himself
		it	its	it	–	itself
복수	1	we	our	us	ours	ourselves
	2	you	your	you	yours	yourselves
	3	they	their	them	theirs	themselves

CHECK-UP

( ) 안에서 가장 알맞은 것을 고르시오.

1 Let's go and watch the play. (He / She / It) will be very exciting.

2 This backpack is (my / me / mine). (You / Your / Yours) is over there.

3 You look very tired. Did you finish (you / your / yours) project last night?

3 지시대명사는 사람이나 사물을 대신 가리키는 말이다.

	가까이 있는 대상		멀리 있는 대상	
	단수	복수	단수	복수
지시대명사	this	these	that	those
지시대명사+be 동사	This is/was ~	These are/were ~	That is/was ~	Those are/were ~

CHECK-UP

( ) 안에서 가장 알맞은 것을 고르시오.

1 (This / These) T-shirts are clean, but (that / those) shoes are dirty.

2 (This / These) is my new cell phone, and (that / those) is my brother's.

4 부정대명사는 불특정한 대상을 가리킬 때 쓴다.

CHECK-UP

(　　) 안에서 가장 알맞은 것을 고르시오.

1 Would you like (another / the other) cup of hot chocolate?

2 Some people like watching the movies. (Others / The other) like reading books.

3 There are two black suits. (One / It) is my father's, and (another / the other) is my uncle's.

4 There are four books on my desk. (One / It) is my English textbook, (another / the other) is my dictionary, and (others / the others) are novels.

5 비인칭대명사 it은 날짜, 시간, 요일, 날씨, 계절, 명암, 거리 등을 나타낼 때 주어 자리에 쓰며 '비인칭주어'라고 부른다.

	인칭대명사 it	비인칭대명사 it
쓰임	특정한 사물을 대신 지칭	날짜, 시간, 요일, 날씨, 계절, 명암, 거리 등을 나타냄
해석	그것	해석하지 않음
예문	It is my lunchbox.	It snowed in Seoul yesterday.

CHECK-UP

다음 중 밑줄 친 it의 의미가 나머지와 다른 것을 고르시오.

1
① It's 2 p.m.
② It's Sunday.
③ It's a blue T-shirt.
④ It's too bright in here.

2
① It's delicious.
② It's too loose.
③ It's an aquarium.
④ It's freezing outside.

인칭대명사 & 소유대명사

대명사	예문
인칭대명사	All of us went to bed early because **we** had to wake up early the next day to catch a flight. (주격) 우리는 모두 일찍 잠자리에 들었다. 왜냐하면, 다음 날 비행기를 타려면 일찍 일어나야 했기 때문이다.
	William borrowed several DVDs from the library. He has to return **them** by next Monday. (목적격) 윌리엄은 도서관에서 몇 개의 DVD를 빌렸다. 그는 그것들을 다음 주 월요일까지 반납해야 한다.
소유대명사	My bike is sitting next to your bike in the garage. But **mine** has a flat tire. 내 자전거는 차고에 네 자전거 옆에 있는데 내 것은 타이어의 바람이 빠졌어.

1 인칭대명사(personal pronouns)는 앞서 언급된 사람이나 사물의 중복을 피하고자 할 때 사용한다.

Jenny and I are at the ice rink. **We** are practicing a new figure skating routine. (주격)
제니와 나는 스케이트장에 있다. 우리는 새로운 피겨 스케이팅 연기 동작을 연습하고 있다.

James and Nick went camping last Saturday. **They** enjoyed it a lot. (주격)
제임스와 닉은 지난 토요일에 캠핑을 갔다. 그들은 매우 즐거운 시간을 보냈다.

What's Alex been up to? I haven't seen **him** for ages. (목적격)
알렉스는 어떻게 지내고 있니? 그를 오랫동안 못 봤어.

I haven't seen Amanda in quite a long time. Have you seen **her** lately? (목적격)
아만다를 꽤 오랫동안 못 봤어. 최근에 그녀를 본 적이 있니?

|주의| 전치사 다음에 대명사가 단독으로 오면 목적격을 사용한다.
I went swimming with **him** last Saturday. 나는 지난 토요일에 그와 함께 수영하러 갔다.

|참고| 1. '~의'라는 소유의 의미를 나타내는 my, our, your(너의), your(너희의), his, her, its, their는 소유한정사(possessive determiners)로 명사 앞에만 쓸 수 있다.
Will Tasha bring **her** guitar to the party? 타샤가 파티에 기타를 가져올까?
My brother and I have to finish **our** homework before watching TV. TV를 보기 전에 형과 나는 숙제를 끝내야 한다.

2. 둘 이상의 인칭대명사를 나열할 때 보통 2인칭, 3인칭, 1인칭의 순서로 쓴다.
He and I are good friends. 그와 나는 좋은 친구다.
You and he are good friends. 너와 그는 좋은 친구다.

2 「대명사의 소유격+명사」는 소유대명사(possessive pronouns)로 바꿔 쓸 수 있으며, '~의 것'이라고 해석한다.

Can you lend me **your umbrella**? (소유격+명사) 당신의 우산을 빌려 줄 수 있나요?

I left **mine** on the subway this morning. (소유대명사: mine = my umbrella) 저는 오늘 아침 지하철에 제 것을 놓고 왔어요.

A: Can you share **your lunch** with me, Jeremy? (소유격+명사) 너의 점심을 나와 나눠 먹을 수 있겠니, 제레미?

B: Where's **yours**? Didn't you bring anything to eat? (소유대명사: yours = your lunch)
네 것은 어디에 있는데? 너는 먹을 것을 아무것도 가져오지 않았니?

A: I left **mine** at home. (소유대명사: mine=my lunch) 내 것을 집에 두고 왔어.

B: Oh, don't worry. Let's share **mine**. 아, 걱정 마. 내 것을 나눠 먹자.

|주의| 소유격은 뒤에 명사를 써야 하지만, 소유대명사는 뒤에 명사를 쓸 수 없다.
Can you share **your lunch** with me? (*NOT* yours lunch)
Where is **yours**? (*NOT* your)

|참고| 1. 앞에 나온 명사의 성별을 알 수 없을 때는 his or her 또는 his/her로 받는다.
요즘은 성차별적인 언어 사용을 피하고자 복수형을 주로 사용한다.
A student should always do **his or her** homework. 학생은 항상 자신의 숙제를 해야 한다.
Students should always do **their** homework. 학생들은 항상 자신들의 숙제를 해야 한다.

2. 한정어와 소유격은 나란히 쓸 수 없으므로 이때에는 이중소유격을 쓴다.
이중소유격의 형태는 [한정어+명사+of+소유대명사]이다.

my a friend (X) — a friend of **mine** 내 친구들 중 한 명
Henry's that violin (X) — that violin of **Henry's** 헨리의 저 바이올린

3 it은 its(그것의)라는 소유격만 있고, 소유대명사는 없다. it's는 it is나 it has를 줄인 말이다.

The company increased **its** profits. (*NOT* it's) 회사가 이익을 증대시켰다.

Their house in Sydney has **its** own swimming pool. 시드니에 있는 그들의 집에는 수영장이 있다.

|참고| 1. it은 인칭대명사로서 앞서 나온 사물을 대신 받는다.
A: Do you like Korean food? 당신은 한국 음식을 좋아합니까?
B: Yes, **it**'s great. I love **it**. (인칭대명사) 네, 그것은 훌륭해요. 저는 그것을 좋아해요.

2. it은 앞서 언급된 명사를 대신하기도 하지만 화자와 청자가 모두 알고 있는 상황이나 사실 자체를 가리키기도 한다.
I've tried my best to fix the problem, but **it** wasn't enough.
(it = the fact that I've tried my best to fix the problem)
나는 그 문제를 해결하기 위해 최선을 다했지만 그것으로는 충분하지 않았어.

3. it이 계절, 날씨, 거리, 시간 등을 나타내는 경우, '비인칭주어 it'이라고 부르며 '그것'이라고 해석하지 않는다.
If **it**'s too cold, you can turn off the air conditioning. (비인칭주어) 너무 추우면, 에어컨을 꺼도 됩니다.

4. it은 주어나 목적어를 대신하는 가주어, 가목적어로도 쓰인다.
It is easy for her to solve the math problem. (it = to solve the math problem: 가주어)
그녀에게 있어서 그 수학 문제를 푸는 것은 쉬운 일이다.
She found **it** easy to solve the math problem. (it = to solve the math problem: 가목적어)
그녀는 그 수학 문제가 풀기 쉽다는 것을 알았다.

EXERCISES

정답 및 해설 P. 28

wag (개가 꼬리를) 흔들다
tail 꼬리
though (비록) ~이긴 하지만
pleasant 즐거운, 쾌적한
accomplished (기예 등이) 뛰어난; 성취된
turn (어떤 나이가) 되다; 돌다
homeroom teacher 담임 선생님
run into ~를 우연히 만나다

A ( ) 안에서 가장 알맞은 것을 고르시오.

1 Isn't that girl over there a friend of (your / yours)?

2 (They / Their / Theirs) house is about two blocks from here.

3 My dog wags (it / its / it's) tail whenever (it / its / it's) sees me.

4 Give the cell phone back to (I / my / me / mine). It's (I / my / me / mine).

5 I offered her my telephone number, but she didn't offer me (she / her / hers).

6 Though (we / our / us) rooms are small, (their / them / they) are pleasant.

7 Jim has already eaten (he / him / his) lunch, but I'm saving (me / my / mine) until later.

8 (He / His / Him) is an accomplished musician. (He / His / Him) music is quite popular.

9 My mother just turned fifty this year. (She / Her / Hers) is starting to get a few gray hairs.

10 Ms. Lee is (I / my / me) homeroom teacher. I ran into (she / her) at the mall a few days ago.

feature 특징, 특성
beyond repair 수리할 수 없을 정도로(의)
own 자신의; 소유하다
back and forth 앞뒤(좌우)로
championship 결승전, 선수권 대회
be into ~에 관심이 있다, ~을 좋아하다
extreme 과격한; 극도의
risk-taker 모험가, 위험을 무릅쓰는 사람
voucher 상품권

B 주어진 대명사를 가장 적절하게 바꿔 문장을 완성하시오.

1 I'm Korean. My name's Jihun. What's __________ (you)?

2 You can't have any of my ice cream. It's all __________ (I)!

3 Your camera has more useful features than __________ (I).

4 John's car wouldn't start. __________ (it) was broken beyond repair.

5 Each student has __________ (he or she) own locker in the classroom.

6 My dog wagged __________ (it) tail back and forth when I came home.

7 Robert is into all kinds of extreme sports. __________ (he) is a risk-taker.

8 __________ (we) ice hockey team is in the championships. We're very excited.

9 My parents' wedding anniversary is coming. I'll give __________ (they) a spa voucher.

10 I met Kelly in the workshop for the first time. __________ (she) and I have been best friends since then.

C 밑줄 친 부분을 알맞은 소유대명사로 바꿔 쓰시오.

1 The car parked in front of our house is his car.

2 Your project was more creative than his project.

3 We have a reservation. Which room is our room?

4 That's your chair over there. This one is my chair.

5 They kept insisting that our seats were their seats.

6 I think the painting on the wall is one of her paintings.

7 How funny! Your son is exactly the same age as my son.

8 Finally we've bought this house. This house is our house!

9 You should do the assignment by yourself because it's your assignment.

10 I think I lost my notebook. Can I borrow your notebook for the final exam?

creative 창의적인
have a reservation 예약이 되어 있다
insist 고집하다
assignment 과제, 임무

D 대화를 읽고, 밑줄 친 부분을 대명사로 바꿔 쓰시오.

A: Hi, Sue. Are you going to Mark's party this weekend?
B: I haven't decided yet. I'm not speaking to Mark's sister right now.
A: Why? What happened? Did you and Jenny have a fight? I'm kind of surprised. I thought you and Jenny were very close friends.
B: Didn't you hear? Jenny totally betrayed my trust by lying to me.
A: Really? That doesn't sound like Jenny at all. Can you tell me what happened?
B: I'd love to, but I've got to run. I'll call you tonight and explain the whole story.

totally 완전히, 모두
betray ~을 배반하다
have got to ~해야 한다

E 빈칸 ① ~ ④에 it's(It's), its(Its) 중 알맞은 것을 써넣으시오.

In most countries where there are mountains, people enjoy the unique appeal of skiing. In ① __________ simplest form, skiing is sliding down a snow-covered slope on a pair of long, slim plates called skis. ② __________ one of the few sports that enable people to move at high speed without any power-producing device. In ③ __________ most advanced form, ④ __________ a highly skilled sport in which experts can slide down a mountain trail at more than 60 miles an hour, soar through the air for several hundred feet, or make quick turns through an obstacle course.

appeal 매력
slide down 미끄러져 내려가다
slope 비탈, 경사
enable ~할 수 있게 하다, 가능하게 하다
power-producing 동력을 발생하는
device 장치; 설비
skilled 숙련된
trail 산길
soar 날아오르다
obstacle 장애물

재귀대명사

쓰임	예문	생략
강조적 용법	The doctor told me the results of the test **herself.** (주어 강조) 의사가 나에게 직접 검사 결과를 말해 주었다. I saw Mike **himself** at the restaurant last night. (목적어 강조) 나는 어젯밤에 식당에서 바로 그 마이크를 직접 봤어.	○
재귀적 용법	My mother cut **herself** on some broken glass. (타동사 cut의 목적어) 우리 엄마는 깨진 유리에 손을 베었다. You should take better care of **yourself.** (전치사 of의 목적어) 너는 너 자신을 더 잘 돌봐야 한다.	×

1 재귀대명사는 소유격이나 목적격에 -self나 -selves를 붙인 형태로, '~ 자신, 스스로, 직접'이라는 뜻이다.

I have to do everything **myself.**
나는 모든 일을 스스로 해야 한다.

We built these bookshelves **ourselves.**
우리가 직접 이 책장들을 만들었어요.

The children seemed very pleased with **themselves.**
아이들은 자신들에게 매우 만족스러운 듯이 보였다.

2 재귀대명사가 대명사나 명사를 강조하기 위해 쓰여 생략해도 되는 경우를 '강조적 용법'이라고 한다.

You have nothing to fear but fear (**itself**).
너는 두려움 그 자체를 제외하고는 두려워할 것이 없다.

Catherine decorated the room (**herself**).
캐서린은 그 방을 직접 장식했다.

Mike was going to buy a new desk, but in the end he made one (**himself**).
마이크는 새 책상을 사려고 했지만 결국에는 직접 책상을 만들었다.

3 재귀대명사가 타동사나 전치사의 목적어로 쓰여 생략할 수 없는 경우를 '재귀적 용법'이라고 한다.

I looked at **myself** in the mirror for a long time. (전치사 at의 목적어)
나는 오랫동안 거울에 비친 나 자신을 바라보았다.

Her Korean name is Soyoung, but she calls **herself** Jackie. (타동사 calls의 목적어)
그녀의 한국 이름은 소영이지만, 그녀는 자신을 '재키'라고 부른다.

4 재귀적 용법 중, 전치사와 재귀대명사가 함께 쓰여 관용적인 의미를 지니는 경우가 있다.

by oneself 스스로(without help) / 혼자서(alone)
in itself 그것 자체가, 본질적으로
between ourselves 우리끼리 얘긴데

My father built the whole cabin **by himself**.
우리 아버지는 혼자서 그 오두막을 다 지었다.

The decision wasn't bad at all **in itself**.
그 결정은 그것 자체로는 전혀 나쁘지 않았다.

This is just **between ourselves**. Please do not tell anybody about it.
이건 그냥 우리끼리 하는 얘기야. 그것에 대해 아무에게도 말하면 안 돼.

5 재귀적 용법 중, 동사와 재귀대명사가 함께 쓰여 관용적인 의미를 지니는 경우가 있다.

burn oneself 화상을 입다
cut oneself 베이다
enjoy oneself 즐거운 시간을 보내다
help oneself (to ~) ~을 마음껏 먹다
hurt oneself 다치다, 상처를 입다
introduce oneself 자기소개를 하다
kill oneself 자살하다
make oneself at home 편하게 있다
talk/say to oneself 혼잣말하다
teach oneself 독학하다
make oneself understood 자기 말을 남에게 이해시키다

I was a bit careless and **burned myself** ironing a shirt yesterday.
나는 다소 조심성이 없어서 어제 셔츠를 다림질하다가 화상을 입었다.

Did you **enjoy yourself** at the dance? I heard it was a lot of fun.
너는 댄스파티에서 즐거운 시간을 보냈니? 무척 재미있었다고 들었어.

Help yourself to a snack. There's some pizza in the fridge, too.
스낵을 마음껏 먹어. 냉장고에 피자도 있어.

I walked straight over and **introduced myself** to him at the party.
나는 파티에서 그에게 곧장 걸어가 내 소개를 했다.

Sadly, the news reported that he tried to **kill himself** at his home last night.
애석하게도 뉴스에서 어젯밤 그가 집에서 자살을 시도했다는 것을 보도했다.

She **taught herself** English without ever leaving her own country.
그녀는 조국을 떠나 본 적도 없이 영어를 독학했다.

Please **make yourself at home** while I change my clothes.
제가 옷을 갈아입는 동안 편히 계세요.

He has a habit of **talking to himself** when he's frustrated.
그는 좌절했을 때 혼잣말하는 습관을 가지고 있다.

He was happy that he could **make himself understood** in English at last.
그는 마침내 영어로 의사소통을 할 수 있게 되어 기뻤다.

EXERCISES

정답 및 해설 P. 28

before ~하려면, ~(하기) 에 앞서서, ~보다 전에
be ashamed of ~을 부끄러워하다
fuss 소동; 야단법석

A ( ) 안에서 알맞은 것을 모두 고르시오.

1 I (me / myself) saw the giant statue.

2 He made (him / himself) a cup of coffee.

3 We can't move this rock (us / ourselves).

4 You must love (you / yourself) before you can love another.

5 You need to forgive (you / yourself) even though it is not easy.

6 We should be ashamed of (us / ourselves) for making such a fuss.

7 She looked at (her / herself) in the mirror while she was drying her hair.

blame oneself 자책하다, 자신을 책망하다
behavior 행동
admiringly 감탄하여

B 빈칸에 알맞은 재귀대명사를 써넣으시오.

1 She can do it ________________.

2 We introduced ________________ to each other.

3 Daniel bought ________________ a new digital camera.

4 They should learn to update their computers ________________.

5 The woman blamed ________________ for her son's bad behavior.

6 David looked at ________________ admiringly in the exercise room mirror.

organic 무공해의; 유기체의
go on holiday 휴가를 가다
ill 아픈; 나쁜
confidence 자신감

C 〈보기〉에서 밑줄 친 재귀대명사의 용법을 고르시오.

보기 ⓐ 타동사의 목적어 ⓑ 전치사의 목적어 ⓒ 강조

1 I myself prefer fresh organic vegetables. __________

2 I hope you like the gift. I chose it myself. __________

3 Why don't you go on holiday by yourself? __________

4 "Where is Lily?" she talked to herself. __________

5 If Cathy doesn't rest more often, she will make herself ill. __________

6 They had a great time and enjoyed themselves in Sydney. __________

7 Come on in. Welcome to my house. Make yourself at home. __________

8 She needs to develop a bit more confidence in herself. __________

D 빈칸에 알맞은 재귀대명사를 써넣으시오.

1 A: You need to set __________ a few manageable goals.
B: I agree. Having some short-term goals will help me focus.

2 A: I heard you and Jess are going to the Maldives on vacation.
B: Yeah. We promised __________ a good holiday this year.

3 A: I just got a call from Mr. Nicolas. Did you fax him the contract?
B: Yes, I did. I faxed the contract to him this morning __________.

4 A: I've bought __________ a new pair of boots. Do you like them?
B: Yes, I do. They really suit you.

5 A: Why are you all so late today? Would you care to explain __________?
B: We're really sorry. Ms. Choi's class finished ten minutes late.

6 A: What's the matter with you?
B: I hurt __________ while I was getting out of the bathtub last night. It's really embarrassing.

7 A: Do you have a bandaid? Mom cut __________ while she was chopping up some meat.
B: Wait a minute. It should be somewhere in my room.

8 A: There's nothing you can do about it. Don't be too hard on __________.
B: I know, but I feel that it's all my fault.

manageable 처리하기 쉬운; 다루기 쉬운
short-term 단기간의
focus (관심, 노력 등을) 집중하다
Maldives 몰디브(인도양의 섬나라)
contract 계약서, 계약; 계약하다
suit (의복 등이) 어울리다; 정장
care to 애를 쓰다, 노력하다
bathtub 욕조
embarrassing 당혹스러운
bandaid 반창고
chop up 잘게 썰다
be hard on ~를 심하게 대하다[나무라다]
fault 잘못; 책임

E 밑줄 친 ① ~ ⑤ 중, 어법상 어색한 것을 고르시오.

During the day, Louise Wilkinson works as a librarian. Once the sun goes down, she transforms ① her into a vampire. Louise has even got some vampire teeth. For ten years as a vampire, she ② has collected a houseful of horror movie videos, skulls, and bats. She enjoys ③ frightening people, although she knows it is just a game. As a secretary of the Dracula Society, which has 110 members, Louise has even been to the town of Dracula's birth. She loves to dress up as the "Mistress of the Dark" and go to parties ④ where she pretends to bite the necks of the other guests. Sometimes she dresses up as one of Dracula's victims and ⑤ wears a white dress covered with artificial blood.

librarian 도서관 사서
go down (해가) 지다
transform (형태, 외견 등을) 바꾸다; 변형시키다
vampire 흡혈귀
houseful 집안 가득
skull 두개골
secretary (협회의) 사무국장; 비서
mistress 여왕; 여주인
pretend ~인 체하다
dress up ~로 변장하다
victim 희생자, 피해자
artificial 가짜의; 인공적인

지시대명사

지시대명사의 종류	예문
this 이것, 이 사람, 이 ~	This is my cousin from New York. 이 사람은 뉴욕에서 온 제 사촌입니다. This girl is my younger sister. 이 소녀가 제 여동생입니다.
these 이것들, 이 사람들, 이 ~들	Are these your new sneakers? 이것이 너의 새 운동화니? Are these sneakers yours? 이 운동화가 네 것이니?
that 저것, 저 사람, 저 ~	That is my aunt, Judy. 저 사람은 우리 이모 주디예요. That lady is my aunt. 저 숙녀는 우리 이모입니다.
those 저것들, 저 사람들, 저 ~들	Those are my parents' bags. 저것들은 우리 부모님의 가방입니다. Those bags are my parents'. 저 가방들은 우리 부모님의 것입니다.

FOCUS

1 지시대명사(demonstrative pronouns)는 특정한 사람이나 사물을 대신 가리키는 말이다. this와 these는 비교적 가까이 있는 것을, that과 those는 각각 멀리 있는 것을 가리킨다. 지시대명사는 명사를 꾸며 주는 지시형용사로도 쓰이고 this, that은 단수 명사를, these, those는 복수 명사를 수식한다.

This is my friend from the UK. **These** are my friends from France. (지시대명사)
이 사람은 영국에서 온 내 친구입니다. 이 사람들은 프랑스에서 온 내 친구들입니다.

That ski slope is too dangerous for you. **Those** ski slopes are for beginners. (지시형용사)
저 스키 슬로프는 너에게 너무 위험해. 저 스키 슬로프들이 초보자들을 위한 거야.

2 this와 that은 앞에서 언급된 내용이나 앞으로 언급될 내용을 대신할 수 있다.

You'll be surprised to hear **this**. Dave and Vicky are getting married! 이 얘기 들으면 놀랄 거야. 데이브와 비키가 결혼을 한대!

The train departs at 9 o'clock sharp, so we must be there before **that**. (= before 9)
열차는 정확히 9시에 출발할 거니까 우리는 그 전에 도착해야 해.

3 앞에 나온 지시대명사를 다시 받을 때 사람이면 she, he, they로 받고, 사물이면 it, they로 받는다.

This is my friend, Kelly. **She**'s from Canada. 이 사람은 내 친구 켈리야. 그녀는 캐나다에서 왔어.

This is my new English textbook. **It** is more challenging than the last one.
이것은 나의 새 영어책이야. 이것은 지난번 것보다 더 어려워.

These are your teammates. **They** were looking forward to meeting you.
이 사람들이 당신의 팀 동료들입니다. 그들은 당신을 만나는 것을 기대하고 있었습니다.

4 문장 속에서 앞서 언급된 명사를 받을 때 그 명사가 단수이면 that, 복수이면 those로 받는다.

The climate of Korea is not unlike **that** of Europe. (that = The climate) 한국 날씨는 유럽 날씨와 다르지 않다.

Airplane tickets to the UK in October are cheaper than **those** in December. (those = Airplane tickets to the UK)
영국행 10월 항공권은 12월 항공권보다 싸다.

EXERCISES

정답 및 해설 P. 29

 ( ) 안에서 가장 알맞은 것을 고르시오.

1 Can you sign (this / these) form for me?

2 I'm sorry, but I believe (this / these) coat belongs to me.

3 Did you see (that / those) crazy driver? He almost hit me!

4 Did you see (that / those)? Something flashed like lightning.

5 (That / Those) are the books that must be returned to the library.

6 Come here and watch (this / these)! Our team is winning at the moment.

sign 서명하다; 징후; 표지판
belong to ~의 것이다, ~에 속하다
flash 번쩍이다
lightning 번개

B 빈칸에 알맞은 인칭대명사를 써넣으시오.

1 A: These are the people who you'll team up with for a month.
B: Wow. __________ all seem to be nice.

2 A: These look good, don't __________? Why don't we order a few?
B: Are you sure? You don't even know what __________ are.

3 A: Is this your dog? __________ is so cute!
B: No, __________ belongs to my sister. She's out of town this week.

4 A: This one is too small. That is the kind of tree I want.
B: That tree is a maple. __________ grows to a height of about 20 meters.

5 A: Who is that boy? I can't quite place him, but I've seen him before.
B: __________ is my cousin from Melbourne. You met him a few years ago.

team up ~와 한 팀이 되다
maple 단풍나무
place ~을 생각해내다, 알아차리다

C 빈칸에 알맞은 지시대명사를 써넣으시오.

1 The number of skyscrapers in China is greater than __________ of Australia.

2 The soles of my sneakers are more durable than __________ of your sneakers.

3 Children today are generally heavier than __________ of only a generation ago.

4 Harris's performance was much more improved than __________ of his classmates.

5 The layout of the first edition is completely different from __________ of the second edition.

6 The monitors from the company are much more expensive than __________ from other companies.

skyscraper 고층 건물
sole (구두 등의) 바닥
durable 견고한, 튼튼한
generation 세대
layout 배치
edition (출간된 책 등의) 판

부정대명사 I

종류	예문
one 같은 종류의 불특정한 것 it 바로 그것	A: Where is my camera that I lent you last week? 내가 지난주에 너에게 빌려 주었던 카메라는 어디에 있니? B: I'm sorry, but I broke **it** by mistake. I'll buy you a new **one**. 미안하지만, 내가 실수로 그것을 부서뜨렸어. 내가 너에게 새것을 사줄게.
one 하나 the other 나머지 하나	There are two pictures on the wall. **One** is of me. **The other** is of my older sister. 벽에는 두 개의 사진이 있다. 하나는 나의 사진이고, 나머지 하나는 우리 누나의 사진이다.
one 하나 another 또 다른 하나 the others 나머지 모두	There are five colored pencils in the box. **One** is yellow. **Another** is green. **The others** are red. 그 상자에는 다섯 개의 색연필이 있다. 하나는 노란색이고, 또 하나는 초록색이고, 나머지 것들은 빨간색이다.
some 일부 others 또 다른 일부	**Some** like hot and spicy food. **Others** like sweet and sour food. 어떤 사람들은 맵고 자극적인 음식을 좋아한다. 또 다른 사람들은 새콤달콤한 음식을 좋아한다.

1 앞서 언급된 것과 같은 종류의 불특정한 것(들)을 가리킬 때는 one(s)을 쓰고, 앞서 언급된 바로 그것(들)을 가리킬 때는 it이나 they[them]을 쓴다.

I lost my wallet the other day. I guess I should buy a new **one**. (불특정한 것)
나는 며칠 전에 지갑을 잃어버렸다. 새것을 사야 할 것 같다.

I lost my wallet the other day. I am still looking for **it**. (이미 언급된 특정한 것)
나는 며칠 전에 지갑을 잃어버렸다. 나는 아직도 그것을 찾고 있다.

These athletic shoes are too expensive. Do you have cheaper **ones**? (불특정한 것들)
이 운동화는 너무 비싸네요. 좀 싼 것도 있나요?

These donuts taste good. Where did you buy **them**? (이미 언급된 특정한 것들)
이 도넛은 맛있네요. 어디서 샀나요?

|참고| one과 you는 일반적인 사람을 나타내기도 하는데, 일상회화에서는 you를 더 많이 사용한다. one의 소유격은 one's, 재귀대명사는 oneself이다.
One must learn from **one's** mistakes. 사람은 자신의 실수로부터 배워야 한다.
You must learn from **your** mistakes. 사람은 자신의 실수로부터 배워야 한다.

2 another는 같은 종류의 또 다른 하나를 가리키며, '또 다른 하나, 하나 더'로 해석한다.

I just missed the bus, but **another** will be along shortly.
나는 방금 버스를 놓쳤어. 하지만, 다른 버스가 곧 올 거야.

This towel is wet. Hand me **another**, please.
이 수건은 젖었어요. 다른 것을 주세요.

3 another, the other, other는 형용사나 대명사로 쓰인다.

	형용사	대명사
단수 복수	Another book is interesting. 또 다른 책은 재미있다. Other books are boring. 다른 책들은 지루하다.	Another is interesting. 또 다른 것은 재미있다. Others are boring. 다른 것들은 지루하다.
단수 복수	The other book is yours. (나머지) 다른 책은 너의 것이다. The other books are mine. (나머지) 다른 책들은 나의 것이다.	The other is his. 나머지는 그의 것이다. The others are hers. 나머지 것들은 그녀의 것이다.

4 부정대명사를 이용하여 다음과 같이 사람이나 사물을 나타낼 수 있다.

I have two kittens. **One** is white, and **the other** is black.
(one은 두 개 중 하나, the other는 나머지 하나) 나는 두 마리의 고양이를 갖고 있다. 하나는 하얀색이고, 다른 하나는 검은색이다.

I bought three mufflers. **One** is for my father, **another** is for my mother, and **the other** is for my sister.
(one은 세 개 중 하나, another는 다른 하나, the other는 나머지 하나) 나는 목도리 세 개를 샀다. 하나는 아빠를 위해, 다른 하나는 엄마를 위해, 나머지 하나는 언니를 위한 것이다.

We have several plants on the balcony. **One** is an aloe. **Another** is a cactus. **The others** are rosemary.
(one은 여러 개 중 하나, another는 또 다른 하나, the others는 나머지 모두)
우리는 발코니에 몇 개의 식물을 기른다. 하나는 알로에이고, 또 다른 하나는 선인장이고, 나머지는 모두 로즈메리이다.

Some people admire professional athletes; **others** don't.
(some은 전체 중 일부, others는 그 나머지 중 일부) 어떤 사람들은 프로 운동선수들을 동경하지만, 또 다른 사람들은 그렇지 않다.

5 -one, -body, -thing은 some 또는 any와 함께 쓰여 불특정한 사람이나 사물을 가리키며, 항상 단수 취급한다. some으로 시작하는 부정대명사는 주로 긍정문과 권유(부탁)문에, any로 시작하는 부정대명사는 주로 부정문과 의문문, 조건문에 사용된다.

Somebody is calling you, Claire. 클레어, 누군가가 너를 부르고 있어.

Would you like **something** more to eat? 뭐 좀 더 드실래요?

He doesn't know **anything** about me. 그는 나에 대해 아무것도 모른다.

Did **anyone** hear my phone ring while I was out? 내가 나가 있는 동안 누군가 내 전화벨 소리를 들었니?

|주의| -thing의 경우 형용사가 뒤에서 수식해 준다.
I don't like this one. I want **something different**. 이것이 마음에 들지 않아요. 저는 다른 것을 원해요.

6 no one, nobody, nothing은 '아무(것)도[누구(것)도] ~이 아니다'라는 전체 부정을 의미한다. no one, nobody는 「not ~ anyone/anybody」로, nothing은 「not ~ anything」으로 바꿔 쓸 수 있다.

There was **nobody** around. 주변에 아무도 없었다.

→ There was**n't anybody** around.

We have **nothing** very good to eat. 우리는 먹을 만한 변변한 것이 하나도 없어.

→ We do**n't** have **anything** very good to eat.

|주의| 1. No one, Nobody, Nothing으로 시작하는 문장 뒤에는 부정어가 오지 않고, 해석은 부정문으로 한다.
Nothing is more important than love. 사랑보다 더 중요한 것은 아무것도 없다.
2. everyone, everything, everybody는 '모든 사람(것)'을 의미하고 항상 단수 취급한다.
Everyone is looking at you. 모든 사람이 너를 보고 있다.

EXERCISES

정답 및 해설 P. 30

plaid 격자무늬의
pleated 주름이 잡힌
ragged 남루한, 낡아 해진
replace (새것으로) 바꾸다, 대체하다
shorts 반바지
fitting room 탈의실

( ) 안에서 가장 알맞은 것을 고르시오.

1 This subway train is full. Let's wait for the next (it / one).

2 Red apples often taste better than green (them / ones).

3 Which do you prefer, the plaid skirt or the pleated (it / one)?

4 These shoes are too tight. Do you have larger (them / ones)?

5 These socks are too thin. Do you have thicker (them / ones)?

6 Your jacket looks a bit ragged. Why don't you replace (it / one)?

7 Is this your dictionary? Do you mind if I use (it / one) for a minute?

8 Can you see the red book on the desk? Please hand (it / one) to me.

9 You bought a new pair of sunglasses. Can you show (them / ones) to me?

10 I've got a few books on Korea. You can borrow (it / one) of them if you like.

11 If you like these shorts, why don't you try (them / ones) on? The fitting room is over there.

dead 다 닳은; 죽은
respect 존경하다, 존중하다
be concerned about ~에 대해 염려하다
mosquito 모기
interest 관심, 흥미
recession 불황, 경기 침체
afford (경제적으로) ~할 여유가 있다
arrogant 거만한, 오만한
go through (카드를) 긁다; ~을 경험하다

B 빈칸에 another, other, others 중 가장 알맞은 것을 써넣으시오.

1 This marker is dead. Have you got ___________ one?

2 Some people prefer fish while ___________ prefer meat.

3 Parents must teach their children to respect ___________.

4 Don't be concerned about what ___________ people are doing.

5 I'm going to have ___________ cup of coffee. Can I get you one?

6 I've just found ___________ mosquito. Close the window, please!

7 Go and ask your brother if he'll lend you ___________ five-dollar bill.

8 Gary would like to meet ___________ people with the same interests.

9 Because of the recession, Jack couldn't afford ___________ trip abroad.

10 Arrogant people are those who believe they are better than ___________.

11 Sorry, sir. Your credit card isn't going through. Do you have ___________ one?

12 Some people like to see movies in the theater while ___________ prefer to see them at home.

C 〈보기〉에서 알맞은 것을 골라 빈칸에 써넣으시오. [중복 사용 가능]

보기 one another the other others the others

1 I bought three bottles of water. Do you want ___________?

2 One of my tropical fish has died, but ___________ are still alive.

3 Some people want red wine while ___________ want white wine.

4 I have two sisters. ___________ lives in Seoul. ___________ lives in Busan.

5 We ordered two different pizzas. ___________ was Margherita, and ___________ was Neapolitan.

6 He has several cats. ___________ is a brown tabby. ___________ are snow-white Persians.

7 The CEO uses two cell phones. ___________ is for private use, and ___________ is for work.

8 He has three daughters. ___________ is a teacher. ___________ is a lawyer. ___________ is a violinist.

9 She can speak three languages. ___________ is Korean, ___________ is English, and ___________ is Spanish.

10 I've received three Christmas cards. ___________ is from my parents, ___________ is from my teacher, and ___________ is from my best friend.

tropical fish 열대어
alive 살아 있는
tabby 얼룩 고양이
private 사적인, 개인 소유의
lawyer 변호사

D ( ) 안에서 가장 알맞은 것을 고르시오.

1 Mary hasn't spoken to (anybody / nobody) all day.

2 Couldn't you wait in line like (everybody / nobody) else?

3 It's a bit boring. There is (anything / nothing) much to do.

4 I think that (everyone / no one) should contribute equally.

5 He rang several times, but (somebody / nobody) answered.

6 I was a little upset that (someone / no one) offered to help me.

7 (Something / Anything) in the fridge smells off. We'd better clean it out.

8 Why would (someone / anyone) ever want to hurt a defenseless animal?

9 (Someone / Anyone) is calling you. Would you like me to take a message?

10 That's an interesting point. I think you've got (something / anything) there.

wait in line 줄을 서서 기다리다
contribute 기부하다, 기여하다
equally 동등하게, 똑같이
fridge 냉장고
off (음식이) 상한
clean out 깨끗이 정리하다
defenseless 방어할 수 없는; 무방비의

부정대명사 II

종류	예문
all	All the people were dancing. 모든 사람이 춤을 추고 있었다. All of the people at the party were dancing. 파티에 있는 모든 사람이 춤을 추고 있었다.
each	Each student has his or her own learning style. 각각의 학생들은 자신만의 학습 방법을 가지고 있다. Each of us has a different idea. 우리는 각자 다른 의견을 가지고 있다.
every	Every room is empty. 모든 방이 비어 있다.

FOCUS

1

all은 '모든 사람(것), 모두의, 전체의'라는 의미로, 단독으로 쓰거나 명사를 수식한다. 수의 일치는 of 뒤에 나오는 명사에 따른다.

all+불특정명사

All students are going to learn how to ski. 모든 학생이 스키 타는 법을 배울 것이다.

All wood tends to expand when it is soaked in water. 모든 나무는 물에 젖으면 팽창하는 경향이 있다.

all(+of)+특정명사[the/소유격+명사]

All (of) the cakes were eaten by a mob of hungry children. 배고픈 아이들 한 무리가 케이크를 모두 먹어 치웠다.

All (of) my relatives were at the airport to see me off. 모든 친척들이 나를 배웅하기 위해 공항에 있었다.

| 주의 | all과 불특정한 명사 사이에는 of가 올 수 없다. 이때 불특정한 명사란 관사나 소유격 등으로 한정되지 않은 명사를 말한다.
All metal rusts when it is exposed to water. (*NOT* All of metal) 모든 금속은 물에 닿으면 녹이 슨다.

2

both는 '둘 다'라는 의미로, 단독으로 쓰거나 복수 명사를 수식한다.

Both are fine with me. 저에게는 둘 다 괜찮아요.

Both books look interesting to me. 두 책 모두 나에게는 흥미 있어 보여.

Both (of) the houses have been sold. 그 두 집은 팔렸어요.

| 주의 | 「all/both of+복수대명사」에서 of는 생략할 수 없다.
All of us can come tomorrow. (*NOT* All us) 우리 모두 내일 올 수 있어요.
Both of them are going to the conference. (*NOT* Both them) 그들 둘 다 회의에 갈 거예요.

3

each는 '각각, 각자'라는 의미로, 단독으로 쓰거나 단수 명사를 수식한다. 단, each of 뒤에는 복수(대)명사와 단수 동사가 온다.

Each girl is wearing what she likes best. 소녀들은 각자 가장 좋아하는 것을 입고 있다.

Each of my children writes me a letter once a week. 우리 아이들은 각자 나에게 일주일에 한 번씩 편지를 써요.

I have five brothers, and each of them is unique. 나에게는 다섯 명의 형제들이 있는데, 그들은 각자 다 독특하다.

| 참고 | each는 부사로 쓰여 '각각'이라는 의미를 나타낸다.
We paid 10 dollars each for admission. 우리는 입장료로 각각 10 달러씩 냈다.

4 every는 '모든'이라는 의미로, 단수 명사를 수식한다.

Every student is tested twice a year. 모든 학생들은 일 년에 두 번씩 시험을 본다.

Every member of the team is going to receive a medal. 그 팀의 모든 선수가 메달을 받을 것이다.

|주의| 1. every는 단독으로 쓰지 않는다.

Every child is leaving the classroom. (*NOT* Every is) 모든 아이들이 교실을 떠나고 있다.

2. each, every는 셀 수 없는 명사를 수식하지 않는다.

All luggage must be checked in at least one hour before departure. (*NOT* Each/Every luggage)
모든 짐은 적어도 출발하기 한 시간 전에 체크인 되어야 한다.

|참고| 「every+복수 시간 명사」는 '매 ~ 마다'라는 의미이다.

There's a meeting **every six weeks.** 6주마다 회의가 있다.

5 none은 '아무(것)도 없다'라는 뜻으로, 단독으로 쓰거나 none of 뒤에 단수 명사나 복수 명사를 쓴다. none of 뒤에 복수 명사가 온 경우에도 단수 동사를 써야 한다. 단, 일상 회화에서는 복수 동사를 쓸 수 있다.

Half a loaf is better than **none.** 반쪽의 빵이라도 없는 것보다 낫다.

None of the information was very useful. 어떤 정보도 아주 유용하지는 않았다. (아주 유용한 정보가 없었다.)

None of the children was late for school. 아이들 중 누구도 학교에 늦지 않았다. (학교에 늦은 아이는 없었다.)

|참고| 1. no는 단독으로 쓸 수 없고, 단수 명사 또는 복수 명사를 수식한다.

Mark has **no** book with him. 마크는 어떤 책도 없다.

No bicycles are allowed on the grass. 어떤 자전거도 잔디 위에 놓으면 안 된다.

2. none of, neither of 뒤에 복수 명사가 온 경우에도 문법적으로는 단수 동사를 써야 한다. 하지만, 일상 회화 등에서는 복수 동사를 쓰기도 한다.

None of the children **were** late for school. / Neither of my sisters **are** married.

6 either는 '(둘 중) 어느 한 쪽의', neither는 '(둘 중) 어느 쪽도 아닌'이라는 의미로 단독으로 쓰거나 단수 명사를 수식한다. either of, neither of 뒤에는 복수 명사를 쓴다.

Come on Monday or Tuesday. **Either day** is fine with me. 월요일이나 화요일에 와. 나는 둘 중 어떤 날도 괜찮아.

If **either of the boys** phones, tell him I'll be in this evening. 그 소년들 중 한 명이 전화하면, 내가 오늘 저녁에 갈 거라고 전해 줘.

I asked Tom and Jane, but **neither one** was able to explain the process.
나는 톰과 제인에게 물어보았지만 아무도 그 과정을 설명할 수 없었다.

Neither of my sisters is married. 우리 누나들 중 아무도 결혼하지 않았다.

|주의| 「either A or B」는 'A와 B 둘 중 하나', 「neither A nor B」는 'A와 B 둘 다 아닌'이라는 뜻이다. 둘 다 B에 동사의 수를 맞춘다.

Either the teachers **or** the principal is to blame for the low test scores. 선생님들과 교장 선생님 중 한쪽이 낮은 시험 성적에 대한 책임이 있다.

Neither the president **nor** his representatives are to attend the meeting. 대통령도 그의 대리인들도 모두 회의에 참가하지 않을 것이다.

7 most는 '대부분의'라는 의미로 단수 명사와 복수 명사 모두를 수식할 수 있다. most of는 '~의 대다수'라는 의미로 역시 단수 명사와 복수 명사를 모두 쓸 수 있다.

Most high school students in Korea wear school uniforms. 한국에서 대부분의 고등학생들은 교복을 입는다.

Most of the test takers said the test was more difficult than they expected.
대부분의 시험 응시자들은 시험이 예상보다 어려웠다고 말했다.

EXERCISES

정답 및 해설 P. 30

빈칸에 of가 필요하면 of를, 생략이 가능하면 (of)를, 필요 없으면 X를 써넣으시오.

1 I have two sisters. Both ________ them are nurses.

2 Have you eaten all ________ the popcorn by yourself?

3 Each ________ problem requires its own unique solution.

4 All ________ the new furniture has arrived. Let's unpack it.

5 None ________ them in the meeting room is for his idea.

6 Each ________ student will be given a school uniform this Friday.

7 I have three tests this week. Each ________ them is going to be difficult.

8 Each ________ our customers is important to us here at ABC Company.

9 Mr. Jones has three sons. All ________ them have enlisted in the Air Force.

10 Both ________ us really enjoyed the trip. It will be remembered for a lifetime.

11 All ________ new drivers must pass a hearing test before they can be licensed.

12 All ________ her dogs used to be street dogs that were abandoned by their owners.

solution 해결책; 해결
unpack (풀어서) 내용물을 꺼내다, ~을 풀다
for ~에 찬성하여
enlist in (군에) 입대하다; 적극적으로 협력하다
air force 공군
license 면허를 내주다; 면허(장)
abandon 버리다; 포기하다

(   ) 안에서 가장 알맞은 것을 고르시오.

1 Neither of the (recipe / recipes) is very good.

2 Each of the children (want / wants) to win the prize.

3 Every child at our school (has / have) his or her own locker.

4 Every writer (learn / learns) to write by practicing every day.

5 Each applicant (are / is) required to fill out an application form.

6 Both of the students (has / have) completed their assignments.

7 I think either (candidate / candidates) would be ideal for the job.

8 Each rug (are / is) individually handmade by one of our weavers.

9 (All / Each) wild animals in Africa learn to hunt through trial and error.

10 Every member of the debate team (is / are) going to receive a scholarship.

11 All public libraries (was / were) closed last Monday because of the holiday.

applicant 지원자
fill out 작성하다
application form 지원서
assignment 과제; 임무
candidate 후보자
ideal 이상적인
individually 하나하나; 개인적으로
handmade 수제의
weaver (천 등을) 짜는 사람
trial and error 시행착오
debate 토론
receive ~을 받다
scholarship 장학금

C 밑줄 친 부분을 바르게 고치시오.

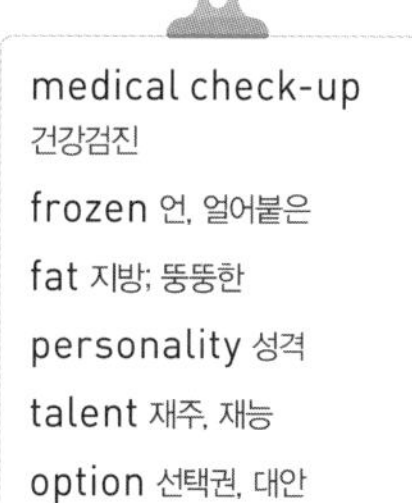

medical check-up 건강검진
frozen 언, 얼어붙은
fat 지방; 뚱뚱한
personality 성격
talent 재주, 재능
option 선택권, 대안

1 Neither Becky nor Tom have a smartphone yet.

2 All of the team member receive training every day.

3 Jake is very popular. Most his classmates like him.

4 Every students get a medical check-up once a year.

5 Bus 501 and Bus 511 stop here. You can take either ones.

6 Larry hates most of vegetables, but he loves tomatoes.

7 The frozen yogurt which tastes like ice cream has none fat.

8 Each of my classmates have a different personality and talents.

9 I have two options, but I can't choose only one because I like both them.

D be동사를 이용하여 과거 시제로 문장을 완성하시오.

national holiday 국경일
show up 나타나다
disappointed 실망한
hard 딱딱한; 어려운; 힘든; 열심히

1 None of the staff ___________ late for the event.

2 He called Judy's, but no one ___________ there.

3 As it was a national holiday, most of the shops ___________ closed.

4 Both of them ___________ invited to the party, but none of them showed up last night.

5 Either my father or my mother ___________ going to pick me up at 6 p.m.

6 I was very disappointed because most of the pizza ___________ already cold and hard.

E 주어진 단어를 이용하여 현재 시제로 문장을 완성하시오.

drop by (~에) 잠깐 들르다
participant 참가자
spend on ~에 (돈·시간을) 쓰다
private 개인 소유의; 사적인
corporate 회사의, 기업의
donor 기부자, 기증자
assistant 조수
promote 승진시키다, 홍보하다

1 If either of them ___________, please give this to him. (drop by)

2 Neither applicant ___________ to be confident. (seem)

3 Each of the participants ___________ given three chances in total. (be)

4 All of the money I saved ___________ been spent on a laptop computer. (have)

5 Every book in this library ___________ from private or corporate donors. (be)

6 Either the coach or her assistants ___________ going to be promoted at the end of the season. (be)

REVIEW

정답 및 해설 P. 31

belong to ~의 것이다, ~에 속하다
witty 재치 있는
colleague 동료
treat 대우하다; 치료하다
equal 동등한 사람
boost (사기 등을) 돋우다; 밀어 올리다
ego 자존심; 자아

A 주어진 대명사를 알맞게 바꿔 문장을 완성하시오.

1 I think that mug belongs to __________ (she).

2 This apartment is much larger than __________ (me).

3 I forgot to bring the textbook. Can I share __________ (you)?

4 We all agree that Peter is doing the best job __________ (he) can.

5 I've known Mike since middle school. __________ (he) is a very witty guy.

6 Has Tim told __________ (you) about __________ (he) plan to marry Ann?

7 Sarah wants __________ (she) colleagues to treat __________ (she) as an equal.

8 If you tell __________ (he) he is handsome, it will boost __________ (he) ego even more.

essentially 본질적으로
pursuit 수행; 추적
discipline 수양; 훈련하다
self-control 자제(심)
degree 정도; 학위
dress shirt 와이셔츠
in time for ~에 좋은 때에
a variety of 갖가지
checkout counter 계산대
wrap 포장하다
regular 보통의; 정기적인

B ( ) 안에서 가장 알맞은 것을 고르시오.

1 < Interview with Po, star of *Kung Fu Panda* >

Reporter: Please explain to (us / ourselves) what kung fu is.
Po: Sure, I'd be happy to. Kung fu is essentially the pursuit of excellence of self through hard work, discipline, and self-control. (It / One) is not just about fighting. One can have great kung fu in many areas of life, for example, cooking, singing, gardening, and anything that requires some degree of skill.

2 < In the men's department >

A: Good afternoon, sir. How may I help you?
B: I'm looking for a few dress shirts for (mine / myself) and a birthday present for my father.
A: Well, these shirts have just arrived in time for spring. (It / They) come in a variety of colors and patterns.

3 < At the checkout counter >

A: I'll take these three dress shirts, this necktie, and this belt.
B: Certainly, sir. Would you like me to wrap them for (you / yours)?
A: Only the belt—(it / one) is a gift. Please, put (others / the others) in a regular bag.

C 〈보기〉에서 알맞은 재귀대명사를 골라 빈칸에 써넣으시오. [중복 사용 가능]

보기 myself yourself ourselves herself himself themselves

1 We have to solve these problems __________.

2 If you are that curious, go and ask Tony __________.

3 Did your sister make her evening gown __________?

4 Would you like to introduce __________ to the group?

5 He was writing something down and talking to __________.

6 Come and join me for dinner. I don't want to eat by __________.

7 I'm in the bathroom. Could you answer the phone __________?

8 The students really enjoyed __________ at the amusement park.

9 He has lived by __________ since he graduated from high school.

10 I taught __________ French. I haven't learned it from anyone else.

11 I hope you make __________ at home while you are staying here.

12 According to the survey, a lot of women consider __________ overweight.

curious 궁금한, 호기심이 많은
amusement park 놀이공원
graduate 졸업하다
according to ~에 따르면
survey (설문) 조사; 조사하다
overweight 과체중의, 비만의

D 밑줄 친 부분을 바르게 고치시오.

1 Is there someone here by the name of Jeremy?

2 Each of our company supports at least one local charity.

3 My father ran him own textile business before he retired.

4 The economic crisis of 2008 was more serious than it of 1971.

5 A lion spends most of it's time sleeping, up to twenty hours every day!

6 Every of the visitors expressed their thanks after the closing ceremony.

7 When the man entered the hotel, they asked to speak with the manager.

8 I am looking for a drugstore. Can you point myself in the right direction?

9 My friend and I had to leave early so that you could catch the train on time.

10 I got my driver's license last month, but my brother got him over a year ago.

11 Compare the freedoms we enjoy today with these of previous generations.

12 James asked to borrow my notebook because he was not complete.

13 What is this dish that the lady over there is having? I'll have the same one.

charity 자선단체; 자선기금; 자선
run 운영하다, 경영하다
textile 직물, 옷감; 섬유산업
retire 은퇴하다
economic crisis 경제 위기[공황]
up to ~까지
closing ceremony 폐막식
drugstore 약국
direction 방향; 지시; 목표
license 면허(장); 면허를 내주다
compare A with B A와 B를 비교하다
previous 이전의
generation 세대
complete 완전한, 빠진 것이 없는

REVIEW PLUS

정답 및 해설 P. 33

cupboard 찬장
earthquake 지진

A 다음 (A), (B), (C)에 들어갈 말이 바르게 짝지어진 것을 고르시오.

- I ___(A)___ saw what happened.
- She will have to do the work ___(B)___.
- ___(C)___ of the plates in the cupboard were broken after the earthquake.

	(A)		(B)		(C)
①	myself	···	herself	···	Every
②	me	···	her	···	All
③	me	···	herself	···	Every
④	myself	···	her	···	Every
⑤	myself	···	herself	···	All

degree in ~ 분야의 학위
interest 관심, 흥미
get through ~을 통과하다, 지나가다

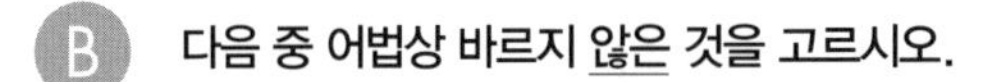

B 다음 중 어법상 바르지 않은 것을 고르시오.

① A: Have these walls been painted recently?
B: No, but this furniture has. Please don't touch something.

② A: Would you like to borrow another comic book?
B: Yes. The ones that you lent me were really entertaining.

③ A: Could you tell me something about someone in your family?
B: Well, my cousin Jane is very smart. She has a degree in electrical engineering.

④ A: I always see you and Jill together. You must be best friends.
B: We like spending time together because we ourselves share many interests.

⑤ A: This door is locked. I can't open it.
B: Try the other one. You can get through there.

researcher 연구원, 조사자
collect 수집하다
find out 발견하다, 알아내다
pattern (사고, 행동 등의 일정한) 형태, 양식, 패턴
make sure 확인하다; 을 확실히 하다

C 다음 밑줄 친 부분이 어법상 바르지 않은 것을 고르시오.

Researchers in the UK have begun collecting data to learn whether driving while talking on cell phones is dangerous. Now, whenever there is a car accident, police officers have been asked to find out if any of the drivers were using a cell phone. ① They will write ② this information in their accident reports. Researchers will then study ③ these reports, looking for patterns. ④ Each the researchers and the police department want to make sure that the roads are safe for ⑤ everyone.

PART 8

부정사
Infinitives

명사적 역할

역할	예문
주어(진주어)	To learn a foreign language is difficult. 외국어를 배우는 것은 어렵다. → It is difficult to learn a foreign language. 가주어 / 진주어
목적어	I decided to stay home. 나는 집에 머물기로 결정했다.
주격보어	My dream is to become a famous entertainer. 내 꿈은 유명한 연예인이 되는 것이다.
목적격보어	I don't want my mom to know about this. 나는 우리 엄마가 이것에 대해 아는 것을 원하지 않는다.
의문사+to부정사	What to do next is to study English grammar for the test. 다음에 해야 할 일은 시험을 위해 영문법을 공부하는 것이다.

FOCUS

1 to부정사(to-infinitives)의 기본 형태는 「to+동사원형」이고, 부정형은 「not+to+동사원형」이다.

We love to walk along the riverside. 우리는 강가를 따라 걷는 것을 좋아한다.

They decided not to buy an expensive car. 그들은 비싼 차를 사지 않기로 결정했다.

2 to부정사는 문장에서 주어 역할을 한다. 주어로 쓰인 to부정사가 길어지는 경우 가주어 it으로 바꿔 쓸 수 있다.

To finish the essay in time is almost impossible. 시간 내에 수필을 끝내는 것은 거의 불가능하다.

→ It is almost impossible to finish the essay in time.
가주어 / 진주어

3 그 외에 to부정사는 문장에서 목적어, 보어의 역할을 한다.

I want to finish my work as soon as possible. (목적어) 나는 내 일을 가능한 한 빨리 끝내고 싶어요.

Her job is to choose neckties that match suits. (주격보어)
그녀의 직업은 양복과 어울리는 넥타이를 골라 주는 것이다.

|참고| 1. afford, agree, ask, decide, expect, hope, learn, manage, plan, promise, want, wish 등의 동사는 to부정사를 목적어로 취한다.

2. 목적어로 쓰인 to부정사가 길어지는 경우 가목적어 it으로 바꿔 쓸 수 있다.
I found it difficult to persuade him to give up. (it = to persuade~) 나는 그를 포기하도록 설득하는 것이 힘들다는 것을 알았다.
가목적어 / 진목적어

3. to부정사는 문장에서 목적격보어의 역할을 할 수 있다. to부정사를 목적격보어로 취하는 동사는 want, tell, ask, allow, advise, expect, order 등이 있다.
My parents want me to get a good score on the final exam. (목적격보어)
우리 부모님은 내가 기말고사에서 좋은 점수를 받기를 원하신다.

4 「의문사+to부정사」는 문장에서 주어, 보어, 목적어로 쓰여 명사적 역할을 한다. 목적어로 쓰인 「의문사+to부정사」는 「의문사+주어+should+동사원형」으로 바꿔 쓸 수 있다.

「how+to부정사」 어떻게 ~ 할지, ~하는 방법

How to make pasta is the subject of this book. (주어) 파스타를 만드는 방법이 이 책의 주제이다.

What we have to decide is **how to get** there. (보어) 우리가 결정해야 하는 것은 거기에 가는 방법이다.

Please tell me **how to choose** the best book. (목적어) 저에게 가장 좋은 책을 고르는 방법을 말씀해 주세요.

→ Please tell me **how I should choose** the best book.

「what+to부정사」 무엇을 ~ 할지, ~하는 것

I don't know **what to do** next. 나는 다음에 무엇을 해야 할지 모르겠어.

→ I don't know **what I should do** next.

「where+to부정사」 어디로/어디에서 ~ 할지

I don't know **where to go**. I'm not good at directions. 나는 어디로 가야 할지 모르겠어. 나는 방향 감각이 좋지 않아.

→ I don't know **where I should go**. I'm not good at directions.

「when+to부정사」 언제 ~ 할지

I don't know **when to start.** 나는 언제 시작해야 할지 모르겠어.

→ I don't know **when I should start.**

「whether+to부정사」 ~ 할지 말지

I don't know **whether to take** this part-time job or not. 나는 이 아르바이트를 해야 할지 말아야 할지 모르겠어.

→ I don't know **whether I should take** this part-time job or not.

「which(+명사)+to부정사」 어느 것을 ~ 할지

I can't decide **which book to choose.** 나는 어떤 책을 골라야 할지 결정할 수 없어.

→ I can't decide **which book I should choose.**

|주의| 「why+to부정사」는 쓰지 않는다.

EXERCISES

정답 및 해설 P. 33

afford (경제적으로) ~할 여유가 있다
competition 경쟁
cut in line 새치기하다

A 〈보기〉와 같이 문장을 완성하고 to부정사의 쓰임을 밝히시오.

보기 We cannot afford __to buy__ (buy) that expensive villa. __목적어__

1 My favorite hobby is ____________ (read) mystery novels. ________

2 I never expected him ____________ (enter) the competition. ________

3 It was lucky ____________ (find) money in my old notebook. ________

4 Most people expected Michelle ____________ (win) the game. ________

5 Our class is planning ____________ (go) to Kyungju next month. ________

6 It's wrong ____________ (cut) in line. Look at all these people. ________

doze 졸다, 선잠 자다
expert 전문가
punish 벌주다, 처벌하다
self-esteem 자존심
downstairs 아래층에서
run around 뛰어다니다

B 주어진 동사를 to부정사의 긍정형이나 부정형으로 바꿔 문장을 완성하시오.

1 We were so happy that Sally agreed ________________ (take) a picture with us.

2 Our teacher always tells us ________________ (sleep) in class.

3 Evan wants to be a soccer player. His dream is ________________ (play) soccer in Europe.

4 Experts say that it is important ________________ (punish) children in front of others for their self-esteem.

5 My aunt Margaret lives downstairs. She said we are too noisy and asked us ________________ (run) around.

trouble 문제; 곤경

C 〈보기〉에서 알맞은 동사를 골라 to부정사로 바꿔 문장을 완성하시오.

보기 ski be forget make help finish use

1 I would like ____________ this copy machine.

2 I hope ____________ writing this final report by 11 o'clock.

3 The teacher told the students not ____________ late for the exam.

4 Youngin and Sherry like ____________ in Colorado on winter vacations.

5 Mom asked me ____________ her clean the house before the guests come.

6 James didn't want ____________ his troubles because he didn't want ____________ the same mistakes again.

D 주어진 문장을 「It(가주어) ~ to부정사(진주어)」 문장으로 바꿔 쓰시오.

1 To design and build a model robot is very interesting.

→ ______________________________

2 To organize all the books on this shelf is difficult.

→ ______________________________

3 To please our parents is sometimes difficult.

→ ______________________________

4 To study in the library all day is not good for your health.

→ ______________________________

5 To watch the World Cup final match at the stadium is very thrilling.

→ ______________________________

6 To let children swim in the sea by themselves is dangerous.

→ ______________________________

7 To become fluent in foreign languages in a short time is not easy.

→ ______________________________

organize 정리하다; 조직하다
shelf 선반
task 임무, 과제
match 시합, 경기; 성냥
thrilling 감동적인, 스릴 만점의

E 〈보기〉에서 알맞은 것을 골라 대화를 완성하시오. [한 번씩만 쓸 것]

보기 what to whether to how to where to

1 A: Excuse me. Could you tell me ____________ catch the bus to the airport?
B: Sure. The airport bus stops just at the end of this block.

2 A: Do you know ____________ make kimchi? I've heard it's very difficult.
B: Actually, I've never made it myself. But I'm sure my mother would love to show you.

3 A: I don't know ____________ do about my art project. It's due tomorrow, and I haven't even started it.
B: You should start working on it right away. Next time, don't put it off to the last minute.

4 A: I'm trying to decide ____________ go to Vancouver or Toronto on vacation.
B: Well, I think you should go to Vancouver because you can enjoy the mountains and seaside there.

be due (기한이) ~까지 이다
put off 미루다, ~을 연기하다
the last minute 최후의 순간, 막판
seaside 해안

형용사적 역할

명사+to부정사	Do you have something to say to me? 나에게 뭔가 할 말이 있니?
to부정사+전치사	We are looking for a house to live in. 우리는 살 집을 찾고 있다.
be+to부정사	Julia is to have a concert in Beijing next month. 줄리아는 다음 달에 베이징에서 콘서트를 열 예정이다. The students are to finish the test by 4 p.m. 학생들은 오후 4시까지 시험을 끝내야 한다.

FOCUS

1

to부정사는 (대)명사를 수식하는 형용사 역할을 한다. 이때 to부정사는 수식하는 (대)명사 뒤에 위치한다.

I have a book. 나는 책을 가지고 있다. → I have a book to read. 나는 읽을 책을 가지고 있다.

There is something. 무언가가 있다. → There is something to eat. 먹을 것이 있다.

|참고| 「It's time+to부정사」는 '~할 시간이다'라는 의미로, to부정사가 time을 수식해 주는 관용 표현이다.

It's time to go to sleep. 잘 시간이다.

It's time to have lunch. 점심 먹을 시간이다.

2

to부정사가 형용사 역할을 할 때 전치사를 꼭 수반해야 하는 경우가 있다.

I need a pencil to write with. (write with a pencil) 나는 쓸 연필이 필요하다.

They bought a house to live in after they got married. (live in a house) 그들은 결혼 후에 살 집을 샀다.

|참고| to부정사가 전치사를 수반해야 하는지 아닌지는 to부정사 뒤에 목적어를 놓아 보면 알 수 있다.

They need a piece of paper to write on. (write on a piece of paper) 그들은 쓸 종이가 필요하다.

We bought some chairs to sit on. (sit on some chairs) 우리는 앉을 의자를 좀 샀다.

The kid doesn't have many friends to play with. (play with many friends) 그 아이는 놀 친구가 많지 않다.

I bought a computer to work on. (work on a computer) 나는 작업할 컴퓨터를 샀다.

3

「be+to부정사」가 예정, 의무, 운명, 가능, 의도 등의 뜻을 나타낼 때도 to부정사는 형용사 역할을 한다.

That store is to open next Wednesday. (예정 = be supposed to) 저 가게는 다음 주 수요일에 문을 열 예정이다.

You are to finish your homework by eight. (의무 = should) 너는 8시까지 숙제를 끝내야 한다.

They were never to meet again. (운명 = be destined to) 그들은 다시는 만나지 못할 운명이었다.

Nobody was to be seen. (가능 = can) 아무도 볼 수 없었다.

If you are to pass the exam, you must study hard. (의도 = intend to) 시험에 통과하고 싶으면, 공부를 열심히 해야만 한다.

EXERCISES

정답 및 해설 P. 34

A 〈보기〉에서 알맞은 동사를 골라 to부정사로 바꿔 문장을 완성하시오.

보기 paint please put lend relax spend

1 Please give me a vase ______________ these flowers in.

2 Many Seoulites would like more parks ______________ in.

3 Melissa was looking for a friend ______________ time with.

4 I think blue is the perfect color ______________ the bedroom.

5 Jennifer was looking for a present ______________ her mother.

6 I'm sorry, but I don't have any money ______________ you at the moment.

relax 편하게 쉬다
vase 꽃병
Seoulite 서울 시민[사람]
at the moment 지금 당장은

B ( ) 안에서 가장 알맞은 것을 고르시오.

1 Jiny gave me a CD (to listen / to listen to).

2 Sharks can go days with no food (to eat / to eat in).

3 The LA Dodgers need a new stadium (to play / to play in).

4 At the airport, Monica bought a novel (to read / to read with).

5 I need some more boxes (to put those books / to put those books in).

6 Samuel often picks strawberries (to have / to have for) after dinner.

7 The boy was lonely because he didn't have friends (to play / to play with).

8 I was disappointed because there were no beautiful buildings (to take pictures / to take pictures of).

pick (꽃·과일을) 따다; 고르다
disappointed 실망한

C 밑줄 친 to부정사의 쓰임을 〈보기〉에서 골라 쓰시오.

보기 ⓐ 예정 ⓑ 의무 ⓒ 가능 ⓓ 의도 ⓔ 운명

1 You are never to run in the hallways at school. ______

2 Bill Gates was to become the richest man in America. ______

3 The next flight to San Francisco is to take off at 8 a.m. ______

4 She searched everywhere, but her locker key was not to be found. ______

5 If you are to take a seat in the front row, you'll need to get up early. ______

hallway 복도
take off 이륙하다
in the front row 앞줄에

부사적 역할

목적	Justin invited his friend Bill to the beach **to play** volleyball. 저스틴은 배구를 하려고 바닷가로 친구 빌을 초대했다.
판단의 근거	She must be very nice **to hold** the door for me. 나를 위해 문을 잡아 주다니 그녀는 매우 친절함이 틀림없다.
감정의 원인	I'm happy **to go** with you. 나는 너와 함께 가서 기뻐.
결과	He grew up **to be** the first African-American president in the USA. 그는 자라서 미국의 첫 번째 아프리카계 미국인 대통령이 되었다.
형용사 수식	My brother is quick **to see** the good of others. 내 남동생은 다른 사람들의 장점을 잘 본다.

1 to부정사는 문장에서 〈목적〉을 나타내는 부사 역할을 하고, '~하기 위해서, ~하려고'라고 해석한다.

I studied very hard **to get** a perfect score on the mid-term exam.
나는 중간고사에서 만점을 받으려고 매우 열심히 공부했다.

Fred went to the café **to meet** his friend.
프레드는 친구를 만나려고 카페에 갔다.

She went to Italy **to study** vocal music.
그녀는 성악을 공부하러 이탈리아에 갔다.

|참고| 〈목적〉을 나타내는 to부정사는 in order to, so as to, 「in order that+주어+can/could+동사원형」, 「so that+주어+can/could+동사원형」으로 바꿔 쓸 수 있다.

Fred went to the café **to meet** his friend.
→ Fred went to the café **in order to meet** his friend.
→ Fred went to the café **so as to meet** his friend.
→ Fred went to the café **in order that he could meet** his friend.
→ Fred went to the café **so that he could meet** his friend.

2 to부정사는 문장에서 〈판단의 근거〉가 되는 부사 역할을 하고, '~하다니/~하는 것을 보니'라고 해석한다.

Sumi must be a genius **to solve** the problem. 그 문제를 풀다니 수미는 천재임이 틀림없어.

She was nice **to share** pizza with us. 피자를 우리와 나눠 먹다니 그녀는 좋은 사람이었어.

He was very generous **to donate** money to charity. 자선 단체에 돈을 기부하다니 그는 매우 관대한 사람이었어.

|참고| 〈판단의 근거〉를 나타내는 to부정사는 「It+형용사+of+목적격+to부정사」로 바꿔 쓸 수 있다.

She was **nice to share** pizza with us.
It was **nice** of her **to share** pizza with us.

3 to부정사는 문장에서 〈결과〉가 되는 부사 역할을 하고, '~해서 그 결과로 ~하다'라고 해석한다. 즉, to부정사의 내용이 앞의 본동사의 내용보다 나중에 일어난 일이라는 것을 의미한다.

Hazel grew up **to be** a top model in America. 헤이즐은 자라서 미국에서 최고의 모델이 되었다.

I awoke **to find** myself famous. 나는 잠에서 깨어보니 유명해져 있었다.

I opened the box, only **to find** it empty. 나는 그 상자를 열었지만, 비어있는 것을 발견했다.

I tried hard, only **to fail**. 나는 열심히 노력했지만 실패했다.

4 to부정사는 문장에서 〈감정의 원인〉이 되는 부사 역할을 하고, '~하게 되어'라고 해석한다.

I was surprised **to see** Kevin, my old friend, in New Zealand last year.
나는 작년에 뉴질랜드에서 내 옛 친구인 케빈을 보게 되어 놀랐다.

Yuki is excited **to go** to a concert after school.
유키는 방과 후에 콘서트에 가게 되어 신났다.

|참고| to부정사를 자주 취하는 형용사에는 다음과 같은 것들이 있다.

1. happy류: happy, pleased, delighted, relieved
   I am **happy to inform** you that you have been promoted. 당신이 승진하게 되었다는 것을 알리게 되어 기쁩니다.
2. sad류: sad, sorry, ashamed, disappointed
   She was very **disappointed to hear** that her best friend wouldn't come. 그녀는 친한 친구가 못 온다는 이야기를 듣고 매우 실망했다.
3. surprised류: surprised, shocked, amazed, astonished
   We were **surprised to hear** that he had migrated to Germany. 우리는 그가 독일로 이민 갔다는 말을 듣고 놀랐다.
4. afraid류: afraid, careful, hesitant, likely
   She was very **afraid to reveal** the truth to everybody. 그녀는 모든 사람에게 진실을 밝히는 것이 매우 두려웠다.

5 to부정사는 문장에서 단순하게 형용사를 수식하는 부사 역할을 하기도 한다.

Magazines are good **to read** when we are in the beauty salon. 잡지는 미용실에 있을 때 읽기에 좋다.

Ms. Jones is very easy **to please**. 존스 씨는 기분 좋게 만들기 매우 쉽다.

EXERCISES

정답 및 해설 P. 34

attend
~에 다니다; 참석하다
relieve
안도하는, 다행으로 여기는
car crash 교통사고
talented 재능이 있는
male 남자; 남자의

A 밑줄 친 to부정사의 쓰임을 〈보기〉에서 고르시오.

보기 ⓐ 목적 ⓑ 판단의 근거 ⓒ 감정의 원인 ⓓ 결과

1 I was so foolish to trust you again. ______
2 She always wears black jeans to look slim. ______
3 He awoke to find himself alone in the house. ______
4 I'm very happy to return to Seoul in November. ______
5 Sylvia's parents came to the library to pick her up. ______
6 Joyce is sad to leave her family to attend university. ______
7 She must be an angel to have been helping the poor. ______
8 We were very relieved to know that no one got hurt in the car crash. ______
9 Tobey Maguire must be very talented to make such a successful movie. ______
10 Justin Timberlake grew up to be one of the most popular male singers. ______

appointment 약속
thorough 철저한, 완전한
examination 검사; 조사
postpone
연기하다, 미루다
fairy tales 동화
high note 고음
appointment 약속; 임명
disappointed 실망한
enthusiastically
매우 열심히; 열광적으로
keep in shape
건강을 유지하다
Chinese character
한자

B 〈보기〉에서 알맞은 동사를 골라 to부정사로 바꿔 문장을 완성하시오.

[1-5] 보기 understand make pass get hear

1 Bonnie was happy ____________ the exam.
2 I'm calling ____________ an appointment with the doctor.
3 I went to the hospital ____________ a thorough examination.
4 I'm happy ____________ that the midterms have been postponed.
5 Fairy tales are popular in all cultures because they are easy ____________.

[6-10] 보기 read learn remind sing keep

6 This song is hard ____________ because of its high notes.
7 She called ____________ me about the appointment.
8 My parents were very disappointed ____________ that I lied to them.
9 Every morning, my mother swims enthusiastically ____________ in shape.
10 Too many Chinese characters are used in this book, so it's hard for me ____________.

C 밑줄 친 부분에 유의하여 해석을 완성하시오.

1 He grew up to be a famous movie director.
→ 그는 자라서 유명한 영화감독이 ______________.

2 I was very pleased to watch the fireworks with you.
→ 나는 너와 함께 불꽃놀이를 ______________ 매우 기뻤다.

3 I ran as fast as I could not to be late for school.
→ 나는 학교에 늦지 ______________ 할 수 있는 한 빨리 달렸다.

4 Sean went to the pier to take the ferry to Long Island.
→ 숀은 롱아일랜드로 가는 페리를 ______________ 부두로 갔다.

5 I called to apologize for canceling our meeting at the last minute.
→ 나는 마지막 순간에 회의를 취소한 것에 대해 ______________ 전화했다.

6 She must be a very independent person to finish the project by herself.
→ 혼자 힘으로 그 프로젝트를 ______________ 그녀는 매우 독립적인 사람임이 틀림없다.

director 감독
fireworks 불꽃놀이
pier 부두
ferry 페리[여객선]
apologize 사과하다
independent 독립적인

D 우리말과 같은 뜻이 되도록 주어진 단어를 이용하여 문장을 완성하시오.

1 그는 체중을 줄이려고 하루에 두 시간씩 운동을 한다. (lose, weight)
→ He exercises two hours a day __________ __________ __________.

2 나는 내 수업을 따라잡기 위해 학교에 남아서 공부했다. (catch up on, classes)
→ I stayed late at school __________ __________ __________ __________ __________ __________.

3 그는 부드럽고 깊은 음성을 가지고 있어서 듣기 좋다. (pleasant, hear)
→ He has a soft and deep voice, so __________ is __________ __________ __________.

4 우리는 그가 올림픽에서 금메달을 따는 것을 보아서 기뻤다. (be delighted, see)
→ We __________ __________ __________ __________ that he won the gold medal in the Olympics.

5 그 목마른 아이는 냉장고 문을 열었지만, 빈 병 하나를 발견했을 뿐이다. (find, empty bottle)
→ The thirsty child opened the refrigerator __________ __________ __________ __________ __________.

6 그렇게 짧은 시간 안에 그 퍼즐을 풀다니 그녀는 똑똑한 것이 틀림없다. (must, be, smart, solve, puzzle)
→ She __________ __________ __________ __________ __________ __________ __________ in such a short time.

pleasant 기분 좋은, 즐거운
catch up on ~을 따라잡다
delighted 기뻐하는
refrigerator 냉장고

의미상의 주어, 시제, 태

의미상의 주어	for+목적격	It was lucky for me to meet you. 내가 너를 만난 건 행운이었다.
	of+목적격	It's generous of you to treat me to dinner. 저녁을 사주다니 당신은 인심이 좋군요.
부정사의 시제	to+동사원형	He seems to be very intelligent. 그는 매우 똑똑한 것처럼 보인다. = It seems that he is very intelligent.
	to+have p.p.	She seemed to have spent a long time in Korea. 그녀는 오랫동안 한국에서 지낸 것처럼 보였다. = It seemed that she had spent a long time in Korea.
부정사의 태	능동태	Ted went to San Diego to play baseball. 테드는 야구를 하려고 샌디에이고로 갔다.
	수동태	Everyone wants to be loved. 모든 사람은 사랑받기를 원한다.

FOCUS

1 to부정사는 동사에서 온 것이므로 동사의 행위자가 존재한다. to부정사의 행위자가 주어 또는 목적어와 같거나 일반인일 경우 특별히 따로 나타내지 않는다. 그러나 그 외는 to부정사 앞에 주로 「for+목적격」을 사용하여 나타내며 '의미상의 주어'라고 부른다.

We like to eat Chinese food. (행위자가 주어와 동일)
우리는 중국 음식 먹는 것을 좋아한다.

Everyone expects Dennis to be the next tennis champion. (행위자가 목적어와 동일)
모두 데니스가 다음 테니스 챔피언이 될 거라고 예상하고 있다.

The books were too easy for me to read. (행위자가 따로 존재)
그 책들은 내가 읽기에 너무 쉬웠다.

|참고| 「It+takes+목적격+시간+to부정사」 구문의 경우 takes 다음에 나오는 목적격이 to부정사의 의미상 주어가 된다. 이 구문은 「It+takes+시간+(for+목적격)+to부정사」의 형태로도 쓸 수 있다.

It takes me a long time to go to my grandfather's house.
= It takes a long time for me to go to my grandfather's house.
내가 우리 할아버지네 집에 가는 데에는 오랜 시간이 걸린다.

2 가주어(it) 뒤에 사람의 성격이나 태도를 나타내는 형용사가 올 경우 「for+목적격」 대신에 「of+목적격」을 사용한다. 주로 사람을 칭찬하거나 비난하는 문장이 여기에 속한다.

사람의 성질이나 태도를 나타내는 형용사: kind, nice, clever, foolish, silly, rude, polite, generous ...

It was foolish of you to stay up so late the night before the exam.
시험 전날 그렇게 늦게까지 잠을 자지 않다니 너는 어리석었다.

It is impossible for him to finish the work in time.
그가 제시간에 그 일을 끝낸다는 것은 불가능하다.

|참고| 부사적 용법 중 〈판단의 근거〉가 되는 to부정사는 「It+be동사+형용사+of+목적격+to부정사」 형식으로 바꿔 쓸 수 있다.

She was very kind to help us.

→ It was very kind of her to help us.
우리를 도와주다니 그녀는 매우 친절했어.

He was foolish not to listen to the teacher.

→ It was foolish of him not to listen to the teacher.
선생님 말씀을 듣지 않다니 그는 어리석었어.

3 seem은 '~처럼 보이다'라는 의미이고, 「seem to+동사원형」은 문장의 동사와 같은 시점에 발생한 일을, 「seem+to have p.p.」는 문장의 동사보다 이전에 일어난 일을 나타낸다.

「seem to+동사원형」

Ted seems to know a lot about pop songs.

→ It seems that Ted knows a lot about pop songs.
테드는 팝송에 대해서 많이 아는 것처럼 보인다.

Kelly seemed to need a lot of attention.

→ It seemed that Kelly needed a lot of attention.
켈리는 많은 관심을 필요로 하는 것처럼 보였다.

「seem to+have p.p.」

He seems to have lived in France.

→ It seems that he was [has lived] in France.
그는 프랑스에서 살았던 것처럼 보인다.

Tanya seemed never to have eaten galbi before.

→ It seemed that Tanya had never eaten galbi before.
타냐는 전에 갈비를 먹어 보지 못한 것처럼 보였다.

4 wish, hope, expect, promise 등 의지나 소망을 나타내는 동사와 함께 사용된 to부정사는 미래의 일을 나타낸다.

Paul expects his younger sister to pass the exam.

→ Paul expects that his younger sister will pass the exam.
폴은 여동생이 시험에 합격할 것이라고 예상하고 있다.

Hanna is hoping to study law at Harvard.

→ Hanna is hoping that she will study law at Harvard.
한나는 하버드에서 법을 공부하기를 바라고 있다.

5 to부정사의 수동은 「to+be+p.p.」, 「to+have been+p.p.」로 나타낸다.

His homework had to be done. 그의 숙제는 마무리되어야 한다.

He didn't expect to be invited to the housewarming party. 그는 집들이 파티에 초대될 거라고 예상하지 못했다.

I was thrilled to have been chosen. 나는 선택 받아서 매우 기뻤다.

EXERCISES

정답 및 해설 P. 35

stay up
(평소보다 늦게까지) 깨어있다
hesitate 망설이다

A 밑줄 친 부분의 의미상의 주어를 찾아 쓰시오.

1 It is difficult for me to solve this puzzle. ________

2 Americans want Peter to win a gold medal. ________

3 The teacher asked me to clean the classroom. ________

4 It is hard for me to stay up late at night without coffee. ________

5 These days it is expensive for many students to study abroad. ________

6 I urge you not to hesitate to ask me questions about the project. ________

play 연극
make a decision
결정하다
appear 출연하다; 나타나다
commercials
광고 (상업) 방송
popularity 인기, 평판

B 빈칸에 for와 of 중 알맞은 것을 써넣으시오.

1 Matthew's race was exciting ________ us to watch.

2 It was so kind ________ you to help us with our school play.

3 It is very sweet ________ you to help me during this difficult time.

4 It is wise ________ you to think carefully before making a decision.

5 It is very thoughtful ________ you to visit your grandmother in the hospital.

6 It is very nice ________ you to share your room with your uncle.

7 It may be dangerous ________ women to travel in that country alone.

8 It is easy ________ Tom to appear in commercials because of his popularity.

apology 사과
sign 서명하다, 서명; 표시
for some time
얼마 동안
unusual 흔치 않은, 드문

C ( ) 안에서 가장 알맞은 것을 고르시오.

1 Chris is sad (to leave / to be left) his friends.

2 He expects his apology (to accept / to be accepted).

3 Lisa needs a pen (to sign / to be signed) her name with.

4 We decided not (to see / to be seen) each other for some time.

5 My boss wants the report (to finish / to be finished) by this Friday.

6 He failed (to win / to be won) two gold medals in the Olympic Games.

7 My father wanted our house (to paint / to be painted) by last weekend.

8 It's very unusual for four world records (to set / to be set) by one person.

D 두 문장의 의미가 통하도록 시제에 주의하여 〈보기〉와 같이 고쳐 쓰시오.

보기	Yesterday, Daniel seemed to be very sad.
	→ Yesterday, it seemed that Daniel was very sad.

tan 선탠; (피부가) 햇볕에 타다
seaside 해안

1 Kate seems to have finished her homework early.
→ ______________________________

2 My father seems to be tired after a long day at work.
→ ______________________________

3 We seem to have everything we need for our school trip.
→ ______________________________

4 No one seemed to listen to the teacher because of the beautiful weather.
→ ______________________________

5 Because of his tan, David seems to have been to the seaside.
→ ______________________________

6 He seems to have done terribly on the test because he looks unhappy.
→ ______________________________

E 두 문장의 의미가 통하도록 동사에 주의하여 〈보기〉와 같이 고쳐 쓰시오.

보기	I expect him to be back within an hour.
	→ I expect that he will be back within an hour.

invitation 초대장, 초대
do well 잘하다; 성공하다
dominate 우위를 차지하다; 지배[위압]하다
archery 양궁

1 I hope to make a lot of friends in the new school.
→ ______________________________

2 Minsu is hoping to get an invitation to the party.
→ ______________________________

3 We expect Beyonce to win a Grammy for her new song.
→ ______________________________

4 Everyone expects William to do well at the Olympics.
→ ______________________________

5 Many people expect Black Hole to be the most popular band of the year.
→ ______________________________

6 Most experts expect Korea to dominate Olympic archery for many years.
→ ______________________________

기타 부정사의 쓰임

지각동사 + 목적어 + 동사원형	We saw a firefighter enter the school. 우리는 소방관이 학교에 들어가는 것을 보았다.
사역동사 + 목적어 + 동사원형	Please let me finish it. 제가 그것을 끝내게 해주세요.
help + 목적어(+to) + 동사원형	Terry helped the kid (to) stand up. 테리는 아이가 일어서도록 도와주었다.
too + 형용사 + to + 동사원형 = so + 형용사 + that + 주어 + can't + 동사원형	This box is too heavy for you to lift. → This box is so heavy that you can't lift it. 이 상자는 네가 들기에 너무 무겁다.

1 see, watch, hear, listen to, feel, notice, observe 등의 지각동사는 목적격보어로 동사원형을 쓴다.

I saw a girl play the violin in a café. 나는 한 소녀가 카페에서 바이올린을 연주하는 것을 보았다.

Vicky didn't notice her little son go out. 비키는 자신의 어린 아들이 나가는 것을 눈치채지 못했다.

Gary heard children shout at the corner. 게리는 아이들이 모퉁이에서 소리치는 것을 들었다.

|참고| 지각동사는 목적격보어로 분사를 쓸 수 있다.

Gary heard children shouting at the corner. (소리치는 행동이 진행되고 있음을 강조)
게리는 아이들이 모퉁이에서 소리치고 있는 것을 들었다.

I heard my name called. (목적어와 목적격보어가 수동의 관계)
나는 내 이름이 불리는 소리를 들었다.

2 make, let, have의 사역동사는 '~에게 …을 하도록 시키다'라는 의미이고 목적격보어로 동사원형을 쓴다.

My friend Jungmin always makes me laugh.
내 친구 정민이는 항상 나를 웃게 만든다.

Would you let me introduce myself, please?
제 소개를 하게 해 주시겠어요?

I'm ready to see Ms. Brown. Have her come in, please.
저는 브라운 씨를 만날 준비가 되어 있어요. 그녀를 들어오게 해 주세요.

|주의| 1. 지각동사와 사역동사는 목적격보어로 to부정사를 쓸 수 없다.
(×) Would you let me ~~to introduce~~ myself, please?

2. get은 사역동사의 의미로 쓰이더라도 목적격보어로 to부정사를 쓴다.
I'll get my sister to call you. 내 여동생이 너에게 전화하도록 할게.

3. have는 목적격보어로 분사를 쓸 수 있다.
She had the boy laughing. 그녀가 그 소년을 웃게 만들었다.
He had his hair cut. 그는 이발을 했다.

3 help는 목적격보어로 to부정사와 동사원형 모두를 쓸 수 있다.

His sister **helped** him **(to) choose** some new shirts. 그의 여동생은 그가 새 셔츠 고르는 것을 도와주었다.

The boy **helped** the woman **(to) carry** her heavy bags to her car. 그 소년은 그 여자가 무거운 가방을 차로 옮기는 것을 도와주었다.

4 「too+형용사+to+동사원형」 너무 ~해서 …할 수 없다

= 「so+형용사+that+주어+can't/couldn't+동사원형」

He is **too** young **to** ride the bumper cars.

→ He is **so** young **that** he **can't** ride the bumper cars. 그는 너무 어려서 범퍼카를 탈 수 없다.

5 「형용사+enough to+동사원형」 ~할 만큼 충분히 …한

= 「so+형용사+that+주어+can/could+동사원형」

It's **warm** enough **to** swim in the lake. 호수에서 수영할 수 있을 만큼 충분히 따뜻하다.

I am **tall** enough **to** reach the top shelf.

→ I am **so** tall **that** I **can** reach the top shelf. 나는 꼭대기 선반에 닿을 만큼 충분히 키가 크다.

「enough+명사+to+동사원형」 ~할 만큼 충분한…

I have **enough** money **to** buy the suit in the show window. 나는 진열장에 있는 정장을 살 수 있을 만큼 충분한 돈을 가지고 있다.

6 to부정사 중 목적이나 의도를 나타내는 to부정사는 다음과 같이 바꿔 쓸 수 있다.

「to+동사원형」 = 「in order to+동사원형」 = 「so as to+동사원형」

= 「in order that+주어+can/could+동사원형」 = 「so that+주어+can/could+동사원형」

I hurried to the train station **to catch** the last train.

→ I hurried to the train station **in order to catch** the last train.

→ I hurried to the train station **so as to catch** the last train.

→ I hurried to the train station **in order that I could catch** the last train.

→ I hurried to the train station **so that I could catch** the last train. 나는 마지막 기차를 타려고 기차역으로 서둘러 갔다.

「not to+동사원형」 = 「in order not to+동사원형」 = 「so as not to+동사원형」

= 「in order that+주어+won't/wouldn't+동사원형」 = 「so that+주어+won't/wouldn't+동사원형」

I got up early **not to miss** the school bus.

→ I got up early **in order not to miss** the school bus.

→ I got up early **so as not to miss** the school bus.

→ I got up early **in order that I wouldn't miss** the school bus.

→ I got up early **so that I wouldn't miss** the school bus. 나는 학교 버스를 놓치지 않으려고 일찍 일어났다.

|참고| in order to/in order that은 일상 회화에서는 잘 쓰지 않는다.

7 to부정사의 기타 표현에는 다음과 같은 것들이 있다.

「be likely to+동사원형」 ~할 것 같다

The rain **is likely to stop** soon. 곧 비가 그칠 것 같다.

Daniel **is likely to show up** here. 대니얼이 이곳에 나타날 것 같다.

「be supposed to+동사원형」 ~하기로 되어 있다, ~할 의무가 있다

He **was supposed to go** to see a movie with Jennifer. 그는 제니퍼와 영화를 보러 가기로 되어 있었다.

Jenny **was supposed to come** here. What happened to her? 제니는 여기에 오기로 되어 있었어. 그녀에게 무슨 일이 있었던 거야?

「It takes+시간(+for+목적격)+to+동사원형」 ~하는 데 … 시간이 들다

It takes two hours for me to read a chapter. 나는 한 챕터를 읽는 데 두 시간이 걸린다.

8 문장에 삽입구처럼 들어가서 문장 전체를 수식하는 것을 '독립부정사'라고 한다.

strange to say 이상한 이야기지만

to begin with = to start with 우선, 첫째로

to make matters worse 설상가상으로, 공교롭게도

to tell the truth = to be frank with you = to be honest with you 솔직히 말하면

not to mention = not to speak of = to say nothing of ~은 말할 것도 없이

Strange to say, I like lukewarm food.
이상한 이야기지만, 나는 미지근한 음식이 좋아.

To begin with, I am going to tell you the story in brief.
우선, 내가 당신에게 그 이야기를 간략하게 해줄게요.

He fell down on the street. **To make matters worse**, he broke his arm.
그는 길거리에서 넘어졌고, 설상가상으로, 팔도 부러졌다.

To tell the truth, I didn't do my homework.
솔직히 말해서, 나는 숙제를 하지 않았어요.

To be frank with you, I made some mistakes.
솔직히 말하면, 내가 실수를 좀 했어요.

The weather is fantastic here, **not to mention** the delicious food.
맛있는 음식은 말할 것도 없고, 여기는 날씨도 환상적이다.

EXERCISES

정답 및 해설 P. 36

A ( ) 안에서 알맞은 것을 모두 고르시오.

take care of ~을 돌보다
deadline 최종 마감 시한
turkey 칠면조
Thanksgiving Day 미국의 추수 감사절(11월의 넷째 주 목요일)
crawl 기어가다
closet 옷장
house chore 집안일

1 Mary listens to the birds (sing / to sing / singing) at night.

2 Junghyun always helps me (take / to take / taking) care of the dogs.

3 We all managed (finish / to finish / finishing) the project before the deadline.

4 Baked turkey always makes me (think / to think) of Thanksgiving Day.

5 Could you please let me (know / to know) which bus to take to COEX?

6 Joyce watched the girls (practice / to practice / practicing) volleyball.

7 I really enjoy reading comic books because they make me (laugh / to laugh / laughed).

8 Jessica decided (study / to study / studying) engineering when she starts college in the fall.

9 When I was a child, my mother would watch me (crawl / to crawl / crawling) into the closet.

10 This weekend was so busy because my parents asked me (help / to help / helping) with the house chores.

B 주어진 단어를 알맞게 배열하여 문장을 완성하시오.

catch up 따라잡다
accomplish ~을 성취하다, 이룩하다
go around 모든 이에게 돌아가다
luxurious 호화로운

1 Tommy ran ______________ for me ______________.
(too, to, fast, catch up)

2 No one is ______________________________ him.
(enough, to, foolish, believe)

3 Rachel is ______________________________ into those pants.
(too, to, tall, fit)

4 There is ______________________________ everything we want.
(enough, to, time, accomplish)

5 The pizza was ______________________________ for everyone.
(too, to, small, go around)

6 He told her that he didn't have ______________________________ such a luxurious wedding. (enough, to, money, have)

jaywalk 무단 횡단하다
house chore 집안일
notice 알아차리다; 주목하다
make sure ~을 확실히 하다
domestic 국내의
compete ~와 경쟁하다
manufacture 제품; 제조하다

C 주어진 단어를 알맞은 형태로 바꿔 문장을 완성하시오.

1 I saw a man ______________ on the street. (jaywalk)

2 I helped my mother ______________ the house chores. (do)

3 My mother made me ______________ how to play the piano. (learn)

4 I noticed a stranger ______________ into my neighbor's window. (stare)

5 We must make sure that there is enough cake ________________. (share)

6 The domestic car industry is growing fast enough ________________ (compete) with foreign car manufacturers.

talented 재능이 있는
physics 물리학
stay up (평소보다 늦게까지) 깨어있다
doze off 졸다

D 문장의 의미가 통하도록 주어진 표현을 이용하여 문장을 바꿔 쓰시오.

1 You are too short to ride this roller coaster.
→ ____ (so ~ that)

2 My little brother is so young that he can't watch that scary movie.
→ ____ (too ~ to)

3 David is talented enough to be a professional boxer.
→ ____ (so ~ that)

4 My friend Jiho is so smart that he can study physics.
→ ____ (enough ~ to)

5 She stayed up late to study for the final exam.
→ ____ (so as to)
→ ____ (in order to)
→ ____ (so that)
→ ____ (in order that)

6 I ran to school to be in time for the first class.
→ ____ (so as to)
→ ____ (in order to)
→ ____ (so that)
→ ____ (in order that)

7 She had enough sleep not to doze off in class.
→ ____ (so as not to)
→ ____ (in order not to)
→ ____ (so that ~ not)
→ ____ (in order that ~ not)

E 우리말과 같은 뜻이 되도록 주어진 단어를 이용하여 문장을 완성하시오.

be supposed to ~하기로 되어 있다
briefly 간단히; 잠시
politics 정치
portion 양; 부분
fall off 떨어지다
taste 취향; 맛, 맛이 ~하다
step in ~에 빠지다; 발을 딛다
puddle 웅덩이
get wet 젖다

1 우선, 몇 가지 쉬운 질문으로 시작할게요. (start)

→ ________ ________ ________, I will ask you several easy questions.

2 이상한 이야기지만, 나는 정말 추울 때 아이스크림을 먹는 것을 좋아해. (say)

→ ________ ________ ________, I like to have ice cream when it is very cold.

3 그것은 시간 낭비는 말할 것도 없고, 너무 비싸다. (say, nothing)

→ It is too expensive, ________ ________ ________ ________ the time it wastes.

4 우리는 오후 1시에 극장 앞에서 만나기로 했어. (supposed, meet)

→ We ________ ________ ________ ________ in front of the cinema at 1 p.m.

5 우선 제가 우리가 오늘 토론하게 될 주제를 간단하게 소개하겠습니다. (begin)

→ ________ ________ ________, I'll briefly introduce the topics we will be discussing today.

6 솔직히 말해서, 나는 정치에 별로 관심이 없어. (frank)

→ ________ ________ ________ ________ ________, I'm not very interested in politics.

7 많은 양은 말할 것도 없고, 이 식당의 음식은 맛있고 싸다. (mention)

→ The meals of this restaurant are delicious and cheap, ________ ________ ________ large in their portions.

8 조심해! 그 책들이 선반에서 떨어질 것 같아. (likely, fall off)

→ Be careful! Those books ________ ________ ________ ________ ________ the bookshelf.

9 솔직히 말하면 그의 음악은 내 취향이 아니야. 그래서 그의 콘서트에 가지 않았던 거야. (tell)

→ ________ ________ ________ ________, his music is not to my taste. That's why I didn't go to his concert.

10 미안하지만, 솔직히 말해서 오늘 저녁은 외식하고 싶지 않아. (honest)

→ I'm sorry but, ________ ________ ________ ________ ________, I don't want to eat out for dinner tonight.

11 월요일에 내 여동생은 학교에 지각을 했어. 설상가상으로 웅덩이를 밟아서 다 젖었어. (make)

→ On Monday, my sister was late for school. ________ ________ ________ ________, she stepped in a puddle and got all wet.

REVIEW

정답 및 해설 P. 37

persuade 설득하다
accept 받아들이다
offer 제안, 제의, 제공하다
harsh (기후, 조건 등이) 가혹한
arctic 북극의

A 〈보기〉에서 밑줄 친 to부정사의 쓰임을 골라 쓰시오.

보기 ⓐ 명사적 역할 ⓑ 형용사적 역할 ⓒ 부사적 역할

1 Please give me some paper to write on. ______

2 My brother hopes to enter a good college. ______

3 She wished to exercise at least three times a week. ______

4 He sent me a letter to persuade me to accept his offer. ______

5 Could you give me a fashion magazine to read, please? ______

6 The boys in our class really want to go and see the new action film. ______

7 If you don't have olive oil to use for the cooking, use butter instead. ______

8 African-Americans were pleased to have Barack Obama as President. ______

9 All of the children were amazed to see the pandas for the first time. ______

10 Polar bears must eat large amounts during the spring and summer to survive the harsh arctic winters. ______

gracious 인자한; 상냥한
apology 사과
dye one's hair 머리를 염색하다
gracefully 기품 있게
allowance 용돈; 할당액
Finland 핀란드(북유럽의 공화국)
white night 백야(白夜)
self-development 자기 (능력) 개발
leave someone behind 뒤에 ~을 남겨 놓다

B ( ) 안에서 가장 알맞은 것을 고르시오.

1 It is my dream (speak / to speak) English fluently.

2 It is very gracious (for her / of her) to accept my apology.

3 Yesterday, my brother had me (dye / to dye) his hair blond.

4 Jason saw her (to skate / skating) gracefully across the ice.

5 This is the best hotel (to stay / to stay at) during summer holidays.

6 They are saving money to buy an apartment (to live / to live in).

7 It is very difficult (say / to say) no when the others are saying yes.

8 I'd like to meet some new friends (to play soccer / to play soccer with).

9 My mother doesn't like me (to receive / to be received) my allowance early.

10 It was difficult (for me / of me) to decide which game to buy for my brother.

11 Finland is a beautiful country (to visit / to visit in) in the summer because of the white nights.

12 We must spend a lot of time on self-development if we don't want (to leave / to be left) behind.

C 〈보기〉에서 알맞은 단어를 골라 어법에 맞게 바꿔 문장을 완성하시오.

[1-5] 보기 take rely on study send disturb

1 Jane saved money ______________ abroad after graduation.

2 My parents never allow me ______________ a trip by myself.

3 I didn't want ______________, so I was looking for a quiet place.

4 You are lucky if you have at least three friends ______________.

5 He promised ______________ the product I ordered as soon as possible.

[6-10] 보기 live in walk climb get move

6 He asked me to help him ______________ his stuff.

7 I saw someone ______________ through a window of the building.

8 My mom had me ______________ my dog in the park after dinner.

9 If someone has no place ______________, we call him or her homeless.

10 I was disappointed ______________ the lowest score for the finals.

rely on ~에 의지[의존]하다
disturb 방해하다
allow 허락하다, 허용하다
as soon as possible 가능한 한 빨리, 신속하게
stuff 물건
homeless 노숙자들; 노숙자의
disappointed 실망한

D 〈보기〉에서 알맞은 단어를 골라 어법에 맞게 바꿔 대화를 완성하시오.

보기 get fix enjoy read eat win

1 A: Brian likes his job. He's really lucky.
B: That's good. It's important ____________ what you do.

2 A: Misu is studying Japanese ____________ Japanese comics.
B: Well, if she finds them interesting, she should learn quickly.

3 A: Our teacher told us ____________ a healthy breakfast every day.
B: That's right. Breakfast is the most important meal of the day.

4 A: Nick is training for more than six hours a day ____________ the game.
B: I know. But I'm so worried that he was pushing himself so hard.

5 A: I'm late for my flight. What's the fastest way ____________ to the airport?
B: I think the fastest way would be to take the subway. At this hour, the traffic is horrible.

6 A: Sue, our TV needs ____________. Would you please call the repairman?
B: Don't worry. I'll do that.

push oneself ~ (하도록) 스스로 채찍질하다
horrible 끔찍한

REVIEW PLUS

정답 및 해설 P. 38

be supposed to ~하기로 되어 있다
be likely to ~인 것 같다
continue 계속하다
mow (풀 등을) 베다
chopsticks 젓가락

A 다음 (A), (B), (C)에 들어갈 말이 바르게 짝지어진 것을 고르시오.

1

- It is very fun ____(A)____ to play computer games.
- My mother always makes me ____(b)____ my teeth before bed.
- You ____(c)____ check the document before you fax it.

(A)		(B)		(C)
① for me	···	brush	···	are supposed to
② of me	···	to brush	···	are supposed to
③ for me	···	to brush	···	are likely to
④ of me	···	to brush	···	are likely to
⑤ for me	···	brush	···	are likely to

2

- Kevin decided ____(A)____ dinner early so he could continue studying.
- Did Donald have you ____(b)____ mowing the grass before lunch?
- Terry seems never ____(c)____ chopsticks before.

(A)		(B)		(C)
① to have	···	to finish	···	to have used
② have	···	to finish	···	to use
③ to have	···	finish	···	to use
④ have	···	finish	···	to use
⑤ to have	···	finish	···	to have used

ignore 무시하다
such as 요컨대, 이를테면
headlines (방송 뉴스의) 주요 제목
lyrics 가사, 노랫말
Korean Wave 한류
spread 퍼지다

B 다음 글의 밑줄 친 ①~⑤ 중 어법상 바르지 않은 것을 고르시오.

For years, young people in many countries wanted only ① to listen to music from such countries as the USA and Britain. However, these days, pop singers from other nations have become too popular ② to ignore. In East Asian countries such as China and Thailand, some of the Korean bands have become popular enough ③ to make headlines. Even parents often prefer to let their children ④ to listen to them instead of American pop music because of their cute image and clean lyrics. This helps ⑤ explain the growing Korean Wave spreading across Asia.

PART 9

동명사
Gerunds

동명사의 형태와 쓰임

역할	예문
주어	Collecting postcards is my hobby. 우편엽서를 모으는 것이 내 취미이다.
주격보어	My hobby is singing songs in English. 내 취미는 영어로 노래를 부르는 거예요.
동사의 목적어	I love taking a short nap after lunch. 나는 점심 식사 후에 잠깐 낮잠을 자는 것을 매우 좋아한다.
전치사의 목적어	Thank you for giving me a unique opportunity to see all of your works. 나에게 당신의 모든 작품을 볼 수 있는 특별한 기회를 제공해 주셔서 감사합니다.

FOCUS

1 동명사(gerunds)의 기본 형태는 「동사원형+ing」이며, 부정형은 「not+동사원형+ing」이다.

I like **eating** Japanese food. 나는 일식을 먹는 것을 좋아한다.

She apologized sorry for **not coming** on time. 그녀는 제시간에 오지 못한 것에 대해 미안하다고 말했다.

|참고| 동명사는 동사에서 나온 것이므로 동사의 성격을 가진다. 즉, 동명사는 목적어를 취할 수 있다.

Reading novels is my hobby. 소설을 읽는 것은 내 취미이다.

I enjoy **reading** novels whenever I am free. 나는 한가할 때마다 소설을 읽는 것을 즐긴다.

2 동명사는 문장에서 주어 역할을 하며, 동명사 주어는 단수 취급한다.

Exercising regularly is good for your health. 규칙적으로 운동하는 것은 너의 건강에 좋다.

Eating junk food makes us sick. 정크 푸드를 먹는 것은 우리를 병들게 만든다.

|참고| 동명사 주어는 to부정사로 바꿔 쓸 수 있다.

Exercising regularly is good for your health.

→ **To exercise** regularly is good for your health.

→ It is good for your health **to exercise** regularly.

3 동명사는 문장에서 주격보어의 역할을 한다.

Her hobby is **writing** screenplays. (Her hobby = writing screenplays)
그녀의 취미는 시나리오를 쓰는 것이다.

His job is **giving** service to passengers. (His job = giving service to passengers)
그의 직업은 승객들에게 서비스를 제공하는 것이다.

|참고| 동명사 보어는 to부정사로 바꿔 쓸 수 있다.

Her hobby is **writing** screenplays.

→ Her hobby is **to write** screenplays.

4 동명사는 문장에서 목적어 역할을 한다.

You had better avoid **spending** too much money over the holidays. 휴가 동안 돈을 너무 많이 쓰지 않는 것이 좋겠다.

Many young people enjoy **listening** to music. 많은 젊은이들은 음악 듣는 것을 즐긴다.

Would you mind **turning** off the TV? TV를 좀 꺼주시겠어요?

|참고| admit, avoid, consider, delay, deny, discuss, enjoy, finish, give up, go on, keep (on), mind, miss, postpone, quit, suggest 등의 동사는 동명사를 목적어로 취한다.

5 동명사는 전치사의 목적어 역할을 한다.

I'm sorry about **hurting** her feelings. 나는 그녀의 감정을 다치게 해서 유감스럽다.

They thanked everyone for **coming** to the party. 그들은 파티에 온 모든 사람에게 고마워했다.

Jacob is interested in **studying** sea animals. 제이콥은 해양 동물을 연구하는 데 관심이 있다.

6 「동사원형+ing」는 문맥에 따라 동명사 또는 현재분사의 역할을 한다. 동명사란 명사처럼 쓰이는 것을 말하고, 현재분사란 형용사처럼 쓰이는 것을 말한다.

쓰임	현재분사	동명사
-ing+명사	a **sleeping** baby 잠자는 아기 **waiting** people 기다리는 사람들 a **swimming** fish 헤엄치는 물고기 (-ing가 명사를 수식할 때는 현재분사)	a **sleeping** bag 침낭(잠자기 위한 주머니) a **waiting** room 대기실(기다리기 위한 방) a **swimming** pool 수영장(수영하기 위한 풀) (-ing가 명사의 용도를 설명할 때는 동명사)
be+-ing	He is **teaching** math in school. (현재진행: is teaching) 그는 학교에서 수학을 가르치고 있다.	His job is **teaching** math. (주격보어: his job=teaching math) 그의 직업은 수학을 가르치는 것이다.
주어	–	**Smiling** can improve your quality of life. 미소는 당신의 삶의 질을 향상시킬 수 있다.
목적어	–	I love **keeping** a diary in English. 나는 영어로 일기 쓰는 것을 좋아한다.
목적격보어	I saw a boy **eating** ice cream. 나는 아이스크림을 먹고 있는 소년을 보았다.	–
전치사의 목적어	–	Flying is one of the safest ways of **traveling**. 비행은 가장 안전한 여행 방법 중 하나이다.

|참고| 1. 현재분사는 주로 현재 진행되고 있는 동작을 의미한다.

The **crying** boy over there is my nephew. 저기서 울고 있는 소년이 내 조카이다.

The **crying** boy over there가 주어이고, 이 주어 안에서 crying은 boy를 수식해 주는 현재분사이다.

2. 현재분사인지 동명사인지 구분하려면 명사와 -ing형의 관계를 잘 파악해야 한다.

- a **sleeping** baby 잠자는 아기 (a baby is **sleeping**): 아기가 잠을 자는 것이므로 현재분사이다.
- a **sleeping** bag 침낭 (a bag **for sleeping**: 잠자기 위한 주머니): 가방이 잠을 잘 수는 없으므로 동명사이다.

EXERCISES

정답 및 해설 P. 39

wakeboard 물 위에서 즐기는 스포츠의 한 종류
audience (음악회, 강연 등의) 청중, 관중
youth 청년기; 젊음
humpback whale 혹등고래
be well known for ~으로 유명하다
distance 거리, 먼 곳
reduce 줄이다, 낮추다
backpack 배낭여행을 하다

A 밑줄 친 부분의 역할을 〈보기〉에서 골라 쓰시오.

보기 ⓐ 주어 ⓑ 동사의 목적어 ⓒ 보어 ⓓ 전치사의 목적어

1 Taehyun's hobby is wakeboarding. ______
2 My greatest fear is speaking in front of a large audience. ______
3 Sending text messages is an important part of youth culture. ______
4 The humpback whale is well known for swimming long distances. ______
5 To keep a pet is a great way of reducing stress and staying healthy. ______
6 Young people enjoy backpacking through Europe during the summer. ______

letup 정지, 약화, 감소
lose weight 체중이 줄다
presentation 발표, 제출
be famous for ~로 유명하다
achieve one's goal 목표를 달성하다
rush hour 러시아워, (출퇴근) 혼잡 시간대
be (at) the center of attention 관심의 대상이 되다

B 주어진 동사를 to부정사 또는 동명사로 바꿔 문장을 완성하시오. [두 개 이상 답 가능]

1 After a short letup, it started ____________ (rain) again.
2 She gave up ____________ (exercise) every day to lose weight.
3 Thank you for ____________ (help) me to prepare for my presentation.
4 ____________ (start) our own restaurant without any help was not easy.
5 Jisun really enjoys ____________ (play) with her hamster in her free time.
6 Minhee is famous for ____________ (work) very hard to achieve her goals.
7 ____________ (take) the subway during rush hour is much faster than driving.
8 My sister doesn't like ____________ (be) the center of attention.

remain 유지하다; 남다
calm 냉정한; 차분한
in a crisis 위기에 처한
get used to ~에 익숙해지다, 적응하다
take care of ~를 돌보다
at the same time 동시에

C 〈보기〉에서 알맞은 동사를 골라 동명사로 바꿔 문장을 완성하시오.

보기 eat get paint remain take travel

1 John often reads books about ____________.
2 The difficult thing is ____________ calm in a crisis.
3 Jill and Tom have started ____________ the living room.
4 ____________ a healthy breakfast will give you energy all day long.
5 ____________ used to life at a new school can be difficult for many students.
6 ____________ care of twins at the same time was more difficult than I thought.

D 주어진 단어를 이용하여 〈보기〉와 같이 문장을 완성하시오.

보기 Computer games are very fun. (play)
→ Playing computer games is very fun.

1 He likes bagels for breakfast. (eat)
→ He likes ______________________.

2 My friend Susan is interested in the stock market. (work)
→ My friend Susan is interested in ______________________.

3 Languages and cultures are important to all countries. (preserve)
→ ______________________ is important to all countries.

4 He's lived in Canada for a year, but he's still poor at English. (speak)
→ He's lived in Canada for a year, but he's still poor at __________.

5 You have to quit late-night snack to lose weight. (eat)
→ You have to quit ______________________ to lose weight.

6 He complained of poor service in the restaurant. (get)
→ He complained of ______________________ in the restaurant.

7 I am embarrassed about such a big mistake. (make)
→ I am embarrassed about ______________________.

stock market 주식 시장
preserve 지키다, 보존하다
be poor at ~에 서투르다, ~을 못하다
quit 그만두다
late-night snack 야식
poor 형편없는; 가난한
embarrass 당황하게 하다

E 밑줄 친 '-ing형'이 동명사면 G(gerunds), 현재분사면 PP(present participles)를 쓰시오.

1 I saw a <u>dancing</u> bird in the mall. ______

2 My father's hobby is <u>fishing</u> in the ocean. ______

3 We've been <u>traveling</u> for hours, but I'm still not tired. ______

4 Jeffrey is <u>preparing</u> to give his presentation to the class. ______

5 My mother likes <u>watching</u> television while she is cooking. ______

6 This novel is <u>being</u> read by thousands all over the country. ______

7 I was very impressed when I first heard Sohee <u>singing</u> *Arirang*. ______

8 It'll be a long trip to Beijing, so let's try to get seats in the <u>sleeping</u> car. ______

9 A <u>fitting</u> room is a place where you try on clothes before you buy them. ______

10 When Ann has free time, she prefers <u>riding</u> her bike to playing video games. ______

impress 감명을 주다; ~에게 깊은 인상을 주다
fitting room 탈의실
try on ~을 입어보다
prefer A to B B보다 A를 좋아하다

의미상의 주어, 시제, 태

의미상의 주어	소유격+동명사	I can't understand **his behaving** in such a rude way. 나는 그가 그렇게 무례한 행동을 하는 것을 이해할 수 없다.
시제	동사원형+ing	Jeonghun **feels** sorry for **being** late. = Jeonghun **feels** sorry that he **is** late. 정훈이는 늦어서 미안해하고 있다.
	having+p.p.	Ian **denied having broken** the vase on the table. = Ian **denied** that he **broke**[**had broken**] the vase on the table. 이안은 테이블 위에 있는 꽃병을 깬 것을 부인했다.
수동태	being+p.p.	She **was** tired of **being pursued** by paparazzi. = She **was** tired that she **was pursued** by paparazzi. 그녀는 기자들의 추적을 받는 것이 피곤했다.
	having been +p.p.	She **is** angry at **having been deceived**. = She **is** angry that she **was**[**has been**] **deceived**. 그녀는 속은 것에 화가 나 있다.

1 동명사는 동사에서 온 것이므로 행위자가 존재한다. 동명사의 행위자가 주어, 목적어와 같거나 일반인인 경우 의미상의 주어를 따로 쓰지 않지만, 그 외에는 동명사 앞에 소유격을 사용하여 나타낸다.

I like **singing** when I am alone at home. (행위자가 주어와 동일)
나는 집에 혼자 있을 때 노래하는 것을 좋아한다.

Thank you for **giving** us this important information. (행위자가 목적어와 동일)
우리에게 이 중요한 정보를 주셔서 감사합니다.

Smoking in this building is not permitted. (행위자가 일반인)
이 건물에서 흡연하는 것은 허용되지 않습니다.

Would you mind my **opening** the window?
제가 창문을 열어도 될까요?

|주의|
- Would you mind **opening** the window? (you가 창문을 여는 것, opening의 의미상 주어는 you) 창문 좀 열어 주실래요?
- Would you mind my **opening** the window? (I가 창문을 여는 것, opening의 의미상 주어는 my) 제가 창문을 열어도 될까요?
  → Would you mind if I **opened** the window?

|참고|
1. 격식체에서는 동명사의 의미상의 주어로 소유격을 써야 하지만, 일상 회화에서는 소유격 대신 목적격을 사용하기도 한다.
   He insists on **my[me] meeting** her. 그는 내가 그녀를 만나야 한다고 주장한다.
2. 동명사의 의미상의 주어가 문장의 목적어와 일치할 경우 따로 표기하지 않기 때문에 「목적어+전치사+동명사」의 어순이 된다.
   Would you forgive **me for forgetting** your birthday? (내가 너의 생일을 잊은 것) 당신의 생일을 잊은 것을 용서해 주시겠어요?
3. 동명사의 의미상의 주어가 무생물일 경우 명사의 소유격이 아닌 명사 그대로 쓴다.
   They objected to **the housing policy** being put into effect. 그들은 그 주택정책이 시행되는 것을 반대했다.

2 「동사원형+ing」는 문장의 동사와 같은 시제를 나타내고, 「having+p.p.」는 문장의 동사보다 앞선 시제, 즉 먼저 일어난 일을 나타낸다.

「동사원형+ing」

I **am** sure of the news **being** true.

→ I **am** sure that the news **is** true.
나는 그 소식이 사실이라고 확신한다.

I **didn't mind traveling** without a tour guide.

→ I **didn't mind** that I **traveled** without a tour guide.
나는 관광 가이드 없이 여행하는 것을 싫어하지 않았다.

「having+p.p.」

I'**m** sorry for **not having read** that book.

→ I'**m** sorry that I **didn't [haven't] read** that book.
그 소설을 읽지 않은 것이 아쉽다.

Peter **was** proud of **having got** a perfect score in the final exam.

→ Peter **was** proud that he **had got** a perfect score in the final exam.
피터는 기말고사에서 만점을 받았던 것을 자랑스러워했다.

| 참고 | 시간의 전후 관계가 명확한 경우, 기본형 동명사로 완료형을 대신하기도 한다. 이때 기본형 동명사는 문장의 동사보다 먼저 일어난 일을 나타낸다.

He **remembers meeting** my sister once.

→ He **remembers having met** my sister once.

→ He **remembers** that he **met [has met]** my sister once.
그는 내 여동생을 한 번 만났던 것을 기억한다.

3 동명사의 수동태는 「being+p.p.」, 「having been+p.p.」로 나타낸다.

I don't like **being disturbed** when I watch movies. 나는 영화 볼 때 방해받는 것을 싫어한다.

She appreciated **having been selected** for the All-Star Team. 그녀는 올스타 팀에 뽑힌 것에 대해 감사했다.

| 참고 | deserve, need, require 다음에 동명사가 쓰이면 수동의 의미를 가진다.

The baby threw up on the carpet. It **needs cleaning**. (= It **needs to be cleaned**.)
아기가 양탄자 위에 토했다. 양탄자를 빨아야 한다.

EXERCISES

정답 및 해설 P. 40

forgive 용서하다
appreciate ~에 감사하다
would like to ~하고 싶다
be proud of ~을 자랑스러워하다
object to ~에 반대하다
linguistics 언어학
practical 실용적인

A 밑줄 친 부분의 의미상의 주어를 찾아 쓰시오.

1 I can't understand his wanting to leave here. ____________

2 You should forgive him for giving you so much trouble. ____________

3 Actually I didn't like the idea of her going on a bicycle trip. ____________

4 He was happy about her getting accepted into the university. ____________

5 Grandma appreciates our helping her with the house chores. ____________

6 We would really like to thank you for babysitting for us tonight. ____________

7 Americans are proud of Brandon's winning of the gold medal in swimming. ____________

8 My father objected to my studying linguistics because he didn't think it was practical. ____________

admit (범행, 잘못 등을) 자백하다; 인정하다
cheat on the exam 시험에서 부정행위를 하다
police investigation 경찰 조사
lead to (어떤 결과)로 이어지다

B 두 문장의 의미가 통하도록 동명사를 이용하여 문장을 완성하시오.

1 Chris admitted that he helped his friends cheat on the exam.
→ Chris admitted ____________ his friends cheat on the exam.

2 They're very proud that they have developed their business so quickly.
→ They're very proud of ____________ their business so quickly.

3 He admitted that he had robbed the bank in the police investigation.
→ He admitted ____________ the bank in the police investigation.

4 He was proud that he had received straight As for this semester.
→ He was proud of ____________ straight As for this semester.

5 I don't remember that I promised to meet you for a movie tonight.
→ I don't remember ____________ to meet you for a movie tonight.

6 I am so excited that I will work with him in the same team.
→ I am so excited about ____________ with him in the same team.

7 I don't mind that I practice a lot because it'll lead to my future success.
→ I don't mind my ____________ a lot because it'll lead to my future success.

C 주어진 단어를 이용하여 <보기>와 같이 고쳐 쓰시오.

보기 Would you mind if I checked my email on your computer? (I)
→ Would you mind ___my checking my email on your computer___?

1 Imagine that you are relaxing on the beach. (you)
→ Imagine ______________________.

2 Alison dislikes that her husband works until late at night. (her husband)
→ Alison dislikes ______________________.

3 I remember that Tom won the marathon. (Tom)
→ I remember ______________________.

4 She insisted that I should stay at her house while I was in Paris. (I)
→ She insisted on ______________________ while I was in Paris.

5 Kelly was angry that he played a mean trick on her. (he)
→ Kelly was angry at ______________________ on her.

6 Eric is proud that his son is attending college on a full scholarship. (his son)
→ Eric is proud of ______________________ on a full scholarship.

imagine 상상하다
dislike ~을 싫어하다; 싫음
insist 주장하다
play a mean trick on ~에게 비열한 속임수를 쓰다
scholarship 장학금

D 두 문장의 의미가 통하도록 문장을 완성하시오.

1 He was sure of her being a musician.
→ He was sure that ______________________.

2 She was ashamed of being unable to read.
→ She was ashamed that ______________________.

3 He felt happy about being employed at a world-renowned company.
→ He felt happy that ______________________.

4 She was worried about her son's playing computer games too much.
→ She was worried that ______________________.

5 Jake admitted feeling jealous of Garry's looks and popularity.
→ Jake admitted that ______________________.

6 He admitted having used inappropriate language before.
→ He admitted that ______________________.

7 He denied having copied someone else's writing from the Internet.
→ He denied that ______________________.

be sure of ~에 확신을 가지다
be ashamed of ~을 부끄러워하다
world-renowned 세계적으로 유명한
be worried about ~에 대해 걱정하다
feel jealous of ~을 질투하다
look 외모, 모양; ~해 보이다
popularity 인기
inappropriate 부적절한, 부적합한
deny 부인하다

동명사 vs. to부정사

구분	예문
동사+to부정사	We all **hope** to arrive on time. 우리는 모두 정시에 도착하기를 희망한다.
동사+동명사	She **enjoys** playing the guitar. 그녀는 기타 치는 것을 즐긴다.
동사+to부정사 동사+동명사	He **likes** to go fishing on weekends. He **likes** going fishing on weekends. 그는 주말에 낚시하러 가는 것을 좋아한다.

1

to부정사를 목적어로 취하는 동사는 다음과 같다.

afford	agree	ask	choose	decide	expect	hope	learn	manage
need	offer	plan	pretend	promise	refuse	seem	want	wish ...

George **plans** to study in Seoul beginning in February. 조지는 2월부터 서울에서 공부할 계획이다.

Joon **decided** to go to the movies. 준은 영화를 보러 가기로 결심했다.

She **agreed** to sell the old convertible. 그녀는 그 낡은 컨버터블을 파는 데 동의했다.

|참고| 1. want와 need는 동명사를 목적어로 가질 경우 수동의 의미이다.

This room **needs** cleaning. 이 방은 청소가 필요하다.

→ This room **needs** to be cleaned.

2. 「동사+목적어+to부정사」의 형태를 취하는 동사는 allow, advise, ask, expect, tell, want, warn 등이 있다.

I **expected** him **to come** on time. 나는 그가 정시에 올 거라고 기대했다.

2

동명사를 목적어로 취하는 동사는 다음과 같다.

admit	avoid	consider	delay	deny	discuss	dislike
enjoy	finish	give up	go on	insist on	keep (on)	mind
postpone	put off	quit	stop	suggest ...		

My grandmother **gave up** knitting because of her poor eyesight. 할머니께서는 시력이 안 좋아서 뜨개질을 그만두셨다.

Suji **finished** painting the self-portrait. 수지는 자화상 그리기를 끝마쳤다.

He **suggested** leaving early. 그는 일찍 떠날 것을 제안했다.

3 to부정사와 동명사 모두를 목적어로 취하고 뜻도 거의 달라지지 않는 동사는 다음과 같다.

begin continue hate like love prefer start ...

I **like** going to concerts. 나는 콘서트에 가는 것을 좋아한다.

→ I **like** to go to concerts.

Her ankle **began** swelling. 그녀의 발목이 부어오르기 시작했다.

→ Her ankle **began** to swell.

|주의| prefer는 to부정사와 동명사를 모두 취할 수 있지만, 그 형태에 주의해야 한다.

He **prefers** taking a bus **to** taking the subway. 그는 지하철을 타는 것보다 버스를 타는 것을 선호한다.

→ He **prefers** to take a bus **(rather) than** (to) take the subway.

4 remember, forget, try, regret은 동명사와 to부정사 모두를 목적어로 취하지만 뜻이 달라진다.

remember+to부정사 ~할 것을 기억하다 vs. remember+동명사 ~했던 것을 기억하다

I must **remember** to visit the CN Tower. (아직 CN 타워를 방문하지 않았음) 나는 CN타워를 방문해야 하는 것을 기억해야 한다.

I **remember** visiting the CN Tower. (CN 타워를 방문했음) 나는 CN타워를 방문했던 것을 기억한다.

forget+to부정사 ~할 것을 잊다 vs. forget+동명사 ~했던 것을 잊다

I **forgot** to give her the keys, so she couldn't go in. (열쇠를 주어야 한다는 사실을 잊어버리고 그녀에게 열쇠를 주지 않았음)
내가 그녀에게 열쇠를 주는 것을 잊어버려서 그녀는 안으로 들어갈 수가 없었다.

I **forgot** giving her the book, and I was looking for it everywhere. (그녀에게 책을 주었으나, 책을 주었다는 사실을 잊어버렸음)
나는 그녀에게 그 책을 준 것을 잊어버리고 사방으로 그것을 찾고 있었다.

try+to부정사 ~을 하려고 노력하다 vs. try+동명사 ~을 시도하다

Why don't you **try** to help others when you can? 네가 할 수 있을 때 다른 사람들을 도우려고 노력하는 게 어때?

Why don't you **try** asking for help when you need it? 도움이 필요할 때 도움을 청해 보는 게 어때?

regret+to부정사 ~하게 되어 유감이다 vs. regret+동명사 ~했던 것을 후회하다

I **regret** to inform you that your position has been eliminated. 당신이 해고되었음을 통보하게 되어 유감입니다.

I **regret** going to the party on Saturday. 나는 토요일에 파티에 갔던 것을 후회한다.

|주의| 1. 「stop+to부정사」 ~하기 위해 멈추다 vs. 「stop+동명사」 ~하던 것을 멈추다

「stop+to부정사」에서 to부정사는 stop의 목적어로 쓰인 것이 아니라 '~하려고'라는 의미의 목적으로 쓰인 것이다.

I **stopped** to talk to Esther. 에스더와 이야기하려고 멈췄다.

I **stopped** talking to Esther. 나는 에스더와 이야기하던 것을 멈췄다.

EXERCISES

정답 및 해설 P. 40

nonsense 터무니없는 말, 허튼소리
hold (경기 등을) 열다, 개최하다
honeymoon 신혼여행
giant tortoise (동물) 코끼리 거북(뭍에 사는 대형 거북의 총칭)
appreciate ~에 감사하다
lesson 교훈; 수업
pour down 비가 내리 퍼붓다

( ) 안에서 알맞은 것을 모두 고르시오.

1 She began (talking / to talk) nonsense after a while.

2 I hate (wasting / to waste) time and money on useless stuff.

3 Paris Hilton considered (holding / to hold) a concert in Seoul.

4 Sybil and Jason planned (spending / to spend) their honeymoon in Hawaii.

5 Giant tortoises seem (living / to live) a very long time without food or water.

6 Natalie had to give up (playing / to play) basketball because she was too short.

7 Learning (appreciating / to appreciate) your family is a lesson that we all have to learn.

8 The rain started early in the morning and continued (pouring / to pour) down all afternoon.

9 Dr. Lim, could I bring my baby to see you today? He keeps (crying / to cry), and I don't know why.

rainforest 열대 우림
delay 미루다, 연기하다
get on board 승차하다
insist on ~을 요구하다
install 설치하다
safety device 안전장치
pretend to ~인 체하다
come on (극, 영화 등이) 상영되다, 시작되다
deny 부인하다
evidence 증거; 흔적
prove one's guilt ~의 유죄를 입증하다

B 주어진 동사를 to부정사 또는 동명사로 바꿔 문장을 완성하시오.

1 Dean offered __________ (help) us study for our test.

2 I need your help to finish __________ (write) an essay on rainforests.

3 She and I delayed __________ (get) on board for as long as we could.

4 The dentist insisted on my __________ (brush) my teeth after every meal.

5 They promised __________ (install) a safety device after the accident.

6 She didn't like the food she ordered, but she pretended __________ (be) enjoying it.

7 Mio decided __________ (move) to the USA in order to work with a famous coach.

8 Would you mind __________ (change) the channel? My favorite drama is coming on at 8 p.m.

9 He denied __________ (have) stolen the cell phones so far, but the police already had evidence to prove his guilt.

C 〈보기〉에서 알맞은 동사를 골라 to부정사 또는 동명사로 바꿔 문장을 완성하시오.

보기 | do | eat | rescue | move | go | play | reduce

1 She learned ______________ the piano when she was young.

2 They postponed ______________ camping because of bad weather.

3 Kelly avoids ______________ too much meat because she wants to stay healthy.

4 Jason pretended ______________ his homework when he was really surfing the Internet.

5 Our teacher refused ______________ class outside even though it was such a beautiful day.

6 The government should consider ______________ carbon emissions to stop global warming.

7 The firefighters managed ______________ residents from the burning apartment building.

rescue (위험에서) 구하다, 구조하다
postpone 연기하다, 미루다
pretend ~인 체하다
refuse 거절하다
government 정부
carbon emission 탄소 배출
global warming 지구 온난화
resident 거주자, 주민
burn ~을 태우다

D ( ) 안에서 가장 알맞은 것을 고르시오.

1 ① I tried (taking / to take) a shower with cold water, but I was still too hot.
② We should try (reducing / to reduce) noise pollution.

2 ① I remember (buying / to buy) the balloons for the party, but I can't find them now.
② Remember (taking / to take) the roast out of the oven. If not, you'll burn it.

3 ① Although she was late, she stopped (buying / to buy) coffee.
② The doctor said that I should stop (eating / to eat) fried food because it is not good.

4 ① My father forgot (buying / to buy) me a bike for my birthday, so, he promised to buy one next year.
② My sister forgot (leaving / to leave) her mobile phone at home, so she is looking for it everywhere.

5 ① Rick couldn't wait to become president of his class. Now, he regrets (becoming / to become) president of his class.
② Will received a letter from Yale. The letter said, "We regret (informing / to inform) you that your application has not been accepted."

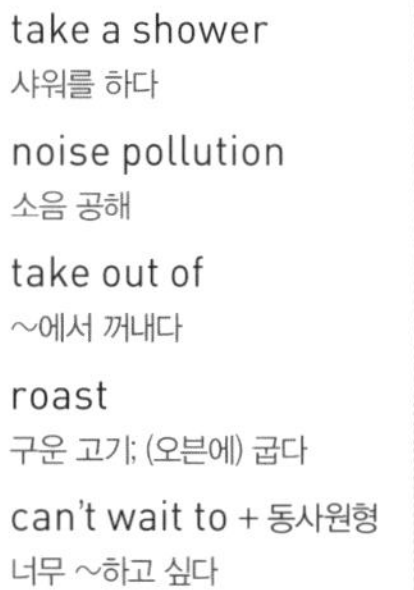

동명사의 관용 표현

1 동명사를 포함하는 관용 표현에는 다음과 같은 것들이 있다.

go -ing ~하러 가다	Nancy often **goes shopping** with her mom. 낸시는 엄마와 자주 쇼핑을 간다.
be busy -ing ~하느라 바쁘다	My brother **is busy making** a model airplane for a contest. 우리 형은 대회에 나갈 모형 비행기를 만드느라 바쁘다.
can't help -ing = cannot (help) but+동사원형 ~하지 않을 수 없다	I **couldn't help laughing** when I saw the kids. = I **couldn't but laugh** when I saw the kids. 나는 그 아이들을 봤을 때 웃지 않을 수 없었다.
have trouble[difficulty] -ing ~하는 데 곤란을 겪다	I **have** no **trouble reading** your handwriting. So don't worry. 네 글씨를 읽는 데 문제없어. 그러니까 걱정하지 마.
be worth -ing ~할 가치가 있다	The play **is worth performing** in the theater. 그 연극은 극장에서 공연할 가치가 있다.
spend+돈/시간+-ing ~하는 데 돈, 시간 등을 소비하다	I **spent** all my money **buying** new books for the next semester. 나는 다음 학기를 위해 새 책을 사는 데 돈을 다 썼다.
be good at -ing ~을 잘하다 vs. be poor at -ing ~에 서투르다	My father **is good at carving** sculptures, but he **is poor at painting**. 우리 아빠는 조각품을 만드는 것을 잘하시지만, 그림은 잘 못 그리신다.
feel like -ing ~하고 싶다	I don't **feel like going** to see a movie tonight. 나는 오늘 밤에 영화 보러 가고 싶지 않아.
never ~ without -ing ~하지 않고는 절대로 …않다	She **never** goes out **without putting** on a scarf in winter. 그녀는 겨울에 목도리를 하지 않고는 절대로 밖에 나가지 않는다.
look forward to -ing ~하기를 고대하다	My grandmother **looks forward to seeing** you. 우리 할머니는 너를 보는 것을 고대하고 계셔.
be[get] used to -ing = be accustomed to -ing ~에 익숙하다, 익숙해지다	She **is used to watching** movies alone. = She **is accustomed to watching** movies alone. 그녀는 혼자서 영화를 보는 데 익숙하다.
object to -ing ~에 반대하다	The workers **objected to working** overtime. 근로자들은 초과 근무하는 것에 반대했다.
It is no use -ing ~해도 소용없다 = It is of no use to+동사원형 = It is useless to+동사원형	**It is no use regretting** what you have already said. = **It is of no use to regret** what you have already said. = **It is useless to regret** what you have already said. 이미 한 말을 후회해봤자 소용없다.
keep[prevent, prohibit, stop] 사람 from -ing ~가 …하지 못하게 하다	My father **kept** me **from** playing outside during the yellow dust season. 우리 아버지는 황사 철에 내가 밖에 나가 노는 것을 못하게 했다.

|주의| look forward to -ing, be[get] used to -ing(= be accustomed to -ing), object to -ing 등의 「to+-ing」 구문에서 to는 전치사이다. 「to+동사원형」 구문처럼 동사원형과 함께 써야 하는 to와 혼동하지 말자.

EXERCISES

정답 및 해설 P. 41

( ) 안에서 가장 알맞은 것을 고르시오.

tax 세금
mow (풀 등을) 베다
vividly 생생하게
portray 묘사하다; 그리다
Great Depression 대공황
kill time 시간을 보내다[때우다]
particularly 특히

1 Many people object (to pay / to paying) higher taxes.

2 Michael is busy (to mow / mowing) the grass in the garden.

3 I think the movie is worth (to watch / watching). It vividly portrays life during the Great Depression.

4 Tom uses his cell phone to listen to music when he's traveling. Perhaps it would be better if he got used (to read / to reading) to kill time instead.

5 My family looks forward (to spend / to spending) a week at the beach in July. This year, my father is particularly eager to relax during the vacation.

B 〈보기〉에서 동사를 골라 알맞은 형태로 바꿔 문장을 완성하시오.

set the table 식탁을 차리다
beaver (동물) 비버
fell (나무 등을) 베어 넘어뜨리다
dam 댐; 댐을 만들다
celebrity 유명 인사
attention 관심
indoor 실내의

보기	receive	wear	build	hike	prepare	stay

1 Mom was busy ___________ dinner. I helped her by setting the table.

2 Beavers are good at felling tall trees and ___________ dams out of them.

3 Sue isn't accustomed to ___________ glasses. She loses them sometimes.

4 Many celebrities have trouble getting used to ___________ lots of attention.

5 I don't feel like ___________ indoors when the weather is so nice. Why don't we go ___________?

C 우리말과 같은 뜻이 되도록 주어진 단어를 이용하여 문장을 완성하시오.

slip on 미끄러지다
latest 최신의

1 우리는 독서에 많은 시간을 투자해야 한다. (spend, time, read)
→ We need to ___________ ___________ ___________ ___________.

2 나는 아침 식사로 토스트를 먹고 싶지 않다. (feel, have)
→ I ___________ ___________ ___________ ___________ toast for breakfast.

3 그녀는 자신의 남동생이 얼음에서 미끄러졌을 때 웃지 않을 수 없었다. (help, laugh)
→ She ___________ ___________ ___________ when her brother slipped on the ice.

4 에이미는 줄리아의 최신 노래 듣는 것을 몹시 고대하고 있다. (look, hear)
→ Amy is really ___________ ___________ ___________ ___________ Julia's latest song.

REVIEW

정답 및 해설 P. 41

prefer A to B
B보다 A를 선호하다
skip
(수업을) 빼먹다, 건너뛰다
admit (범행, 잘못 등을) 자백하다; 인정하다
pretend to ~인 체하다
give up 포기하다
injure 부상을 입다
knee 무릎
go on 계속해서 ~하다
model ship
모형선[모형배]
renegotiate
~을 재교섭하다
treaty 조약, 협정; 조약문
protest 항의; 항의하다

A ( ) 안에서 알맞은 것을 모두 고르시오.

1 Eunji prefers doing yoga to (play / playing) tennis.

2 I wonder why Clair keeps (skipping / to skip) class.

3 Samantha hopes (buying / to buy) a new apartment soon.

4 One of the boys finally admitted (starting / to start) the fire.

5 Wendy pretended not (noticing / to notice) the “No Parking” sign.

6 Mark gave up (playing / to play) basketball when he injured his knee.

7 Jaemin told Miranda that he couldn’t go on (living / to live) without her.

8 My brother promised to help me (put / to put) the model ship together.

9 Jaehoon suggested (going / to going) to the library to study for the math test.

10 Peter enjoys (watching / to watch) English Premier League football on TV.

11 I couldn’t help (thinking / think) about soccer during the World Cup season.

12 The president agreed (renegotiating / to renegotiate) the treaty after many days of protest.

be well known for
~로 잘 알려져 있다
humorous
재미있는; 익살스러운
dependence 의존
fossil fuel 화석 연료
expand into
~로 확장하다
spare time 여가시간
popularity 인기
aspirin 아스피린, 해열제
allow 허용하다
search for ~을 찾다

B 밑줄 친 부분을 어법에 맞게 고치시오.

1 Youtube is well known for have humorous videos.

2 We need reducing our dependence on fossil fuels.

3 The American IT company hopes expanding into Korea.

4 It is worth to volunteer with your friends in your spare time.

5 Barbara didn’t like kimchi at first, but she got used to eat it.

6 The Korean singer started to growing in popularity in China.

7 She is looking forward to see Brian’s next concert in Busan.

8 Mr. Smith regrets to behave badly when he was young.

9 If you have a headache, why don’t you try to take an aspirin?

10 Elizabeth remembered to go to Disneyland when she was little.

11 Keeping your promises are a very important part of being a friend.

12 An Internet search engine allows people searching for interesting information.

C 주어진 단어를 이용하여 대화를 완성하시오.

intend to ~할 작정이다
last 지속되다; 마지막의; 최근의
drop by (~에) 잠깐 들르다
help oneself 스스로를 어떻게 하다

1 A: Where do you want to go on vacation?
B: I intended __________ (go) to Las Vegas.

2 A: Today, I don't feel like __________ (eat out).
B: If so, why don't we get some food delivered?

3 A: I've given up __________ (drink) soda to lose weight.
B: Really? Well, I wonder how long it will last.

4 A: Mom, did you get some cereal and milk?
B: Sorry, I forgot __________ (drop by) the grocery store on my way home.

5 A: You should stop __________ (eat) sweets. They're bad for your health.
B: I know, but I just can't help myself.

6 A: Why did you get up so early?
B: Jeff and I plan __________ (go) fishing. I'm meeting him at seven.

7 A: Jessica, don't you remember __________ (promise) to help me with the dishes?
B: But Dad, I just want to go out and ride my bike.

D 우리말과 같은 뜻이 되도록 주어진 단어를 이용하여 문장을 완성하시오.

be famous for ~로 유명하다
recipe 요리법
save 저축하다; 절약하다; 구하다

1 소피는 가족을 위해 요리하는 것을 좋아한다. (love, cook)
→ Sophie __________ __________ __________ for her family.

2 그는 자신만의 요리법을 개발한 것으로 유명하다. (famous, develop)
→ He __________ __________ __________ __________ his own recipes.

3 재키는 가능한 한 오래 배우로서 계속 일할 것이다. (continue, work)
→ Jackie will __________ __________ __________ as an actor as long as he can.

4 샐리는 밤 늦게까지 TV를 본 것을 후회했다. (regret, watch)
→ Sally __________ __________ __________ until late at night.

5 메리는 방과 후에 바로 숙제를 하는 것이 익숙하다. (accustomed, do)
→ Mary __________ __________ __________ __________ her homework right after school.

6 로빈은 해외에 나가기로 결정했고 돈을 저축하기 시작했다. (decide, go, start, save)
→ Robin __________ __________ __________ abroad and __________ __________ __________ money.

REVIEW PLUS

정답 및 해설 P. 43

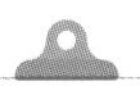

count on
기대하다; ~에 의존하다
go out 외출하다
insist on
~을 하겠다고 고집을 부리다
delay 연기하다, 미루다
join the army 입대하다
cheat on an exam
시험에서 부정행위를 하다

A 다음 중 어법상 바르지 않은 것을 고르시오.

1 ① Betty counts on going out this weekend.
② Sujin looks forward to visit her grandmother.
③ Debbie insists on wearing that blue dress to his wedding.
④ Yunji suggests going to the beach for the holiday.
⑤ Hyunjin delayed joining the army until after graduation.

2 ① He denies to have cheated on the exam.
② Jill expects to watch a film with her boyfriend.
③ Jaemin asked to leave class to go to the bathroom.
④ William discussed playing basketball for the school team.
⑤ Harry finished washing the car before his father got home.

ballet 발레
The Nutcracker
호두까기 인형 (발레)
be supposed to
~하기로 되어 있다

B 다음 중 대화가 자연스럽지 않은 것을 고르시오.

① A: Do you enjoy going to the ballet?
B: Yes. And I've heard *The Nutcracker* is playing this weekend.
② A: Mom, can I go to the mall with Sally on Saturday?
B: I'm sorry, but you promised to help your brother doing his science project.
③ A: Would you like to see *Spiderman* with me this weekend?
B: I prefer watching romantic comedies. How about seeing *Love Actually*?
④ A: What are you planning to do this weekend?
B: I hope to play tennis if I can find someone to play with me.
⑤ A: It's supposed to be a beautiful, sunny day today. What would you like to do?
B: I'd love to go to Riverside Park.

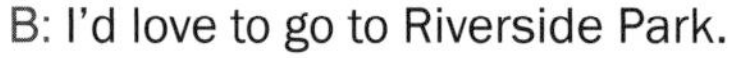

relieve ~을 경감하다
modern 현대의
lie 위치해 있다; 거짓말하다; 눕다
coast 해안
breathtaking
넋을 잃고 바라볼 만한; 숨 막히게 하는
scenery 경치, 풍경
indoor 실내의
district 구역
stylish 멋진, 우아한

C 다음 밑줄 친 부분이 어법상 바르지 않은 것을 고르시오.

Winter sports like skiing are great for ① relieving the stress of modern life. Whistler lies on the west coast of British Columbia, and it has breathtaking scenery. Many visitors come ② to enjoy all types of winter sports. There's something for everyone, whether it's hiking, skiing, listening to nature or simply relaxing. For those visitors who prefer ③ being warm, there are also indoor activities such as the wonderful shopping district and stylish restaurants. If you are considering ④ taking a winter vacation, let me suggest ⑤ to try the best ski resort in North America, Whistler.

PART 10

수동태
The Passive

시제에 따른 수동태

능동태 → 수동태

Frank Lloyd Wright designed the Guggenheim Museum.

→ The Guggenheim Museum was designed by Frank Lloyd Wright.

프랭크 로이드 라이트가 구겐하임 박물관을 디자인했다.

FOCUS

1 문장에서 주어가 동작이나 행위의 주체가 되어 '주어가 ~하다'라는 의미이면 '능동태'라고 하고, 주어가 동작이나 행위를 당하는 대상이 되어 '주어가 ~ 당하다, ~하여지다'라는 의미이면 '수동태'라고 한다.

My uncle **repaired** the bicycle yesterday. (능동태) 우리 삼촌은 어제 자전거를 수리했다.

→ The bicycle **was repaired** by my uncle yesterday. (수동태) 자전거가 어제 삼촌에 의해 수리되었다.

|주의| 수동태와 능동태를 구분하려면 주어가 동작을 하는 주체인지, 동작을 당하는 대상인지를 파악하는 것이 중요하다.

The wall was painted by me. 그 벽은 나에 의해 페인트칠이 되었다.

(×) ~~The wall painted me.~~ (벽이 나를 페인트칠할 수 없으므로 문장이 성립하지 않음)

2 수동태의 시제는 「be+p.p.」의 'be' 부분을 바꿔 표현한다.

현재 「am/are/is+p.p.」

Our mail **is delivered** by the mailman. 우리 우편물은 집배원에 의해 배달된다.

Rice **is grown** in Korea. 쌀은 한국에서 재배된다.

과거 「was/were+p.p.」

The document **was faxed** by the secretary. 서류가 비서에 의해 팩스로 보내졌다.

The game **was postponed** due to rain. 우천으로 경기가 연기되었다.

미래 「will[be going to]+be+p.p.」

The letter **will[is going to] be mailed** by Mom. 그 편지는 엄마에 의해 발송될 것이다.

The reports **will[are going to] be collected** by Tom. 보고서는 톰에 의해 취합될 것이다.

현재진행 「be+being+p.p.」

Her new novel **is being printed** now. 그녀의 새 소설이 지금 인쇄되고 있다.

The movie **is being played** now. 그 영화가 지금 상영되고 있다.

현재완료「have/has+been+p.p.」

A new hospital **has been built** by them. 새 병원은 그들에 의해 지어졌다.

A strange rumor **has been spread** around the country. 이상한 소문이 온 나라에 퍼졌다.

과거완료「had+been+p.p.」

When I got home, the house **had** already **been broken** into. 내가 집에 왔을 때 집은 이미 도둑이 든 상태였다.

Before he left the office, all lights **had been switched** off. 그가 사무실을 떠나기 전에 모든 불은 꺼진 상태였다.

3 조동사를 포함한 수동태는 「조동사+be+p.p.」 어순으로 나타낸다.

All rules **must be obeyed.** 모든 규칙은 지켜져야 한다.

The assignment **can be completed** over the weekend. 그 과제는 주말 동안 끝마칠 수 있다.

My homework **should be finished** before my parents come home. 내 숙제는 부모님이 집에 오시기 전에 끝나야 한다.

4 수동태의 부정문은 be동사나 조동사 뒤에 not을 붙인다.

The birdseed **wasn't eaten** by the greedy brown squirrel. 새 모이는 욕심 많은 갈색 다람쥐에게 먹힌 것이 아니었다.

Food and drinks **will not be allowed** in the library. 도서관에서는 음식물 반입이 허용되지 않을 것이다.

5 수동태의 의문문은 be동사나 조동사를 문장의 맨 앞에 놓는다.

Was Michael **taken** to the hospital after the accident? 사고 후에 마이클이 병원으로 보내졌니?

Should the project **be done** by Friday? 그 프로젝트는 금요일까지 끝나야 하나요?

|참고| 의문사가 있는 문장의 수동태는 다음과 같다.

What **is** this fruit **called** in English? 이 과일은 영어로 뭐라고 불리니?

Where **can** the hidden treasure **be found**? 숨겨진 보물이 어디에서 발견될 수 있을까?

By whom **was** the building **attacked**? → Who **attacked** the building? 그 건물은 누구에게 공격을 받았을까?(누가 그 건물을 공격했니?)

6 수동태는 동작을 당하는 대상에 초점을 둔 문장이므로 동작을 하는 대상인 「by+행위자(목적격)」는 흔히 생략된다. 특히, 행위자가 we, you, they, people, one 등 특정하지 않은 일반인인 경우이거나 추측할 수 있어서 나타낼 필요가 없는 경우 생략된다.

Robert **is called** Bob for short. 로버트는 짧게 줄여서 밥이라고 불린다.

The stem cells **were kept** in a refrigerator. 그 줄기세포는 냉장고에 보관되었다.

One of my neighbor's sons **was killed** in Iraq. 내 이웃의 아들 중 하나가 이라크에서 사망했다.

EXERCISES

정답 및 해설 P. 43

envelope 봉투
modern 현대의
serve (음식 등을) 대접하다; 제공하다
exotic 이국적인, 별난
reception 환영회, 환영; (호텔의) 프런트, 접수처
mess 엉망인 상태
ad campaign 광고 캠페인
proficiency level 능숙도

( ) 안에서 가장 알맞은 것을 고르시오.

1 An address (write / is written) on the back of the envelope.

2 Pablo Picasso (painted / was painted) *Massacre in Korea* in 1951.

3 The modern toothbrush (didn't invent / was not invented) until 1938.

4 Mr. Lee (taught / was taught) science at the local high school in 2014.

5 Many different exotic dishes (served / were served) at the reception.

6 This mess had better (clean up / be cleaned up) before Mom comes home and sees it.

7 The company's ad campaign (designed / was designed) by a freshman college student.

8 The professor (organized / was organized) the English speaking classes by proficiency level.

raise 모으다; 올리다; 기르다
charity 자선단체; 자선기금; 자선
conquer 정복하다
tutor ~에게 개인 교수를 하다; 가정 교사
housewarming 집들이
devastate ~을 황폐시키다
compose 작곡하다
beloved 가장 사랑하는, 소중한
symphony 교향곡

B 주어진 능동태 문장을 수동태 문장으로 바꿔 쓰시오.

1 Junsu didn't mail the package.
→ ______________________________

2 Brian raised a lot of money for charity.
→ ______________________________

3 The Ottoman Empire conquered Egypt in 1517.
→ ______________________________ in 1517.

4 Jenny's sister tutors Minji in math and science.
→ ______________________________ in math and science.

5 Did Ryan invite Julia to the housewarming party?
→ ______________________________

6 Hurricane Katrina devastated the Gulf Coast of the USA in 2005.
→ ______________________________ in 2005.

7 Mozart composed many of the world's most beloved symphonies.
→ ______________________________

8 Did they deliver the product I ordered last night?
→ ______________________________

C 〈보기〉에서 알맞은 단어를 골라 어법에 맞게 바꿔 문장을 완성하시오.

보기 send exhibit attend invite discover delay

1 I __________ __________ to Brenda's birthday party last Saturday.

2 The event will not __________ __________ unless it rains that day.

3 Penicillin __________ __________ by Alexander Fleming in the 1920s.

4 The museum __________ __________ Picasso's sketches since May 1st.

5 The package must __________ __________ to him as quickly as possible.

6 Hundreds of people __________ __________ the movie star's funeral so far.

exhibit 전시하다
discover 발견하다
penicillin 페니실린(항생 물질의 하나)
funeral 장례식

D 우리말과 같은 뜻이 되도록 주어진 단어를 이용하여 문장을 완성하시오.

1 잃어버린 반지가 침대 밑에서 발견되었다. (find)
→ The missing ring __________ __________ under the bed.

2 내 손목시계는 그 보석상에 의해서 수리되고 있는 중이다. (repair)
→ My wristwatch __________ __________ __________ __________ the jeweler.

3 아이들은 이번 여름에 캠프에서 말 타는 법을 배우게 될 것이다. (teach)
→ The children __________ __________ __________ __________ __________ how to ride a horse at the camp this summer.

4 그 건물의 공사는 내일까지 완공되어야 합니다. (must, complete)
→ The construction of the building __________ __________ __________ by tomorrow.

wristwatch 손목시계
jeweler 보석상
how to ~하는 방법
construction 공사; 건설

E ( ) 안에서 가장 알맞은 것을 고르시오.

1 My best friend Leo is in the hospital. He (is treating / is being treated) for a rare, but curable, heart defect.

2 On October 3, 2003, Roy Horn (bit / was bitten) on the neck by the tiger he had trained. But fortunately, crew members (separated / were separated) Horn from the tiger and rushed him to the hospital.

3 Calculus (independently discovered / was independently discovered) by two brilliant mathematicians around the same time: Isaac Newton and Gottfried Leibniz. But it was Leibniz who first (published / was published) the discovery.

treat ~을 치료하다; 다루다
rare 드문, 희박한
curable 치료할 수 있는
heart defect 심장병
crew 팀; 승무원
separate A from B B에서 A를 분리하다
rush 급히 수송하다
calculus (수학) 미적분
independently 독립하여, 자주적으로
mathematician 수학자
discovery 발견

문장의 형태에 따른 수동태

문장의 형태	능동태	수동태
주어+동사	He **arrived** at the airport. 그는 공항에 도착했다.	×
주어+동사+보어	He **became** a doctor. 그는 의사가 되었다.	×
주어+상태동사 +목적어	I **have** something to do. 나는 해야 할 일이 있다.	×
주어+동사 +목적어	The owner **posted** the menu. 주인이 메뉴를 게시했다.	The menu **was posted** by the owner. 메뉴는 주인에 의해 게시되었다.
주어+동사 +간접목적어 +직접목적어	Jihye **teaches** Tom Korean. 지혜는 톰에게 한국어를 가르친다.	Tom **is taught** Korean by Jihye. 톰은 지혜에게 한국어를 배운다. Korean **is taught** to Tom by Jihye. 한국어는 지혜에 의해서 톰에게 가르쳐진다.
주어+동사 +목적어+보어	People **elected** Obama president. 사람들이 오바마를 대통령으로 선출했다.	Obama **was elected** president. 오바마는 대통령으로 선출되었다.

1 목적어를 갖지 않는 동사는 수동태로 바꿔 쓸 수 없다.

appear 나타나다 | become ~이 되다 | belong to ~에 속하다 | die 죽다 | disappear 사라지다
fall 떨어지다 | happen 발생하다 | occur 일어나다 | rise 뜨다

John **appeared** on local television. (*NOT* was appeared) 존이 지역 방송 TV에 나왔다.

The accident **happened** right in front of us. (*NOT* was happened) 그 사고는 우리 바로 앞에서 일어났다.

2 목적어를 갖는 동사라도 다음의 뜻으로 쓰일 때는 수동태로 바꿔 쓰지 않는다.

cost 비용이 ~가 들다 | have ~을 가지고 있다, 소유하다 | resemble ~을 닮다

It **cost** me ten dollars. 십 달러가 들었다.
(×) I ~~was cost~~ ten dollars by it.

I **have** a book. 나는 책을 가지고 있다.
(×) A book ~~is had~~ by me.

The twins **resemble** their grandfather. 쌍둥이는 그들의 할아버지를 닮았다.
(×) Their grandfather ~~is resembled~~ by the twins.

3 간접목적어와 직접목적어가 있는 문장은 두 가지 형태의 수동태 문장을 만들 수 있다.

Jenna's grandmother gave her a golden bracelet. 제나의 할머니는 그녀에게 금팔찌를 주었다.
→ Jenna **was given** a golden bracelet by her grandmother.
→ A golden bracelet **was given to** Jenna by her grandmother.

4 직접목적어를 주어로 하여 만든 수동태 문장은 간접목적어 앞에 주로 to나 for 등의 전치사를 쓴다.

to를 쓰는 동사 : bring, give, lend, pass, send, show, teach, tell ...

The pictures **were shown to** her friends by her mother. 그 사진들은 그녀의 어머니가 그녀의 친구들에게 보여줬다.

The flowers **were sent to** her by him this morning. 그 꽃들은 오늘 아침에 그가 그녀에게 보낸 것이다.

|참고| 간접목적어가 대명사인 경우 to를 생략하기도 한다.

The flowers were sent **her** by him this morning.

for를 쓰는 동사 : build, buy, cook, find, get, make ...

Pajeon **was made for** my Australian friends by me. 파전은 호주 친구들을 위해 내가 만든 것이다.

The sand castle **was built for** David by his father. 그 모래성은 데이비드를 위해 그의 아버지가 지은 것이다.

|주의| buy, cook, get, make 등의 동사가 쓰인 문장에서는 직접목적어를 주어로 하여 수동태를 만드는 것이 일반적이다.

Tina **bought** me a cute watch. 티나는 나에게 귀여운 시계를 사 주었다.

→ A cute watch **was bought for** me by Tina.

5 「주어+동사+목적어+목적격보어」로 된 문장의 수동태는 다음과 같다.

We named the yacht *Atlantis*. 우리는 그 요트를 아틀란티스라고 이름 지었다.

→ The yacht **was named** *Atlantis* by us. 그 요트는 우리에 의해 아틀란티스라고 이름 지어졌다.

He **asked** me to write down my name and phone number. 그는 나에게 이름과 전화번호를 적도록 요청했다.

→ I **was asked** to write down my name and phone number by him. 나는 그에게 이름과 전화번호를 적도록 요청받았다.

|주의| 목적격보어를 주어로 하여 수동태를 만들지 않는다.

(×) ~~Atlantis was named the yacht by us.~~

목적격보어가 동사원형인 경우 「지각동사/사역동사+목적어+동사원형」

My mother **made** me **visit** my grandfather's house after class.
우리 어머니는 나에게 방과 후에 할아버지 댁을 방문하도록 시켰다.

→ I **was made to visit** my grandfather's house after class by my mother. (동사원형을 to부정사로 바꾼다.)

목적격보어가 분사인 경우 「지각동사+목적어+분사」

We **saw** Yuna **skating**. 우리는 연아가 스케이트 타는 것을 보았다.

→ Yuna **was seen skating** (by us). (과거분사나 현재분사를 그대로 써 준다.)

|참고| 1. 절을 목적어로 하는 문장의 수동태: say, believe, know, think, consider, expect 등의 동사의 경우, 두 가지 형태의 수동태 문장을 만들 수 있다.

People **say that** smartphones **have** a bad effect on children. 스마트폰이 아이들에게 나쁜 영향을 미친다고들 한다.

→ **It is said that** smartphones **have** a bad effect on children.

→ Smartphones **are said to have** a bad effect on children.

2. 사역동사 let이 쓰인 문장의 수동태: 「be allowed to+동사원형」의 형태이다.

She **let** me **borrow** her car while she was on vacation. 그녀는 휴가 동안 내가 자신의 차를 빌리는 것을 허락해 주었다.

→ I **was allowed to borrow** her car while she was on vacation.

EXERCISES

정답 및 해설 P. 44

spoil 망치다
disappear into ~속으로 사라지다
crowd 사람들, 군중
tourism industry 관광산업
boom 급속히 발전하다
complex 복잡한
management 경영
structure 구조
establish ~를 설립하다, 창설하다
corporation 법인(法人), 주식회사
reschedule 일정을 변경하다

A 주어진 능동태 문장을 수동태 문장으로 바꿀 수 있다면 바꾸고, 바꿀 수 없다면 ×표를 하시오.

1 Bad weather spoiled my trip to Jejudo.
→ ____________________

2 The man quickly disappeared into the crowd.
→ ____________________

3 The tourism industry is booming in Malaysia.
→ ____________________

4 Someone closed all of the windows in my room.
→ ____________________

5 The company has a complex management structure.
→ ____________________

6 Kiichiro Toyoda established Toyota Motor Corporation in 1937.
→ ____________________

7 The manager has rescheduled the meeting for tomorrow afternoon.
→ ____________________

tutor 가정교사; ~에게 개인 교수를 하다
ancient 고대의
ruin 유적, 폐허

B 주어진 능동태 문장을 수동태 문장으로 바꿔 쓰시오.

1 Jake told me the good news.
→ I ____________________.
→ The good news ____________________.

2 My tutor bought me a notebook.
→ A notebook ____________________.

3 Sally sent Inhye a postcard from Vatican City.
→ A postcard from Vatican City ____________________.

4 Rachel gave Mark some advice about dating.
→ Mark ____________________.
→ Some advice about dating ____________________.

5 The tour guide showed us the way to the ancient ruins.
→ We ____________________.
→ The way to the ancient ruins ____________________.

C 주어진 능동태 문장을 수동태 문장으로 바꿔 쓰시오.

invention 발명품
miracle 기적
chairman (회의의) 의장, 회장
recite ~을 낭송하다
touching 감동적인

1 Diana's father saw her playing basketball.

→ ______________________________

2 Everyone called the new invention a miracle.

→ ______________________________

3 They elected William the new chairman through the vote.

→ ______________________________

4 My mother told me to have breakfast before I went to school.

→ ______________________________

5 Rebecca washed her hair clean in the shower after the food fight.

→ ______________________________

6 We heard Eunhye recite a touching poem at her sister's wedding.

→ ______________________________

D ( ) 안에서 가장 알맞은 것을 고르시오.

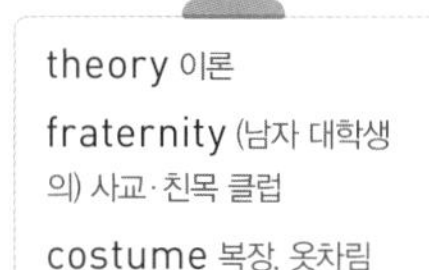
theory 이론
fraternity (남자 대학생의) 사교·친목 클럽
costume 복장, 옷차림

1 ① I heard the baby (cry / to cry) for most of the night.
② The baby was heard (cry / to cry) for most of the night.

2 ① They asked the professor (explain / to explain) the theory.
② The professor was asked (explain / to explain) the theory.

3 ① We all saw the star (shooting / to shoot) across the night sky.
② The star was seen (shooting / shoot) across the night sky.

4 ① The fraternities made new members (wear / to wear) silly costumes.
② New members were made (wear / to wear) silly costumes by the fraternities.

5 ① My teacher allowed me (leave / to leave) school because I was sick.
② I was allowed (leave / to leave) school because I was sick.

6 ① Someone noticed two masked men (to break / breaking) into a house.
② Two masked men were noticed (break / breaking) into a house.

7 ① The teacher saw his students (play / to play) soccer in the playground.
② The students were seen (play / to play) soccer in the playground by the teacher.

다양한 전치사를 사용하는 수동태

by 대신 다른 전치사를 쓰는 경우 (with, at, to, in 등)	Joe's eyes **were filled with** tears. 조의 눈에 눈물이 가득 찼다.
동사구의 수동태	My sister **is taking care of** my cat during my vacation. 내 여동생이 휴가 동안 내 고양이를 돌봐주고 있다. → My cat **is being taken care of** by my sister during my vacation.

1 수동태의 행위자는 일반적으로 「by+행위자」로 나타낸다. 그러나 by 대신에 at, with, in, to 등의 전치사가 사용되기도 한다.

be associated with ~와 관련되다	be bored with/by ~에 지루해하다
be concerned with ~에 관심이 있다	be contented with ~에 만족하다
be covered with/by ~으로 덮여 있다	be crowded with ~으로 붐비다
be disappointed with/in ~에 실망하다	be equipped with ~을 갖추다
be filled with ~으로 가득 차 있다	be provided with ~가 제공되다
be pleased with ~에 기뻐하다	be satisfied with ~에 만족하다

Elisha **was disappointed with** her friend. 엘리샤는 친구에게 실망했다.

Most of the customers **were satisfied with** the service. 대부분의 손님들이 서비스에 만족했다.

be amazed at ~에 놀라다	be frightened at ~에 깜짝 놀라다
be surprised at ~에 놀라다	be shocked at ~에 충격을 받다

The groom **was amazed at** the sight of his bride wearing her wedding dress.
신랑은 웨딩드레스를 입은 신부의 모습에 몹시 놀랐다.

I **was frightened at** the sight of the accident.
나는 사고 광경을 보고 깜짝 놀랐다.

be married to ~와 결혼하다	be known to ~에게 알려지다
be related to ~에 관련되다	be seen to ~에게 보이다
be accustomed to ~에 익숙하다	be expected to ~가 기대되다

The sheriff **was known to** many people in town. 그 보안관은 마을에서 많은 사람들에게 알려졌다.

These crimes could **be related to** each other. 이 범죄들은 서로 연관이 있을 수 있다.

He **is not accustomed to** using chopsticks yet. 그는 아직 젓가락을 사용하는 것에 익숙하지 않다.

|참고| be known for ~으로 유명하다 be known by ~에 의해 알 수 있다 be known as ~으로 알려져 있다

be engaged in ~에 참여하다, 관련되다, 종사하다
be involved in ~에 관련되다
be interested in ~에 관심이 있다
be located in ~에 자리 잡고 있다

My brother has **been interested in** Julia for years.
내 남동생은 여러 해 동안 줄리아에게 관심을 가지고 있다.

He must **be involved in** everything my department does.
그는 우리 부서가 하는 모든 일에 관련되어 있음이 틀림없다.

be composed of ~으로 구성되다
be made of (물리적 변화) ~으로 만들어지다
be tired from ~ 때문에 지치다
be ashamed of ~을 부끄러워하다
be prepared for ~에 대해 준비하다
be made from (화학적 변화) ~으로 만들어지다
be tired of ~에 지치다[지겹다]
be worried[concerned] about ~에 대해 걱정하다

Many parents **are worried about** school safety.
많은 부모들이 학교 안전에 대해 걱정한다.

The drug **is made from** a number of different chemical combinations.
그 약은 수많은 다른 화학적 배합으로 만들어진다.

The statue of David **was made of** marble.
다비드 상은 대리석으로 만들어졌다.

|참고| be made of와 be made from은 모두 '~으로 만들어지다'라는 의미이지만, be made of는 재료의 성분이 변화하지 않고 만들어진 것을 의미하고, be made from은 화학적 과정을 통해 재료의 성분이 변해서 만들어진 경우를 의미한다.

2 「동사+전치사」가 동사 역할을 하는 경우, 이 동사구는 하나의 동사로 취급하여 수동태 문장을 만든다.

agree with ~에게 동의하다
deal with ~을 다루다
pass out ~을 나눠주다
run over (차가) ~을 치다
take away ~을 가져가다
carry out ~을 수행하다, 실행하다
laugh at ~을 비웃다
put off ~을 미루다
send for ~을 부르러 보내다
take care of ~을 돌보다

The teacher will **carry out** the survey. 선생님은 설문 조사를 할 것이다.
→ The survey will **be carried out** by the teacher.

Everybody **laughed at** the architect at first. 처음에는 모두가 그 건축가를 비웃었다.
→ The architect **was laughed at** (by everyone) at first.

Somebody **took away** the flowerpot last night. 어젯밤 누군가가 화분을 가져갔다.
→ The flowerpot **was taken away** (by somebody) last night.

EXERCISES

정답 및 해설 P. 45

cancer 암
engage 약혼하다
flyer 전단지; 비행사
passerby 행인, 오가는 사람

( ) 안에서 알맞은 것을 고르시오.

1 John's cancer is related (at / to) his smoking.

2 The meeting will be put (off / out) until the CEO returns.

3 You need to be prepared (by / for) the coming hurricane.

4 We were very satisfied (to / with) our hotel room in Guam.

5 I was amazed (at / to) the size of Jim's apartment in London.

6 You will be happy if you are content (with / for) what you have.

7 She got married (to / with) an Australian man named Joshua.

8 I was a bit disappointed (with / for) the B+. I was hoping for an A.

9 Suhee's friends were surprised (at / in) the news she was engaged.

10 The streets were covered (with / at) snow when I woke up this morning.

11 Why don't you get some sleep? You may be tired (with / from) the long flight.

12 The flyers from the mall are being passed (by / out) to shoppers.

unfortunately 불행하게도; 유감스럽게도
house chore 집안일
courier 배달원, 배송원; 배송회사, 택배회사

B 주어진 능동태 문장을 수동태 문장으로 바꿔 쓰시오.

1 I'll take care of your dog tonight.
→ Your dog ______________________ tonight.

2 The teacher silently passed out the exam papers.
→ The exam papers ______________________.

3 Unfortunately, we cannot put off the house chores forever.
→ Unfortunately, the house chores ______________________.

4 A bicycle courier almost ran over my pet downtown today.
→ My pet ______________________ downtown today.

5 They are going to deal with Isaac Newton's life in the documentary.
→ Isaac Newton's life ______________________.

6 They will carry out the speaking test for two hours through computers.
→ The speaking test ______________________.

7 His mother took away his motorcycle after she saw him riding without a helmet.
→ His motorcycle ______________________
after she saw him riding without a helmet.

C 빈칸에 공통으로 들어갈 말을 써넣으시오.

1
- Every customer must be provided ________ good service.
- Smoking is associated ________ lung cancer.

2
- I was surprised ________ my nephew's knowledge.
- She said she was laughed ________ in school for being overweight.

3
- This side dish case is made ________ glass, so it's a little heavy.
- When he was young, he was taken care ________ by his grandmother.

4
- The director is famous, so his movies are known ________ many people.
- She is hesitant to take the job because her major is not related ________ the position.

5
- She realized that she was engaged ________ a serious dispute.
- I have been involved ________ this project for two months, but it doesn't seem to progress.

lung cancer 폐암
nephew (남자) 조카
overweight 과체중의, 비만의
side dish case 반찬 통
be hesitant to ~하는 것을 망설이다
major 전공; 주요한
position (일)자리; 위치
dispute 분쟁, 논쟁
progress 진전을 보이다

D 우리말과 같은 뜻이 되도록 주어진 단어를 이용하여 문장을 완성하시오.

1 내 차가 견인차에 의해 견인되었다. (take away)
→ My car ______________________________ a tow truck.

2 해변은 피서객들로 붐볐다. (crowded)
→ The beaches ______________________________ summer vacationers.

3 공항은 저스틴의 해외 팬들로 가득 찼다. (fill)
→ The airport ______________________________ Justin's overseas fans.

4 사람들은 비행기 실종 소식을 듣고 충격을 받았다. (shock)
→ People ______________________________ the news of the missing plane.

5 그 전쟁 때문에, 회담은 무기한 연기되었다. (put off)
→ Because of the war, the talks have ____________________ indefinitely.

6 회의 시작 전에 자료가 배포되어야 한다. (pass out)
→ The materials need to ____________________ before the meeting starts.

7 학생들 중 몇몇은 시험 준비가 되어 있지 않은 듯했다. (prepare)
→ Some of the students seemed not to ____________________ the exam.

8 뇌물 수수 사건에 연루된 사람들은 처벌받아야 한다. (involve, punish)
→ People who have ____________________ the bribery scandal must ____________________.

tow truck 견인차
vacationer 피서객
missing 실종된, 없어진
talks 회담
indefinitely 무기한으로
bribery scandal 뇌물 수수 사건
punish 처벌하다

REVIEW

정답 및 해설 P. 45

polish ~을 닦다
resemble 닮다
homecoming 귀국
political prisoner 정치범
release ~을 석방하다, 해방하다

A ( ) 안에서 알맞은 것을 고르시오.

1 His hair is going to (cut / be cut) by his mom today.

2 A lot of food (ate / was eaten) by the football team.

3 The car (is polishing / is being polished) by my father.

4 The children (resemble / are resembled) their parents.

5 Hilton (described / was described) the situation to me.

6 Rare stamps and coins (collect / are collected) by John.

7 Mom (is preparing / is being prepared) a hot cup of cocoa.

8 Will our English (test / be tested) by the teacher next week?

9 Is she (organizing / being organized) the homecoming parade?

10 By whom was the car (driving / being driven) at the time of the accident?

11 The elephant was seen (attack / to attack) several people in the crowd.

12 A number of political prisoners (will release / will be released) within the next few days.

mixture 혼합물
put into ~에 넣다, (어떤 특질을) 더하다
scold 야단치다
luxurious 호화로운
candidate 지원자
fill in ~을 작성하다, 채우다
application form 지원서[신청서]
serve 제공하다, 차려 주다
transfer (돈을) 이체하다
bank account 은행계좌
chef 요리사
exhibit 전시하다

B 주어진 단어를 문맥에 맞도록 써넣어 문장을 완성하시오.

1 ________________ planted ________________. (our class, these trees)

2 ________________ was handed to ________________. (the boy, the plate)

3 ________________ were worn by ________________. (Victoria, these clothes)

4 ________________ has been lost by ________________. (Nicole, the house key)

5 ________________ was put into the oven by ________________. (Tim, the mixture)

6 ________________ was being scolded by ________________. (her mother, Jane)

7 ________________ didn't buy ________________. (the man, that luxurious ship)

8 ________________ must fill in ________________. (candidates, the application form)

9 ____________ will be served by ____________ at 7 a.m. (the waiter, breakfast)

10 ____________ has been transferred to my bank account by ____________. (Nicky, the money)

11 ______________ are being prepared for the wedding by ______________. (our top chefs, nice meals)

12 ____________________ will be exhibited in ____________________. (the art museum, paintings by Edgar Degas)

C 문장을 읽고, 밑줄 친 「by+행위자」를 생략할 수 있으면 ( )로 표시하시오.

1 That book was written by Haruki Murakami.

2 Is our luggage being brought up by the bellhop?

3 His favorite coat was stolen by someone last night.

4 The man was caught for speeding by the police officer.

5 The NBA finals were watched by millions of people last night.

6 Large areas of forest are being destroyed every day by people.

bellhop (호텔·클럽의) 벨 보이, 급사
for speeding 속도위반으로
final 결승전
destroy ~을 파괴하다

D ( ) 안에서 가장 알맞은 것을 고르시오.

1 ① I doubt I will (find / be found) the missing earring.
② I doubt the missing earring will (find / be found).

2 ① Millions of donuts (eat / are eaten) daily around the world.
② My mom (made / were made) donuts for the party.

3 ① The street (cleans / is cleaned) by street cleaners every day.
② The children (clean / are cleaned) their room every day.

4 ① Bees (have / are had) an excellent sense of smell.
② Our food crops (mostly pollinate / are mostly pollinated) by bees.

5 ① Milk chocolate (invented / was invented) by Daniel Peter.
② An ounce of chocolate (contains / is contained) about 20 mg of caffeine.

6 ① Julius Caesar (knew / was known) as a great swimmer.
② I (know / am known) that Julius Caesar was a Roman military and political leader.

doubt 의심하다, 확신하지 못하다
missing 없어진; 실종된
street cleaner 환경미화원
sense of smell 후각
food crop 식용 작물
pollinate (식물) ~에 수분(授粉)하다
contain ~을 포함하다, ~이 들어 있다
caffeine 카페인
military 군대; 군사의, 육군의
political leader 정치 지도자

E 빈칸에 at, in, with, to 중 알맞은 전치사를 써넣으시오.

1 We are related ___________ each other by marriage.

2 Jim was amazed ___________ the talent of his new students.

3 Our new head office is located ___________ the heart of the city.

4 The mall downtown was crowded ___________ holiday shoppers.

5 Everyone was interested ___________ learning more about his life.

6 My parents have been engaged ___________ agriculture all their lives.

7 I'm pleased ___________ my test results, even though I didn't get an A+.

marriage 결혼
talent 재능, 소질
head office 본사
heart 중심(부); 심장
agriculture 농업

REVIEW PLUS

정답 및 해설 P. 47

document 서류, 문서
burglar 강도
arrest 체포하다
try 재판하다

다음 중 어법상 어색한 것을 고르시오.

① The CD shop was not closed.
② Little yellow fish swam past.
③ Your documents have printed.
④ The blackboard has been cleaned.
⑤ The burglar will be arrested and tried.

B 다음 중 어법상 바른 것을 고르시오.

① When were you told about the new rules?
② The waiter has been brought us the menu.
③ Millions of people will be visited the new Olympic stadium.
④ I'm sorry, madam. This carpet has already been selling.
⑤ Over a thousand people are used this swimming pool each week.

Jack-o'-lantern 호박 초롱(미국 핼러윈 축제 때 쓰는 호박으로 만든 등)
empty (속을) 비우다
content 내용물
scrap out 도려내다
felt-tip pen 펠트펜
potato peeler 감자 껍질 벗기는 도구
tricky 다루기 힘든, 까다로운
creation 창작품, 대조
thrill ~을 오싹하게 하다

다음을 읽고, ( ) 안에서 가장 알맞은 것을 고르시오.

Making your own Jack-o'-lantern is as easy as 1-2-3. Start by cutting a hole in the top of a pumpkin and emptying its contents. Once the seeds (have scraped out / have been scraped out), use a felt-tip pen and draw a scary face on the outside. Then, carefully begin cutting out the face with a small kitchen knife. A potato peeler (should use / should be used) for the trickier areas. Finally, drop in a candle and you're all done. Your creation (is going to thrill / is going to be killed) the neighborhood trick-or-treaters.

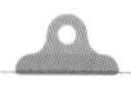

recycle 재활용하다
protect 보호하다
environment 환경
citizen 시민
separate 분리하다
garbage bag 쓰레기 봉투

다음 글의 밑줄 친 부분 중, 어법상 어색한 것을 고르시오.

Recycling helps protect the environment. For example, fifty kilograms of ① recycled paper saves one tree. Some cities ② have trained their citizens to separate garbage. People have to put cans and plastic bottles in different garbage bags. Paper also ③ is keeping separate. The plastic, metal, and paper ④ are taken to special centers for ⑤ recycling.

NEXUS Edu

LEVEL CHART

	초1	초2	초3	초4	초5	초6	중1	중2	중3	고1	고2	고3
VOCA	초등필수 영단어 1–2 · 3–4 · 5–6학년용									WORD PASS		
VOCA					The VOCA + (플러스) 1~7							
VOCA			THIS IS VOCABULARY 입문 · 초급 · 중급					고급 · 어원 · 수능 완성 · 뉴텝스				
VOCA							WORD FOCUS 중등 종합 5000 · 고등 필수 5000 · 고등 종합 9500					
Grammar			초등필수 영문법 + 쓰기 1~2									
Grammar			OK Grammar 1~4									
Grammar			This Is Grammar Starter 1~3									
Grammar					This Is Grammar 초급~고급 (각 2권: 총 6권)							
Grammar						Grammar 공감 1~3						
Grammar						Grammar 101 1~3						
Grammar						Grammar Bridge 1~3 (NEW EDITION)						
Grammar						The Grammar Starter, 1~3						
Grammar							한 권으로 끝내는 필수 구문 1000제					
Grammar								구사일생 (구문독해 Basic) 1~2				
Grammar									구문독해 204 1~2 (개정판)			
Grammar										고난도 구문독해 500		
Grammar								그래머 캡처 1~2				
Grammar									[특급 단기 특강] 어법어휘 모의고사			

THIS IS GRAMMAR

Workbook

넥서스영어교육연구소 지음

내신·토익·토플·텝스 등 각종 시험 완벽 대비, 이것이 **현대 영문법의 결정판**이다!

★원어민이 사용하는 생생한 문장들로 구성된 예문

★단계별, 유형별로 구성된 연습문제와 리뷰문제

1

중급

NEXUS Edu

주어+동사(+수식어)

A **보기** 에서 알맞은 동사를 고르고 시제에 맞게 바꿔 문장을 완성하시오.

보기	go	set	work	appear	rain	arrive	walk

1 그가 모퉁이에서 나타났다.
→ He ____________ around the corner.

2 겨울에는 해가 빨리 진다.
→ In winter, the sun ____________ early.

3 그녀는 이번 휴가 때 집에 갈 것이다.
→ She ____________ ____________ home for this holiday.

4 Brian은 일주일에 세 번 시간외 근무를 한다.
→ Brian ____________ overtime three times a week.

5 학생들 대부분은 학교에 시간 내에 도착한다.
→ Most students ____________ at school in time.

6 올 여름에는 이 지역에 비가 많이 왔다.
→ It ____________ a lot in this region this summer.

7 노부부가 손을 잡고 나란히 걷고 있었다.
→ An old couple ____________ ____________ hand in hand.

B **밑줄 친 단어에 유의하여 해석을 완성하시오.**

1 The wine business pays well.
→ 와인 사업은 ________________ 많다.

2 This medicine works well on colds.
→ 이 약은 감기에 잘 ________________.

3 One hundred dollars will do for you two.
→ 100달러면 너희 둘에게 ________________ 것이다.

4 This phone battery lasts up to 80 hours.
→ 이 전화 배터리는 80시간까지 ________________.

5 English skills count above all in this field.
→ 이 분야에서는 무엇보다도 영어 실력이 ________________.

6 The escalator doesn't work after midnight.
→ 에스컬레이터는 자정 이후에는 ________________ 않는다.

C 우리말과 같은 뜻이 되도록 주어진 말을 이용하여 문장을 완성하시오.

1 그 꼬마가 갑자기 사라졌다. (suddenly, disappear)

→ The little boy ________ ________.

2 그의 사무실은 은행 맞은편에 있다. (be, opposite the bank)

→ His office building ________ ________ ________ ________.

3 학생들 몇 명이 수업 후에 학교에 있었다. (stay, in the school)

→ Some of the students ________ ________ ________ ________ after class.

4 그 사고는 일요일 아침에 발생했다. (happen, on Sunday morning)

→ The accident ________ ________ ________ ________.

5 경제가 빠른 속도로 회복되고 있는 중이다. (recover, very quickly)

→ The economy ________ ________ ________ ________.

6 우리 부모님은 한적한 시골에서 산다. (live in, the quiet countryside)

→ My parents ________ ________ ________ ________ ________.

7 공연이 다음 주 금요일 대강당에서 있을 것이다. (be, in the main hall)

→ The concert ________ ________ ________ ________ ________ ________ next Friday.

D 우리말과 같은 뜻이 되도록 주어진 단어를 배열하시오.

1 정직이 항상 이로운 것은 아니다. (all the time, honesty, pay, doesn't)

→ ____

2 리모컨이 제대로 작동을 안 한다. (work, the remote control, properly, doesn't)

→ ____

3 Emily는 소파에서 TV를 보고 있었다. (on the couch, TV, was watching)

→ Emily ____.

4 신생아는 하루에 17시간가량 잔다. (17 hours a day, sleep, newborn, about, babies)

→ ____

5 그 샌드위치 가게는 매일 아침 8시에 문을 연다. (at 8, the sandwich shop, every morning, opens)

→ ____

6 우리 아버지는 월요일과 금요일을 제외하고 자가용으로 출근한다.
(drives, except on Mondays and Fridays, work, to)

→ My father ____.

주어+동사+주격보어(+수식어)

A 보기 에서 알맞은 말을 골라 우리말과 같은 뜻이 되도록 문장을 완성하시오.

보기	fresh	rich	president	bitter	sour	empty

1 그 노부인은 매우 부자인 듯 보인다.
→ The old lady appears very ____________.

2 그는 젊은 나이에 대통령이 되었다.
→ He became ____________ at a young age.

3 이 우유는 상한 것 같다. 시큼한 냄새가 난다.
→ This milk seems spoiled. It smells ____________.

4 그 건물은 여러 해 동안 비어 있었다.
→ The building stood ____________ for several years.

5 초콜릿을 먹은 후에 커피는 더 쓴 맛이 났다.
→ After I had some chocolate, coffee tasted ____________.

6 그녀는 냉장고를 청소했지만 상쾌한 향기가 나지 않았다.
→ She cleaned the refrigerator, but it didn't smell ____________.

B 밑줄 친 부분을 바르게 고쳐 문장을 다시 쓰시오.

1 I hope your wish comes <u>truly</u>.
→ ____

2 We've run <u>shortly</u> of sugar and eggs.
→ ____

3 She looked <u>beautifully</u> in the blue dress.
→ ____

4 While I was cooking dinner, she fell <u>sleepy</u>.
→ ____

5 The singer seemed <u>nervously</u> on the stage.
→ ____

6 Almost half of the tomatoes have gone <u>badly</u>.
→ ____

7 As soon as she heard the news, she turned <u>paleness</u>.
→ ____

C 우리말과 같은 뜻이 되도록 [A], [B]에서 알맞은 말을 골라 문장을 완성하시오. [시제에 따라 동사를 변형할 것]

보기	[A] 동사			[B] 형용사		
	appear	sound	grow	open	available	intelligent
	get	become	stay	dark	angry	familiar

1 어두워지기 전에 갑시다.
→ Let's go before it ____________ ____________.

2 그 학생은 매우 지적으로 보였다.
→ The student ____________ very ____________.

3 그녀의 전화 목소리는 내게 친숙하게 들렸다.
→ Her voice on the phone ____________ ____________ to me.

4 온라인 예약은 다음 달부터 가능할 것입니다.
→ Online booking will ____________ ____________ next month.

5 그는 그들이 그 결과에 대해 자신을 비난하자 점점 화가 났다.
→ He ____________ ____________ when they criticized him for the result.

6 많은 상점이 월드컵 기간 동안 늦게까지 문을 열 것이다.
→ Many shops will ____________ ____________ late during the World Cup season.

D 우리말과 같은 뜻이 되도록 주어진 단어를 배열하시오.

1 눈이 온 뒤 날씨가 매우 추워졌다. (cold, it, very, got)
→ After it snowed, ____.

2 그들의 아이들은 매우 무례해 보였다. (rude, appeared, very)
→ Their children ____.

3 시간이 지남에 따라 학생들은 지루해졌다. (grew, the students, bored)
→ As time went on ____.

4 Daniel은 이내 소파에서 잠이 들었다. (on the sofa, asleep, fell)
→ Daniel soon ____.

5 Lisa는 토론 시간 동안 조용히 있었다. (the debate, remained, during, silent)
→ Lisa ____.

6 시험을 앞두고 그들은 깨어 있으려고 애쓰고 있다. (awake, are fighting, keep, to)
→ They ____ before the test.

7 그는 동시에 여러 프로젝트에 참여하게 되었다. (involved, projects, became, in, several)
→ He ____ at the same time.

주어+동사+목적어(+수식어)

A 우리말과 같은 뜻이 되도록 주어진 단어를 이용하여 문장을 완성하시오.

1 거리에서 낯선 사람이 내게 다가왔다. (approach)
→ A stranger __________ __________ in the street.

2 모두가 언젠가 죽는다는 사실을 알고 있다. (know)
→ Everyone __________ __________ they are going to die someday.

3 그는 집에 오자마자 자신의 코트를 옷걸이에 걸었다. (put, coat)
→ He __________ __________ __________ on the hanger as soon as he got home.

4 나는 그 일이 나에게 어렵다는 것을 설명해야 했다. (explain)
→ I had to __________ __________ the task was too difficult for me.

5 우리는 이번 주 금요일까지 최종 결정을 내려야 한다. (need, reach)
→ We __________ __________ __________ a final decision by this Friday.

6 당신을 위해 해줄 수 있는 게 없어 유감입니다. (regret, say)
→ I __________ __________ __________ that there's nothing I can do for you.

B 우리말과 같은 뜻이 되도록 [A], [B]에서 알맞은 말을 골라 문장을 완성하시오. [시제에 따라 동사를 변형할 것]

보기	[A]			[B]		
	pour	lay	put	to know	anything	his dirty clothes
	send	steal	want	her eyes	some hot coffee	a gift with a card

1 그는 상점에서 아무것도 훔치지 않았다.
→ He didn't __________ ____________________ in the shop.

2 그녀는 뜨거운 커피를 컵에 따랐다.
→ She __________ ____________________ in a cup.

3 그녀는 사랑스러운 딸아이를 바라보았다.
→ She __________ ____________________ on her lovely baby daughter.

4 그는 더러운 옷을 세탁기에 넣었다.
→ He __________ ____________________ into the washing machine.

5 나는 Brad와 그의 가족에 대해 더 많이 알고 싶었다.
→ I __________ ____________________ more about Brad and his family.

6 그녀는 가장 친한 친구에게 카드와 함께 선물을 보냈다.
→ She __________ ____________________ to her best friend.

C 어법상 어색한 부분을 바르게 고쳐 문장을 다시 쓰시오.

1 He didn't mention about the problem.

→ ____________________

2 She married with Michael on Christmas Eve.

→ ____________________

3 The houses in this town resemble with one another.

→ ____________________

4 The phone kept ringing, but she didn't answer to it.

→ ____________________

5 The salesperson explained about how to use the machine.

→ ____________________

6 I won't be at home because I have to attend to a wedding.

→ ____________________

7 Feel free to call me if you want to discuss about the matter.

→ ____________________

8 Don't forget to knock before you enter into the professor's office.

→ ____________________

D 우리말과 같은 뜻이 되도록 주어진 단어를 배열하시오.

1 그녀는 부끄러움에 양손으로 머리를 감쌌다. (buried, in her hands, her head,)

→ She ____________________ out of shame.

2 엄마가 오시기 전에 방을 치우는 게 좋을 거야. (your room, had better, clean)

→ You ____________________ before your mom gets home.

3 Brian은 여자 친구를 부모님께 소개했다. (to his parents, introduced, his girlfriend)

→ Brian ____________________.

4 그녀는 학교를 졸업하자마자 커피숍을 열었다. (left, opened, school, a coffee shop)

→ She ____________________ right after she ____________________.

5 나는 교통 체증으로 제시간에 올 수 없었다고 설명했다. (that, couldn't, I, come, I, explained, on time)

→ ____________________ because of the heavy traffic.

6 Jessica가 거기 가는 길을 아니까 우리는 그녀를 따라가기만 하면 된다. (get there, how to, knows, her, follow)

→ Jessica ____________________, so we can just ____________________.

주어+동사+간접목적어+직접목적어

A **보기** 에서 알맞은 전치사를 골라 문장을 완성하시오. [중복 사용 가능]

보기	to	for	of

1 Can I ask a favor __________ you?
2 He handed his business card __________ me.
3 She wrote a letter of apology __________ me.
4 My friend lent her lecture notes __________ me.
5 They promised support __________ me for a year.
6 My father bought a laptop __________ me for my birthday.
7 He will get the receipt and your credit card __________ you.
8 The flight attendant brought some cookies and juice __________ us.
9 My grandmother cooked curry and rice __________ me and my sister.
10 Someday I will build a house __________ my parents in the countryside.

B **보기** 와 같이 어법상 어색한 부분을 바르게 고쳐 문장을 다시 쓰시오.

보기
I've emailed the related data for you.
→ I've emailed the related data to you.

1 Will you show the painting for me?
→ ______________________________

2 She taught to me how to cook spaghetti.
→ ______________________________

3 He needed to ask a few questions her.
→ ______________________________

4 Will you get a glass of iced water of me?
→ ______________________________

5 The artist sold her paintings for an old lady.
→ ______________________________

6 Maria teaches basic cooking skills for young children.
→ ______________________________

7 My father makes simple dishes like sandwiches to us on weekends.
→ ______________________________

C 보기 와 같이 두 문장이 같은 뜻이 되도록 문장을 완성하시오.

보기	The police officer found me my lost wallet. → The police officer found my lost wallet for me.

1 Mike handed me some books at the station.

→ ______________________________

2 She made her newborn baby a black and white mobile.

→ ______________________________

3 They showed their tickets to a crew member at the gate.

→ ______________________________

4 You'd better tell the truth to him before he gets more upset.

→ ______________________________

5 My grandmother sent me gloves and a muffler this Christmas.

→ ______________________________

6 During the class, a few students asked the teacher some questions.

→ ______________________________

D 우리말과 같은 뜻이 되도록 주어진 단어를 이용하여 문장을 완성하시오.

1 나가기 싫으면, 내가 너를 위해 룸서비스를 주문해 줄게. (order, room service)

→ If you don't want to go out, I'll ______ ______ ______ ______.

2 그녀는 우리에게 앨범에 있는 자신의 가족 사진들을 보여주었다. (show, her family photos)

→ She ______ ______ ______ ______ ______ in the album.

3 그가 큰 실수를 저질렀음에도 나는 그에게 또 한 번 기회를 주었다. (give, another chance)

→ I ______ ______ ______ ______ even though he made a big mistake.

4 우리 어머니는 내 생일파티를 위해 내게 훌륭한 저녁을 만들어주셨다. (cook, a great dinner)

→ My mother ______ ______ ______ ______ ______ for my birthday party.

5 그 싱어송라이터는 자신의 아내에게 아름다운 음악을 만들어주었다. (make, wife, a beautiful)

→ The singer-song writer ______ ______ ______ ______ ______ song.

6 그녀는 자신의 딸에게 아름다운 웨딩드레스를 만들어주었다. (make, a beautiful wedding dress)

→ She ______ ______ ______ ______ ______ ______ her daughter.

주어+동사+목적어+목적격보어

A 밑줄 친 부분을 바르게 고쳐 쓰시오.

1 I found his lecture interestingly. ____________

2 They named their son to Peter. ____________

3 His defeat made me to feel disappointed. ____________

4 She heard them to argue in the living room. ____________

5 She asked me return the book to the library. ____________

6 They call their youngest daughter to "Princess." ____________

7 We thought her very nicely and warm-heartedly. ____________

8 They elected him to the leader of the Reading Club. ____________

9 I believed him very honestly, responsibly and reliably. ____________

B 보기 에서 알맞은 말을 골라 우리말과 같은 뜻이 되도록 문장을 완성하시오.

보기 participate take show up adjust grow make

1 나는 그가 제시간에 나타나는 것을 본 적이 없다.
→ I've never seen him ____________ on time.

2 그들은 내가 새로운 곳에 적응하도록 도와주었다.
→ They helped me ____________ to a new place.

3 그는 내가 그 콘테스트에 참여하도록 격려했다.
→ He encouraged me ____________ in the contest.

4 우리 부모님은 내게 빠른 결정을 내리도록 강요했다.
→ My parents forced me ____________ a quick decision.

5 우리 선생님은 내게 컴퓨터 수업을 들으라고 말씀하셨다
→ My teacher told me ____________ the computer class.

6 태양은 식물을 자라게 하고, 식물은 우리에게 식량을 제공한다.
→ The sun makes plants ____________, and plants give us food.

C 우리말과 같은 뜻이 되도록 주어진 단어를 이용하여 문장을 완성하시오.

1 그가 사무실로 돌아오면 알려드릴게요. (let, know)

→ I will ____________ ____________ ____________ when he's back in the office.

2 나는 네가 똑같은 실수를 하지 않았으면 좋겠어. (want, make)

→ I don't ____________ ____________ ____________ ____________ the same mistake.

3 그 충격적인 소식은 나를 종일 잠 못 들게 했다. (keep, awake)

→ The shocking news ____________ ____________ ____________ all night.

4 우리 어머니는 내게 정원의 꽃에 물을 주도록 시켰다. (have, water)

→ My mother ____________ ____________ ____________ the flowers in the garden.

5 우리 아버지는 우리 오빠에게 내 숙제를 돕도록 시켰다. (make, help)

→ My father ____________ ____________ ____________ ____________ me with my homework.

6 나는 악취가 완전히 사라질 때까지 창문을 열어두었다. (keep, open)

→ I ____________ ____________ ____________ ____________ until the bad smell disappeared completely.

7 나는 네가 이번 주 금요일까지 프로젝트를 마쳤으면 한다. (want, finish)

→ I ____________ ____________ ____________ ____________ the project by this Friday.

D 우리말과 같은 뜻이 되도록 주어진 단어를 배열하시오.

1 우리는 그 회의가 유익하다고 생각했다. (found, we, useful, the meeting)

→ ____

2 그녀는 그를 두 시간이나 커피숍에서 기다리게 했다. (in the coffee shop, kept, waiting, him)

→ She ____ for two hours.

3 그의 부모님은 그를 설득하여 법학을 전공으로 선택하게 했다. (to, persuaded, choose, law, him)

→ His parents ____ as his major.

4 많은 사람들이 약 5분 동안 땅이 흔들리는 것을 느꼈다. (shake, for about five minutes, felt, the earth)

→ Many people ____.

5 그는 많은 사실을 알고 있어서 나는 그를 걸어 다니는 백과사전이라 부른다. (him, a walking encyclopedia, call)

→ He knows many facts, so I ____.

6 우리 부모님은 내가 친구 집에서 자고 오는 것을 절대 허락하지 않는다.
(to, me, at my friend's place, allow, sleep over)

→ My parents never ____.

현재 시제

A 우리말과 같은 뜻이 되도록 주어진 동사를 알맞게 바꿔 쓰시오.

1 내가 돌아올 때까지 여기 있을래? (come)
→ Can you stay here until I ___________ back?

2 그녀는 손톱을 깨무는 버릇이 있다. (have)
→ She ___________ a habit of biting her fingernails.

3 내가 런던에 도착하면 너에게 전화할게. (arrive)
→ I'll call you when I ___________ in London.

4 나는 그녀가 이 선물을 좋아할지 궁금하다. (like)
→ I wonder if she ___________ ___________ this present.

5 내일 비가 온다면 우리는 그냥 집에 있을 것이다. (rain)
→ We'll just stay home if it ___________ tomorrow.

6 그는 일어나자마자 물 한 잔을 마신다. (get up)
→ He drinks a glass of water as soon as he ___________ ___________.

7 도서관 카드가 없으면 책을 빌릴 수 없습니다. (have)
→ You can't borrow a book unless you ___________ a library card.

8 엄마가 집에 오기 전에 너는 숙제를 끝내야 한다. (get)
→ You need to finish your homework before your mom ___________ home.

B 보기 에서 알맞은 말을 골라 우리말과 같은 뜻이 되도록 문장을 완성하시오.

보기 buy give start blend depart

1 기름과 물은 서로 섞이지 않는다.
→ Oil and water _______________ together.

2 다음 부산행 비행기는 오후 3시에 출발한다.
→ The next flight to Busan _______________ at 3 p.m.

3 우리 아빠는 매일 아침 나를 차로 학교에 데려다 주신다.
→ My dad _______________ me a ride to school every morning.

4 연극은 7시에 시작하니까 지금 저녁을 먹는 게 어때?
→ The play _______________ at 7, so why don't we have dinner now?

5 미리 표를 사지 않는다면 뮤지컬을 볼 수 없을 것이다.
→ We won't be able to see the musical unless we _______________ tickets in advance.

C 우리말과 같은 뜻이 되도록 주어진 단어를 이용하여 문장을 완성하시오.

1 인간의 몸의 60–70%는 물로 구성되어 있다. (human body, consist of)

→ 60-70% of ______ ______ ______ ______ ______.

2 우리 가족은 모두 한 달에 한 번 모인다. (my whole family, get together)

→ ______ ______ ______ ______ ______ once a month.

3 구명조끼를 입지 않으면 수영장에 들어갈 수 없다. (wear, a life jacket)

→ You can't go in the pool unless ______ ______ ______ ______ ______.

4 나는 다른 사람들 앞에서 이야기를 하는 것이 편하지 않다. (be comfortable with)

→ I ______ ______ ______ ______ talking in front of others.

5 대전행 기차가 3번 플랫폼에서 9시 30분에 출발합니다. (the train for Daejeon, leave)

→ ______ ______ ______ ______ ______ at 9:30 from platform 3.

6 그녀는 일주일에 7시간씩 학교 도서관에서 자원봉사를 한다. (volunteer, at the school library)

→ ______ ______ ______ ______ ______ ______ for seven hours a week.

7 우리 부모님은 일 년에 한 번 건강 검진을 받으신다. (my parents, receive, medical checkups)

→ ______ ______ ______ ______ ______ once a year.

D 우리말과 같은 뜻이 되도록 주어진 단어를 배열하시오.

1 많은 사람들이 신의 존재를 믿는다. (God, believe in, many people)

→ ______________________________

2 그는 유명한 배우를 떠올리게 한다. (me, a famous actor, of, reminds, he)

→ ______________________________

3 회의가 끝나면 우리는 함께 저녁을 먹을 것이다. (the meeting, after, ends)

→ We're going to have dinner together ______________________________.

4 나는 일주일에 세 번 개를 산책시킨다. (I, a week, my dog, three times, walk)

→ ______________________________

5 만약 네가 내 컴퓨터를 고쳐준다면 근사한 저녁을 대접할게. (fix, if, my computer, you)

→ I'll treat you to a fabulous dinner ______________________________.

6 태양은 동쪽에서 뜨고 서쪽으로 진다. (in the east, the sun, sets, and, rises, in the west)

→ ______________________________

7 우리 아이들은 대개 오후 5시면 집에 돌아온다. (are, at 5 p.m., my children, usually, back home)

→ ______________________________

과거 시제

A 우리말과 같은 뜻이 되도록 주어진 동사를 알맞게 바꿔 쓰시오.

1 나는 전공을 영문학으로 바꿨다. (change)
→ I ___________ my major to English literature.

2 누군가 어젯밤에 내 차를 긁어놓았다. (scratch)
→ Somebody ___________ my car last night.

3 공룡은 수백만 년 전에 멸종했다. (become)
→ Dinosaurs ___________ extinct millions of years ago.

4 Chris는 보통 버스를 타고 등교하지만, 어제는 지하철을 탔다. (go, take)
→ Chris usually ___________ to school by bus, but she ___________ the subway yesterday.

5 나는 10분 전에 책상 위에 두었다. 근데 지금 어디 있는 거지? (put, be)
→ I ___________ my wallet on the desk 10 minutes ago. But where ___________ it now?

B 보기 에서 알맞은 말을 골라 우리말과 같은 뜻이 되도록 문장을 완성하시오.

[1-3] 보기 hurt wait break out be ended show up slip

1 우리 어머니는 눈길에 미끄러져서 팔을 다쳤다.
→ My mother ______________ on a snowy road and ______________ her arm.

2 나는 그를 두 시간 동안 기다렸으나 끝내 나타나지 않았다.
→ I ______________ for him for two hours, but he never ______________.

3 한국 전쟁은 1950년에 발발하여 1953년에 중단되었다.
→ The Korean War ______________ in 1950 and ______________ in 1953.

[4-6] 보기 be worried fall off be move into be able to reach live

4 그는 Judy에게 휴대폰으로 연락이 되지 않아 걱정했다.
→ He ________________ because he ________________ Judy on her cell phone.

5 우리는 이 아파트로 이사 오기 전에 시골에 살았다.
→ We ________________ in the countryside before we ________________ this apartment.

6 버스 한 대가 한 시간 전에 다리에서 떨어졌고, 많은 승객들이 지금 병원에 입원해 있다.
→ A bus ________________ a bridge an hour ago, and many passengers ________________ in the hospital now.

C 우리말과 같은 뜻이 되도록 주어진 단어를 이용하여 문장을 완성하시오.

1 어제 네게 전화하는 것을 잊어버려서 미안해. (forget, to call)

→ I'm sorry I ________ ________ ________ ________ yesterday.

2 갈릴레오는 지구가 태양 주위를 돈다고 믿었다. (believe, move)

→ Galileo ________ that the earth ________ around the sun.

3 대공황은 1929년에 시작되어 1939년까지 계속되었다. (begin, last)

→ The Great Depression ________ in 1929, and it ________ until 1939.

4 김연아는 2010년 밴쿠버 올림픽에서 금메달을 땄다. (win, the gold medal)

→ Kim Yu-na ________ ________ ________ ________ in the 2010 Vancouver Winter Olympics.

5 나는 그에게 수차례 사과했지만 그는 쉽게 화를 풀지 않았다. (say sorry, let go)

→ I ________ ________ to him many times, but he ________ ________ ________ of his anger easily.

6 그는 2004년에 대학에 입학했고 2009년에 졸업했다. (get into college, graduate)

→ He ________ ________ ________ in 2004 and ________ in 2009.

7 나는 장을 보러 가야 했지만, 시장은 일요일에 6시에 닫는다. (need, to do the shopping, the market, close)

→ I ________ ________ ________ ________ ________, but ________ ________ ________ at 6 on Sundays.

D 우리말과 같은 뜻이 되도록 주어진 단어를 배열하시오.

1 여름휴가 때 어디 갔었어? (on your summer vacation, did, go, you)

→ Where ________________________________?

2 작년에는 춥고 눈이 많이 왔다. (last year, cold, and, a lot, was, snowed)

→ It ________________________________.

3 나는 마지막 순간에 마음을 바꿨다. (changed, at the last minute, my mind)

→ I ________________________________.

4 대공황 동안에 많은 사람들이 일자리를 잃었다. (lost, many people, their jobs)

→ During the Great Depression, ________________________________.

5 너는 어제 너무 운동을 많이 했어. 그래서 온 몸이 쑤신 거야. (yesterday, did, exercise, too much)

→ You ________________________________. That's why you ache all over.

6 모차르트는 다섯 살 때 첫 작품을 작곡했다. (5 years old, when, composed, was, he, his first work)

→ Mozart ________________________________.

7 그녀는 대학 시절에 공부를 잘해서 학기마다 장학금을 받았다. (a scholarship, did, got, in college, well)

→ She ________________, so she ________________ every semester.

Unit 08 미래 시제

A 주어진 단어와 will 또는 be going to를 이용하여 문장을 완성하시오.

1 집에 오는 길에 빵 좀 사오겠니? (buy)

→ ______ you ______ some bread on the way home?

2 너 정말 피곤해 보여. 내가 집까지 태워다줄게. (give)

→ You look so tired. I ______ ______ you a ride home.

3 상자가 정말 무거워 보여. 상자 나르는 것을 도와줄게. (help)

→ The box seems so heavy. I ______ ______ you with it.

4 어떻게 할지 이미 결정했어. 난 일을 그만두지 않을 거야. (not, quit)

→ I've already made up my mind. I ______ ______ ______ ______ ______ my job.

5 호텔 방을 예약하는 것을 잊어버릴 뻔 했다. 지금 예약해야겠다. (book)

→ I almost forgot to book a hotel room. I ______ ______ it now.

6 공항에 갈 필요 없어. Sarah가 내 여동생을 마중 나가기로 했어. (pick up)

→ You don't have to go to the airport. Sarah ______ ______ ______ ______ ______ my sister.

7 이번 휴가는 이미 모든 게 계획되어 있어. 우리는 특별한 파티를 열기로 했어. (have)

→ Everything is already planned for this holiday. We ______ ______ ______ ______ a special party.

B 두 문장의 의미가 통하도록 be going to 또는 진행형을 사용하여 문장을 완성하시오.

1 He will get promoted next year.

→ He ______ ______ ______ ______ ______ next year.

2 Will you come to Jennie's birthday party tonight?

→ ______ ______ ______ to Jennie's birthday party tonight?

3 What time are you going to meet your tutor tomorrow?

→ What time ______ ______ ______ your tutor tomorrow?

4 According to the weather forecast, it will snow tomorrow.

→ According to the weather forecast, it ______ ______ ______ ______ tomorrow.

C 우리말과 같은 뜻이 되도록 주어진 말을 이용하여 문장을 완성하시오.

1 그는 64세이다. 그는 내년에 은퇴할 것이다. (retire, next year)

→ He is 64 years old. ________ ________ ________ ________ ________ ________ ________.

2 비행기가 막 이륙하려는 참이야. 안전벨트 매. (the plane, take off)

→ ________ ________ ________ ________ ________ ________ ________. Fasten your seatbelt.

3 너 오늘밤 뭐 할 거니? 나랑 같이 저녁 먹을래? (do, tonight)

→ What are ________ ________ ________? Do you want to have dinner with me?

4 영화는 6시 30분에 시작해. 그러니까 늦지 마. (the movie, start at, 6:30)

→ ________ ________ ________ ________ ________, so don't be late.

5 그녀의 비행기는 내일 모레 11시 정각에 도착한다. (plane, arrive at, 11 o'clock)

→ ________ ________ ________ ________ ________ the day after tomorrow.

6 나는 이번 주말에 계획이 있어. 야구 경기를 볼 예정이야. (watch, a baseball game)

→ I have a plan for the weekend. ________ ________ ________ ________ ________ ________ ________ ________.

7 오늘 오후에 사무실로 돌아오지 않을 겁니다. 그러니 무슨 일이 생기면 전화하세요. (come back, anything, happen)

→ I am ________ ________ ________ to the office this afternoon. So call me if ________ ________.

D 우리말과 같은 뜻이 되도록 주어진 단어를 배열하시오.

1 정말 미안해. 다시는 그런 일 없을 거야. (won't, again, it, happen)

→ I'm so sorry. ________________________________

2 그녀 걱정은 하지 마. 곧 괜찮아질 거야. (soon, be, she, will, okay)

→ Don't worry about her. ________________________________

3 Lisa는 내년 3월에 결혼할 예정이다. (getting, next March, is, married)

→ Lisa ________________________________.

4 지갑을 잃어버렸어. 돈을 좀 빌려줄래? (you, me, will, some money, lend)

→ I've lost my purse. ________________________________

5 너무 피곤해서 이번 주말에는 외출하지 않을 거야. (going out, am, this weekend, I, not)

→ I'm too tired, so ________________________________.

6 네가 올 수 있을지 없을지 확실하지 않으면 내가 모임을 취소할게. (the meeting, I, cancel, will)

→ If you're not sure whether you can come, ________________________________.

7 우리 어머니는 이번 주 토요일에 고등학교 동창회에 나갈 예정이다.
(to, this Saturday, is going, her high school reunion)

→ My mother ________________________________.

현재진행

A 주어진 말을 현재나 현재진행으로 바꿔 문장을 완성하시오. [미래는 진행으로 쓸 것]

1 ____________ you ____________ abroad every year? (travel)

2 Please be quiet. Ally ____________ ____________ in her room. (study)

3 He ____________ to work overtime, especially on Friday. (hate)

4 We ____________ ____________ a break from our homework now. (take)

5 ____________ you ____________ to Brian's birthday party tomorrow? (go)

6 We ____________ ____________ a teaching practice next semester. (have)

7 It ____________ ____________ outside. We must bring an umbrella. (pour)

8 She usually ____________ a hot bath when she ____________ tired after workouts. (take, feel)

9 My cousin came to my house, and she ____________ ____________ with me this month. (stay)

B 밑줄 친 부분을 바르게 고쳐 문장을 다시 쓰시오.

1 William is resembling his father very much.

→ ____

2 August is being the hottest month of the year.

→ ____

3 Tommy is having breakfast at 7 every morning.

→ ____

4 Where is Mr. Park? Does he meet a client now?

→ ____

5 This pizza is tasting too greasy. I need some more soda.

→ ____

6 We are belonging to a hiking club and meet once a month.

→ ____

7 I think she is knowing why they had a fight last Wednesday.

→ ____

8 I am appreciating that you were not badly hurt in the accident.

→ ____

9 I am preferring to study in the library rather than at home.

→ ____

C 우리말과 같은 뜻이 되도록 주어진 단어를 이용하여 문장을 완성하시오.

1 실은 네 이름이 영어로는 웃기게 들려. (sound, funny)

→ Actually, your name ________ ________ in English.

2 나 이번 주 토요일에 집들이를 할 거야. (have, a housewarming party)

→ I ________ ________ ________ ________ ________ this Saturday.

3 나중에 얘기할 수 있을까? 나는 지금 저녁을 먹고 있어. (have, dinner)

→ Can we talk about it later? I ________ ________ ________ now.

4 나는 이번 학기에 경제학 수업을 듣고 있다. (take, an economics class)

→ I ________ ________ ________ ________ ________ this semester.

5 전공이 나에게 맞지 않아 전공을 바꿔 볼까 생각 중이다. (think of, change)

→ I ________ ________ ________ ________ my major because it doesn't suit me.

6 그녀는 항상 욕실 불 끄는 것을 잊어버린다. (always, forget, to turn off, the light)

→ She ________ always ________ to turn off the light in the bathroom.

7 그녀는 언제나 자신이 아들이 10시 전에 잠자리에 들도록 하고 있다. (always, have)

→ She ________ ________ her son go to bed before 10.

D 우리말과 같은 뜻이 되도록 주어진 단어를 배열하시오.

1 나는 이번 주에 야간 근무를 하고 있다. (the night shift, am, on, working)

→ I ________________________________ this week.

2 학생들은 방과 후에 햄버거를 먹을 것이다. (after school, having, are, hamburgers)

→ The students ________________________________.

3 그는 지금 고기 한 덩이의 무게를 재고 있다. (now, weighing, a piece of, is, meat)

→ He ________________________________.

4 그녀는 긴 금발머리를 가진 소녀를 부러워한다. (long blonde hair, envies, with, girls)

→ She ________________________________.

5 나는 내일 처음으로 댄스스포츠 수업을 들을 거야. (taking, dance sports lesson, am, my first)

→ I ________________________________ tomorrow.

6 Henry는 일요일에는 주로 교회에서 대부분의 시간을 보낸다. (most of the time, usually, in church, spends)

→ Henry ________________________________ on Sundays.

7 내 친구들이 내일 우리 집에 올 것이다. 그래서 나는 청소하고 있다.
(to my house, cleaning up, are, am, coming, tomorrow)

→ My friends ________________. So I ________________.

과거진행

A 보기 에서 동사를 골라 시제에 맞게 바꿔 대화를 완성하시오.

보기 argue sleep snowboard walk watch help

1 A What were you doing at 10 last night?
  B I ____________ a movie with my sister at home.

2 A What were you doing after class yesterday?
  B I ____________ my dog in the park.

3 A What were you doing when I called you yesterday?
  B I ____________ my mother prepare dinner.

4 A I called you at 9:30 p.m. Why didn't you answer my call?
  B I couldn't answer it because I ____________ then.

5 A Do you know why they haven't been speaking for an hour?
  B I don't know. They ____________ when I got home.

6 A What happened to your leg?
  B While I ____________, I bumped into someone and fell down.

B 보기 와 같이 두 문장을 하나의 문장으로 만드시오.

보기
• I hurt my finger.
• I was opening a can of cola.
→ I ___hurt___ my finger while I ___was opening___ a can of cola.

1 • I was taking a shower.
  • My mother made a snack for me.
  → While I ____________, my mother ____________ a snack for me.

2 • I was working on my laptop.
  • The electricity suddenly went off.
  → When I ____________ on my laptop, the electricity suddenly ____________.

3 • I was walking to school this morning.
  • I ran into an old friend.
  → When I ____________ to school this morning, I ____________ an old friend.

C 우리말과 같은 뜻이 되도록 주어진 단어를 이용하여 문장을 완성하시오.

1 그녀는 수영을 하다가 다리에 쥐가 났다. (have a cramp, swim)

→ She ________ ________ ________ in her leg while ________ ________ ________.

2 길을 걷고 있는데 천둥이 치기 시작했다. (walk, begin)

→ I ________ ________ down the street when it ________ to thunder.

3 그녀는 당근을 잘게 썰다가 손가락을 베었다. (cut, her finger, while, chop, carrots)

→ She ________ ________ ________ ________ ________ ________ ________ ________.

4 그녀는 어젯밤 중간고사 시험공부를 하고 있었다. (study, last night)

→ She ________ ________ for the midterms ________ ________.

5 작년 이맘때 그녀는 런던에서 영어를 가르치고 있었다. (at this time, last year, teach)

→ ________ ________ ________ ________ ________, she ________ ________ ________ in London.

6 어제 내가 집에 늦게 들어왔을 때, 엄마는 주무시고 있었다. (sleep, when, get, home, late, yesterday)

→ Mom ________ ________ ________ ________ ________ ________ ________ ________.

7 어머니가 그녀를 불렀을 때 Jessica는 음악을 듣고 있었다. (listen to, when, her mother, call)

→ Jessica ________ ________ ________ music ________ ________ ________ ________ ________.

D 우리말과 같은 뜻이 되도록 주어진 단어를 배열하시오.

1 친구가 전화했을 때, 그는 운전 중이었다. (his friend, him, was driving, called, when)

→ He ________________________________.

2 작년 이맘때쯤 그녀는 유럽 여행 중이었다. (around Europe, was traveling, at this time last year)

→ She ________________________________.

3 거리를 걷고 있었는데 갑자기 누가 나를 따라오는 것을 느꼈다. (when, the street, was walking down, I)

→ ________________________________, I suddenly sensed somebody following me.

4 Lily는 상사랑 이야기 중이어서 어떤 전화도 받을 수 없었다. (her boss, she, was talking to, call, take, couldn't)

→ Lily ________________________________, so ________________________________.

5 그가 집에 도착했을 때 나는 설거지를 하고 있었다. (the dishes, he, home, was washing, when, arrived)

→ I ________________________________.

6 그 사고가 났을 때, 그는 친구들과 축구를 하고 있었다.
(happened, was playing, with his friends, the accident, soccer, when)

→ He ________________________________.

미래진행

A 보기 에서 알맞은 동사를 골라 대화를 완성하시오.

보기 attend use visit work teach study pack

1 A What will you be doing next Saturday?
B I ____________ ____________ ____________ to move out.

2 A What will you be doing in 10 years?
B I ____________ ____________ ____________ English to young students.

3 A ____________ you ____________ ____________ your bicycle tomorrow?
B No, I won't. Do you want to use it?

4 A Are you going to be home this Sunday?
B No. I ____________ ____________ ____________ my friend in the hospital.

5 A What will you be doing this time next year?
B I ____________ ____________ ____________ abroad this time next year.

6 A Don't call me before 6. I ____________ ____________ ____________ in the office.
B Okay. I will call you at 7.

7 A Why doesn't he answer the phone?
B He is at the airport. He ____________ ____________ ____________ his uncle's wedding next week in New York.

B 보기 와 같이 두 문장을 하나의 문장으로 만드시오.

보기
The tests begin at 9 and end at 4. + I will take the tests.
→ I ____will be taking the tests____ at 3.

1 (a) A repair person will come to my home at 3.
(b) He will fix my computer until 4.
→ A repair person ________________________________ at 3:30.

2 (a) Her parents promised her a cell phone.
(b) She will use a new cell phone next month.
→ She ________________________________ next month.

3 (a) He is going to drive across the country for a month.
(b) He will begin the trip tomorrow.
→ He ________________________________ in a week.

C 우리말과 같은 뜻이 되도록 주어진 동사를 이용하여 문장을 완성하시오.

1 나는 다음 달까지 내 사촌 집에 머무를 것이다. (stay, until)
→ I ________ ________ ________ at my uncle's house ________ ________ ________.

2 그는 오늘 밤에 거실에서 자고 있을 것이다. (sleep)
→ He ________ ________ ________ in the living room tonight.

3 그녀는 가족과 함께 크리스마스를 보내고 있을 것이다. (spend, Christmas)
→ She ________ ________ ________ ________ with her family.

4 공항에 도착하면 내가 너를 기다리고 있을 거야. (wait, when, arrive)
→ I ________ ________ ________ for you ________ ________ ________ at the airport.

5 그는 이번 여름 방학 때 스페인어를 공부할 예정이다. (study, summer vacation)
→ He ________ ________ ________ Spanish ________ ________ ________.

6 그녀는 친구와 함께 점심을 먹을 예정이다. (have, lunch)
→ She ________ ________ ________ ________ with her friend.

7 내년 이맘때 우리는 LA에서 즐거운 시간을 보내고 있을 것이다. (have, this time)
→ We ________ ________ ________ a great time in LA ________ ________ ________ ________.

D 우리말과 같은 뜻이 되도록 주어진 단어를 배열하시오.

1 우리 딸은 내년 봄에 대학에 다니고 있을 것이다. (be, next spring, will, to college, going)
→ My daughter ________________________________.

2 우리 할머니는 오늘 밤에 우리와 함께 지내고 있을 것이다. (staying, be, will, tonight, with us)
→ My grandmother ________________________________.

3 천천히 와. 커피 한 잔 하면서 너를 기다리고 있을게. (will, over a cup of coffee, for you, be, waiting)
→ Take your time. I ________________________________.

4 그녀를 쉽게 찾을 수 있을 거야. 그녀는 파란 드레스를 입고 있을 거야. (a blue dress, will, wearing, be)
→ You will be able to find her easily. She ________________________________.

5 내일 아침 네가 일어나면, 밖에는 눈이 오고 있을 거야. (outside, will, it, snowing, be, tomorrow morning)
→ When you get up ________________, ________________.

6 그 신형 비행기는 800명 이상의 승객을 실어 나를 것이다. (carrying, 800 passengers, be, will, more than)
→ The new plane ________________________________.

7 선생님이 교실에 안 계실 때 그들은 공부하고 있지 않을 것이다. (be, their teacher, won't, isn't, studying, while)
→ They ________________________________ in the classroom.

현재완료

A 두 문장의 의미가 통하도록 문장을 완성하시오.

1 John lost his wallet, and he still doesn't have it.
→ John ________ ________ his wallet.

2 I bought this cell phone last year, and I'm still using it.
→ I ________ ________ this cell phone since last year.

3 Mr. Choi just went out, and he won't be here for an hour.
→ Mr. Choi ________ ________ ________.

4 I moved to Busan three years ago, and I still live there.
→ I ________ ________ in Busan for three years.

5 My aunt gave me a dog 10 years ago, and I still have it.
→ I ________ ________ my dog for 10 years.

6 I started to study Japanese three years ago, and I'm still studying it.
→ I ________ ________ Japanese for three years.

7 I put my report card on the table a few minutes ago, and it's still there.
→ I ________ just ________ my report card on the table.

B 밑줄 친 부분을 바르게 고쳐 문장을 다시 쓰시오.

1 I have <u>gone</u> to Africa once.
→ ________________________________

2 He <u>has gone</u> to Canada two years ago.
→ ________________________________

3 The shop <u>doesn't open</u> for business yet.
→ ________________________________

4 Someone <u>have broken</u> a window yesterday.
→ ________________________________

5 She hasn't eaten anything <u>since</u> eight hours.
→ ________________________________

6 I <u>have had</u> a lobster for the first time yesterday.
→ ________________________________

C 우리말과 같은 뜻이 되도록 주어진 동사를 이용하여 문장을 완성하시오.

1 유럽의 몇 개 국가에 가봤어요? (be, to)

→ How many European countries ______ ______ ______ ______?

2 우리는 2008년 이후로 이 아파트에 살고 있다. (live, 2008)

→ We ______ ______ in this apartment ______ ______.

3 신분증을 집에 놓고 왔어요. (leave, my identification card)

→ I ______ ______ ______ ______ ______ at home.

4 경찰은 절도 혐의로 17세 소년을 체포했다. (arrest, a 17-year-old boy)

→ The police ______ ______ ______ ______ ______ on the charge of theft.

5 우리는 이 프로젝트를 진행하며 지금까지 많은 문제가 있었다. (have, so far)

→ We ______ ______ ______ ______ on this project ______ ______.

6 나는 이달에 돈을 너무 많이 썼어. (spend, this month)

→ I ______ ______ too much money ______ ______.

7 그는 이틀 전에 그녀에게 사과 이메일을 보냈지만 아직 그녀는 확인하지 않았다. (email, check)

→ He ______ his apology to her ______ ______ ______, but she ______ ______ it ______.

D 우리말과 같은 뜻이 되도록 주어진 단어를 배열하시오.

1 그녀는 해외여행을 해 본 적이 없다. (abroad, traveled, has, never)

→ She ______________________________.

2 네 전화기를 써도 될까? 내 것을 잃어버렸거든. (have, I, lost, mine)

→ Can I use your phone? ______________________________.

3 그는 방금 기차를 놓쳤다. 다음 기차를 기다려야 한다. (just, the train, has, missed)

→ He ______________________________. He needs to wait for the next one.

4 나는 이미 저녁을 먹었어. 그러니 내 것은 주문하지 마. (already, dinner, had, have)

→ I ______________________________, so do not order a meal for me.

5 그 야구 선수는 작년 이후로 수술을 세 번이나 받았다. (last year, had, three times, has, surgery, since)

→ The baseball player ______________________________.

6 다른 것을 주문하면 안 될까? 이번 달에 면을 너무 많이 먹었어. (this month, had noodles, too many times, have)

→ Can't we order a different one? I ______________________________.

7 우리는 한 시간 전에 음식을 주문했지만, 아직도 나오지 않았다. (the food, come, ordered, hasn't, yet, it)

→ We ______________________________ an hour ago, but ______________________________.

현재완료진행

A 보기 에서 동사를 골라 알맞은 형태로 바꿔 쓰시오.

[1-3] 보기 receive rain argue

1 하루 종일 비가 오고 있다. 금방 그칠 것 같지 않다.
→ It ________ ________ ________ all day. It doesn't seem that it will stop soon.

2 나는 다리가 아파서 최근에 물리 치료를 받고 있다.
→ My leg hurt, so I ________ ________ ________ the physical therapy recently.

3 그들은 30분 동안 언쟁을 벌이고 있다. 둘 중 아무도 멈추려 하지 않는다.
→ They ________ ________ ________ for half an hour. Neither of them will stop.

[4-6] 보기 cook work watch

4 나는 노트북을 사고 싶다. 그래서 아르바이트를 하고 있는 중이다.
→ I want to buy a laptop computer, so I ________ ________ ________ part time.

5 엄마는 두 시간 째 요리 중인데, 아직 저녁이 준비가 되지 않았다!
→ Mom ________ ________ ________ for two hours, but dinner isn't ready yet!

6 Alicia는 TV를 보고 있다. 그녀는 3시간 동안 TV를 보고 있다.
→ Alicia is watching TV. She ________ ________ ________ it for three hours.

B 주어진 상황을 읽고, 현재완료 또는 현재완료진행 중 가장 적절한 것 하나를 이용하여 문장을 완성하시오.

1 I started to read a book two hours ago. I am still reading it now.
→ I ________________ the book for two hours. (read)

2 I put my watch on the desk in the library, but I can't find it now.
→ Somebody ________________ my watch! (steal)

3 You lent me a DVD two days ago, and I watched it yesterday.
→ I ________________ the DVD you lent me, so I'll return it to you. (watch)

4 He started waiting for the bus 40 minutes ago, and he's still waiting for it.
→ He ________________ for the bus for 40 minutes. (wait)

5 She joined the voluntary service club a year ago, and she's still a member.
→ She ________________ a member of the voluntary service club for a year. (be)

6 He started to do his homework this morning, and he's still doing it in the evening.
→ He ________________ his homework all day. (do)

C **우리말과 같은 뜻이 되도록 주어진 단어를 이용하여 문장을 완성하시오.**

1 너는 언제 수화를 가르치기 시작했니? (start)

→ ________ ________ ________ ________ teaching sign language?

2 지금까지 얼마나 많은 우표를 수집했니? (collect, so far)

→ How many stamps ________ ________ ________ ________ ________?

3 같은 호텔에서 얼마나 오랫동안 머무르고 있는 거야? (stay)

→ ________ ________ ________ ________ ________ ________ at the same hotel?

4 누가 그 쪽지를 버렸어! 아무데도 없어. (throw, away)

→ Somebody ________ ________ the memo ________! I can't find it anywhere.

5 그녀는 작년부터 Tim과 사귀고 있다. (see, last year)

→ She ________ ________ ________ Tim ________ ________ ________.

6 Cathy는 지난달부터 운동을 하고 있다. (work out)

→ Cathy ________ ________ ________ ________ since last month.

7 나는 30분 동안 이 기계를 고치려고 하고 있는데 여전히 작동을 안 한다. (try, half an hour)

→ I ________ ________ ________ to fix this machine ________ ________ ________ ________, but it still doesn't work.

D **우리말과 같은 뜻이 되도록 주어진 단어를 배열하시오.**

1 그녀는 한 시간 넘게 화장을 하고 있다. (putting on, has, her make-up, been)

→ She ________________________ for more than an hour.

2 몇 년째 그들은 독거노인들을 돕고 있다. (senior citizens, been, helping, have)

→ For years, they ________________________ who live alone.

3 그는 10년 동안 같은 회사에서 일하고 있다. (the same company, been, has, working, at)

→ He ________________________ for ten years.

4 나는 작년부터 학생들에게 수학과 과학을 가르치고 있다. (teaching, been, math and science, have)

→ I ________________________ to students since last year.

5 우리는 세 시간 동안 발표 준비를 하고 있다. (the presentation, have, three hours, been, for, preparing)

→ We ________________________.

6 그는 한 시간이나 지루한 주제에 대해 계속 이야기를 하고 있다. (been, a boring topic, has, talking about)

→ He ________________________ for an hour.

과거완료와 과거완료진행

A 밑줄 친 부분을 어법에 맞게 고쳐 쓰시오.

1 The class has already begun when I arrived. ______________
2 She said she has never been abroad before. ______________
3 He has just had a shower when his wife got home. ______________
4 I have never had a blind date until I was 22 years old. ______________
5 He was very tired because he has done a lot of work. ______________
6 She had never lived in an apartment before she had gotten married. ______________
7 When Eric arrived at the hospital, his father has already passed away. ______________
8 She can't go into her house because she had lost her key somewhere. ______________
9 The boy has never learned English before he entered elementary school. ______________
10 I have been thinking about his offer for a long time, but I decided not to take it. ______________

B 두 문장의 의미가 통하도록 과거완료 또는 과거완료진행을 이용하여 문장을 완성하시오.

1 He lost his puppy but found it later.
→ He found the puppy he __________ __________.

2 When I got home, I saw my mother cleaning the house.
→ My mother __________ __________ __________ the house when I got home.

3 Ten minutes after we began washing the car, it started to rain.
→ We __________ __________ __________ the car for 10 minutes when it started to rain.

4 He forgot to fill up the car, so it stopped in the middle of the road.
→ He realized he __________ __________ to fill up the car.

5 It had been raining all night, but when I got up next day, the sky was clear.
→ By the time I got up, it __________ __________ raining.

6 A few years after he began to work as a salaried person, he became a businessman.
→ He __________ __________ as a salaried person for a few years before he became a businessman.

7 I saw him watching TV in the morning yesterday. When I was back home late at night, he was still watching TV.
→ He __________ __________ __________ TV all day long yesterday.

C 우리말과 같은 뜻이 되도록 주어진 동사를 이용하여 문장을 완성하시오.

1 밤새 내내 눈이 내렸다. (snow, all night long)

→ It ____________ ____________ ____________ ____________ ____________ ____________.

2 그녀는 집에 휴대폰을 놓고 왔음을 깨달았다. (realize, leave)

→ She ____________ that she ____________ ____________ her cell phone at home.

3 그녀는 어제 하루 종일 음악을 듣고 있었다. (listen to, all day long)

→ She ____________ ____________ ____________ ____________ music ____________ ____________ ____________ yesterday

4 전기가 나가기 전까지 그 컴퓨터는 잘 작동되고 있었다. (work, well, go out)

→ The computer ____________ ____________ ____________ ____________ before the power ____________ ____________.

5 태국에 오기 전에 나는 두리안을 먹어본 적이 없었다. (never, eat, come to)

→ I ____________ ____________ ____________ durian before I ____________ ____________ Thailand.

6 그는 중학생이 될 때까지 과외를 받아본 적이 없었다. (never, have, become)

→ He ____________ ____________ ____________ private lessons until he ____________ a middle school student.

7 Glen은 이미 피자를 충분히 먹었다. 한 조각 더 먹고 싶지 않았다. (already, have, not, want)

→ Glen ____________ ____________ ____________ enough pizza. He ____________ ____________ to have another piece.

D 우리말과 같은 뜻이 되도록 주어진 단어를 배열하시오.

1 눈이 많이 내렸는지 오늘 아침 세상은 온통 하얗게 변해 있었다. (snowed, it, a lot, had)

→ ____, and the world turned white this morning.

2 나는 중학교 3학년이 되기 전에 그와 이야기를 나눠본 적이 없었다. (him, to, had, talked, never)

→ I ____ before I became a 9th grader.

3 어제 그녀는 학교에 지각했다. 그 전에 그녀는 지각을 해본 적이 없었다. (had, she, been, never, late)

→ Yesterday she was late for school. Before that, ____.

4 그녀는 세 시간 동안 공부를 하고 있었기 때문에 매우 피곤했다. (been, three hours, had, for, studying)

→ She ____, so she was very tired.

5 올 겨울은 매우 추웠다. 그렇게 추운 겨울은 처음 경험해봤다. (experienced, never, like that, had, cold weather)

→ It was very cold this winter. I ____.

6 전화벨이 몇 분 동안 계속 울리고 있었지만, 아무도 전화를 받지 않았다.
(ringing, the phone, been, for minutes, had)

→ ____, but nobody answered it.

셀 수 있는 명사

A 밑줄 친 부분을 어법에 맞게 고쳐 쓰시오.

1 There was many deer in this forest. ____________
2 Her foot are swollen from walking too much. ____________
3 The financial crisis of Asia were very serious. ____________
4 The two thiefs ran away when the alarm went off. ____________
5 Statistic is the last thing I want to study in college. ____________
6 Even though eels are fishs, they don't have scales. ____________
7 Salmons live in the sea but swim upriver to spawn. ____________

B 보기 에서 알맞은 말을 골라 어법에 맞게 바꿔 문장을 완성하시오.

[1-4] 보기 phenomenon oasis short match

1 사막 곳곳에 많은 오아시스들이 산재해있다.
→ There are many ____________ all over the desert.

2 상자 안에 있는 저 성냥들을 갖고 놀지 마라.
→ Please don't play with those ____________ in the box.

3 사원에 들어가고 싶으면 반바지가 무릎 밑 길이여야 한다.
→ ____________ must reach below the knees if you want to enter the temple.

4 많은 과학자들이 기상 이변들에 대해서 걱정하고 있다.
→ Many scientists are worried about unusual weather ____________.

[5-8] 보기 mouse glass parent series

5 쥐들에게 많은 약물 실험이 시행되고 있다.
→ Many drugs are tested on ____________.

6 많은 TV 드라마 시리즈가 DVD로 출시되었다.
→ Many TV drama ____________ are out on DVD.

7 내가 안경을 바닥에 떨어뜨려서 부서졌다.
→ I dropped my ____________ on the floor, and they broke.

8 Julie는 파티에 가기 전에 부모님에게 허락을 받았다.
→ Before Julie went to the party, she got permission from her ____________.

C 우리말과 같은 뜻이 되도록 주어진 단어를 이용하여 문장을 완성하시오.

1 나는 안경 없이는 작은 활자를 읽을 수 없다. (glass)

→ I can't read the fine print without my ___________.

2 평균적으로 여자가 남자보다 더 오래 산다. (woman, man)

→ On average, ___________ ___________ longer than ___________.

3 수학은 내게 가장 어려운 과목이었다. (mathematics, be)

→ ___________ ___________ the most difficult subject for me.

4 우리는 많은 물고기를 잡았지만 모두 다시 강에 놓아주었다. (fish, river)

→ We caught ___________ ___________, but we released all of them back to the ___________.

5 소와 염소, 양의 젖으로 다양한 치즈를 만들 수 있다. (cow, goat, sheep)

→ You can make various cheeses from the milk of ___________, ___________, or ___________.

6 가위와 칼은 아이들의 손이 닿지 않는 곳에 두어야 한다. (scissors, knife, child)

→ You need to put ___________ and ___________ beyond your ___________ reach.

7 어제 음주 운전 사고가 일어났지만, 나는 그런 종류의 사고들은 예방할 수 있다고 생각한다. (accident)

→ A drunk-driving ___________ happened yesterday, but I think those kinds of ___________ can be prevented.

D 우리말과 같은 뜻이 되도록 주어진 단어를 배열하시오.

1 나는 검은 양말 한 쌍을 잃어버렸다. (black, lost, have, socks, a pair of)

→ I ______________________________________.

2 내 여동생은 잠자리에 들기 전에 언제나 양치질을 한다. (brushes, always, her teeth, my sister)

→ ______________________________________ before she goes to bed.

3 우리 삼촌은 시골에서 소와 염소, 거위를 기른다. (my uncle, cows, goats and geese, raises)

→ ______________________________________ in the countryside.

4 내 전공은 경제학이고, 부전공은 정치학이다. (economics, is, politics, my major, is, my minor)

→ ___________________, and ___________________.

5 양 떼 한 무리가 들판에서 평화롭게 풀을 뜯고 있었다. (grazing peacefully, a flock of, sheep, was)

→ ______________________________________ in the field.

6 흠집이 나는 것을 막기 위해 선글라스는 케이스에 보관해야 한다. (in the case, your sunglasses)

→ You need to keep ______________________________ to prevent scratches.

7 나는 나무 꼭대기에 있는 새들을 보기 위해서 쌍안경을 사용했다.
(the birds, used, to watch, binoculars, at the top of the tree)

→ I ______________________________________.

셀 수 있는 명사와 셀 수 없는 명사

A 밑줄 친 부분을 어법에 맞게 고쳐 쓰시오.

1 Ice in Antarctica are melting fast. ____________
2 Happiness lie first of all in health. ____________
3 You can leave your valuable at the counter. ____________
4 She thinks money don't matter in happiness. ____________
5 About 20% of oxygen are produced in the Amazon. ____________
6 Please put two spoonful of sugars into my coffee. ____________
7 Fresh fruit are high in vitamin, so I eat lots of kiwis. ____________
8 Grammar are the most difficult part, so I don't want to study it. ____________
9 Salt are important for your body, but too much salt are bad for you. ____________
10 His hair are quite thin on top, so he is sensitive about his hair style. ____________

B 보기 에서 알맞은 말을 골라 어법에 맞게 문장을 완성하시오.

[1-4] 보기 arm furniture shoes cocoa

1 나는 침대를 포함해서 가구를 바꾸기로 결정했다.
→ I decided to change the ____________ including my bed.

2 그녀는 어제 구두 한 켤레를 사기 위해 쇼핑을 갔다.
→ She went shopping to buy a pair of ____________ yesterday.

3 그 무기 제조업체는 전쟁으로 큰 수익을 올렸다.
→ The ____________ manufacturer made a huge profit from the war.

4 나는 오늘 같이 비 오는 추운 날에는 뜨거운 코코아를 마시고 싶다.
→ I would like to drink hot ____________ on a cold, rainy day like today.

[5-7] 보기 clothing / dress mail / letter sunlight / light

5 나는 우편물을 회수하러 나갔는데, 우체통에서 편지 한 통을 발견했다.
→ I went out to pick up my ____________, and I found a ____________ in the mailbox.

6 햇빛이 풍부할 때는 모든 전등을 켜놓을 필요가 없다.
→ When the ____________ is plentiful, you don't have to leave all of the ____________ on.

7 그 상점은 치마와 코트, 드레스, 벨트와 같이 다양한 의류를 판매한다.
→ The shop sells a variety of ____________ such as skirts, coats, ____________, or belts.

C 우리말과 같은 뜻이 되도록 주어진 단어를 이용하여 문장을 완성하시오.

1 고기가 충분히 익은 것 같지 않아요. (meat, be)
→ I don't think the ______ ______ cooked enough.

2 영어는 일본어와 어순이 다르다. (English, have)
→ ______ ______ a different word order from Japanese.

3 차 한 잔 드실래요, 아니면 커피 드실래요? (cup, tea, coffee)
→ Would you like ______ ______ ______ ______ or ______?

4 그의 용기는 회사의 많은 사람들에게 박수를 받았다. (courage, is)
→ His ______ ______ applauded by many people in the company.

5 후추는 한국에서 가장 많이 사용되는 양념 가운데 하나다. (pepper, be)
→ ______ ______ one of the most common seasonings in Korea.

6 가스가 어디선가 새고 있어. 창문을 모두 열어야만 해. (gas, be, window)
→ ______ ______ leaking somewhere. We need to open all of the ______.

7 임신부들은 아기들을 위해 충분한 철분을 섭취해야 한다. (woman, need, iron, baby)
→ Pregnant ______ ______ to take enough ______ for their ______.

D 우리말과 같은 뜻이 되도록 주어진 단어를 배열하시오.

1 물이 끓기 시작하면, 야채를 냄비에 넣으시오. (boil, the water, when, to, starts)
→ ______, put the vegetables into the pot.

2 나는 내 짐이 없어졌다는 것을 깨달았다. (that, realized, was, my luggage, missing)
→ I ______.

3 그는 너무 목이 말라 주스 한 잔을 다 마셔버렸다. (he, juice, a glass of, finished up)
→ He was very thirsty, so ______.

4 당신이 재미있는 시간을 보낼 때에는 시간이 빨리 흘러간다. (when, have, flies, you, fun)
→ Time ______.

5 나는 집에 오는 길에 비누 하나와 우유 한 팩을 샀다. (a carton of, soap, a bar of, milk, bought, and, I)
→ On my way home, ______.

6 나는 수프에서 머리카락을 발견했기 때문에 매니저에게 항의했다. (in my soup, I, a hair, because, found)
→ I complained to the manager ______.

7 나는 돈이 많이 없었다. 내 주머니에는 5달러밖에 없었다. (didn't, much money, have, had, five dollars, only)
→ I ______. I ______ in my pocket.

수량표현

A 밑줄 친 부분을 어법에 맞게 고쳐 쓰시오.

1 He is as smart as a three-years-old boy. ____________

2 There were very little days when I took a nap. ____________

3 Every shops in this town is closed early on weekends. ____________

4 Unfortunately, none of this information are useful to me. ____________

5 Let's rearrange the furnitures to make enough room for the new table. ____________

6 The number of students enrolled in the institute have doubled in two years. ____________

7 People visit the web site because it has a great deal of informations about books. ____________

B much 또는 many와 주어진 말을 이용하여 문장을 완성하시오.

1 그 오디션에 얼마나 많은 지원자들이 몰렸나요? (competitor)
→ How ____________ came to the audition?

2 미국에는 아주 많은 인종과 아주 많은 문화가 존재한다. (race)
→ There are so ____________ and so many cultures in the US.

3 너무 많은 햇빛에 노출되면 화상을 입을 수 있다. (sunlight)
→ If you are exposed to too ____________, you can get sunburn.

4 너는 컴퓨터 게임하는데 너무 많은 시간을 보내는 것 같아. (time)
→ I think you spend too ____________ playing computer games.

C 보기 에서 알맞은 말을 고르고 주어진 단어를 이용하여 우리말과 같은 뜻이 되도록 문장을 완성하시오.

보기 few a few little a little

1 나는 내 차에 설탕을 약간 넣었다. (sugar)
→ I added ____________ ____________ to my tea.

2 우리는 물이 거의 없어요. 사야 해요. (water)
→ We have ____________ ____________ left. We need to buy some.

3 나는 다음 달 쯤에 며칠 휴가를 낼 예정이다. (day off)
→ I'm going to take ____________ ____________ sometime next month.

4 요즘에는 휴대폰을 살 때 현금으로 결제하는 사람들이 거의 없다. (person)
→ Nowadays, ____________ ____________ pay in cash when they buy cell phones.

D **우리말과 같은 뜻이 되도록 주어진 단어를 이용하여 문장을 완성하시오.**

1 서울역까지는 몇 정거장인가요? (stop, be)
→ How ________ ________ ________ it to Seoul Station?

2 나는 그의 능력에 대한 의심이 거의 없다. (have, little, doubt)
→ I ________ ________ ________ about his ability.

3 버스가 출발하기 전 까지 시간이 많이 남지 않았다. (have, time)
→ We ________ ________ ________ ________ before the bus leaves.

4 콘서트가 몇 분 뒤에 시작할 예정입니다. (in, minute)
→ The concert will start ________ ________ ________ ________.

5 이 가게는 많은 유명인이 방문하는 인기 있는 곳이다. (number, celebrity, visit)
→ This store is a popular place that ________ ________ ________ ________ ________.

6 그 학생들은 영어를 공부하는 데 많은 양의 시간을 보낸다. (large amount, time)
→ The students spend ________ ________ ________ ________ ________ studying English.

7 각각의 학생들은 다가오는 핼러윈을 위한 독특한 의상을 준비해야 한다. (student, have to, prepare)
→ ________ ________ ________ ________ ________ unique costumes for the upcoming Halloween.

E **우리말과 같은 뜻이 되도록 주어진 단어를 배열하시오.**

1 약을 너무 많이 복용하면 위험하다. (drugs, too, is, many, taking)
→ ________________________________ dangerous.

2 엄마의 생일까지 며칠 밖에 남지 않았다. (left, are, a few, there, days)
→ ________________________________ until my mother's birthday.

3 냉장고에 콜라가 많이 있다. (there, plenty of, in the refrigerator, is, cola)
→ ________________________________

4 그 호텔의 각 방에는 옷장과 냉장고가 있다. (has, each, in the hotel, room, a closet)
→ ________________________________ and a refrigerator.

5 대량으로 구매하면 얼마를 할인받을 수 있나요? (discount, much, a, volume, how, large, buy)
→ ________________ can I get if I ________________?

6 모든 아이는 저마다의 재능이 있으며 부모들은 그것을 발견하고 개발시켜주어야 한다.
(has, child, talents, every, different)
→ ________________________________, and parents need to find and develop them.

7 오랫동안 우리는 여성의 사회적 지위에 대해 거의 관심을 기울이지 않았다.
(the social status of, attention, to, little, paid, women)
→ We ________________________________ for a long time.

명사의 소유격

A 주어진 말을 소유격이나 전치사 of을 이용하여 문장을 완성하시오.

1 ____________________ is not realistic. (Hines, idea)

2 ____________________ tells us its mood. (the dog, tail)

3 ____________________ blew away in the wind. (the boy, cap)

4 We couldn't stand ____________________ anymore. (James, behavior)

5 The hero rescued the princess at ____________________. (the story, the end)

6 She got ____________________ from work. (three months, maternity leave)

7 ____________________ got a great amount of media spotlight again. (last year, winner)

8 My father has received ____________________. (honorary professor, the title)

9 ____________________ is an hour's drive from my house. (my grandparents, house)

10 The hospital is open until late on Wednesday nights for ____________________.
(the patients, convenience)

B 보기 와 같이 문장의 의미가 통하도록 소유격을 이용하여 문장을 완성하시오.

> **보기** I was a little late for the movie, so I couldn't see the beginning.
> → I missed __the__ __beginning__ __of__ __the__ __movie__.

1 The dog started barking and it made a baby cry.
→ The baby was startled by ________ ________ ________.

2 I heard a beautiful song, and I want to know the title.
→ I want to know ________ ________ ________ ________ ________.

3 Louis has a puppy. He has a long body and short legs.
→ ________ ________ has a long body and short legs.

4 There was a big match last Sunday. It was really a close game.
→ ________ ________ ________ was really close.

5 The boss made a decision about the matter. But nobody agreed to it.
→ Nobody agreed to ________ ________ ________ about the matter.

6 We scheduled a meeting for Thursday. But it has been postponed to next week.
→ ________ ________ has been postponed to next week.

C 우리말과 같은 뜻이 되도록 주어진 말과 소유격을 이용하여 문장을 완성하시오.

1 내일의 파티에는 정장을 입어야 한다. (for)

→ ________ ________ ________, you should be formally dressed.

2 모두가 경기 결과에 실망했다. (the game, the result)

→ Everybody was disappointed with ________ ________ ________ ________ ________.

3 나는 어제 신문에서 그 사고에 대한 기사를 읽었다. (in, newspaper)

→ I read the article about the accident ________ ________ ________.

4 집주인은 내가 미리 두 달 치의 집세를 내주기를 원했다. (pay, rent)

→ The landlady wanted me to ________ ________ ________ ________ in advance.

5 그 남자 중학교와 여자 중학교는 내년에 통합될 것이다. (girls, middle schools)

→ The boys' and ________ ________ ________ ________ will be integrated next year.

6 나는 이번 주 토요일에 딸아이의 방에 페인트칠을 할 예정이다. (paint)

→ I'm going to ________ ________ ________ ________ this Saturday.

7 그녀는 이번 휴가 때 자신의 언니네 집에서 머물 예정이다. (stay, at, sister, house)

→ She's going to ________ ________ ________ ________ ________ for this holiday.

D 우리말과 같은 뜻이 되도록 주어진 단어를 배열하시오.

1 진심으로 사과드립니다. (to you, my heart, apologize, of, the bottom, from)

→ I ________________________________.

2 그녀는 자신의 학생들의 이름을 모두 알고 있다. (all of, knows, names, her students')

→ She ________________________________.

3 아직 아무도 그 질병의 원인에 대해서 모른다. (the disease, knows, of, yet, the cause)

→ Nobody ________________________________.

4 그 상점에서 하나의 가격에 두 개를 살 수 있어. (at the store, two, of, for, the price, one)

→ You can get ________________________________.

5 우리 아버지의 차는 10년이 되었지만 여전히 잘 굴러간다. (ten, my father's, old, is, years, car)

→ ________________________________, but it still runs good.

6 한 남자가 상점 앞에서 내년 달력을 나눠 주고 있다. (giving out, is, calendars, a man, next year's)

→ ________________________________ in front of the shop.

7 TV 리모컨의 버튼을 누르면 물건을 살 수 있다. (the TV remote control, the buttons, by, pressing, of)

→ We can buy things ________________________________.

Unit 19 부정관사 a/an

A 빈칸에 a, an, × 중 알맞은 것을 써 넣으시오. [×는 필요 없는 경우]

1 ____________ cats can jump much higher than ____________ dogs.

2 I take ____________ trip with my family at least once ____________ year.

3 He is ____________ doctor, and his brothers are ____________ doctors, too.

4 How could he buy such ____________ expensive car on his salary?

5 Last summer I took ____________ short trip to Busan with my family.

6 ____________ scale is ____________ instrument that is used for weighing objects.

7 This sweater is made of ____________ wool, so you need to dry-clean it.

8 We take ____________ examination once ____________ month at the English institute.

9 She bought ____________ table and four chairs for the dining area of the house.

10 I met ____________ guy while I was traveling around Europe, and he is my husband now.

B 우리말을 참고하여 밑줄 친 부분을 바르게 고쳐 쓰시오.

1 나는 미래에 아인슈타인과 같은 사람이 되고 싶다.
→ I want to be a Einstein in the future. ____________

2 나는 지금까지 그렇게 아름다운 드레스를 본 적이 없다.
→ I have never seen so a beautiful dress so far. ____________

3 탁자와 책장은 먼지로 덮여 있었다.
→ The tables and the bookshelf were covered with a dust. ____________

4 왜 이렇게 늦었어? 30분 동안 기다렸잖아.
→ Why are you so late? I have been waiting for half a hour. ____________

5 그는 심리학 석사학위가 있는데 유학을 갈까 생각 중이다.
→ He has a M.A. in psychology and is thinking of studying abroad. ____________

6 우리 마을에 대학교가 하나 있는데, 100년 전에 지어졌다.
→ There is an university in my town, and it was built 100 years ago. ____________

7 옛날 옛적 큰 나라에 왕과 그의 딸이 살았어요.
→ Once upon a time, there lived the king and his daughter in big country. ____________

C 우리말과 같은 뜻이 되도록 주어진 단어와 관사를 이용하여 문장을 완성하시오.

1 양과 말은 풀을 먹는다. (sheep, horse, feed)

→ ___________ and ___________ ___________ on grass.

2 문어는 몸 색깔을 바꿀 수 있는 능력이 있다. (octopus, have)

→ ___________ ___________ ___________ the ability to change its skin color.

3 나는 친구들과 한 달에 두 번 영화를 보러 간다. (twice)

→ I go to the movies with my friends ___________ ___________ ___________.

4 돌고래는 매우 영리해서 많은 재주들을 빠른 시간에 배울 수 있다. (dolphin, be)

→ ___________ ___________ very intelligent, so they can learn many tricks quickly.

5 그는 크리스마스에 내게 상당히 비싼 선물을 주었다. (quite, expensive, gift)

→ He gave me ___________ ___________ ___________ ___________ for Christmas.

6 가구는 집안 분위기에 있어서 중요한 역할을 한다. (furniture, play, important role)

→ ___________ ___________ ___________ ___________ ___________ in your home atmosphere.

7 그는 모든 신생 기업에게 스티브 잡스와 같은 사람이 필요하다고 생각한다. (need, Steve Jobs)

→ He thinks every startup company ___________ ___________ ___________ ___________.

D 우리말과 같은 뜻이 되도록 주어진 단어를 배열하시오.

1 나는 언젠가 부모님께 집을 지어 드리고 싶다. (house, want, a, I, to, build)

→ _______________________________ for my parents someday.

2 어제 금과 석유 가격이 20% 이상 올랐다. (went up, the price, oil, of, and, gold)

→ _______________________________ by more than 20% yesterday.

3 어느 날 한 소녀가 숲 속을 혼자 걷고 있었다. (the forest, girl, through, walking, was, a)

→ _______________________________ alone one day.

4 우리 엄마는 내게 하루에 세 번 양치를 하라고 말씀하셨다. (brush, day, my teeth, to, three times, a)

→ My mother told me _______________________________.

5 그녀는 유니폼을 받았고, 가게에서는 그것을 입고 있어야 한다. (the, uniform, has received, a, shop, in)

→ She _______________________________ and has to wear it _______________________________.

6 그녀는 아침으로 계란프라이 하나, 소시지 하나, 우유를 주문했다.
(fried egg, and, sausage, breakfast, a, a, milk, for)

→ She ordered _______________________________.

정관사 The

A 빈칸에 a, an, the, × 중 알맞은 것을 써 넣으시오. [×는 필요 없는 경우]

1 Look at ________ sky. It's so blue and clear.

2 What is ________ largest country in ________ world?

3 Do you know ________ guy standing over there?

4 Let's meet in front of ________ bank at 7 tomorrow.

5 Unfortunately, he wasn't ________ same person I had known.

6 Please bring me ________ book on the table in ________ living room.

7 ________ last person out should turn off ________ lights in the office.

8 ________ Brian lives next door to me. ________ Brians are well known for helping ________ poor.

9 I went to ________ Italian restaurant one day. Since then ________ restaurant became my favorite one.

B 보기 에서 관사를 고르고, 우리말과 같은 뜻이 되도록 주어진 단어를 이용하여 문장을 완성하시오. [관사가 필요 없는 경우 쓰지 말 것]

보기 a an the

1 지구에서 가장 큰 대양은 태평양이다. (largest ocean)
→ ____________ on Earth is the Pacific Ocean.

2 컴퓨터 게임을 하는 것은 그가 가진 유일한 취미다. (only hobby)
→ Playing computer games is ____________ that he has.

3 나는 영화 보는 것을 좋아하지만 어제 본 영화는 별로다. (movies, movie)
→ I like to watch ________ but I don't like ____________ that I saw yesterday.

4 Robert는 아마추어 록밴드에서 기타를 친다. (guitar, amateur rock band)
→ Robert plays ____________ in ____________.

5 프랑스는 서부 유럽에 있고 스웨덴은 북쪽에 있다. (France, Sweden, north)
→ ________ is located in western Europe, and ________ is in ________.

6 나는 자원봉사 동아리에서 한 소녀를 만났다. 그 소녀는 내 가장 친한 친구가 되었다. (girl, girl)
→ I met ________ in a voluntary service club. ________ became my best friend.

7 많은 사람들이 부자는 가난한 사람들을 돕는 데 더 많은 돈을 기부해야 한다고 생각한다. (rich, poor)
→ Many people think that ________ should donate more money to help ________.

C 우리말과 같은 뜻이 되도록 주어진 말과 관사를 이용하여 문장을 완성하시오.

1 햇볕이 매우 뜨거우니 선크림을 발라라. (sun, be)

→ ________ ________ ________ very hot, so put on sunscreen.

2 그는 운전하면서 라디오를 듣고 있었다. (listen to, radio)

→ He ________ ________ ________ ________ ________ while he was driving.

3 너 지난주에 내가 네게 빌려준 그 책 다 읽었니? (finish, book)

→ Have ________ ________ ________ ________ I lent you last week?

4 고기는 그램이나 킬로그램 단위로 판다. (by, gram, kilogram)

→ Meat is sold ________ ________ ________ or ________ ________ ________.

5 내가 탁자 위에 있는 옷들을 세탁소에 맡길게. (take, clothes, on, table)

→ I will ________ ________ ________ ________ ________ ________ to the laundry.

6 내가 설거지를 하는 동안 쓰레기 좀 밖에 내놓아 줘. (garbage, do, dishes)

→ Please take out ________ ________ while ________ ________ ________ ________.

D 우리말과 같은 뜻이 되도록 주어진 단어를 배열하시오.

1 여기 너무 춥네요. 제가 창문을 좀 닫아도 될까요? (close, if, window, I, the)

→ It's too cold in here. Do you mind ________________________?

2 부상자들은 즉시 병원으로 이송되었다. (were taken, injured, the hospital, the, to)

→ ________________________ right away.

3 과거에 사람들은 지구가 둥글지 않다고 믿었다. (not, round, believed, earth, that, the, was)

→ In the past, people ________________________.

4 나는 스테이플러를 책상 세 번째 서랍에 넣어두었다. (the stapler, drawer, placed, in, third, the)

→ I ________________________ of my desk.

5 대부분의 학생들은 마지막 순간까지 숙제를 미룬다. (their homework, until, leave, very, the, last minute)

→ Most students ________________________.

6 나는 프랑스를 여행했을 때, 프랑스 사람들이 매우 친절하다고 생각했다.
(around, traveled, were, France, very kind, French, the)

→ When I ________________, I thought that ________________.

Unit 21 관사의 생략

A 빈칸에 a, an, × 중 알맞은 것을 써 넣으시오. [×는 필요 없는 경우]

1 He said to me "I wish you ______ luck".

2 We need more daycare centers for ______ working mothers.

3 Before going to ______ bed, I set the alarm for seven o'clock.

4 My father watches ______ TV all day long during the weekends.

5 She has been learning ______ English for ______ year.

6 My father goes to work by ______ car, and I go to school by ______ bus.

7 Germany exports ______ machinery and ______ equipment to many countries.

8 Dad is ______ member of a soccer club and he plays ______ soccer every Sunday.

9 I didn't have ______ time to eat ______ lunch, so I had ______ sandwich for ______ lunch.

10 My brother is ______ tennis player, and he goes to ______ school ______ hour early for practice.

B 우리말을 참고하여 밑줄 친 곳을 바르게 고쳐 문장을 다시 쓰시오.

1 Could you show me a that skirt? (저 치마 좀 보여주시겠어요?)
→ ______

2 My mother prepared special dinner for my birthday. (우리 엄마는 내 생일날 특별한 저녁을 준비했다.)
→ ______

3 I'm meeting my mother in front of church. (나는 그 교회 앞에서 엄마를 만나기로 했다.)
→ ______

4 My family goes to a church by the car on Sundays. (우리 가족은 일요일마다 차를 타고 예배를 드리러 간다.)
→ ______

5 It is hard for young to find a work these days. (요즘에는 젊은이들이 일을 구하는 것이 어렵다.)
→ ______

6 He went to the prison because he stole a jewelry. (그는 보석을 훔쳐 교도소에 갔다.)
→ ______

C 우리말과 같은 뜻이 되도록 주어진 말을 이용하여 문장을 완성하시오.

1 사고는 언제 어디서든 발생할 수 있다. (accident, happen)

→ ___________ ___________ ___________ anytime and anywhere.

2 나는 딸기를 좋아해서 딸기 케이크를 종종 굽는다. (like, strawberry)

→ ___________ ___________ ___________, so I often bake strawberry cakes.

3 그녀는 배탈이 나서 저녁을 먹지 않았다. (upset stomach, skip)

→ She had ___________ ___________ ___________, so ___________ ___________ dinner.

4 우리 딸이 독감으로 열이 있어 누워 있다. (be, in, bed, fever, with, flu)

→ My daughter ___________ ___________ ___________ because she has ___________ ___________ ___________ ___________.

5 세미나가 그 호텔의 한 회의실에서 열릴 것이다. (conference room, in, hotel)

→ A meeting will be held in ___________ ___________ ___________ ___________ ___________ ___________.

6 오늘 교통이 혼잡하니 지하철로 출근하는 것이 좋겠어. (traffic, be, work, subway)

→ ___________ ___________ heavy today, so you'd better go ___________ ___________ ___________ ___________.

D 우리말과 같은 뜻이 되도록 주어진 단어를 배열하시오.

1 비가 내리기 시작했을 때 그는 농구를 하던 중이었다. (basketball, was, playing, he)

→ ___________________________ when it started to rain.

2 나는 매일 아침 식사를 간단하게 먹는 것을 즐긴다. (having, breakfast, enjoy, light, a)

→ I ___________________________ every morning.

3 그녀는 이번 학기에 언어학 101을 듣고 있다. (is taking, this semester, Linguistics 101)

→ She ___________________________.

4 Nick과 Kelly는 물과 기름처럼 잘 어울리지 못한다. (and, like, get along well, water, oil)

→ Nick and Kelly don't ___________________________.

5 그는 축구를 하다가 허리를 다쳐서 한 달 동안 입원해야 했다. (a, soccer, he, was, playing, month, for)

→ He hurt his back while ___________________ and had to stay in the hospital ___________.

6 우리 어머니는 라디오 듣는 것은 좋아하지만, TV 보는 것은 좋아하지 않는다.
(the radio, like, listening to, TV, watching)

→ My mother enjoys ___________________, but she doesn't ___________________.

7 그녀는 해외에서 공부 중이어서 친구들과 이메일로 연락을 유지하고 있다.
(by, stays, her friends, email, in contact with)

→ She is studying abroad, so she ___________________________.

인칭대명사 & 소유대명사

A 밑줄 친 부분을 알맞은 인칭대명사 또는 소유대명사로 바꿔 쓰시오.

1 This is not my umbrella. My umbrella is a new one. ______________

2 I have lost my calculator. Can I borrow your calculator? ______________

3 Cindy has a driver's license, but Cindy doesn't have a car. ______________

4 He has a cat. Her name is Kiki. Kiki has beautiful blue eyes. ______________

5 I saw Jack in the theater yesterday. Jack was with his girlfriend. ______________

6 Peter took a chocolate cake to school. Peter ate it with his friends. ______________

7 My parents want me to be a doctor. But it is their dream, not my dream. ______________

8 When Mark and I were in high school, Mark and I went to school together. ______________

9 Henry and Emma got married two years ago. Henry and Emma have been married for two years. ______________

B 인칭대명사 또는 소유대명사를 이용하여 대화를 완성하시오.

1 **A** Don't touch the diary. It's not __________.
B I'm sorry. This is similar to mine.

2 **A** Greg! Wake up. The next stop is __________.
B Sorry. Are we there already?

3 **A** Today is my wife's birthday. What should I do for __________?
B Why don't you send __________ some flowers and a cake?

4 **A** Glen and I are going out for dinner. Would you like to come with __________?
B No, thanks. I have a lot to do. You guys go ahead.

5 **A** Jack! Do you know who the women are?
B __________ are Ashley and Lira. Their office is directly beneath __________.

6 **A** I can't find my grandparents' house. All the houses here look the same!
B The house with a blue roof is __________!

7 **A** Alice! What are you going to do this weekend?
B You know Brian, right? He asked __________ out last week. I'm going to the movies with __________.

C 우리말과 같은 뜻이 되도록 주어진 말을 이용하여 문장을 완성하시오.

1 나 펜을 잃어버렸어. 네 펜을 좀 빌릴 수 있을까? (can, borrow)

→ I've lost my pen. ________ ________ ________ ________?

2 그 회사는 곧 전략을 변경할 것이라고 발표했다. (change, strategy)

→ The company announced that it would ________ ________ ________ soon.

3 친구가 캐나다로 이사 갔다. 나는 그것을 믿을 수가 없다. (believe)

→ My friend moved to Canada. ________ ________ ________ ________.

4 우리 할아버지와 할머니의 집은 우리 집 바로 맞은편에 있다. (across from)

→ My grandparents' house is directly ________ ________ ________.

5 그 개는 자신의 꼬리를 좌우로 흔들고 있었다. (wag, tail)

→ The dog was ________ ________ ________ side to side.

6 Sally가 힘든 시간을 겪고 있을 때, 그녀의 남자 친구가 그녀를 위로했다. (boyfriend, comfort)

→ When Sally was having a hard time, ________ ________ ________ ________.

7 그는 자신의 인생의 거의 절반을 가르치는 데 보냈다. (spend, life)

→ ________ ________ almost half of ________ ________ teaching.

D 우리말과 같은 뜻이 되도록 주어진 단어를 배열하시오.

1 나는 어제 Bob을 우연히 만났는데, 그는 하나도 변하지 않았다. (changed, he, a bit, hasn't)

→ I happened to meet Bob yesterday, and ________________.

2 우리 이모는 지난달에 아기를 낳았고, 지금은 출산 휴가 중이다. (is, maternity leave, she, on)

→ My aunt had a baby last month, and ________________ now.

3 Jordan과 Mark는 너무 어리다. 그래서 그들은 롤러코스터를 탈 수 없다. (a roller coaster, can't, they, ride)

→ Jordan and Mark are too young. So ________________.

4 내년에 공항이 지어질 것이다. 그것은 세계에서 가장 큰 규모가 될 것이다. (it, in the world, be, will, the biggest)

→ An airport is going to be built next year. ________________.

5 아이들을 데리러 갈 시간이 없어서 그에게 아이들을 데려오라고 부탁했다. (him, I, to, them, asked, pick, up)

→ I didn't have time to pick up my children, so ________________.

6 비록 내 상황이 심각하긴 하지만, 그것은 그녀의 문제에 비하면 아무것도 아니다.
(it, hers, nothing, is, compared to)

→ Even though my situation is serious, ________________.

7 나는 언니와 방을 같이 쓴다. 우리는 이층 침대를 쓰는데, 언니가 아래층을 쓴다.
(use, the lower bunk, uses, we, she, a bunk bed)

→ I share a room with my sister. ________________, and ________________.

재귀대명사

A 빈칸에 알맞은 재귀대명사를 써 넣으시오.

1 I repaired the broken computer ____________.

2 She cut ____________ while she was cooking.

3 I like the song ____________, but I don't like the singer.

4 He started to blame ____________ for failing the examination.

5 It's you ____________ who chose to live in a foreign country.

6 My sister has lived by ____________ since she entered college.

7 His behavior is bad in ____________, but we can understand him.

8 He confidently introduced ____________ in front of many students.

9 Many young women consider ____________ to be overweight.

10 My family and I enjoyed ____________ on Jeju island for this holiday.

B 우리말을 참고하여 어법상 어색한 곳을 바르게 고쳐 문장을 다시 쓰시오.

1 Take a seat here. Make you at home. (여기 앉으세요. 편하게 계세요.)

→ ______________________________

2 My daughter smiled at her in the mirror. (내 딸은 거울에 비친 자신을 보며 미소 지었다.)

→ ______________________________

3 The actress tried to kill her because of her depression. (그 여배우는 우울증으로 자살을 시도했다.)

→ ______________________________

4 He devoted him to taking care of his sick parents. (그는 아픈 부모님을 돌보는 데 자신을 헌신했다.)

→ ______________________________

5 Please leave me alone. I can take care of me. (제발 저 좀 내버려 두세요. 저는 제 앞가림을 할 줄 알아요.)

→ ______________________________

6 My sister is on a diet, but she can't control her around sweets.
(우리 언니는 다이어트 중이지만 단 것을 보면 자신을 절제하지 못한다.)

→ ______________________________

C 우리말과 같은 뜻이 되도록 주어진 단어와 재귀대명사를 이용하여 문장을 완성하시오.

1 학생들은 놀이 공원에서 정말 즐거워했다. (enjoy)

→ The ________ ________ ________ at the amusement park.

2 강의는 지루했지만, 나는 억지로 깨어 있으려고 애썼다. (force)

→ The lecture was boring, but ________ ________ ________ to stay awake.

3 사람들은 그가 프랑스어를 독학했다고 이야기한다. (teach, French)

→ People say that ________ ________ ________ ________.

4 나는 이번 겨울을 맞아 내 코트를 사려고 백화점에 갔다. (get, a coat, for)

→ I went to the department store to ________ ________ ________ ________ ________ ________ ________.

5 벽에 못을 박을 때에는 다치지 않게 조심해야 한다. (not to hurt)

→ You should be careful ________ ________ ________ ________ when you hammer a nail in the wall.

6 우리는 탁자의 디자인이 마음에 들지 않아서 하나를 직접 만들기로 결심했다. (decide, to, make)

→ We didn't like the design of the table, so ________ ________ ________ ________ ________ ________.

D 우리말과 같은 뜻이 되도록 주어진 단어를 배열하시오.

1 Mary! 쿠키를 마음껏 먹어라. (to, help, the cookies, yourself)

→ Mary! ________________________________.

2 앉아서 편하게 있어. 금방 돌아올게. (at home, make, sit down, yourself, and)

→ ________________________________. I'll be right back.

3 우리 어머니는 케이크를 굽다가 오븐에 화상을 입었다. (burned, my mother, herself)

→ ________________________________ while she was baking a cake.

4 그녀가 30분 동안 혼잣말을 하고 있다. (for, talking to, she, half an hour, herself, is)

→ ________________________________

5 너는 내게 거짓말을 했어! 너는 너 자신을 부끄러워해야 해! (should, yourself, you, be, of, ashamed)

→ You lied to me! ________________________________!

6 기타 치는 법을 네가 독학으로 배웠다니 믿을 수가 없어. (how to, you, the guitar, taught, play, yourself)

→ I can't believe that ________________________________.

7 우리는 일손이 부족합니다. 이 프로젝트를 우리 인원만 가지고 끝낼 수가 없어요.
(this project, finish, can't, ourselves, we, by)

→ We are short handed at work. ________________________________.

지시대명사

A **우리말과 같은 뜻이 되도록 빈칸에 알맞은 지시대명사를 써 넣으시오.**

1 노트북이 필요하다면 네게 이걸 빌려줄게.
→ If you need a laptop computer, I'll lend you ___________.

2 네게 줄 게 있어. 이건 네 생일을 위해 준비한 거야.
→ I have something for you. ___________ is for your birthday.

3 아프리카 코끼리의 귀는 아시아 코끼리들의 그것보다 훨씬 더 크다.
→ The ears of African elephants are much bigger than ___________ of Asian elephants.

4 저것 좀 봐! 길 잃은 불쌍한 강아지가 무척 배가 고픈 것 같아.
→ Look at ___________! I think that poor stray dog is very hungry.

5 도시의 삶은 전원의 삶 보다 빠르게 흘러간다.
→ Life in the city is more fast-paced than ___________ in the countryside.

6 동쪽 해안의 바닷물이 서쪽 바닷물보다 더 맑다.
→ The sea water on the east coast is clearer than ___________ on the west.

7 이 목걸이는 매우 비싼데, 그 이유는 이것들이 다 진짜 다이아몬드이기 때문이다.
→ This necklace is very expensive because ___________ are real diamonds.

B **빈칸에 알맞은 인칭대명사 또는 지시대명사를 써 넣으시오.**

1 A How do you like this house?
B I think ___________ is a bit small.

2 A Vicky took first place in the examination.
B Wow, I guess ___________ studied very hard this time.

3 A Do you know that guy talking with Garry?
B Who? Oh, ___________ is Nick from Australia. ___________'s Garry's friend.

4 A Do not throw away that cup. ___________'s only been used once.
B Are you going to recycle this?

5 A Do you know who owns ___________ on that table?
B They're Clara's stamps. She collects foreign stamps.

6 A Jenny, come and try this cake. I made ___________ myself.
B Wow! ___________ tastes so good!

C 우리말과 같은 뜻이 되도록 주어진 단어를 이용하여 문장을 완성하시오.

1 호주와 한국은 계절이 정반대다. (Korea)

→ The seasons in Australia are opposite to ________ ________ ________.

2 나는 이 케이크를 먹어 봤어요. 이것이 저것보다 더 나아요. (one)

→ I tasted these cakes. ________ ________ is better than ________ ________.

3 아기의 심장 박동 수는 어른의 심장 박동 수보다 더 빠르다. (of, adults)

→ Babies' heart rate is faster than ________ ________ ________.

4 그 극장의 2층 좌석은 1층 좌석보다 싸다. (first)

→ The seats on the second floor are cheaper than ________ ________ ________ ________ ________.

5 어머니들은 자신의 아이와 다른 아이를 비교하지 말아야 한다. (of, other women)

→ Mothers must not compare their kids with ________ ________ ________ ________.

6 또 피자와 콜라를 먹고 있구나. 이것들은 네 건강에 좋지 않아. (be, not, good)

→ You're eating pizza and drinking Coke again. Listen, ________ ________ ________ ________ for your health.

7 그녀의 피아노 연주는 아마추어의 연주 수준을 넘는다. (of, an amateur)

→ Her piano playing is beyond ________ ________ ________ ________.

D 우리말과 같은 뜻이 되도록 주어진 단어를 배열하시오.

1 나는 이것보다 더 아름다운 그림을 본 적이 없다. (more, is, than, beautiful, this)

→ I've never seen a painting that ________________________.

2 이것들은 샴 고양이인데, Sam이 키우고 있는 것들이야. (Siamese, these, cats, are)

→ ________________________, and they belong to Sam.

3 저 재킷들은 내 취향이야. 저것들 중 하나를 살 거야. (my, jackets, those, are, type)

→ ________________________. I'll buy one of them.

4 저기에 있는 저 남자는 누구니? 나에게 그를 소개시켜줄 수 있니? (that, is, who, over there, man)

→ ________________________? Can you introduce him to me?

5 그들의 주가는 다른 회사의 주가보다 더 빨리 상승하고 있다. (than, other companies, faster, of, those)

→ Their stock prices are rising ________________________.

6 이 동물들의 지능은 인간의 지능만큼 높다. (animals' intelligence, is, these, that, as high as, of humans)

→ ________________________

7 이 식당이 저 식당보다 점심시간에 더 많이 붐빈다. (this, that, restaurant, one, is, than, more crowded)

→ ________________________ during lunch hours.

부정대명사 I

A 보기 에서 알맞은 말을 골라 대화를 완성하시오 [중복 사용 가능]

보기	one(s)	another	the other	the others	others

1 A How many puppies do you have?
B I have two. ___________ is black, and ___________ is white.

2 A Where did you buy this chocolate cake? It tastes so good.
B My sister baked it herself. Will you have ___________ piece?

3 A Some like his opinion. ___________ don't like it. How about you?
B I think his idea is brilliant.

4 A Somebody stole my shoes.
B That's too bad. Why don't you ask your parents to buy new ___________?

5 A What did you shop for?
B I bought three candles. ___________ is for me, ___________ is for my sister, and ___________ is for my mother.

B 밑줄 친 부분을 어법에 맞게 고쳐 쓰시오.

1 I don't want no one to see my diary. ___________

2 One must try hard to become successful in your business. ___________

3 My youngest son broke the window, so I had to pay for one. ___________

4 A We have ten teachers in our institute. Another is a man and others are all women.
B Wow. You have more female than male teachers in your institute. ___________

C 두 문장의 의미가 통하도록 주어진 단어를 이용하여 문장을 완성하시오.

1 There is nobody in that old house. (anybody)
→ There ___________ ___________ ___________ in that old house.

2 I don't want anything to eat at the moment, and I'm not hungry. (nothing)
→ I ___________ ___________ ___________ ___________ at the moment, and I'm not hungry.

3 I have a hard time now, but I don't have anyone to ask for advice. (one)
→ I have a hard time now, but I ___________ ___________ ___________ to ask for advice.

D 우리말과 같은 뜻이 되도록 부정대명사와 주어진 단어를 이용하여 문장을 완성하시오.

1 위층에는 아무도 없었다. (upstairs)
→ There ________ ________ ________ ________.

2 이 쿠키는 내가 직접 구운 거야. 좀 먹어보겠니? (will, try)
→ I baked these cookies myself. ________ ________ ________ ________?

3 한 가게만 열려 있고 나머지는 다 문을 닫았다. (be, closed)
→ Only one store was open, and ________ ________ ________ all ________.

4 나는 오늘 아무것도 먹지 않아서 배가 매우 고프다. (eat, today)
→ I'm very hungry because I haven't ________ ________ ________.

5 이 라디오는 작동이 안 돼요. 다른 것으로 교환할 수 있을까요? (exchange, for)
→ This radio doesn't work. Can I ________ ________ ________ ________?

6 운이 좋게도 그 교통사고에서 아무도 다치지 않았다. (be injured)
→ Luckily, ________ ________ ________ in the car accident.

7 이 반바지는 안 맞네요. 같은 색깔로 좀 더 큰 것이 있나요? (larger)
→ These shorts don't fit me. Do you have ________ ________ in the same color?

E 우리말과 같은 뜻이 되도록 주어진 단어를 배열하시오.

1 주변에 아무도 없다면 성공은 아무 의미도 없다. (nobody, you, around, have, you)
→ Success doesn't mean anything if ________________________.

2 학생들 중 3분의 1만이 깨어 있었고, 나머지는 졸고 있었다. (were, the, dozing off, others)
→ Only one third of the students were awake, and ________________________.

3 그 센터의 노인들은 배움에는 나이가 없다는 것을 보여주었다. (too old, is, to learn, no one)
→ The senior citizens at the center showed that ________________________.

4 검은 색 목도리를 원하시나요, 아니면 하얀색을 원하시나요? (black, white, or, scarf, want, a, a, one)
→ Do you ________________________?

5 이 귀걸이들은 너무 비싸네요. 좀 더 싼 것으로 보여주시겠어요? (show, ones, can, me, you, cheaper)
→ These earrings are too expensive. ________________________?

6 나는 언니가 두 명 있다. 한 명은 영어 교사이고 다른 한 명은 피아니스트이다.
(an English teacher, a pianist, is, the other, one, is)
→ I have two sisters. ________________ and ________________.

7 어떤 사람들은 맑은 날을 좋아하지만 또 다른 사람들은 비 오는 날을 좋아한다.
(some people, like, rainy days, like, sunny days, others)
→ ________________, but ________________.

부정대명사 II

A 보기 에서 알맞은 말을 골라 문장을 완성하시오.

보기 either neither all every both each none

1 영어에서 모든 문장은 대문자로 시작한다.
→ ___________ sentence begins with a capital letter in English.

2 내 여동생과 나는 그 둘 중 어느 편도 들고 싶지 않았다.
→ My sister and I didn't want to take sides of ___________ one.

3 팬들이 보낸 편지에 전부 답장을 하고 있다는 것이 확실한가요?
→ Are you sure that you are answering ___________ of your fans' letters?

4 날씨가 너무 덥지도 않고 춥지도 않아서 거기 머무는 것이 좋았다.
→ It was good to stay there because it is ___________ too hot nor too cold.

5 그들에게는 네 명의 자식이 있지만 그들 중 아무도 근처에 살지 않는다.
→ They have four children, but ___________ of them live near them.

6 나는 둘 다 마음에 들었기 때문에 이 파란색 머그잔과 저 빨간색을 샀다.
→ I bought this blue mug and that red one because I wanted ___________ of them.

7 농구 경기에서 다섯 명으로 구성된 각 팀은 점수를 획득하기 위해서 골대에 공을 넣는다.
→ In a basketball game, ___________ team of five players tries to throw a ball through a hoop in order to score points.

B 밑줄 친 부분을 어법에 맞게 고쳐 쓰시오.

1 I don't like neither science or economics. ___________
2 Is it true that you have spent all of money? ___________
3 Both them are old friends from high school. ___________
4 You need to answer each questions in no more than 50 words. ___________
5 I'd like to give you some more cake, but there's no left. ___________
6 Every student have to take the examination to graduate. ___________
7 I bought three T-shirts. Each T-shirt are different in color. ___________
8 Neither of my parents didn't like my plan after graduation. ___________
9 Every equipment needs to be inspected regularly for safety. ___________
10 Nowadays all of cell phones have cameras and MP3 players. ___________

C 우리말과 같은 뜻이 되도록 주어진 단어를 이용하여 문장을 완성하시오.

1 우리는 3주마다 집안 대청소를 한다. (week)

→ We clean the whole house ______ ______ ______.

2 Henry와 Brian 둘 중 하나가 축구팀의 주장이 될 것이다. (either)

→ ______ ______ ______ ______ will become the captain of the soccer team.

3 그 둘 다 해외에 나가본 적이 없었기 때문에 그들은 매우 긴장되었다. (neither)

→ ______ ______ ______ has been abroad, so they were very nervous.

4 비록 그 남자는 양쪽 눈이 다 안 보이지만 결코 좌절한 적이 없다. (blind, in, eyes)

→ Even though the man is ______ ______ ______ ______, he's never discouraged.

5 각각의 학생은 자신만의 주제를 골라야 한다. (student, have to, choose)

→ ______ ______ ______ ______ ______ his or her own topics.

6 줄다리기에서 두 팀은 줄의 각각의 끝을 상대 팀에 대항해서 잡아당긴다. (end of a rope)

→ In a tug-of-war, two teams pull ______ ______ ______ ______ ______ against each other.

7 우리 결혼을 축하하기 위해 와주신 것에 대해 여러분 모두에게 감사드리고 싶습니다. (thank, all, for coming)

→ I would like to ______ ______ ______ ______ ______ ______ to congratulate us on our wedding.

D 우리말과 같은 뜻이 되도록 주어진 단어를 배열하시오.

1 그것은 이제 내 일과 상관없어. (my business, anymore, of, none)

→ It's ______________________.

2 많은 차들이 거리의 양편에 주차되어 있다. (the street, of, are parked, on each side)

→ Many cars ______________________.

3 모든 아이들은 캠프에 참가할 기회를 얻게 됩니다. (a chance, child, every, have, will)

→ ______________________ to take part in the camp.

4 우리는 둘 다 차가 없었기 때문에 차를 빌려야 했다. (a car, because, of, had, neither, us)

→ ______________________, we had to rent one.

5 우리는 우리의 노력으로부터 아무것도 얻지 못해서 실망했다. (our efforts, we, from, got, nothing)

→ We were disappointed because ______________________.

6 날씨가 너무 추워서 나는 두 손을 주머니에 넣고 걸었다. (in my pockets, walked with, I, hands, both)

→ It was too cold, so ______________________.

7 나는 두 가지 선택권이 있었지만 둘 중 어느 것도 마음에 들지 않았다. (of, didn't, them, I, like, either)

→ I had two choices, but ______________________.

Unit 27 명사적 역할

A 주어진 동사를 어법에 맞게 바꿔 문장을 완성하시오.

1 I can't afford ____________ you that much money. (lend)

2 We plan ____________ a trip to Europe for two weeks. (take)

3 We hope ____________ with you again in the near future. (work)

4 My professor advised me ____________ to graduate school. (go)

5 She failed ____________ a gold medal in the Olympic Games. (win)

B 보기 에서 알맞은 말을 골라 어법에 맞게 바꿔 문장을 완성하시오.

보기 go major get solve take

1 He tried ________________ the math question but failed to get the answer.

2 There was a lot of traffic on the road, so we decided ________________ the subway.

3 My plan is ________________ a job as soon as I graduate from high school.

4 They want me ________________ in economics, but my dream is to become a singer.

5 She refused ________________ to the movie with us because she has a dental appointment.

C 보기 에서 알맞은 말을 골라 「의문사+to부정사」로 바꿔 문장을 완성하시오.

보기 read cook get off invite put

1 제가 어디서 내려야 할지 말씀해 주실 수 있나요?
→ Could you tell me ________________?

2 이 탁자를 거실 어디에 놓을지 말씀해 주세요.
→ Please tell me ________________ this table in your living room.

3 요즘 아이들은 매우 어린 나이에 읽는 법을 배운다.
→ Nowadays children learn ________________ at a very young age.

4 우리는 새집에 그들을 언제 초대할지 결정하지 못했다.
→ We haven't decided ________________ them to our new house.

5 나는 유명한 요리사에게서 요리하는 법을 배웠다.
→ I learned ________________ from a famous chef.

D 두 문장이 같은 의미가 되도록 문장을 다시 쓰시오.

1 To drive on icy roads can be very dangerous.

→ ______________________________

2 To change his opinion is almost impossible.

→ ______________________________

3 To admit one's mistake in front of others is difficult.

→ ______________________________

4 To walk around in this area at night is dangerous.

→ ______________________________

5 He hasn't decided whether he should go to the party.

→ He hasn't decided ______________________________.

6 Most fathers don't know what they should do when their babies cry.

→ Most fathers don't know ______________________________.

E 우리말과 같은 뜻이 되도록 주어진 단어를 이용하여 문장을 완성하시오.

1 그는 고객의 불만을 어떻게 처리해야 할지 몰랐다. (deal with)

→ He didn't know ________ ________ ________ ________ customer complaints.

2 그는 자신의 월급으로 아파트를 살 수 없었다. (afford, buy, an apartment)

→ He couldn't ________ ________ ________ ________ ________ on his salary.

3 그는 다음날 있을 시험을 위해 벼락치기를 하기로 결심했다. (decide, cram)

→ He ________ ________ ________ for the next day's exam.

4 우리는 여행하는 동안 어떤 호텔에 묵을지 결정하지 못했다. (hotel, stay in)

→ We haven't decided ________ ________ ________ ________ ________ during the trip.

5 그가 나를 오해한 것 같다. 나는 그를 화나게 할 의도는 없었다. (intend, make, upset)

→ I think he got me wrong, and I didn't ________ ________ ________ ________ ________.

6 무역 회사에서 일하기 위해서는 외국어를 배우는 것이 매우 중요하다. (learn, a foreign language)

→ ________ is very important ________ ________ ________ ________ ________ to work at a trading company.

7 외국에서 공부하는 데 많은 돈이 들지만 많은 부모가 자녀를 해외로 보내고 싶어 한다. (study abroad, want, send)

→ ________ takes lots of money ________ ________ ________, but many parents ________ ________ ________ their children abroad.

형용사적 역할

A 보기 와 같이 문장을 바꿔 쓰시오.

보기	We have made a decision. We're going to move to another city. → We have made ___a decision to move___ to another city.

1 May is a perfect time. I can go on a trip in May.
→ May is ________________.

2 I am thirsty. I want to drink something.
→ I want ________________ because I am thirsty.

3 These street cats need someone. She can feed them.
→ These street cats need ________________ them.

4 She brought a book. She wanted to read it at the cafe.
→ She brought ________________ at the cafe.

5 This coffee is too strong for her. She wants to put some milk in her coffee.
→ She wants ________________ in her coffee.

6 I need to buy some clothes. I have to wear them for tomorrow's entrance ceremony.
→ I need to buy ________________ for tomorrow's entrance ceremony.

B 두 문장의 의미가 통하도록 「be+to부정사」를 이용하여 바꿔 쓰시오.

1 We should make a final decision.
→ We ____.

2 You have to follow many rules in school.
→ You ____.

3 He was destined to become a great artist.
→ He ____.

4 No one could survive in the earthquake.
→ No one ____.

5 My friends and I are going to a concert this evening.
→ My friends and I ____.

6 If you intend to succeed in business, you must not be afraid of challenges.
→ If you ________________________________, you must not be afraid of challenges.

C 우리말과 같은 뜻이 되도록 주어진 단어를 이용하여 문장을 완성하시오.

1 그는 차를 살 충분한 돈이 없다. (money, buy)

→ He doesn't have ________ ________ ________ ________ a car.

2 나는 파티에 같이 갈 사람이 없다. (anyone, go)

→ I don't have ________ ________ ________ to the party with.

3 그는 돈을 빌릴 친구가 한 명도 없다. (any friends, borrow)

→ He doesn't have ________ ________ ________ ________ money from.

4 나는 바닥을 쓸 빗자루가 필요하다. (a broom, sweep, the floor)

→ I need ________ ________ ________ ________ the floor with.

5 우리는 묵을 호텔을 예약했다. (a hotel, stay)

→ We booked ________ ________ ________ ________ ________.

6 물건을 담을 비닐봉지 하나만 주시겠어요? (a plastic bag, put, things)

→ Can I have ________ ________ ________ ________ ________ ________ ________?

7 그녀는 혼자 시간을 보낼 자신만의 방이 필요했다. (her own room, spend)

→ She needed ________ ________ ________ ________ ________ ________ alone.

D 우리말과 같은 뜻이 되도록 주어진 단어를 배열하시오.

1 안타깝지만 작별 인사를 해야 할 시간이다. (time, goodbye, it's, say, to)

→ I'm afraid ______________________________.

2 그는 내년에 전무로 승진될 예정이다. (to, is, be promoted, to, executive director)

→ He ______________________________ next year.

3 모든 것이 잘 될 것이니 걱정할 것은 아무것도 없다. (worry, nothing, there's, to, about)

→ Everything will be all right, so ______________________________.

4 남편이 죽은 뒤로, 그녀는 의지할 사람이 없었다. (have, rely, she, anyone, on, to, didn't)

→ Since her husband passed away, ______________________________.

5 그는 그 나라의 대통령이 될 운명이었다. (become, the country, was, of, the president, to)

→ He ______________________________.

6 나는 들어야 할 무거운 짐이 많아서 택시를 타야 한다. (heavy bags, lots of, I, carry, have, to)

→ I need to take a taxi because ______________________________.

7 먹을 게 하나도 없으니 오늘 저녁은 우리 나가서 먹는 게 어때? (to, we, anything, don't, have, eat)

→ ______________________________, so why don't we eat out this evening?

Unit 29 부사적 역할

A 보기 에서 알맞은 말을 골라 문장을 완성하시오.

보기	hear	borrow	get	be	donate

1 I went to the hair salon __________ __________ a haircut.

2 She grew up __________ __________ a world-famous pianist.

3 She went to the library __________ __________ some books.

4 He must be generous __________ __________ a lot of money for sick children.

5 He was relieved __________ __________ that his father wasn't hurt in the accident.

B 보기 와 같이 문장을 바꿔 쓰시오.

보기

We dropped by a coffee shop to take a break.

→ We dropped by a coffee shop in order to take a break.

→ We dropped by a coffee shop so as to take a break.

1 She cut down on food to lose weight.

→ ______________________________

→ ______________________________

2 He drove faster not to be late for the meeting.

→ ______________________________

→ ______________________________

3 We took the subway not to waste time on the road.

→ ______________________________

→ ______________________________

4 I have to go to bed early to get up early tomorrow morning.

→ ______________________________

→ ______________________________

5 She drank some coffee to stay awake during the boring class.

→ ______________________________

→ ______________________________

C 우리말과 같은 뜻이 되도록 주어진 단어를 이용하여 문장을 완성하시오.

1 우리는 제주도로 졸업여행을 가게 되어 행복했다. (happy, go)

→ We ________ ________ ________ ________ to Jejudo for a graduation trip.

2 나중에 잊어버리지 않도록 그것을 적어놓는 것이 어때? (forget)

→ Why don't you write it down so ________ ________ ________ ________ it later?

3 나는 막차를 잡으려고 죽을힘을 다해 뛰었다. (catch, the last bus)

→ I desperately ran ________ ________ ________ ________ ________.

4 그녀는 괜히 그 문제를 꺼냈다가 그를 화나게 만들었다. (make, upset)

→ She brought up the issue only ________ ________ ________ ________.

5 우리는 그가 심각한 상태라는 이야기를 듣고 충격을 받았다. (shocked, hear)

→ We were ________ ________ ________ that he was in serious condition.

6 그 당시에 그는 기회를 잡을 준비가 되어 있지 않았다. (ready, grab, the chance)

→ At that time, he was not ________ ________ ________ ________ ________.

7 자신을 속인 사람을 용서하다니 그는 관대한 사람임에 틀림이 없다. (forgive, tolerant)

→ He must be ________ ________ ________ the person who deceived him.

D 우리말과 같은 뜻이 되도록 주어진 단어를 배열하시오.

1 우리 할머니는 90세까지 사셨다. (90 years old, lived, be, to)

→ My grandmother ________________________________.

2 그 할머니를 돕다니 너는 무척 친절하구나. (the old lady, of, help, kind, you, to)

→ It is very ________________________________.

3 건강을 유지하기 위해 정기적으로 운동을 해야 한다. (regularly, need to, healthy, work out, to stay)

→ You ________________________________.

4 데이지 않도록 오븐을 조심해서 다뤄야 해요. (not, so as, careful, yourself, burn, with the oven, to)

→ You should be ________________________________.

5 나는 너희와 같은 좋은 친구들이 있어서 매우 운이 좋다고 생각해! (friends, lucky, to, have, like you)

→ I think I am very ________________________________!

6 우리 어머니는 내가 거짓말을 했다는 것을 알고 매우 실망했다. (know, disappointed, very, my mother, to, was)

→ ________________________________ that I lied to her.

7 그녀는 세계적으로 유명한 패션모델이 되기 위해 뉴욕으로 가기로 결심했다.
(in order to, to New York, be, to go, a world-famous fashion model)

→ She decided ________________________________.

의미상의 주어, 시제, 태

A 주어진 단어를 이용하여 빈칸에 알맞은 의미상 주어를 써 넣으시오.

1 The book is too difficult ____________ ____________ to understand. (I)

2 We've arranged ____________ ____________ to see the doctor tomorrow. (you)

3 It is clever ____________ ____________ to answer all the questions so quickly. (she)

4 It is impolite ____________ ____________ to talk back to your mother constantly. (you)

5 It's very sweet ____________ ____________ to help me even though he is very busy. (he)

B 밑줄 친 부분을 어법에 맞게 고쳐 쓰시오.

1 He wanted his opinion <u>to respected</u> by others. ____________

2 She seemed <u>to have already decide</u> to change jobs. ____________

3 My boss wants this report <u>to finish</u> by tomorrow morning. ____________

4 It's important <u>of you</u> to think deeply before you do something. ____________

5 Due to a different word order, English is difficult <u>of Koreans</u> to learn. ____________

C 두 문장의 의미가 통하도록 문장을 완성하시오.

1 Lisa seems to be sick.

→ ____________ ____________ ____________ Lisa is sick.

2 His handwriting is difficult to read.

→ It is ____________ ____________ ____________ his handwriting.

3 It seems that the criminal has already gone abroad.

→ The criminal seems ____________ ____________ ____________ ____________ ____________.

4 She was silly not to follow the safety regulations.

→ It was ____________ ____________ ____________ ____________ ____________ ____________
the safety regulations.

5 It seemed that all of the students in the classroom had agreed with his idea.

→ All of the students in the classroom seemed ____________ ____________ ____________
____________ ____________ ____________.

D 우리말과 같은 뜻이 되도록 주어진 단어를 이용하여 문장을 완성하시오.

1 나는 노트북을 가져가야 한다. (necessary, take)

→ It is ____ ____ ____ ____ ____ my laptop.

2 돈을 도박에 낭비하다니 그는 어리석었어. (stupid, waste)

→ It was ____ ____ ____ ____ ____ money on gambling.

3 돌고래들은 매우 똑똑해서 훈련시키기가 쉽다. (easy, train)

→ Dolphins are so smart that they are ____ ____ ____.

4 네 방은 당장 치울 필요가 있어. (need, clean)

→ Your room ____ ____ ____ ____ right now.

5 그런 상황에서 싫다고 말하다니 너는 용감했어. (brave, say no)

→ It was ____ ____ ____ ____ ____ ____ in such a situation.

6 그녀는 그 남자를 오랫동안 알고 있었던 것처럼 보였다. (seem, know)

→ She ____ ____ ____ ____ the man for a long time.

7 나는 다음 주 이 시간까지 그 프로젝트를 마칠 거라고 예상한다. (expect, finish)

→ I ____ ____ ____ the project by this time next week.

E 우리말과 같은 뜻이 되도록 주어진 단어를 배열하시오.

1 시키는 대로 다 하다니 너는 바보 같았어. (of, to, foolish, you, do)

→ It was ________________ as you were told to do.

2 그는 요즘 할 일이 많은 것 같다. (have, to do, to, work, a lot of, seems)

→ He ________________ these days.

3 우리 부모님은 내가 여행을 갈 수 있게 허락해 주셨다. (me, a trip, allowed, to, take)

→ My parents ________________.

4 그가 제시간에 도착하는 것은 가능하지 않았다. (him, possible, on time, for, arrive, to)

→ It was not ________________.

5 John 삼촌은 운전면허 시험에 떨어졌던 것 같다. (to, his driving test, have, failed, seems)

→ Uncle John ________________.

6 한 시간이나 나를 기다리게 하다니 그녀는 무례했다. (have kept, rude, waiting, of, me, her, to)

→ It was ________________ for an hour.

7 우리는 그가 그런 사건에 연루될 것이라고는 예상하지 못했다. (him, expect, be involved in, to)

→ We didn't ________________ such an incident.

기타 부정사의 쓰임

A 주어진 말을 어법에 맞게 바꿔 문장을 완성하시오.

1 I'm going to have my car __________ this Saturday. (wash)

2 Please let me __________ if there's anything I can do for you. (know)

3 She watched me __________ basketball in the schoolyard. (play)

4 It takes only an hour __________ this cell phone battery. (recharge)

B 두 문장의 의미가 통하도록 문장을 완성하시오.

1 Her hair is so short that she can't tie her hair in the back.
→ Her hair ______________________________.

2 She was too sick to go to work this morning.
→ She was ______________________________.

3 My father's car is too old to take a long drive with it.
→ My father's car is ______________________________.

4 He was so young that he couldn't ride the rides in the amusement park.
→ He was ______________________________.

C 문장의 의미가 통하도록 주어진 표현을 이용하여 문장을 다시 쓰시오.

1 He is doing a part-time job to make money for tuition.
→ ______________________________ (so as to)
→ ______________________________ (in order to)
→ ______________________________ (so that)
→ ______________________________ (in order that)

2 She ran as fast as she could not to be late for school.
→ ______________________________ (so as to)
→ ______________________________ (in order to)
→ ______________________________ (so that)
→ ______________________________ (in order that)

D 우리말과 같은 뜻이 되도록 주어진 단어를 이용하여 문장을 완성하시오.

1 솔직히 말해서, 나는 그를 만난 기억이 없다. (the truth)
→ ____________ ____________ ____________ ____________, I don't remember meeting him.

2 우선, 이 이야기의 배경부터 말씀드리겠습니다. (begin)
→ ____________ ____________ ____________, I will talk about the background of the story.

3 그녀의 남편은 퇴근 후 그녀가 집안일 하는 것을 도왔다. (help, do, housework)
→ Her husband ____________ ____________ ____________ ____________ after work.

4 오늘 우리 엄마가 방과 후에 나에게 내 남동생을 돌보도록 시켰다. (make, take care of)
→ Today, my mother ____________ ____________ ____________ ____________ ____________ ____________ ____________ after school.

5 도로 한가운데서 내 차가 고장 났고, 설상가상으로 비가 내리기 시작했다. (make, worse)
→ My car broke down in the middle of the road, and ____________ ____________ ____________ ____________, it started to rain.

6 그녀는 그날 밤 한 남자가 담을 뛰어넘어 도망가는 것을 보았다. (see, a man, jump over, run away)
→ She ____________ ____________ ____________ ____________ ____________ a fence and ____________ ____________ that night.

7 이상한 이야기지만 그는 더 높은 월급에 좋은 조건임에도 불구하고 그 일자리 제안을 거절했다. (strange)
→ ____________ ____________ ____________, he refused the job offer despite a higher salary with good benefits.

E 우리말과 같은 뜻이 되도록 주어진 단어를 배열하시오.

1 Tracy는 노래 실력은 말할 것도 없고 춤도 잘 춘다. (her singing ability, to, not, of, speak)
→ Tracy dances well, ____.

2 그는 잘생긴 얼굴뿐만 아니라 인간성도 좋다. (looks, mention, good, not, his, to)
→ He has a great personality ____.

3 그 방은 우리가 잘 수 있을 만큼 충분히 크다. (large, us, enough, sleep in, for, to)
→ The room is ____.

4 솔직히 말해서 이 목걸이는 네 옷에 안 어울리는 것 같아. (you, to, honest, be, with)
→ ____, I don't think this necklace matches your dress.

5 그는 너무 뚱뚱해서 이 빨간 코트를 입을 수 없다. (to, too, red, fat, wear, coat, this)
→ He is ____.

6 인터뷰 준비가 다 되시면 제게 알려주세요. (to be interviewed, let, are, know, you, when, ready, me)
→ Please ____.

동명사의 형태와 쓰임

A 주어진 말을 어법에 맞게 바꿔 문장을 완성하시오.

1 I am interested in ____________ abroad. (study)

2 Would you mind ____________ seats with me? (change)

3 I'm sorry for not ____________ to your email right away. (reply)

4 ____________ various vegetables is good for your health. (eat)

5 ____________ my dog in the park is my favorite pastime. (walk)

6 The couple thanked everyone for ____________ their wedding ceremony. (attend)

7 His dream is ____________ his own house with a beautiful garden. (build)

8 She dislikes ____________ her personal matters with the school counselor. (discuss)

B 보기 와 같이 주어진 문장의 의미가 통하도록 문장을 완성하시오.

보기	I don't like to swim in the sea. I'm afraid of it. → I am afraid of ______ swimming in the sea ______.

1 I often paint pictures. I really enjoy that activity.
→ I really enjoy ________________________________.

2 Do not eat instant noodles. It's bad for your health.
→ ________________________________ is bad for your health.

3 He often plays mobile games. It's his favorite hobby.
→ His favorite hobby is ________________________________.

4 Tom plays tennis with his friend every weekend. He likes it.
→ Tom likes ________________________________.

5 My mother worked overtime all week long. She got very tired.
→ ________________________________ made my mother very tired.

6 She often spends time with her friends chatting in a coffee shop. She loves it.
→ She loves ________________________________ chatting in a coffee shop.

7 He is interested in some language courses. He wants to learn Spanish and French.
→ He is interested in ________________________________.

C 우리말과 같은 뜻이 되도록 주어진 말을 이용하여 문장을 완성하시오.

1 대기실에서 사람들이 많이 있었다. (wait)
→ There were a lot of people in the ________ ________.

2 아침을 거르면 저녁 때 과식으로 이어질 수 있다. (skip breakfast, overeat)
→ ________ ________ can lead to ________ in the evening.

3 그는 엄격한 부모님에게 싫다고 말하는 것이 두려웠다. (be afraid of, say no)
→ He ________ ________ ________ ________ ________ to his strict parents.

4 식사 중 물을 많이 마시는 것은 소화에 도움이 안 된다. (drink, lots of, not, help)
→ ________ ________ ________ ________ ________ ________ your digestion during the meals.

5 스트레스를 받지 않는 것이 건강을 유지하는 데 중요하다. (not, be stressed out, be)
→ ________ ________ ________ ________ ________ important to stay healthy.

6 내 직업에서 가장 좋은 점은 다양한 배경을 가진 사람들을 많이 만나는 것이다. (meet, lots of)
→ The best part of my job is ________ ________ ________ ________ from different backgrounds.

7 아이들은 이번 주 금요일에 야외에 나가서 점심을 먹는 것에 들떠있다. (be excited about, have a picnic)
→ The children ________ ________ ________ ________ ________ ________ this Friday.

D 우리말과 같은 뜻이 되도록 주어진 단어를 배열하시오.

1 그 남자아이는 모자를 훔쳤다는 것을 부인했다. (a hat, denied, stealing)
→ The boy ________________________.

2 그는 내가 문을 열 때까지 계속 문을 두드렸다. (banging, the door, kept, on)
→ He ________________________ until I opened it.

3 나는 점심 식사 후 산책할 것을 제안했다. (after, going, for a walk, lunch, suggested)
→ I ________________________.

4 나는 미국을 여행한다는 생각에 무척 신이 났다. (traveling, the thought of, around the US, made)
→ ________________________ me so excited.

5 우리는 이사를 가는 대신 집을 리모델링하기로 결정했다. (remodel, instead of, decided, moving, our house, to)
→ We ________________________.

6 그는 배우로서의 경력을 발전 시켜나가는 것을 포기했다. (developing, gave up, his career)
→ He ________________________ as an actor.

의미상의 주어, 시제, 태

A 보기 와 같이 동명사의 의미상의 주어를 이용한 문장으로 바꿔 쓰시오.

보기
She talked behind his back. He couldn't stand it.
→ He couldn't stand ____her talking behind his back____.

1 He is always chatting during the group work in class. I dislike it.
→ I dislike ______________________.

2 Some parents let their kids run around in restaurants. I can't tolerate that.
→ I can't tolerate ______________________ in restaurants.

3 My son won first prize in the essay contest. We were surprised at the news.
→ We were surprised at ______________________ in the essay contest.

B 두 문장의 의미가 통하도록 that절을 이용한 문장으로 바꿔 쓰시오.

1 She denied having lied to her parents.
→ She denied ______________________.

2 The couple officially admitted having broken up.
→ The couple officially admitted ______________________.

3 He didn't mind having to pay for the dinner that day.
→ He didn't mind ______________________.

4 She was very proud of his finding a new home for the abandoned dog.
→ She was very proud ______________________.

C 두 문장의 의미가 통하도록 동명사를 이용한 문장으로 바꿔 쓰시오.

1 I regret that I didn't tell you about this earlier.
→ I regret ______________________.

2 Do you mind if I ask you your phone number?
→ Do you mind ______________________?

3 I'm sorry that I didn't call you back immediately.
→ I'm sorry for ______________________.

4 I appreciate that you took care of my kids for two days.
→ I appreciate ______________________.

D 우리말과 같은 뜻이 되도록 주어진 말을 이용하여 문장을 완성하시오.

1 나는 더운 여름날에 아이스크림 먹는 것을 좋아한다. (like, have, ice cream)

→ I ________ ________ ________ ________ on a hot summer day.

2 그는 그녀가 복권을 사야 한다고 주장했다. (insist on, she, buy)

→ He ________ ________ ________ ________ a lottery ticket.

3 우리 어머니는 내가 밤늦게 들어오는 것을 정말 싫어한다. (hate, I, come, home)

→ My mother really ________ ________ ________ ________ late at night.

4 나는 옷에 그렇게 많은 돈을 쓴 것을 후회한다. (regret, spend, too much money)

→ I ________ ________ ________ ________ ________ on clothes.

5 당신과 함께 일할 수 있는 기회를 주셔서 감사합니다. (give, work)

→ Thank you for ________ me a chance ________ ________ with you.

6 박물관 안에서 사진을 찍는 것은 금지되어 있습니다. (take pictures, be, not, allow)

→ ________ ________ ________ ________ ________ in the museum.

7 그녀는 파티에서 그가 그 말을 한 것을 기억을 할 수 없었다. (remember, he, say, that)

→ She couldn't ________ ________ ________ ________ at the party.

E 우리말과 같은 뜻이 되도록 주어진 단어를 알맞게 배열하시오.

1 나는 그에게 돈을 갚지 않아서 미안하다. (sorry, paid, for, I'm, having, not)

→ ________________________________ him back the money.

2 사고가 일어나기 전 그는 나를 만났던 것을 기억하지 못했다. (me, didn't, he, recall, met, having)

→ ________________________________ before the accident.

3 나는 발표하는 동안 큰 실수를 한 것이 부끄럽다. (a big mistake, having, embarrassed, was, I, made, about)

→ ________________________________ during the presentation.

4 그녀는 그날 이후로 엄마와 눈을 마주치는 것을 피했다. (with her mother, making, has avoided, eye contact)

→ She ________________________________ since that day.

5 학생들은 때때로 어른들에게 이해받지 못한다고 불평한다. (not, by adults, understood, about, being, complain)

→ Students sometimes ________________________________.

6 나는 하루 종일 모기 물린 자국 긁고 싶은 것을 참을 수가 없었다. (resist, the mosquito bites, couldn't, I, scratching)

→ ________________________________ all day long.

7 그 두 소년은 서로 싸운 것에 대해 벌을 받을까 봐 두려웠다.
(punished, each other, for, of, afraid, were, fighting with, being)

→ The two boys ________________________________.

동명사 vs. to부정사

A 주어진 단어를 이용하여 문장을 완성하시오.

1 He tried to avoid ____________ overtime. (work)

2 He denied ____________ the false rumor. (spread)

3 The students refused ____________ the classes. (attend)

4 She chose ____________ her job after she had a baby. (quit)

5 I gave up ____________ independent from my parents. (become)

6 They managed ____________ from the burning building. (escape)

7 My uncle hopes ____________ married in his mid-thirties at the latest. (get)

8 They postponed ____________ their own house until they saved enough money. (buy)

B 보기 에서 단어를 골라 어법에 맞게 바꿔 문장을 완성하시오.

[1-5] **보기** comply have smoke join study

1 I am considering ____________ a baseball team.

2 I decided ____________ ____________ regular medical checkups.

3 She regrets not ____________ harder in high school.

4 My father tried to quit ____________, but he failed.

5 They promised ____________ ____________ with the school rules.

[6-10] **보기** hire get know participate take

6 We plan ____________ ____________ in a marathon.

7 They are discussing ____________ a substitute teacher.

8 The boy insisted on ____________ a higher monthly allowance.

9 My sister suggested ____________ a backpacking trip to Europe.

10 He pretended not ____________ ____________ anything about the incident.

C 두 문장의 의미가 통하도록 문장을 완성하시오.

1 I told him my secret, and now I regret it.
→ I regret ________________ my secret.

2 Suddenly the thunder and lightning began to strike.
→ Suddenly the thunder and lightning began ________________.

3 The fire continued to cause great damage to the forest.
→ The fire continued ________________________.

4 I had to turn off the TV before I went to bed, but I forgot.
→ I forgot ________________ before I went to bed.

5 I remembered that I booked the ticket, but I can't find it.
→ I remembered ________________, but I can't find it.

6 I hate to lose games, but I admit that he is hard to beat.
→ I hate ________________, but I admit that he is hard to beat.

7 He prefers studying at the library because he can concentrate more easily there.
→ He prefers ________________________ because he can concentrate more easily there.

D 우리말과 같은 뜻이 되도록 주어진 단어를 이용하여 문장을 완성하시오.

1 그녀가 돌아오면 제게 전화 좀 해달라고 해주세요. (tell, call)
→ When she comes back, please ________ ________ ________ ________ me.

2 그는 우유가 상했는지 보기 위해서 냄새를 맡아봤다. (try, sniff at)
→ He ________ ________ ________ the milk to see if it had turned sour.

3 나는 외출하기 전에 가스를 잠갔던 것을 기억한다. (remember, turn off, the gas)
→ I ________ ________ ________ ________ ________ before I went out.

4 그는 그녀에게 문자메시지를 보내기 위해 멈춰 섰다. (stop, send, a text message)
→ He ________ ________ ________ ________ ________ ________ to her.

5 그녀는 우유를 냉장고에 넣는 것을 깜빡해서 우유가 상해버렸다. (forget, put)
→ She ________ ________ ________ the milk in the refrigerator, so it has gone bad.

6 나는 그녀에게 사과하지 않은 것을 후회한다. (regret, not, apologize, to her)
→ I ________ ________ ________ ________ ________.

7 그는 부모님과 함께 있을 때 자신의 여자 친구에 대해 언급하는 것을 피했다. (avoid, mention)
→ He ________ ________ ________ ________ when he was with his parents.

동명사의 관용 표현

A 보기 에서 알맞은 말을 골라 어법에 맞게 바꿔 문장을 완성하시오.

[1-5] 보기 concentrate go ski mention spend

1 Her attitude is not worth ___________.

2 I don't feel like ___________ to a concert today.

3 I look forward to ___________ time with him next weekend.

4 My brother and I like winter sports, so we go ___________ every winter.

5 She had difficulty ___________ on studying because it's too noisy outside.

[6-10] 보기 conduct play decorate grade wear

6 She never goes out without ___________ makeup.

7 She spent a lot of time ___________ her new house.

8 He totally objects to ___________ experiments on animals.

9 The teacher is busy ___________ students' papers this week.

10 The boy has no brothers and sisters, so he is used to ___________ by himself.

B 두 문장의 의미가 통하도록 주어진 말을 이용하여 문장을 완성하시오.

1 It is useless to regret it now. (no use)

→ It ___________ ___________ ___________ ___________ it now.

2 He is used to staying awake until late at night. (accustomed)

→ He ___________ ___________ ___________ ___________ ___________ until late at night.

3 My mother is not good at cooking, so we often eat out. (poor)

→ My mother ___________ ___________ ___________ ___________, so we often eat out.

4 She couldn't help laughing because his joke was really funny. (but)

→ She ___________ ___________ ___________ because his joke was really funny.

5 He keeps his children from going out after 9:00 p.m. (prevent)

→ He ___________ ___________ ___________ ___________ ___________ ___________ after 9:00 p.m.

C 우리말과 같은 뜻이 되도록 주어진 단어를 이용하여 문장을 완성하시오.

1 이제 변명을 해봐야 소용이 없다. (no use, make, excuses)

→ It is ____________ ____________ ____________ ____________ now.

2 그녀는 아이들에게 소리 지르지 않을 수 없었다. (help, shout)

→ She ____________ ____________ ____________ at her kids.

3 우리 어머니는 서울로 이사 가는 것을 반대하셨다. (object to, move)

→ My mother ____________ ____________ ____________ to Seoul.

4 나는 공부에 집중하는 데 애를 먹었다. (have trouble, concentrate)

→ I ____________ ____________ ____________ on my studies.

5 당신에게서 곧 소식을 들을 수 있기를 기대합니다. (look forward to, hear)

→ We are ____________ ____________ ____________ ____________ from you soon.

6 나는 주말을 도서관에서 공부하며 보낼 것이다. (spend, the weekend, study)

→ I will ____________ ____________ ____________ ____________ in the library.

7 그녀는 이렇게 추운 날에 산책을 가고 싶지 않았다. (feel like, go for a walk)

→ She ____________ ____________ ____________ ____________ ____________ ____________ ____________ on this cold day.

D 우리말과 같은 뜻이 되도록 주어진 단어를 배열하시오.

1 우리 누나는 바이올린 연주를 잘 한다. (playing, is, at, the violin, good)

→ My sister ____.

2 그들은 여행 일정을 짜느라 바빴다. (planning, they, busy, were, their trip)

→ ____

3 고등학생은 매일 일찍 일어나는 것에 익숙하다. (early, are accustomed, getting up, to)

→ High school students ____ every day.

4 네 미래를 위해 이 프로젝트는 참여할만한 가치가 있다. (taking part in, this project, worth, is)

→ ____ for your future.

5 나는 매일 집안 청소를 하는 것에 익숙해졌다. (got used, I, to, cleaning, the house)

→ ____ every day.

6 그 아이는 따뜻한 우유를 마시지 않고는 잠을 자지 않는다. (goes to bed, warm milk, never, drinking, without)

→ The kid ____.

7 그는 도둑고양이를 집 안에 들어오지 못하게 했다. (from, his home, prevented, coming into, the stray cat)

→ He ____.

시제에 따른 수동태

A 능동태 문장을 수동태 문장으로 바꿔 쓰시오.

1 Someone broke the window.
→ The window ______________________________.

2 They have moved back my presentation.
→ My presentation ______________________________.

3 You must do something about the problem.
→ Something ______________________________.

4 They will build a monument for her in her native place.
→ A monument ______________________________.

5 You must keep the important documents in a safe place.
→ The important documents ______________________________.

B 우리말과 같은 뜻이 되도록 보기 에서 알맞은 말을 골라 문장을 완성하시오.

보기 include change follow take unlock delay protect

1 사생활은 무슨 일이 있어도 보호되어야 한다.
→ Privacy must ______________ by all means.

2 당신의 이름은 대기자 명단에 포함되어 있습니다.
→ Your name ______________ on the waiting list.

3 그 결정 사항은 회의 후에 바뀔 수 있다.
→ The decision can ______________ after the meeting.

4 면접은 필기시험 뒤에 있을 것입니다.
→ The interview will ______________ by written examination.

5 악천후로 비행기가 한 시간 지연될 것입니다.
→ The flight will ______________ for an hour due to bad weather.

6 문손잡이를 돌렸을 때 나는 문이 잠겨 있지 않았음을 알았다.
→ When I turned the door knob, I found that the door ______________.

7 시위자들 중 일부는 수갑을 찬 채 경찰서로 끌려갔다.
→ Some of the protestors ______________ to the police station in handcuffs.

C 우리말과 같은 뜻이 되도록 주어진 단어를 이용하여 수동태 문장을 완성하시오.

1 Daniel이 교통사고로 심하게 다쳤다. (seriously, injure)
→ Daniel ______ ______ ______ in the car accident.

2 나는 그녀의 생일 파티에 초대되지 않았다. (not, invite)
→ I ______ ______ ______ to her birthday party.

3 오늘은 내 차를 쓸 수 없다. 내 차는 수리 중이다. (repair)
→ I can't use my car today. It ______ ______ ______.

4 그 도둑이 지난주에 경찰에게 체포되었다. (arrest, the police)
→ The thief ______ ______ last week ______ ______ ______.

5 학생들은 여행이 취소되어서 실망했다. (have, cancel)
→ Students are disappointed because the trip ______ ______ ______.

6 이 버스 노선들 중 일부는 중지될 것입니다. (will, discontinue)
→ Some of these bus lines ______ ______ ______.

7 집에 도착했을 때, 우리는 집에 도둑이 침입했었다는 것을 알았다. (have, break into)
→ When we arrived home, we found that our house ______ ______ ______ ______.

D 우리말과 같은 뜻이 되도록 주어진 단어를 배열하시오.

1 축하해! 네가 대학에 합격했다는 소식 들었어. (been, have, admitted, you, to university)
→ Congratulations! I heard ____________________.

2 이 낡은 타이어는 안전을 위해 교체되어야 합니다. (your safety, must, replaced, be, for)
→ These old tires ____________________.

3 상위 10명의 후보가 다음 주 월요일에 발표될 것입니다. (be, next Monday, will, announced)
→ The list of top 10 candidates ____________________.

4 그 호텔의 모든 방은 이미 꽉 찬 상태다. (already, of the hotel, all the rooms, are, filled up)
→ ____________________

5 죄송합니다만 참고 문헌은 대출이 안 됩니다. (be, cannot, checked out, the reference books)
→ I'm sorry, but ____________________.

6 과제는 이번 주 금요일까지 완료되어야 한다. (by, the assignment, be, must, finished, this Friday)
→ ____________________

7 우리 할머니의 사진이 지하실에서 발견되었다. (was, my grandmother's picture, in the basement, found)
→ ____________________

문장의 형태에 따른 수동태

A 주어진 문장을 수동태 문장으로 바꿔 쓰시오.

1 When I was young, my aunt raised me in Daegu.
→ When I was young, I ______________________________.

2 Mary hasn't returned the book to the library yet.
→ The book ______________________________.

3 I passed him some cookies.
→ Some cookies ______________________________.

4 My parents bought me a new computer.
→ A new computer ______________________________.

5 My mother taught me English songs.
→ I ______________________________.
→ English songs ______________________________.

6 They gave me another chance.
→ I ______________________________.
→ Another chance ______________________________.

B 주어진 문장을 수동태 문장으로 바꿔 쓰시오. [by+행위자 생략]

1 They told me to lock the door when I went out.
→ I ______________________________.

2 My teacher advised me to study art in college.
→ I ______________________________.

3 My parents made me do my homework by myself.
→ I ______________________________.

4 Alicia let me stay in her house while she was away.
→ I ______________________________ while she was away.

5 He asked her to tell Lisa that he would be back in an hour.
→ She ______________________________.

6 The student helped the old lady to go upstairs in the hospital.
→ The old lady ______________________________.

7 He saw his daughter playing with her friends in the playground.
→ His daughter ______________________________.

C 우리말과 같은 뜻이 되도록 주어진 말을 이용하여 문장을 완성하시오.

1 그녀는 진료를 받기 위해 30분 기다리라고 들었다. (tell, wait)
→ She ________ ________ ________ ________ half an hour to see the doctor.

2 비행기 사고가 발생했고 많은 승객들이 죽었다. (occur, kill)
→ A flight accident ________, and many of the passengers ________ ________.

3 우승자에게 메달이 수여될 것입니다. (will, give, the winner)
→ A medal ________ ________ ________ ________ the winner.

4 우리 어머니는 나에게 남동생이 숙제하는 것을 도와주도록 시켰다. (make, help)
→ I ________ ________ ________ ________ my brother do his homework.

5 그는 가능한 한 빨리 수술을 받도록 설득당했다. (persuade, have an operation)
→ He ________ ________ ________ ________ ________ ________ as soon as possible.

6 금요일 밤에 그가 들어가는 것이 목격되었다. (see, enter the theater)
→ He ________ ________ ________ ________ ________ on Friday night.

7 아이가 갑자기 모퉁이에서 나타났고, 오토바이에 거의 치일 뻔했다. (appear, around the corner, hit)
→ A kid suddenly ________ ________ ________ ________ and ________ almost ________ ________ a motorcycle.

D 우리말과 같은 뜻이 되도록 주어진 단어를 배열하시오.

1 컴퓨터를 고치는 데 얼마가 들까요? (me, how much, will, to fix, cost, it)
→ ________________________________ the computer?

2 Judy와 Kelly는 쌍둥이처럼 서로 닮았다. (resemble, like twins, each other)
→ Judy and Kelly ________________________________.

3 그녀는 반장으로 선출되었다. (elected, of her class, been, the president, has)
→ She ________________________________.

4 그 신비한 남자는 군중 속으로 사라졌다. (the crowd, into, disappeared, the mystery man)
→ ________________________________

5 구매 전에 상품 샘플을 고객에게 보여줬다. (before purchase, shown, the customers, was, to)
→ The product sample ________________________________.

6 TV 광고는 그에게 엄청난 인기를 가져다주었다. (him, the TV commercial, brought, by, was, to)
→ A great deal of popularity ________________________________.

7 나는 친구네 집에서 하룻밤 자는 것이 허락되지 않았다. (sleep over, wasn't, at my friend's house, to, allowed)
→ I ________________________________.

다양한 전치사를 사용하는 수동태

A 보기 에서 알맞은 전치사를 골라 빈칸에 써 넣으시오.

[1-4] 보기 from with to in

1 His office is located ____________ the center of the city.

2 This toilet tissue is made ____________ recycled paper.

3 Every school must be equipped ____________ a fire alarm system.

4 She was married ____________ a wealthy man.

[5-8] 보기 with to of at

5 We were all surprised ____________ Mark's story.

6 His first book was known ____________ a few people.

7 He was tired ____________ doing the same thing over and over again.

8 Students will be provided ____________ feedback after they have turned in their reports.

B 주어진 문장을 수동태 문장으로 바꿔 쓰시오.

1 We must carry out the plan secretly.
→ The plan ____.

2 The shop manager should deal with customers sincerely.
→ Customers ____.

3 They called off the baseball game because of the rain.
→ The baseball game ____.

4 Her mother takes care of her kids while she is at work.
→ Her kids ____.

5 My baby was so sick that I called in a doctor last night.
→ My baby was so sick that a doctor ____.

6 A truck almost ran over a drunken man who was jaywalking.
→ A drunken man who was jaywalking ____.

7 A tow truck took away my car because I parked it illegally.
→ My car ____ because I parked it illegally.

C **우리말과 같은 뜻이 되도록 주어진 단어를 이용하여 문장을 완성하시오.**

1 사고 장면을 보고 아이들은 겁을 먹었다. (frighten)
→ The kids ______ ______ ______ the scene of the accident.

2 63대의 차량이 그 사고에 관련돼 있다. (involve, the accident)
→ Sixty-three vehicles ______ ______ ______ ______ ______.

3 그 가게는 세일 기간 동안 사람들로 붐볐다. (crowd)
→ The store ______ ______ ______ ______ during the sale.

4 잠에서 깼을 때, 그녀는 세상이 눈으로 덮여 있음을 보았다. (cover, snow)
→ When she woke up, she found that the world ______ ______ ______ ______.

5 모든 참고자료들이 사람들에게 배포되었다. (pass out)
→ All the reference materials ______ ______ ______ to people.

6 그의 아이디어는 그 방에 있는 모든 사람에게 비웃음을 당했다. (laugh at, everyone)
→ His idea ______ ______ ______ ______ ______ in the room.

7 나는 시험 결과에 만족하지만 우리 엄마는 실망한 듯하다. (satisfy, disappoint)
→ I ______ ______ ______ the test results, but my mother seems to ______ ______ ______ them.

D **우리말과 같은 뜻이 되도록 주어진 단어를 배열하시오.**

1 이 부츠는 진짜 가죽으로 만들어졌다. (made, these boots, are, genuine leather, of)
→ ______________________________

2 시험지는 10분 후에 배포될 것입니다. (passed out, test papers, be, in ten minutes, will)
→ ______________________________

3 그는 산업디자인을 전공하고 있으나 순수 예술에 관심이 있다. (fine arts, in, is, he, interested)
→ He is majoring in industrial design, but ______________________________.

4 많은 건강 문제는 비만과 관련되어 있다. (obesity, health problems, associated, many, are, with)
→ ______________________________

5 학교 폭력은 좀 더 심각하게 다루어져야 한다. (more seriously, school violence, dealt with, be, must)
→ ______________________________

6 교육은 우리나라의 미래와 밀접한 관련이 있다. (to, education, closely related, is, our country's future.)
→ ______________________________

7 우리가 지구 온난화에 대해 준비되어 있지 않다는 것은 사실이다. (global warming, are not, for, prepared)
→ It is true that we ______________________________.

MEMO

MEMO

MEMO

MEMO

THIS IS GRAMMAR

이것이 진화하는 New This Is Grammar다!

- 판에 박힌 형식적인 표현보다 **원어민이 실제 일상 생활에서 바로 쓰는** 생활 영문법
- 문어체뿐만 아니라 **구어체 문법을 강조한 회화, 독해, 영작을 위한** 실용 영문법
- 현지에서 더는 사용하지 않는 낡은 영문법 대신 **시대의 흐름에 맞춘** 현대 영문법

이 책의 특징

★ 실생활에서 쓰는 문장과 대화, 지문으로 구성된 예문 수록
★ 핵심 문법 포인트를 보기 쉽게 도식화 · 도표화하여 구성
★ 다양하고 유용한 연습문제 및 리뷰, 리뷰 플러스 문제 수록
★ 중 · 고등 내신에 꼭 등장하는 어법 포인트의 철저한 분석 및 총정리
★ 회화 · 독해 · 영작 실력 향상의 토대인 문법 지식의 체계적 설명

This Is Grammar (최신개정판)시리즈

초급 1, 2 **기초 문법 강화 + 내신 대비**
예비 중학생과 초급자를 위해 영어의 기본적 구조인 형태, 의미, 용법 등을 소개하고, 다양한 연습문제를 제공하고 있다. Key Point에 문법의 핵심 사항을 한눈에 보기 쉽게 도식화·도표화하여 정리하였다.

중급 1, 2 **문법 요약(Key Point) + 체계적 설명**
중·고등 내신에 꼭 등장하는 문법 포인트를 철저히 분석하여 이해 및 암기가 쉽도록 예문과 함께 문법을 요약해 놓았다. 중급자들이 체계적으로 영문법을 학습할 수 있도록 충분한 콘텐츠를 제공하고 있다.

고급 1, 2 **핵심 문법 설명 + 각종 수험 대비**
중·고급 영어 학습자들을 대상으로 내신, 토익, 토플, 텝스 등 각종 시험을 완벽 대비할 수 있도록 중요 문법 포인트를 분석, 정리하였다. 다양하고 진정성 있는 지문들을 통해 풍부한 배경지식을 함께 쌓을 수 있다.

www.nexusEDU.kr
넥서스 초·중·고등 사이트

www.nexusbook.com
넥서스 홈페이지

책에 대해 궁금한 사항은 넥서스에듀 홈페이지 1:1 고객상담 게시판을 이용하세요.

	초1	초2	초3	초4	초5	초6	중1	중2	중3	고1	고2	고3
Writing				공감 영문법+쓰기 1~2								
						도전만점 중등내신 서술형 1~4						
				영어일기 영작패턴 1–A, B · 2–A, B								
				Smart Writing 1~2								
Reading					Reading 101 1~3							
					Reading 공감 1~3							
					This Is Reading Starter 1~3							
						This Is Reading 전면 개정판 1~4						
						원서 술술 읽는 Smart Reading Basic 1~2						
									원서 술술 읽는 Smart Reading 1~2			
									[특급 단기 특강] 구문독해 · 독해유형			
										[앱솔루트 수능대비 영어독해 기출분석] 2019~2021학년도		
Listening						Listening 공감 1~3						
					The Listening 1~4							
						넥서스 중학 영어듣기 모의고사 25회 1~3						
						도전! 만점 중학 영어듣기 모의고사 1~3						
									만점 적중 수능 듣기 모의고사 20회 · 35회			
TEPS					NEW TEPS 입문편 실전 250+ 청해 · 문법 · 독해							
						NEW TEPS 기본편 실전 300+ 청해 · 문법 · 독해						
							NEW TEPS 실력편 실전 400+ 청해 · 문법 · 독해					
								NEW TEPS 마스터편 실전 500+ 청해 · 문법 · 독해				

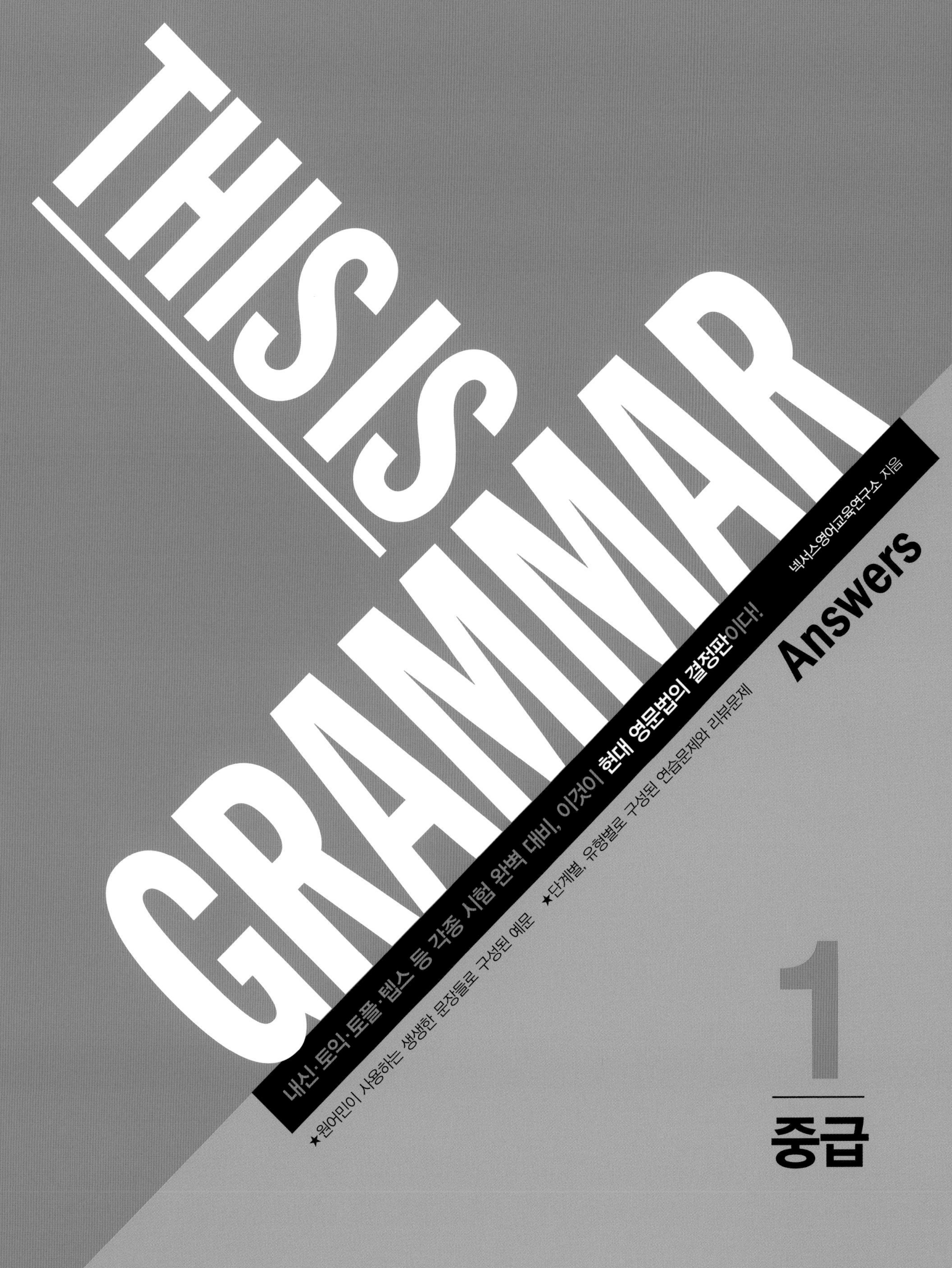
THIS IS GRAMMAR
Answers
넥서스영어교육연구소 지음
내신·토익·토플·텝스 등 각종 시험 완벽 대비, 이것이 현대 영문법의 결정판이다!
★원어민이 사용하는 생생한 문장들로 구성된 예문
★단계별, 유형별로 구성된 연습문제와 리뷰문제
1
중급

NEXUS Edu

PART 1

Unit 01 EXERCISES

p. 15

1 My friends are in the library.
S V M

2 The pharmacy is across from the hospital.
S V M

3 In ten minutes, the cell phone shop will be closed.
M S V

4 The swimming pool is on the fifth floor of the hotel.
S V M

5 The plants are growing nicely in the new greenhouse.
S V M

6 My mother exercises in the park Monday through Friday.
S V M

7 The rehearsal will be in the gymnasium tomorrow afternoon.
S V M

해석

1 내 친구들은 도서관에 있다.
2 그 약국은 병원 건너편에 있다.
3 10분 뒤에 휴대폰 가게는 문을 닫을 것이다.
4 수영장은 호텔 5층에 있다.
5 그 식물들은 새 온실에서 잘 자라고 있다.
6 우리 어머니는 월요일부터 금요일까지 공원에서 운동하신다.
7 예행연습이 체육관에서 내일 오후에 있을 것이다.

1 ① 2 ②

해석

1 ① 나는 도서관에 있었다.
② 그들은 스페인 출신이다.
③ 나의 사촌들이 곧 도착할 것이다.
④ 달은 저녁 7시 30분에 뜬다.

2 ① 서울에 비가 올 것이다.
② 고양이가 내 책상 위에 있다.
③ 그들이 공원에서 걷고 있다.
④ 그가 슈퍼마켓에 갔다.

Ⓒ

1 counts 2 lasted 3 pay
4 do 5 work 6 matter

해석

1 매분(每分)이 중요하다.
2 영화는 거의 세 시간 동안 계속되었다.
3 친절은 때때로 보답을 받지 못한다.
4 이 방은 세 사람이 있기에 충분하지는 않을 것이다.
5 그 금속 탐지기가 제대로 작동하지 않았다.
6 너는 가도 되고 있어도 돼. 내겐 상관이 없어.

Unit 02 EXERCISES

p. 18~19

Ⓐ

1 The boys kept silent.
S V SC

2 The gentleman looked happy after the meal.
S V SC M

3 She became the CEO of the company in 2014.
S V SC M

4 As a result, their problems remained unsolved.
M S V SC

5 The man became the first freely elected president of the country.
S V SC

6 Diana didn't seem happy with the results of the midterm test.
S V SC M

해석

1 그 소년들은 계속 조용히 있었다.
2 식사 후에 그 신사는 행복해 보였다.
3 그녀는 2014년에 그 회사의 최고 경영자가 되었다.
4 결과적으로 그들의 문제는 해결되지 않은 채로 남아 있다.
5 그 남자는 그 나라에서 최초로 자유선거로 뽑힌 대통령이 되었다.
6 다이애나는 중간고사 결과에 기뻐하지 않는 것 같았다.

Ⓑ

1 calm 2 dark
3 beautiful 4 fashionable
5 a professional writer 6 sour
7 dark

해석

1 그들은 차분히 있었다.
2 밖이 어두워지고 있다.
3 크리스틴은 아름다워 보인다.
4 그녀는 매우 유행을 따르는 것처럼 보인다.
5 그 소녀는 전문 작가가 되었다.
6 냉장고 안의 우유는 신 맛이 나니 그것을 마시지 마라.
7 어두워지고 있으니 우리는 지금 당장 집에 가야 한다.

Ⓒ

1 your father 2 strange 3 cheerful
4 sad 5 angry 6 bitter

해석

1 너는 너의 아버지와 닮았다.
2 치즈에서 이상한 냄새가 난다.
3 그녀의 목소리가 쾌활하게 들렸다.
4 나는 그 영화를 보고 슬펐다.
5 내가 그에게 진실을 말했을 때, 그는 화가 난 것처럼 보였다.
6 이 한약은 쓴맛이 난다.

D

1 ran short　　2 grow old
3 kept silent　　4 fall asleep
5 come true　　6 turn pale
7 went wrong　　8 go bad

해석

1 우리는 사무용품이 부족했다.
2 나이가 들면서 너는 많은 경험을 쌓게 될 것이다.
3 나는 무슨 말을 해야 할지 몰라서 그냥 침묵을 지켰다.
4 나는 비행기가 이륙하자마자 잠들 수 있기를 바란다.
5 당신이 계속해서 꿈을 추구한다면, 그 꿈은 이루어질 것이다.
6 나는 피를 보면 창백해지기 때문에 결코 의사가 될 수 없을 것이다.
7 갑자기 모든 것이 잘못되어 우주선이 폭발했다.
8 너무 많은 채소를 사지 말자. 우리가 다 못 먹으면 상할 거야.

E

1 틀린 것 없음　　2 cold　　3 틀린 것 없음
4 sad　　5 calm　　6 tired
7 good　　8 straight　　9 틀린 것 없음
10 틀린 것 없음　　11 impatient　　12 bad
13 salty　　14 happy

해석

1 아이들이 조용히 있었다.
2 그녀는 매우 추웠다.
3 그녀의 목소리가 날카로웠다.
4 아기가 슬퍼 보인다.
5 그는 거의 차분히 있지 못한다.
6 그녀는 매우 피곤해 보였다.
7 피자 냄새가 매우 좋았다.
8 군인들은 똑바로 서 있었다.
9 그는 훌륭한 의사가 될 것이다.
10 그의 동기는 미스터리로 남았다.
11 아이들은 참을성을 잃어가고 있었다.
12 미트볼 스파게티는 상했다.
13 저 레스토랑의 음식은 항상 약간 짠맛이 난다.
14 우리가 어머니께 선물을 드리자, 어머니는 행복해 보였다.

Unit 03 EXERCISES p. 21

1 I met Nick in the library yesterday.
S V O M

2 She didn't mention him all evening.
S V O M

3 John suddenly appeared in the doorway.
S M V M

4 Ben looked cute in his Halloween costume.
S V SC M

5 I had a very strange dream about you last night.
S V O M

6 Your feet smell terrible! You had better wash them.
S V SC S V O

7 Your brother's old leather jacket fits you perfectly.
S V O M

8 They conducted a survey to learn about consumer needs.
S V O M

9 I know that he will accept my offer in the end.
S V O

10 You look exhausted! So, did you finish the work completely?
S V SC S V O M

해석

1 나는 어제 도서관에서 닉을 만났다.
2 그녀는 저녁 내내 그에 대해 언급하지 않았다.
3 존이 갑자기 현관에 나타났다.
4 벤이 핼러윈 의상을 입으니 귀여워 보였다.
5 나는 어젯밤에 너에 관한 아주 이상한 꿈을 꾸었다.
6 네 발 냄새가 지독하구나! 씻고 오는 게 좋겠어.
7 네 형의 오래된 가죽 재킷이 네게 매우 잘 맞구나.
8 그들은 고객 요구를 알아내기 위해서 설문 조사를 실시했다.
9 나는 그가 결국 내 제안을 받아들일 것을 안다.
10 너 지쳐 보여! 그래서 일을 완전히 끝낸 거야?

1 resemble with → resemble
2 answered to → answered
3 married with → married
4 discuss about → discuss
5 explained about → explained
6 enter into → enter
7 attended to → attended

해석

1 사람들은 종종 나에게 내가 우리 어머니를 닮았다고 말한다.
2 나는 재빨리 전화를 받았지만, 그들은 이미 전화를 끊었다.
3 내 동생 폴은 한국에서 3년 전에 지영이와 결혼했다.
4 나는 네 아이디어에 매우 관심이 있어. 저녁을 먹으면서 그것에 대해 논의해 보자.
5 선생님이 아이들에게 그 게임의 규칙을 설명해 주었다.
6 그 나라에 입국하기에 앞서 유효한 여권을 가지고 있어야 한다.
7 4만 명이 넘는 사람들이 김 추기경의 장례식에 참석했다.

EXERCISES p. 24~25

1 Everyone looks tired.
S V SC

2 She handed me the bill.
S V IO DO

3 He built a nice house for his parents.
S V O M

4 I had to walk home alone late at night.
S V M

5 Brandon showed me his family photos.
S V IO DO

6 I have spilt something on my new pants.
S V O M

7 I have emailed the list of addresses to you.
S V O M

8 Would you send a postcard to me in Europe?
S V O M

9 My friend sent me a Christmas card last week.
S V IO DO M

10 I would like to pour you some more grapefruit juice.
S V IO DO

11 The university has awarded her a $500 scholarship.
S V IO DO

12 You won't regret it. This machine will save you a lot of money.
S V IO DO

13 Frank and his coworker James look really depressed today.
S V SC M

14 My parents promised me a new notebook computer for Christmas.
S V IO DO M

15 During the financial crisis, the family had to manage on just my father's salary.
M S V M

해석

1 모든 사람들이 피곤해 보인다.
2 그녀가 나에게 계산서를 건네주었다.
3 그는 부모님에게 멋진 집을 지어드렸다.
4 나는 밤늦게 혼자 집으로 걸어가야 했다.
5 브랜든이 자신의 가족사진을 나에게 보여 주었다.
6 나는 새 바지에 무언가를 엎질렀다.
7 나는 너에게 주소록을 이메일로 보냈어.
8 너 유럽에서 내게 엽서를 보내주겠니?
9 내 친구가 지난주에 나에게 크리스마스카드를 보냈다.
10 제가 당신에게 자몽 주스를 좀 더 따라 줄게요.
11 그 대학은 그녀에게 500달러의 장학금을 수여했다.
12 후회하지 않을 겁니다. 이 기계는 많은 돈을 절약시켜줄 거예요.
13 프랭크와 그의 동료인 제임스는 오늘 정말 우울해 보인다.
14 우리 부모님은 크리스마스에 내게 새 노트북 컴퓨터를 (사 주겠다고) 약속했다.
15 경제 위기 동안 우리 가족은 아버지의 봉급만으로 생활을 해야 했다.

B

1 She will tell the secret to you.
2 I brought some blankets to them.
3 The boy wrote a fan letter to Jennifer.
4 She will get the concert tickets for me.
5 Julia sometimes buys robots for her son.
6 The teacher asked a few questions of him.
7 He will build a beautiful tree house for her.
8 My father cooked a delicious meal for me.
9 I bought a birthday cake for my grandmother.
10 The tour guide showed many attractions to us.
11 Junsu made a wooden bookshelf for his girlfriend.
12 The boy showed his new toy to us.
13 The computer brought a comfortable life to us.

해석

1 그녀가 너에게 비밀을 말해 줄 것이다.
2 나는 그들에게 약간의 담요를 가져다주었다.
3 그 소년은 제니퍼에게 팬레터를 썼다.
4 그녀는 나에게 콘서트 표를 구해 줄 것이다.
5 줄리아는 가끔 아들에게 로봇을 사준다.
6 선생님이 그에게 몇 가지 질문을 했다.
7 그는 그녀에게 나무 위에 아름다운 집을 지어 줄 것이다.
8 우리 아버지가 나에게 맛있는 음식을 요리해 주셨다.
9 나는 우리 할머니께 생일 케이크를 사드렸다.
10 여행 가이드가 우리에게 많은 관광 명소를 안내해 주었다.
11 준수는 여자 친구에게 나무로 된 책장을 만들어 주었다.
12 그 소년은 우리에게 자신의 새로운 장난감을 보여 주었다.
13 컴퓨터는 우리에게 편안한 삶을 가져다주었다.

Unit 05 EXERCISES

p. 28~29

A

1 She heard Harry go out.
S V O OC

2 Sally allowed me to use her cell phone.
S V O OC

3 He asked his mom to make galbi for dinner.
S V O OC

4 My luggage is large, heavy, and awkward to carry.
S V SC

5 Suzy rubbed the blackboard clean for the teacher.
S V O OC

6 Nowadays, companies advertise their services on the Internet.
S V O

해석

1 그녀는 해리가 나가는 소리를 들었다.
2 샐리는 자기 휴대 전화를 내가 사용하도록 허락했다.
3 그는 엄마에게 저녁으로 갈비를 만들어 달라고 부탁했다.
4 나의 짐은 크고, 무겁고, 들고 다니기에도 불편하다.

5 수지는 선생님을 위해 칠판을 깨끗이 닦았다.
6 요즈음에는 회사들이 인터넷에 자기들의 서비스를 광고한다.

Ⓑ

1 busy	2 to be	3 talk
4 warm	5 to finish	6 cry
7 feel	8 wash	9 watch
10 to take	11 to smoke	12 difficult
13 enter		

해석

1 그녀는 온종일 우리를 바쁘게 했다.
2 우리 엄마는 내가 변호사가 되기를 원하신다.
3 나는 오늘 그가 그녀와 말하는 것을 보지 못했다.
4 벽난로의 불이 우리를 따뜻하게 만들었다.
5 그녀는 그들이 그 프로젝트를 끝내도록 할 수 없었다.
6 우리는 이른 아침에 아기가 우는 소리를 들었다.
7 내가 어제 본 영화는 나를 슬프게 만들었다.
8 그의 아버지는 그에게 새로 산 가족용 차를 닦게 했다.
9 그녀의 부모님은 그녀가 열 시까지 TV를 보도록 내버려 두었다.
10 의사가 나에게 하루에 세 번 약을 먹으라고 말했다.
11 우리는 그 고객들에게 식당 안에서는 담배를 피우지 말아 달라고 부탁했다.
12 나는 그 문제들이 어렵다고 생각했지만 모든 문제를 다 풀었다.
13 나는 월터가 카메라를 들고 그 방에 들어가는 것을 보았다.

Ⓒ

1 named, Sarah	2 elected, president
3 made, angry	4 found, more serious
5 asked, to buy	6 helped, finish

해석

1 그들은 딸의 이름을 '사라'라고 지었다.
2 학생들이 나를 우리 반의 반장으로 선출했다.
3 일부 무례한 학생들이 존스 씨를 화나게 했다.
4 나는 그 상황이 예상보다 더 심각하다고 느꼈다.
5 우리 엄마는 내게 집에 오는 길에 우유를 사오라고 부탁했다.
6 그녀의 아버지는 그녀가 나가서 놀기 전에 숙제를 끝낼 수 있게 도와주었다.

Ⓓ

1 want you to heat this muffin
2 I'll let you know
3 elected him president of the board
4 keep you healthy
5 heard somebody call her name
6 helped me choose my college major
7 got the company to sign the contract
8 He encouraged me to try a difficult task

REVIEW

p. 30~31

Ⓐ

1 The gift(S) made(V) me(O) happy(OC).

2 Alex(S) put(V) his dog(O) on the chair(M).

3 Jason(S) lent(V) Jack(IO) his old snowboard(DO).

4 John(S) finished(V) blowing up the balloon(O).

5 He(S) told(V) us(O) to come over to his house(OC).

6 This oven(S) will make(V) you(O) a great cook(OC).

7 Policemen(S) are guarding(V) the entrance(O).

8 The leaves(S) are(V) red, yellow, and orange(SC).

9 The train from Paris(S) arrived(V) four hours late(M).

10 She(S) took(V) a hammer(O) and knocked(V) a hole(O) in the wall(M).

11 After the earthquake(M), the city(S) resembled(V) a war zone(O).

12 I(S) sent(V) my mother(IO) a bouquet of flowers(DO) on her birthday(M).

해설/해석

1 The gift가 주어, made가 동사, 목적어 me의 기분을 보충 설명해 주는 happy는 목적격보어
그 선물이 나를 행복하게 했다.

2 Alex가 주어, put이 동사, his dog는 '그의 개를'이라는 의미로 '~을 놓다'의 대상이 되므로 목적어
알렉스는 그의 개를 의자 위에 놓았다.

3 Jason이 주어, lent가 동사, Jack과 his old snowboard는 '잭에게 그의 스노보드를'이라는 의미이므로 Jack은 간접목적어, his old snow board는 직접목적어
제이슨은 잭에게 자신의 낡은 스노보드를 빌려주었다.

4 John이 주어, finished가 동사, blowing up the balloon은 '풍선 부는 것을'이라는 의미로 'finished(~을 끝내다)'의 대상이 되므로 목적어
존은 풍선 부는 것을 끝냈다.

5 He가 주어, told가 동사, us와 to come over to his house는 우리가 그의 집에 가는 것이므로 us는 목적어, to come over to his house는 목적격보어
그는 우리에게 그의 집에 오라고 말했다.

6 This oven이 주어, will make가 동사, 목적어 you를 보충 설명해주는 a great cook은 목적격보어
이 오븐은 너를 훌륭한 요리사로 만들어줄 것이다.

7 Policemen이 주어, are guarding이 동사, the entrance는 '입

구를'이라는 의미로 'are guarding(~를 지키다)'의 대상이 되므로 목적어
경찰이 입구를 지키고 있다.

8 The leaves가 주어, are가 동사, red, yellow, and orange는 주어(The leaves)의 상태를 보충 설명해 주는 주격보어
나뭇잎들은 빨간색, 노란색, 오렌지색이다.

9 The train from Paris가 주어, arrived가 동사
파리발 기차가 네 시간 늦게 도착했다.

10 She가 주어, took과 knocked가 동사, a hammer와 a hole이 각각 took(~을 가져오다)과 knocked(~을 만들다)의 대상이 되므로 목적어이다.
그녀가 망치를 가져다가 벽을 쳐서 구멍을 냈다.

11 the city가 주어, resembled가 동사, a war zone은 '전쟁 지역을'이라는 의미로 'resemble(~을 닮다)'의 대상이 되므로 목적어
그 지진 후에 도시는 전쟁터와 닮아 있었다.

12 I가 주어, sent가 동사, my mother와 a bouquet of flowers는 '어머니께 꽃 한 다발을'이라는 의미로 my mother는 간접목적어, a bouquet of flowers는 직접목적어
나는 엄마 생신 때 엄마께 꽃 한 다발을 보내 드렸다.

1 to go → go
2 of → for
3 easily → easy
4 lightly → light
5 for → for 삭제
6 to → to 삭제

해설/해석

1 사역동사 let은 목적격보어로 동사원형을 취하므로 go가 적절
그는 그녀가 떠나도록 놔두지 않을 것이다.

2 '~에게 …해 주다'라는 의미를 갖는 수여동사(make)가 있는 문장에서 간접목적어(my parents)가 직접목적어(sandwiches) 뒤에 오는 경우 간접목적어 앞에 전치사를 사용해야 하는데 buy, get, make, cook 등의 동사에는 전치사 of가 아니라 for가 적절
나는 부모님을 위해 샌드위치를 만든다.

3 목적어 grammar의 특성을 설명하는 목적격보어 자리이므로 easy가 적절, 부사(easily)는 목적격보어가 될 수 없음
어떤 학생들은 문법이 쉽다고 생각한다.

4 주어인 Jerry's new cell phone을 보충 설명하는 보어 자리이므로 light가 적절, 부사(lightly)는 주격보어가 될 수 없음
제리의 새 휴대 전화는 작고 가볍다.

5 주어, 동사, 간접목적어, 직접목적어의 구조이므로 전치사가 필요 없음
아버지는 내 여동생에게 생일 선물로 새 차를 사주었다.

6 주어, 동사, 간접목적어, 직접목적어의 구조에서는 직접목적어 앞에 전치사를 쓰지 않음
선생님이 학생들에게 엄중한 경고를 했다.

1 The play was very good.
2 I found the puzzle difficult.
3 He painted his room a soft shade of blue.
4 They didn't allow me to leave the room.
5 He called me a fool in class yesterday.
6 I saw Jeremy sleeping at his desk.
7 Ms. William's children were arguing with each other.
8 The baseball player hit the ball over the fence.
9 I've sent him two tickets for the musical *Cats*.
10 My sister finally became a doctor last year.
11 My mother had her hair permed at the near beauty shop.
12 My father cooked breakfast for Mom on her birthday.

해설

1 the play가 주어, was는 동사, very는 형용사 good을 꾸며 주는 부사, very good은 주어를 보충 설명해 주는 주격보어, 「S+V+SC」 구조

2 I가 주어, found가 동사, 형용사 difficult는 the puzzle을 보충 설명해 주는 목적격보어, 「S+V+O+OC」 구조

3 he가 주어, painted가 동사, a soft of blue는 his room을 보충 설명해 주는 목적격보어, 「S+V+O+OC」 구조

4 they가 주어, didn't allow가 동사, to leave the room은 목적어 me가 하는 행동으로 목적격보어, 「S+V+O+OC」 구조

5 he가 주어, called가 동사, a fool은 목적어 me에 대한 보충 설명이므로 목적격보어, 「S+V+O+OC+M」 구조

6 I가 주어, saw가 동사, sleeping은 목적어인 Jeremy의 행동을 나타내므로 목적격보어, 「S + V + O + OC+M」 구조

7 Ms. William's children이 주어, were arguing이 동사, 「S+V+M」 구조

8 the baseball player가 주어, hit이 동사, the ball은 hit(~을 치다)의 대상이 되므로 목적어, 「S+V+O+M」 구조

9 I가 주어, 've가 동사, him이 간접목적어, two tickets가 직접목적어, 「S+V+IO+DO+M」 구조

10 my sister가 주어, became이 동사, a doctor는 주어를 설명해 주는 주격보어, 「S+V+SC+M」 구조

11 my mother가 주어, had가 동사, permed는 목적어인 her hair의 상태를 보충 설명해 주는 목적격보어, 「S+V+O+OC+M」 구조

12 my father가 주어, cooked가 동사, breakfast가 목적어, 「S+V+O+M」 구조

REVIEW PLUS

p. 32

1 ③ 2 ⑤

해설/해석

1 감각동사 (A) look(~하게 보이다), (B) sound(~처럼 들리다), (C) smell(~한 냄새가 나다)은 형용사를 보어로 취하므로 kind,

interesting, strange가 적절
• 그는 친절해 보인다.
• 너의 아르바이트는 흥미로울 것 같다.
• 이 소스에서 이상한 냄새가 난다.

2 (A) want는 to부정사를 목적격보어로 취하므로 to heat이 적절, (B) make는 형용사를 목적격보어로 취하고 부사는 목적격보어가 될 수 없으므로 angry가 적절, (C) 나를 회장으로 뽑았다는 의미이므로 목적어 me, 목적격보어 leader가 적절
• 나는 네가 이 머핀을 데우기를 원한다.
• 소란스러운 학생들이 존스 선생님을 화나게 했다.
• 우리 학급이 나를 회장으로 뽑았다.

1 ① 2 ①

해설/해석

1 ① He is my father.
S V SC

② Chanwoo came late.
S V (M)

③ Cheetahs run very fast.
S V (M)

④ Your opinion doesn't count.
S V

⑤ The bus arrived earlier today.
S V (M)

① 그는 우리 아버지이다.
② 찬우가 늦게 왔다.
③ 치타는 매우 빨리 달린다.
④ 너의 의견은 중요하지 않다.
⑤ 버스가 오늘 더 일찍 도착했다.

2 ① The car was repaired.
S V

② The cook added salt to the soup.
S V O (M)

③ The hunter fired his gun at the deer.
S V O (M)

④ Jenny broke the dish by mistake.
S V O (M)

⑤ James ordered takeout food for lunch.
S V O (M)

① 그 차는 수리되었다.
② 요리사가 수프에 소금을 넣었다.
③ 사냥꾼이 사슴을 향해 총을 쐈다.
④ 제니가 실수로 접시를 깨뜨렸다.
⑤ 제임스는 점심으로 포장음식을 주문했다.

PART2

REPLAY

p. 34~35

1 CHECK-UP

1 loves 2 is 3 watches 4 carries

2 CHECK-UP

1 ate 2 carried 3 found 4 left
5 sang 6 began 7 knew 8 wore
9 thought 10 ran 11 wrote 12 spent

3 CHECK-UP

1 will arrive 2 studied
3 met 4 didn't[did not] take
5 won't[will not] be 6 volunteers
7 Will, send, will send 8 Do, help, clean

Unit 06 EXERCISES

p. 38~39

A

1 ⓐ 2 ⓒ 3 ⓓ 4 ⓒ 5 ⓐ
6 ⓑ 7 ⓓ 8 ⓐ 9 ⓑ 10 ⓓ

해석

1 나는 요즘에는 거의 고향을 방문하지 않는다.
2 우리의 회의는 돌아오는 금요일에 시작한다.
3 내가 집에 늦게 가면 우리 어머니가 화를 내실 것이다.
4 노르웨이행 배가 여덟 시에 출발한다.
5 프랜시스는 점심 식사 후에 가끔 커피를 마신다.
6 에베레스트 산은 높이가 8,848미터에 달한다.
7 내가 거기에 도착하면 전화할게. 전화기를 계속 켜놔.
8 너는 월요일마다 규칙적으로 체육관에서 운동하니?
9 고래와 돌고래는 해양 포유류에 속한다.
10 오늘 숙제를 제출하지 않으면 너는 벌을 받을 것이다.

B

1 practices 2 vacuums 3 doesn't go
4 comes 5 stick to 6 spend
7 watch 8 want 9 Does, begin
10 travels 11 ends 12 listens

해석

1 사라는 매일 아침 요가를 연습한다.
2 우리 형은 매일 밤 진공청소기로 집을 청소한다.
3 내 친구 제레미는 걸어서는 아무 데도 가지 않는다.
4 시내로 가는 다음 버스가 20분 후에 온다.
5 이 저지방 식사를 고수하면 너는 살이 빠질 것이다.
6 피터의 조부모님은 자주 미국에서 겨울을 보내신다.

7 너는 TV를 보기 전에 저녁 식사를 마쳐야 한다.
8 큰 곤경에 빠지고 싶지 않다면 그와 논쟁하지 마라.
9 그 축제가 내일 여덟 시에 시작하니?
10 지구는 약 365일에 한 번 태양 주위를 돈다.
11 연극은 8시에 끝난다. 그리고 너는 배우들과 셀카를 찍을 수 있다.
12 그녀는 아침을 준비하면서 항상 라디오를 듣는다.

1 connects 2 harms 3 start
4 arrives 5 goes 6 comes
7 does 8 are 9 need
10 returns

해석

1 그 철도는 서울과 대구를 연결한다.
2 간접흡연은 비흡연자들에게 해를 끼친다.
3 네 연주회가 여덟 시에 시작하니, 아니면 여덟 시 반에 시작하니?
4 존이 인천 공항에 도착하면 내가 너에게 전화할게.
5 그레그는 건강을 유지하기 위해 매일 아침 조깅을 하러 간다.
6 박 선생님께서 사무실에 돌아오시면 알려 드릴게요.
7 론은 누군가의 도움 없이는 거의 숙제를 하지 않는다.
8 이 상품에 관심이 없으시다면 저건 어떠세요?
9 비행기 출발 두 시간 전에는 공항에 도착해야 한다.
10 다음 주에 팀이 돌아오면, 시(市)가 그들에게 행진을 하게 해 줄 것이다.

D

1 The next semester starts in September.
2 My sister prefers herbal tea to black tea.
3 You are always late and never apologize.
4 The train to Munich leaves in five minutes
5 The Peace Conference takes place every four years.
6 the term 'cider' refers to non-alcoholic apple juice
7 assigns customers to tables

Unit 07 EXERCISES

p. 41

1 worried 2 imagined
3 bragged 4 waited, showed up
5 forgot, left 6 watched
7 broke out, ceased 8 supplied, started

해석

1 메리는 지난주에 자신의 성적에 대해 지나치게 걱정했다.
2 나는 내가 세계여행을 하리라고는 상상하지 못했다.
3 마이클은 경기가 끝나고 자신의 경기 실력을 자랑했다.
4 나는 그녀를 기다렸지만, 그녀는 결코 나타나지 않았다.
5 나는 집을 나서기 전에 열쇠를 챙기는 것을 잊어버렸다.
6 제이콥은 카페에서 밖에 사람들이 걸어가는 것을 바라보았다.
7 한국 전쟁은 1950년에 발발하여 1953년에 중단되었다.
8 스미스 부인은 학생들이 그림 그리기를 시작하기 전에 붓을 나눠 주었다.

B

1 is 2 inhabited
3 was 4 lives
5 hurt 6 arranged
7 reached, say 8 skimmed, doesn't need

해석

1 내 남동생의 생일은 돌아오는 목요일이다.
2 수백만 년 전에 공룡이 지구에 살았다.
3 조지 워싱턴은 미국의 첫 번째 대통령이었다.
4 브라이언은 할머니를 거의 찾아뵙지 않았지만, 지금은 할머니와 함께 산다.
5 에이미는 이틀 전에 다리를 다쳐서 파티에 갈 수 없었다.
6 우리 엄마가 어제 꽃병에 꽃을 정성 들여 꽂았다.
7 콜럼버스는 1492년에 미국에 도착했다. 하지만 지금 어떤 사람들은 그가 첫 번째가 아니었다고 말한다.
8 메리는 오늘 아침 회사 가는 길에 신문을 대강 훑어보았다. 그래서 이제 더는 신문이 필요 없다.

① landed ② wasn't ③ was accompanied
④ spent ⑤ announced

해석

닐 암스트롱은 1969년 7월 20일에 달 표면에 착륙했다. 하지만 그는 혼자가 아니었다. 그는 버즈 올드린과 동행했다. 암스트롱과 올드린은 지구로 돌아오기 전에 달 표면에서 하루를 보냈다. 암스트롱은 "그것은 사람에게는 작은 발걸음이지만, 인류에게는 거대한 도약이다."라고 세상에 알렸다.

Unit 08 EXERCISES

p. 44~45

1 미래 2 미래 3 현재진행
4 현재진행 5 미래 6 현재진행

해석

1 존은 오늘 밤에 하키를 할 것이다.
2 이번 주 금요일에 너는 무엇을 할 거니?
3 조용히 해 주세요. 시험공부 중이에요.
4 음악 소리가 정말 크네요. 그들이 파티하고 있나요?
5 캐롤라인은 다음 주말에 친구 집에서 잘 것이다.
6 나는 공부에 집중을 할 수 없다. 내 남동생이 너무 시끄럽게 코를 골고 있다.

1 am going to go
2 will take, will walk
3 will have
4 won't[will not] forget, will, buy
5 are going to see, will meet
6 will buy

해석

1 A: 오늘은 밖에 날씨가 참 좋구나. 잠깐 자전거 타러 가자.
B: 미안. 선약이 있어. 아버지와 함께 등산갈 예정이거든.

2 A: 점점 늦어지고 있어. 나는 택시를 타고 집에 가야 할 것 같아.
B: 그래? 아름다운 밤이잖아. 그러니까 난 걸을게.
A: 알았어. 내일 봐.

3 A: 오늘의 특별 요리는 무엇인가요?
B: 특별 요리는 라자냐와 구운 연어입니다.
A: 그러면 마늘빵을 곁들인 라자냐로 할게요.

4 A: 밖에 나가면 신문 사는 것을 잊지 마.
B: 걱정하지 마. 잊지 않을게.
A: 그리고 집에 오는 길에 빵도 조금 사다 줄래? 고마워!

5 A: 카렌과 나는 내일 밤에 영화 보러 갈 거야. 너도 함께 갈래?
B: 그래. 나는 다른 계획은 없어.
A: 잘됐다! 여섯 시 반에 무비월드 앞에서 보자.

6 A: 엄마! 제이슨이 마지막 남은 주스를 마셨어요.
B: 어쩌지. 오늘 오후에 장 보러 가면 좀 더 사올게. 대신, 두유를 먹으렴.
A: 두유요? 아니요, 괜찮아요!

1 Are, going
2 is, doing, is babysitting
3 am meeting
4 be getting, am leaving
5 is participating

해석

1 A: 아이들이 내일 학교에 가나요?
B: 아니요, 안 가요. 개교기념일이에요.

2 A: 제인은 지금 여기 없어요.
B: 그녀는 무엇을 하고 있나요?
A: 그녀는 이웃집 아이들을 돌보고 있어요.

3 A: 뭘 좀 먹으러 나갈까?
B: 그럴 수 없어. 몇 분 후에 건우를 만나서 점심을 먹을 거야.

4 A: 너는 지금 동해 여행에 신이 났구나.
B: 응! 난 벌써 표를 예매했어. 다음 주 목요일에 떠날 거야.

5 A: 그녀가 수업을 왜 빠졌지?
B: 다음 주 월요일에 수영 대회에 참가한대. 그래서 그녀는 지금 연습 중이야.

D

1 will close
2 are, going to change
3 will go
4 am going to make
5 is going to come

해석

1 A: 창문을 닫아야겠어. 약간 추운 것 같아.
B: 그래. 담요를 갖다 줄까?

2 A: 내 기숙사 방을 다시 장식해야겠어.
B: 그래? 뭘 바꿀 건데?

3 A: TV 소리 좀 줄여 줄래요? 독서를 하려고요.
B: 미안해요. 다른 방에 가서 TV를 볼게요.

4 A: 왜 그렇게 많은 바나나를 샀니?
B: 내일 아침 식사로 바나나 팬케이크를 만들 거야.

5 A: 여기 왜 이렇게 덥지?
B: 냉방 시스템이 또 고장 났어. 내가 이미 서비스 센터에 전화했어. 내일 수리 기사가 와서 고칠 거야.

REVIEW

p. 46~47

1 travels
2 is working, will be
3 finishes, will go
4 was, decided
5 are, last
6 had, aren't speaking
7 called, is coming
8 is going, comes

해설/해석

1 변하지 않는 진리나 일반적 사실을 나타내므로 현재 시제인 travels가 적절
소리는 공기 중보다 액체에서 더 빨리 이동한다.

2 right now는 '바로 지금'이라는 의미이므로 is working이 적절, next week은 미래이므로 will be가 적절
베키는 지금 일을 하고 있다. 그녀는 다음 주에 카리브 해로 휴가를 떠날 것이다.

3 After(~한 후에)가 이끄는 시간 부사절은 미래 시제 대신 현재 시제를 사용
그녀는 내년에 고등학교를 마친 후에, 경제학을 공부하기 위해 대학에 들어갈 것이다.

4 last week은 과거이므로 was가 적절, 두 문장이 서로 연결된 내용이므로 decided가 적절
제니는 지난주에 교사 자리를 제안 받았다. 하지만 이상하게도 그녀는 그것을 받아들이지 않기로 했다.

5 Nowadays는 '요즘'이라는 현재의 상태를 나타내므로, are가 적절, 플라스틱 지폐가 훨씬 더 오래 지속되는 것은 현재사실이므로 last가 적절
요즘 호주 지폐는 플라스틱으로 만들어진다. 그것들은 종이 지폐보다 훨씬 더 오래간다.

6 last night은 과거이므로 had가 적절, Now는 현재이므로 aren't speaking이 적절
어젯밤에 우리 부모님께서 다투셨다. 지금 부모님께서는 서로 이야기하지 않으신다.

7 yesterday는 과거이므로 called가 적절, next month는 가까운 미래를 나타내므로 is coming이 적절
수희가 어제 밴쿠버에서 내게 전화했다. 그녀는 향수병에 걸려서 다음 달에 한국으로 돌아올 것이다.

8 next week은 가까운 미래를 나타내므로 is going이 적절, when(~할 때)이 이끄는 시간의 부사절에서 현재가 미래를 대신하므로 comes가 적절
내 여동생은 다음 주에 두 달간 외국으로 공부하러 갈 것이다. 내 남동생은 여동생이 돌아오면 외국으로 공부하러 갈 것이다.

1 do, go
2 send
3 didn't, call, was, went
4 will get
5 Will, join
6 Did, meet, did, went, didn't enjoy

해설/해석

1 How often은 빈도를 묻는 의문사이고, 대답에서 현재 시제를 사용했으므로 go가 적절
A: 너는 얼마나 자주 영화를 보러 가니?
B: 나는 한 달에 한 번 영화를 보러 가.

2 After(~한 후에)가 이끄는 시간 부사절에서는 현재가 미래를 대신하므로 send가 적절
A: 너 한동안 깨어 있을 거니?
B: 아니, 존에게 이 이메일 보내고 나서 잘 거야.

3 last night은 과거를 나타내므로 didn't와 call이 적절. A의 질문에 대한 답변이므로 was와 went가 적절
A: 왜 어젯밤에 나에게 전화 안 했어?
B: 미안해. 너무 피곤해서 일찍 잤어.

4 '잠깐 쉬자'는 상대방의 말을 듣고 그 순간에 결정한 일이므로 will get이 적절
A: 나 졸려. 잠깐 쉬자.
B: 좋아. 내가 널 위해 커피 좀 갖다 줄게.

5 상대의 의향을 묻고 있으므로 will과 join이 적절
A: 오늘 저녁은 혼자 먹고 싶지 않아. 나랑 같이 먹을래?
B: 물론이지. 친구 좋다는 게 뭐겠어.

6 last Saturday는 과거를 나타내므로 Did와 meet이 적절. A의 질문에 대한 답변이므로 모두 과거 시제가 적절
A: 지난 토요일에 제니퍼를 만났니?
B: 응, 만났어. 영화를 봤는데 영화가 재미없었어.

1 cost	2 want	3 raised
4 rains	5 will graduate	6 was
7 join	8 drop by	9 looked
10 start		

해설/해석

1 '비용이 많이 든다(cost)'라는 의미가 되어야 하고 현재의 가격을 나타내므로 cost가 적절
저 신발은 정말 괜찮은데 너무 비싸다.

2 '네가 원한다면(want) 번역을 해주겠다'라는 의미가 되어야 하고, if(~하면)가 이끄는 조건의 부사절 안에서는 현재가 미래를 대신하므로 want가 적절
만약 네가 원한다면 널 위해 문서를 번역해 줄게.

3 '가난한 사람들을 돕기 위해 돈을 모았다(raise)'라는 의미가 되어야 하고, last year는 과거이므로 raised가 적절
우리 자선 단체는 작년에 가난한 사람들을 돕기 위해 2만 달러를 모았다.

4 '비가 내린다(rain)'라는 의미가 되어야 하고, 시애틀의 변하지 않는 기후를 나타내므로 현재 시제 rains가 적절
시애틀은 비가 너무 자주 오기 때문에 나는 정말 시애틀에 사는 것이 즐겁지 않다.

5 '성적을 유지하면 우등으로 졸업할 것이다(graduate)'라는 의미가 되어야 하고, next year는 미래이므로 will graduate가 적절
켈리가 성적을 유지할 수 있다면 내년에 우등으로 졸업할 것이다.

6 '내가 어렸을 때'라는 의미가 되어야 하고, 이것은 과거 시제를 나타내므로 be동사의 과거형인 was가 적절
나는 어렸을 때 춤을 배우지 않았다.

7 상대방의 의향을 묻는 조동사 will 다음에는 동사 원형을 써야 하므로 join이 적절
나는 저녁을 먹으러 갈 거야. 함께 갈래?

8 '마이크의 집에 들를 것이다(drop by)'라는 의미가 되어야 하고, I'll은 I will을 줄인 말이다. 여기서 will이 조동사고 will 뒤에는 동사원형이 나와야 하므로 drop by가 적절
나는 아마 학교에서 집으로 가는 길에 마이크의 집에 들를 것이다.

9 '그녀가 행복해 보였다(look)'라는 의미가 되어야 하고, yesterday는 과거이므로 looked가 적절
나는 오늘 아침 오랜 학교 친구를 만났는데 그녀는 정말 행복해 보였다.

10 '수업이 시작하다(start)'라는 의미가 되어야 하고, until(~할 때까지)이 이끄는 시간의 부사절에서는 현재 시제가 미래 시제를 대신하므로 doesn't 뒤에는 동사원형 start가 적절
그 수업은 9월까지 시작하지 않지만, 일찍 등록해야 할 것이다.

1 reads, gets, gives up, tries, looks
2 roamed, was, uncovered
3 am going to do, are going to go

해설/해석

1 제니퍼의 평상시 영어 공부 습관에 관한 내용으로 현재 시제가 적절, often, never 등의 빈도부사는 흔히 현재 시제와 함께 쓰임
제니퍼는 종종 영어책을 읽을 때 새롭고 낯선 단어를 접한다. 하지만 그녀는 결코 낙담하거나 포기하지 않는다. 대신 그녀는 그 단어가 의미하는 것을 추측해 보려고 애쓰고, 사전을 찾아본다.

2 수백만 년 전에 공룡이 존재했음을 알려주는 내용으로 Millions years ago, a few months ago는 과거이므로 전체적으로 과거 시제가 적절
수백만 년 전, 거대한 공룡들이 지구를 돌아다녔다. 기가노토사우르스라 불리는 41피트의 괴물은 이 포식자들 중 가장 컸다. 하지만 몇 개월 전 피타고니아에 있는 과학자들은 훨씬 더 큰 공룡을 발견했다.

3 Next week에 할 일을 계획한 것이므로 be going to를 이용한 미래 시제가 적절
다음 주가 내 생일이다. 내 생일을 축하하기 위해 나는 정말 흥미진진한 것을 할 예정인데, 바로 번지점프이다. 내 친구 제임스와 나는 함께 번지점프를 할 것이다.

REVIEW PLUS

p. 48

(A) wrote, (B) takes, (C) displays

해설/해석

(A) 모차르트는 역사 속의 인물, 역사적인 사실은 과거 시제로 써야 하므로 wrote가 적절, (B) 매일 아침 지하철을 타고 학교에 간다는 의미이므로 반복적이고 습관적인 행동에는 현재 시제를 사용, 주어가 3인칭 단수인 it이므로 takes가 적절, (C) 미국의 국기가 어떤 사물을 상징한다는 것은 변하지 않는 사실이므로 현재 시제가 적절

- 모차르트는 평생 동안 600곡 이상을 작곡했다.
- 나는 매일 아침 지하철로 학교에 가는 데 한 시간이 넘게 걸린다.
- 미국 국기에 있는 13개의 줄은 각각 최초의 13개 주를 나타낸다.

(A) washes, (B) open, (C) will wear

해설/해석

(A) if(~하면)가 이끄는 조건의 부사절에서는 현재가 미래를 대신하므로 washes가 적절, (B) 은행이 문을 여는 시간은 항상 정해진 일정으로 현재 시제인 open이 적절, (C) next Sunday는 미래를 나타내므로 will wear가 적절

- A: 그 스웨터를 뜨거운 물에 세탁하면 그에게 맞지 않을 거야.
  B: 맞아. 울은 뜨거운 물에서 줄어들어.
- A: 여행자 수표를 현금으로 바꿔야 해요. 은행이 몇 시에 열죠?
  B: 은행은 대부분 정확히 오전 9시 30분에 열어요.
- A: 참 예쁜 드레스구나. 어디에 입고 갈 거니?
  B: 다음 주 일요일에 있는 데이비드와 엠마의 결혼식에 입고 갈 거야.

②

해설/해석

(A) 패스트푸드가 열량이 높다는 것은 이미 과학적으로 입증된 변하지 않는 사실이므로 are가 적절, (B) if(만약 ~하면)가 이끄는 조건 부사절 안에서는 현재가 미래를 대신하므로 skip이 적절, (C) 종속절인 if절이 앞으로 일어날 가능성이 있는 일을 나타내면 주절의 내용은 그 결과에 대해서 예측하는 것이므로 will reduce가 적절

대부분의 패스트푸드는 열량이 높다. 예를 들어, 치즈가 곁들여진 트리플 와퍼는 1,250 칼로리를 함유하고 있다. 그리고 그 안에는 69그램의 지방이 들어 있다! 간단히 마요네즈, 치즈, 베이컨을 모두 빼면 전체적인 칼로리를 줄일 수 있다. 그리고 감자튀김을 먹지 않고 다이어트 콜라를 주문하면, 전체적인 칼로리를 훨씬 더 많이 줄이게 될 것이다.

REPLAY

p. 50~51

1 CHECK-UP

1 eating	2 coming	3 cutting
4 dying	5 riding	6 lying
7 stopping	8 planning	9 crying
10 hurrying	11 setting	12 giving
13 living	14 seeing	

2 CHECK-UP

1 are walking　　2 is chatting
3 is preparing　　4 Is, snowing
5 am not listening

3 CHECK-UP

1 am doing　　2 was sleeping
3 was reading　　4 was raining
5 was taking

1 plays, is playing　　2 walks, is walking
3 cried, was crying　　4 waited, was waiting

Unit 09 EXERCISES

p. 55~57

1 ⓐ　2 ⓑ　3 ⓑ　4 ⓒ　5 ⓒ　6 ⓐ

해석

1 우리는 지금 햄버거를 먹는 중이야. 너도 원하니?
2 내 남편은 요즘 거의 집안일을 하지 않는다.
3 나는 이번 주에 시내에 있는 친구의 아파트에서 머물고 있다.
4 모든 것이 결정되었다. 그들은 10시 기차로 떠날 것이다.
5 나는 오늘 밤 참치 캐서롤을 만들 거야. 저녁 식사 때까지 있을래?
6 실례합니다만, 아내를 위한 기념일 선물을 고르고 있어요.

1 study　　2 drives
3 helps　　4 Is, cleaning up
5 are, spending　　6 am, preparing
7 is, raining　　8 is, changing
9 Do, feed　　10 is, volunteering, is, flying
11 am, trying, am, exercising

해석

1 한국 학생들 대부분이 방과 후에도 공부를 한다.
2 매일 아침, 김 씨는 아이들을 학교에 태워다 준다.
3 진은 일주일에 한두 번씩 엄마의 가게 일을 돕는다.
4 네 남동생은 지금 차고를 청소하고 있니?
5 많은 캐나다 사람들이 올해 멕시코에서 겨울 휴가를 보내고 있다.
6 지금 나는 점심을 준비하고 있어서 말할 시간이 없다.
7 봐! 밖에 비가 오고 있어. 나는 우산이 없으니까 하나 빌려야겠어.
8 사진사가 사진기의 배터리를 바꾸고 있어요. 참고 기다려 주세요!
9 너는 오리에게 주로 빵을 먹이니? 너도 알다시피, 빵은 오리의 건강에 매우 안 좋아.
10 트레이시는 이번 달에 아프리카에서 자원봉사를 하고 있고, 다음 달에는 필리핀으로 비행기를 타고 갈 것이다.
11 나는 여름 전에 살을 빼려고 애쓰고 있다. 그래서 요즘 헬스클럽에서 운동하고 있다.

1 is tasting　　2 smell
3 Are you having　　4 is looking for

5 is tasting
6 cost
7 has
8 don't like
9 contains
10 makes
11 think

해석

1 요리사가 지금 주방에서 수프를 맛보고 있다.
2 이 꽃들은 향기가 매우 좋다. 어머니께 좀 사 드리자.
3 너 지금 커피 마시고 있니? 커피 향이 매우 좋구나!
4 마이크가 지금 너를 찾고 있어. 그에게 문자 메시지를 보내.
5 제빵사가 초콜릿 케이크를 맛보고 있다. 맛있어 보인다.
6 이 신발은 너무 비싸네요. 좀 더 저렴한 것을 찾도록 도와주세요.
7 토미는 두 대의 노트북을 가지고 있지만, 그것들은 작동하지 않는다.
8 런던은 항상 비가 너무 많이 오기 때문에 나는 런던에 사는 것을 좋아하지 않는다.
9 비타민과 미네랄을 많이 함유한 음식을 먹는 것이 좋다.
10 우리 어머니는 내가 학교에서 돌아오자마자 손을 씻도록 시킨다.
11 아직도 눈이 오고 있어! 내 생각에 올해는 화이트 크리스마스가 될 거 같아.

D

1 visit
2 reads
3 is acting
4 answers
5 are studying
6 am making
7 are doing
8 goes

해석

1 매주 일요일에 우리는 지역 벼룩시장에 간다.
2 우리 어머니는 대개 오전 7시에 신문을 읽는다.
3 네 친구가 바보짓을 하고 있구나. 제발 좀 그만두라고 말해 줘.
4 그녀는 선생님의 질문에 항상 정확하게 대답한다.
5 우리는 지금 내일 있을 세계사 시험을 공부하고 있다.
6 나는 지금 쇼핑 목록을 만들고 있어. 냉장고를 열고 우리가 필요한 것을 말해 줘.
7 아이들이 식당에서 너무 시끄럽게 떠들고 있다. 하지만 그들의 부모는 아무것도 하고 있지 않다.
8 제이크는 일요일마다 교회에 가고, 교회가 끝나면 친구들과 농구를 한다.

E

1 believes, know
2 was weighing
3 is fixing
4 was sniffing at
5 is playing, are listening to
6 am doing, makes
7 Are, going, are, staying

F

1 is having lunch at the cafeteria
2 are getting married next month
3 are playing soccer in the schoolyard
4 I appreciate that you gave me a chance
5 My father is reading the newspaper
6 is teaching ballet in a school
7 are swimming in the aquarium, are watching them

Unit 10 EXERCISES

p. 59

A

1 hurt, was, working
2 was, making, stormed, in
3 was, waiting, for, had
4 was, washing, was, blaring
5 wanted, didn't, answer, was, sleeping, called

해석

1 A: 엄마, 무슨 일이세요? 기분이 안 좋아 보여요.
B: 아버지가 오늘 일하시다가 다치셨단다.
2 A: 박 선생님이 화를 내며 들어오셨을 때 내가 반 아이들 모두를 웃게 만들고 있었어.
B: 그러고 나서 무슨 일이 있었는데? 꾸중을 많이 들었니?
3 A: 방과 후에 무엇을 하고 있었니? 나는 너를 기다리고 있었어.
B: 니콜라스 선생님을 보러 잠깐 들렀었어. 역사 숙제에 관해 질문이 있었거든.
4 A: 너는 오늘 오후에 왜 미셸에게 그렇게 화를 냈니?
B: 그녀가 목욕탕에서 머리를 감고 있는데 거실에서 TV 소리가 크게 울렸었거든.
5 A: 빌과 내가 어젯밤 조촐한 파티를 했어. 너를 초대하고 싶었는데 전화를 안 받더라.
B: 아, 네가 전화했을 때 나는 자고 있었어.

B

1 was walking, ran into
2 were having, heard
3 was listening, called
4 were studying, brought
5 saw, was laughing and giggling

해석

1 나는 오늘 집에 걸어가다가 예전 영어 선생님을 우연히 만났다.
2 우리가 즐거운 시간을 보내고 있는데, 라디오에서 그 슬픈 소식이 들렸다.
3 벨 소리를 못 들었어. 네가 내게 전화했을 때, 음악을 듣고 있었거든.
4 우리가 기말고사를 준비하기 위해 역사 공부를 하고 있을 때, 아버지께서 우리에게 약간의 쿠키를 가져다주셨다.
5 에이미는 어제 쇼핑몰에서 제니퍼를 보았다. 그녀는 새 남자 친구인 스티브와 웃으며 낄낄거리고 있었다.

Unit 11 EXERCISES

p. 61

A

1 will be sitting
2 will be waiting for
3 will be watching
4 will be landing
5 will be sleeping
6 Will, be bringing
7 will be freezing
8 will be visiting

해석

1 다음 주 이맘때쯤이면 나는 해변에 앉아 있을 것이다.
2 오후 두 시에 들러. 사무실에서 널 기다리고 있을게.
3 그는 9시에 가장 좋아하는 TV 드라마인 'CSI'를 보고 있을 것이다.
4 이 비행기는 약 10분 후에 착륙할 것입니다.

5 자정에 나는 자고 있을 거야. 그러니 좀 더 일찍 전화해 줘.
6 파티에 너의 제일 친한 친구를 데려올 거니?
7 따뜻한 재킷을 가져가. 오늘 밤엔 몹시 추울 거야.
8 조부모님께서 내일 우리를 방문하실 것이다. 우리는 공항에 조부모님을 모시러 나갈 것이다.

1 Will, be seeing
2 will be going
3 Will, be eating
4 Will, be cooking
5 will be studying
6 will be playing
7 will be working

해석

1 A: 오늘 이따가 마이크를 만날 거니?
B: 응. 너한테 전화하라고 할까?
2 A: 오늘 이따가 슈퍼마켓에 갈 거야.
B: 점심으로 먹을 햄 좀 사다 줘.
3 A: 너는 6시에 저녁 먹고 있을 거니?
B: 아니. 그때면 다 먹었을 거야. 6시 이후에 언제든 들러.
4 A: 아빠, 이제부터 저녁을 준비하실 거예요?
B: 물론이지. 그리고 엄마는 계속해서 아침과 점심을 준비할 것이고.
5 A: 토요일 밤에 와서 영화 볼래?
B: 그러고 싶지만, 그때는 공부하고 있을 거야. 다음 주에 시험이 여러 개 있거든.
6 A: 우리 밴드가 이번 주말에 센테니얼 뮤직홀(100주년 기념 음악당)에서 연주할 거야. 너 올 거니?
B: 물론이야! 너희는 몇 시에 연주할 거니?
7 A: 다음 주에 너 뉴욕으로 출장 갈 거니?
B: 아니. 그때 나는 사무실에서 일하고 있을 거야. 출장이 연기되었어.

REVIEW

p. 62~63

1 prefer
2 is getting
3 needs
4 Do you believe
5 is she looking
6 was sleeping
7 owns
8 was
9 fell off
10 don't seem
11 smells
12 Do you understand

해설/해석

1 감정동사인 prefer가 '~을 더 좋아하다'라는 의미일 때는 진행형을 쓰지 않으므로 현재형 prefer가 적절
나는 집에서 먹는 것이 더 좋아.

2 next month는 가까운 미래를 나타내며 확정된 일정을 나타낼 때는 미래 시제 대신 현재진행을 쓸 수 있으므로 is getting이 적절
박 선생님은 다음 달에 결혼할 것이다.

3 인지동사인 need가 '~을 필요로 하다'라는 의미일 때는 진행형을 쓰지 않으므로 현재형 needs가 적절
케빈은 자신의 자전거를 고치기 위한 연장이 필요하다.

4 인지동사인 believe가 '~을 믿다'라는 의미일 때는 진행형을 쓰지 않으므로 현재형이 적절
너는 UFO나 외계인의 존재를 믿니?

5 now는 현재를 나타내는 부사이므로 현재진행인 is she looking이 적절
왜 그녀가 지금 제시카를 찾고 있는 거지?

6 내가 짐을 싸는 동안 동생이 잠을 자고 있다는 의미로 과거에 어떤 일이 동시에 진행되는 경우, 주절과 부사절에 모두 과거진행을 써야 하므로 was sleeping이 적절
내가 짐을 싸는 동안, 나의 게으른 남동생은 잠을 자고 있었다.

7 소유동사인 own이 '~을 소유하다'라는 의미일 때는 진행형을 쓰지 않으므로 현재형 owns가 적절
내 차고 앞에 있는 산악자전거는 누구의 것이니?

8 when은 시간을 나타내는 종속접속사로 주절과 종속절의 시제는 일치해야 한다. 주절에서 didn't learn이 나왔으므로 종속절에는 was가 적절
나는 2년 전에 이탈리아에 있으면서 이탈리아어를 많이 배우지 않았다.

9 과거의 비슷한 시점에 일어난 일 중 먼저 시작된 일(자전거를 타는 것)에 과거진행 was riding이 쓰였으므로, 나중에 일어난 일(바퀴가 빠진 것)은 과거시제인 fell off가 적절
마이크가 자전거를 타고 길을 가는데 바퀴가 빠졌다.

10 상대방의 상태가 요즘 행복해 보이지 않는다는 의미이므로 don't seem이 적절
너는 요즘 정말 행복해 보이지 않아. 문제가 뭐야?

11 감각동사인 smell이 '~한 냄새가 나다'라는 의미일 때는 진행형을 쓰지 않으므로, 현재형 smells가 적절
방에서 불쾌한 냄새가 나! 창문을 열고 환기시키는 것이 어때?

12 인지동사인 understand가 '~을 이해하다'라는 의미일 때는 진행형을 쓰지 않으므로 현재형 Do you understand가 적절
너는 이 지시사항을 이해하니?

1 contains
2 are
3 are having
4 go
5 will be cramming 등
6 don't mix, floats
7 was lying
8 tastes
9 resemble, resembles
10 is holding/will hold 등

해설/해석

1 contain이 '~이 들어 있다'라는 상태를 나타내는 동사로 쓰일 경우 진행형을 쓰지 않으므로 현재형 contains가 적절
이 병에는 2리터의 물이 들어 있다.

2 돌고래가 포유류라는 것은 변하지 않는 사실이므로 현재 시제 are가 적절
돌고래는 어류가 아닌 포유류이다.

3 지금 즐거운 시간을 보내고 있는 중이므로 진행형인 are having이 적절
우리는 지금 놀이공원에서 즐거운 시간을 보내고 있다.

4 일요일마다 하는 반복적인 행동을 나타내므로 go가 적절
나의 사촌들은 일요일마다 대개 교회에 간다.

5 다음 주에 있을 시험을 위해 주말 내내 공부하고 있을 것이라는 의미이므로 미래진행 will be cramming이 적절
기말고사가 다음 주에 시작된다. 나는 주말 내내 벼락공부를 하고 있을 것이다.

6 일반적 사실은 진행형이 아닌 현재 시제를 써야 하므로 don't mix, floats가 적절
물과 기름은 섞이지 않고 기름이 물 위에 뜬다.

7 그가 침대에 누워 있는 중에 이상한 소리를 들은 것이므로 was lying이 적절
그가 침대에 누워 있는데 밖에서 이상한 소리가 들렸다.

8 감각동사인 taste가 '~한 맛이 나다'의 의미일 때는 진행형을 쓰지 않으므로, 현재 시제 tastes가 적절
이 파이는 맛이 정말 좋구나! 네가 정말 처음부터 만든 거야?

9 resemble은 진행형으로 쓰지 않는 동사이므로 resemble, resembles가 적절
나는 아빠를 닮았고, 우리 언니는 엄마를 닮았다.

10 tomorrow morning은 미래의 확정된 계획을 나타내므로 미래 시제 is holding/will hold 등이 적절
대통령은 내일 아침에 기자 회견을 열 것이다.

1 is, taking
2 will, be, waiting
3 are, speaking
4 am, attending/will, attend
5 are, changing
6 am, going, to, learn

해설/해석

1 현재 그녀가 낮잠을 자고 있기 때문에 말을 할 수 없다는 의미가 되어야 하므로 현재진행 is taking이 적절
A: 그녀는 지금 너와 이야기를 할 수 없어. 낮잠을 자고 있어.
B: 알겠어. 그녀가 일어나면 내게 알려 줘.

2 7시에 사무실에서 기다리는 행위는 미래의 어떤 시점에서 진행될 일이므로 미래 진행인 will be waiting이 적절
A: 7시에 사무실에서 너를 기다리고 있을게.
B: 좋아. 집에서 나갈 때 네게 전화할게.

3 now(지금)로 보아 현재 진행 중인 일임을 알 수 있으므로 are speaking이 적절
A: 그들은 지금 어떤 언어를 쓰고 있는 거지? 친숙하게 들리는데.
B: 확실히는 모르지만 프랑스어처럼 들려.

4 결혼식이 열리는 것은 확정된 가까운 미래를 나타내므로 현재 진행인 am attending이나 will attend가 적절
A: 그 정장을 입으니 멋져 보인다. 무슨 일이야?
B: 오늘 우리 이모의 결혼식에 참석할 거야.

5 부사인 constantly를 현재진행 시제와 함께 써서 불평의 의미를 나타내고 있으므로 are changing이 적절
A: 나 마음이 바뀌었어. 도서관에서 보자.
B: 너는 계속 마음이 왔다 갔다 하는 구나!

6 미래를 나타내는 부사인 this summer가 나왔으므로 am going to learn이 적절
A: 나는 이번 여름에 기타 치는 것을 배울 거야.
B: 정말? 나도 같이 배워도 되겠니?

D

1 will, be, waiting
2 am, having, next, week
3 will, be, studying
4 didn't, see, was, facing
5 were, cleaning, did, see
6 was, playing, started, to, rain

해설

1 미래에 진행 중인 동작을 나타내므로 will be waiting이 적절

2 다음 주에 확정된 계획을 나타내므로 현재 진행인 am having으로 미래를 표현할 수 있음

3 미래의 한 시점에 공부를 진행 중인 상황을 말하는 것이므로 will be studying이 적절

4 보지 못한 것은 과거의 한 동작이고, 다른 쪽을 보고 있었던 것은 과거에 진행 중인 동작이므로 didn't see, was facing이 적절

5 청소를 하는 중에 제임스를 봤는지 묻고 있는 것이므로 먼저 시작된 동작인 clean은 were cleaning, see는 did, see가 적절

6 운동장에서 놀고 있던 것은 과거에 진행 중이던 동작이고, 비가 오기 시작한 것은 과거의 한 시점에 발생한 사건이므로 was playing, started to rain이 적절

REVIEW PLUS

p. 64

④

해설/해석

(A) 먼저 시작된 일(소풍)은 과거진행인 were having, 나중에 일어난 일(지진)은 struck이 적절, (B) 먼저 시작된 일(나무를 베는 것)은 과거진행 was chopping, 나중에 일어난 일(가슴에서 통증을 느낀 것)은 과거 felt가 적절, (C) 빈도부사 never는 일반동사 앞에 오므로 never eat이 적절

- 그들이 공원에 소풍 가서 놀고 있는데 지진이 일어났다.
- 우리 아버지가 나무를 베다가 가슴에서 극심한 고통을 느꼈다.
- 나는 밤 10시 이후에는 아무것도 먹지 않는다. 어디에선가 그렇게 먹는 것이 건강에 좋지 않다고 읽었다.

1 ④
2 ①

해설/해석

1 잭이 청소하는 동안 내가 설거지와 쓰레기를 버리는 두 가지 행동을 한 것이다. 설거지와 쓰레기를 내놓은 일이 과거이므로 청소하는 일은 과거진행 was cleaning이 적절
A: 와! 너희가 모든 집안일을 매우 빨리 끝냈구나.
B: 잭이 거실을 청소하는 동안, 저는 설거지를 하고 쓰레기를 버렸어요.

2 앞에 is looking(~을 보고 있다)이라는 현재진행이 쓰였고, 등위 접속사 and로 연결되었으므로 whispering이 적절
A: 왜 저 소녀가 나를 바라보면서 메리에게 귓속말을 하고 있지?
B: 모르겠어. 아마 그녀가 너에게 관심이 있나 봐.

① witnessed
② were closing
③ were standing

해설/해석

① 오늘 저녁 때 사고를 목격했다는 의미가 되어야 하므로 witnessed가 적절 ② 나중에 일어난 일(비집고 들어오려는 것)이 과거 tried로 쓰였으므로, 먼저 시작된 일(문 닫히는 것)은 과거진행 were closing이 적절 ③ 나중에 일어난 일(할머니가 비집고 들어오려는 것)이 과거 happened로 쓰였으므로 먼저 시작된 일(서 있던 것)은 과거진행 were standing이 적절

미셸은 오늘 저녁 지하철에서 끔찍한 사고를 목격했다. 시청역에서 지하철 문이 막 닫히려고 할 때 한 할머니가 그 사이로 비집고 들어오려고 했지만 끼여 버렸다. 다행히도 그 일이 일어났을 때, 힘센 10대 소년 두 명이 문 옆에 서 있었다. 그들은 문 틈 사이로 물건을 넣고 억지로 열어서 할머니를 무사히 안으로 끌어당길 수 있었다.

REPLAY

p. 66~67

1 CHECK-UP

1 broken
2 brought
3 built
4 bought
5 caught
6 chosen
7 come
8 cost
9 cut
10 drawn
11 drunk
12 fed
13 fallen
14 fought
15 flown
16 sent
17 written
18 begun
19 grown
20 hit
21 held
22 hurt
23 kept
24 lent
25 lost
26 meant
27 paid
28 put
29 read
30 set
31 sat
32 stolen
33 worn
34 gone
35 driven
36 laid

2 CHECK-UP

1 Have, met
2 have never been
3 has lived
4 have been
5 has lost
6 has worked
7 haven't decided
8 Have, visited
9 Have, seen
10 have never tried
11 hasn't attended
12 have watched
13 Has, been
14 has never won

Unit 12 EXERCISES

p. 70~71

A

1 has turned on
2 has ordered
3 have gone
4 have entered
5 has called
6 has been

해석

1 TV가 꺼져 있었다. 지금은 TV가 켜져 있다. → 누군가 TV를 켰다.
2 엄마가 피자하우스에 전화하셨다. 피자가 오는 중이다. → 엄마가 피자를 주문했다.
3 앤은 길버트와 함께 방금 도서관으로 떠났다. 그들은 지금 밖에 있다. → 앤과 길버트는 밖에 나가고 없다.
4 우리 학교는 영어 말하기 대회를 개최할 것이다. 나는 신청서를 보냈다. → 나는 영어 말하기 대회에 참가 신청을 했다.
5 재스퍼는 사라에게 연락하려고 애쓰고 있다. 그는 오전 9시와 11시, 오후 4시에 전화했다. → 재스퍼는 오늘 사라에게 세 번 전화했다.
6 애니카는 9월 초에 한국에 왔다. 그녀는 아직도 한국에 있고, 이제 11월 말이다. → 애니카는 거의 석 달째 한국에 있다.

B

1 have just had
2 have already called
3 Has, stopped, yet
4 Have, shown, yet
5 has already left
6 has stolen

해석

1 A: 너 배고프니? 내가 너에게 먹을 것을 만들어 줄 수 있어.
B: 아니, 괜찮아. 방금 간식을 먹었어.
2 A: 네 여동생에게 전화해서 파티에 대해 상기시키는 것을 잊지 마.
B: 벌써 전화했어.
3 A: 이제 눈 오는 거 멈췄니?
B: 안 멈췄어. 내 생각에는 보도를 삽으로 치우려면 잠시 기다려야 할 것 같아.
4 A: 너는 벌써 너희 부모님께 성적표를 보여 드렸니?
B: 아니, 아직 보여 드리지 않았어. 하지만 그다지 걱정되지는 않아. 수학과 영어를 잘 봤거든.
5 A: 벨라는 이미 떠났어. 몇 분 차이로 그녀를 놓쳤구나.
B: 이거 곤란한데. 나를 위해 그녀에게 메시지를 좀 전해 줄래?
6 A: 누군가 내 지갑을 훔쳐갔어! 어디에서도 찾을 수가 없어.
B: 책상과 사물함은 찾아봤어?

C

1 since
2 since
3 for
4 since
5 for
6 for
7 since
8 since
9 for
10 since
11 for
12 for

해석

1 나는 도착한 이후로 제대로 된 식사를 하지 못했다.
2 나는 오늘 아침부터 아무것도 못 먹었다.
3 나는 지금까지 2년 정도 톰과 신디를 알아 왔다.
4 그들은 결혼한 이후로 해외여행을 해보지 못했다.
5 우리 아버지는 같은 회사에서 15년 동안 일을 하고 계신다.
6 톰슨 씨는 10년 동안 같은 신문을 읽어왔다.
7 런던의 지하철은 1933년부터 운행되어 왔다.

8 팸은 새로운 도시로 이사 오고 난 뒤로 요가 수업에 참여하지 않았다.
9 아빠는 항상 바쁘다. 그래서 그는 5년 동안 휴가를 가지 못했다.
10 우리 아버지는 어렸을 때부터 이 오래된 전축을 갖고 계신다.
11 난 네 동생을 오랫동안 못 봤어. 그녀는 정말 빨리 자라는구나!
12 우리 언니는 몇 달간 농구 팀에 있었다.

D

1	has gone up	2	did, finish
3	has lived	4	have been
5	married	6	have been
7	has treated	8	has been
9	haven't had	10	has never seen
11	heard	12	planted

해석

1 최근에 기름 값이 올랐다.
2 어제 예행연습이 몇 시에 끝났니?
3 조디는 밴쿠버에 산다. 그녀는 평생 그곳에서 살아왔다.
4 나는 한국에 온 후로 부산에 세 번 가봤다.
5 샘은 지난 주말에 라스베이거스에서 여자 친구와 결혼했다.
6 우리 부모님은 30년 넘게 행복한 결혼 생활을 해왔다.
7 에밀리는 20년 넘게 아프리카에서 병든 사람을 치료해왔다.
8 단풍잎기(旗)는 1965년부터 캐나다의 공식 국기였다.
9 우리는 몇 해째 휴가를 가지 못했다. 이제 휴식을 취할 때다.
10 앤은 자메이카에 산다. 그녀는 평생 눈을 본 적이 없다.
11 나는 어젯밤에 옆 아파트에서 이상한 소리를 들었다.
12 엠마는 아름다운 정원을 가지고 있다. 지난주 그녀는 장미와 튤립을 심었다.

Unit 13 EXERCISES

p. 74~75

1	have, been doing	2	has been hanging up
3	has been going	4	has been eating
5	have been waiting	6	has been vacuuming
7	have been playing	8	have been waiting

해석

1 이번 주에 무엇을 하고 있니?
2 빈센트는 젖은 빨래를 널고 있다.
3 요즘 학교에서는 모든 일이 잘 돌아가고 있다.
4 누가 내 팝콘을 먹고 있던 거야? 절반이 없어졌잖아!
5 그들은 티켓을 사려고 30분 동안 줄을 서서 기다리고 있다.
6 네 형이 진공청소기로 카펫을 청소하고 있어. 가구의 먼지를 털어 줘.
7 너는 세 시간 넘게 컴퓨터 게임을 하고 있잖아. 밖에 나가서 운동을 좀 하렴.
8 우리는 7시부터 여기에서 널 기다리고 있었어.

B

1 How long have you been babysitting
2 How much money have you spent
3 How many times have you listened
4 How many people have you invited

해석

1 당신의 친구가 이웃집 아이들을 돌보고 있다. 그에게 물어 보아라.
→ 너는 얼마나 오랫동안 이웃집 아이들을 돌봐 왔니?
2 당신의 친구는 고서(古書)를 모은다. 그녀는 많은 수집품을 가지고 있다. 그녀에게 물어 보아라. → 이 모든 고서를 모으는 데 얼마나 많은 돈을 썼니?
3 당신의 남동생이 방금 그레이트 보이즈의 새 CD를 샀다. 그는 계속해서 그것을 듣고 있다. 그에게 물어 보아라. → 그레이트 보이즈의 새 CD를 몇 번이나 들었니?
4 당신의 여동생이 부모님을 위한 25주년 결혼기념일 파티를 준비하고 있다. 그녀에게 물어 보아라. → 엄마 아빠의 25주년 결혼기념일 파티에 얼마나 많은 사람을 초대했니?

C

1	① did, date	② has, been dating
2	① did, teach	② have, been teaching
3	① did, ring	② has, been ringing
4	① did, talk	② has, been talking
5	① did, lie	② has, been lying
6	① did, work	② has, been working
7	① did, wear	② has, been wearing

해석

1 ① 그가 언제 수지와 데이트를 했니?
② 그가 얼마나 오랫동안 수지와 사귀었니?
2 ① 너는 언제 영어를 가르쳤니?
② 너는 얼마나 오랫동안 영어를 가르쳐왔니?
3 ① 내 휴대폰이 언제 울렸니?
② 내 휴대폰이 얼마나 오랫동안 울렸니?
4 ① 아론이 언제 윤희와 이야기를 했니?
② 아론이 얼마나 오랫동안 윤희와 이야기를 했니?
5 ① 마르코가 언제 일광욕 침대에 누웠니?
② 마르코가 얼마나 오랫동안 일광욕 침대에 누워 있었니?
6 ① 진우가 언제 에버월드에서 일했니?
② 진우가 얼마나 오랫동안 에버월드에서 일했니?
7 ① 지민이가 언제 콘택트렌즈를 꼈니?
② 지민이가 얼마나 오랫동안 콘택트렌즈를 껴 왔니?

D

1	① ⓐ ② ⓑ	2	① ⓐ ② ⓑ
3	① ⓑ ② ⓐ	4	① ⓑ ② ⓐ

해석

1 낸시는 남아메리카 지역을 배낭여행했다. 그녀는 지난달에 여행을 시작했다. 그녀는 칠레, 브라질, 콜롬비아를 여행했다.
① 그녀는 지금까지 세 나라를 여행했다.
② 그녀는 한 달째 여행 중이다.
2 재스민은 열성적인 블로거이다. 그녀는 이번 주에 10개가 넘는 글을 게시할 예정이다. 그녀는 방금 세 개의 글을 게시했다.
① 재스민은 일주일 내내 자신의 블로그에 글을 게시해 왔다.
② 재스민은 지금까지 세 개의 글을 게시했다.
3 브라운 씨는 오늘 아침에 영화를 보기 시작했다. 지금은 오후 3시다. 그는 여전히 영화를 보고 있고, 지금 막 다섯 번째 영화를 보기 시작했다.

① 그는 오늘 아침부터 영화를 보고 있다.
② 그는 지금까지 네 편의 영화를 봤다.

4 마이클은 두 시간 전쯤에 새로 산 휴대 전화의 설명서를 읽기 시작했다. 그는 여전히 그것을 읽고 있고, 지금 막 120쪽을 다 읽었다.
① 그는 두 시간도 넘게 설명서를 읽고 있는 중이다.
② 그는 지금까지 120쪽을 읽었다.

Unit 14 EXERCISES p. 77

1 had never met
2 had expected
3 had heard
4 had already finished
5 had never seen
6 had gone out

해석

1 그녀는 그를 한 번도 만난 적이 없다고 주장했다.
2 실제 크기는 우리가 기대했던 것보다 컸다.
3 그녀는 그 소식을 듣고 매우 행복했다.
4 내가 집에 도착했을 때 우리 엄마는 이미 저녁을 다 해 놓은 상태였다.
5 나는 전에 그를 한 번도 본 적이 없었기 때문에 그가 누구인지 몰랐다.
6 내가 재키를 방문했을 때 그녀는 어머니와 밖에 나가고 없었다.

B

1 remembered, had forgotten
2 missed, had told
3 had eaten, knew
4 came, had gone
5 admitted, had hit
6 had lost, found

해석

1 나는 열쇠를 잊고 두고 왔다는 것을 기억해냈다.
2 아무도 파티에 대해 그에게 말해주지 않았기 때문에 그는 파티에 참석하지 못했다.
3 데이비드는 전에 태국 음식을 먹어 본 적이 있어서 무엇을 주문해야 할지 알았다.
4 케리가 학교에 왔을 때 샐리는 거기에 없었다. 그녀는 집에 가버렸다.
5 토니는 다른 차를 치었다는 것은 인정했지만, 심하게 파손시키지는 않았다고 말했다.
6 나는 오늘 아침에 개를 잃어버렸는데, 나중에 이웃집 쓰레기통에서 발견했다.

C

1 had been crying
2 had been organizing
3 had been napping

해석

1 피트가 혼자 앉아 있었다. 그의 눈이 충혈 되고 젖어 있었다. → 그는 울고 있었다.
2 마크의 여행 사진이 모두 식탁 위에 분류되어 있었다. → 그는 식탁 위에 그것들을 정돈하고 있었다.
3 릭이 거울 속에 비친 자신을 보았을 때 그의 머리는 흐트러져 있었고 눈은 반쯤 감겨 있었다. → 릭은 소파에서 낮잠을 자고 있었다.

REVIEW p. 78~79

1 haven't seen
2 had prepared
3 haven't been
4 has studied
5 had gone
6 have already had
7 had been trying
8 have been warning

해설/해석

1 현재 멀리 떨어져 살고 있어 몇 년 동안 못 본 것은 과거부터 현재까지의 시간을 모두 포함하므로, 현재완료 haven't seen이 적절
프랭크와 나는 멀리 떨어져서 살고 있다. 우리는 몇 년 동안이나 서로 못 봤다.

2 준비가 된 것이 과거의 일이고, 그 전날부터 준비를 해왔기 때문에 과거완료 had prepared가 적절
나는 연설할 준비가 되어 있었다. 나는 전날부터 매우 열심히 준비를 했다.

3 아침 내내 연락이 안 되고 있으므로 현재까지 영향을 미치는 현재완료 haven't been이 적절
아침 내내 수와 연락할 수가 없다. 약간 걱정이 되기 시작했다.

4 대학에 들어간 시점부터 현재까지 공부를 해오고 있으므로, 현재완료 has studied가 적절
앤젤라는 생물학을 공부한다. 그녀는 대학에 들어간 이후로 생물학을 공부해 왔다.

5 도착한 시점이 과거(got to)이며, 그전에 이미 남자 친구가 떠났으므로 과거완료 had gone이 적절
루스가 마침내 극장에 도착했을 때, 그녀의 남자 친구는 거기에 없었다. 그는 집에 가버렸다.

6 이번 학기가 힘들다는 것으로 보아 아직도 학기 중이므로, 학기 초부터 현재까지를 포함한 현재완료 have already had가 적절
이번 학기는 정말 힘들다. 우리는 벌써 마감이 다가온 주요 과제가 다섯 개나 있다.

7 바닥에 쓰레기가 널려진 것은 과거의 일이고, 그 상황이 일어난 것은 그전에 개가 쓰레기통에서 음식물을 뒤지고 있었던 것이므로 과거완료진행형 had been trying이 적절
오늘 아침 나는 부엌 바닥에 쓰레기가 널려 있는 것을 보았다. 내 개가 쓰레기통에서 먹을 것을 찾고 있었던 것이다.

8 과학자들이 1970년대 후반부터 지구 온난화에 대해 지금까지 경고해 온 것이므로 현재완료 진행형 have been warning이 적절
과학자들은 1970년 후반 이래로 지구 온난화의 악영향에 대해 계속 경고해 왔다.

1 have
2 won
3 Have you seen / Did you see
4 splashed
5 was
6 saw
7 has lost
8 have become

해설/해석

1 신문이 방금 여기 있었는데 없어진 것을 보고 한 질문이므로 현재완료가 적절
신문이 바로 여기 있었는데. 신문을 가지고 무엇을 한 거니?

2 last weekend는 과거이므로 won이 적절
우리 학교가 지난 주말에 상을 받았다. 지금 우리는 축하하고 있다.

3 휴대 전화 찾는 것을 도와달라는 것은 현재까지도 휴대 전화를 찾지 못했다는 의미이므로 현재완료가 가장 적절하지만 과거 시제도 사용 가능
내 휴대 전화 본 적 있니? 내가 놓아둔 곳에 없네. 찾는 것 좀 도와줘.

4 시간을 나타내는 종속접속사 when절의 시제와 주절의 시제는 주로 일치한다. 머그컵을 넘어뜨린 것이 과거이므로 주절도 과거 시제 splashed가 적절
내가 머그컵을 넘어뜨려서, 커피가 내 새 신발 위로 다 튀었다.

5 last year는 과거이고, 작년에 그곳에 갔다는 의미가 되어야 하므로 과거 시제 was가 적절
너는 멕시코에 가본 적 있니? 나는 작년 휴가 때 가족과 함께 거기에 갔었어.

6 주절에서 닉을 부른 것이 과거이므로 종속절도 과거가 적절
나는 창밖으로 닉을 보고 소리쳐 불렀다. 그가 나에게 손을 흔들며, '안녕'이라고 외쳤다.

7 실비아가 정크푸드 먹는 것을 그만둔 과거의 시점 이후 현재 살이 빠진 상태이므로 현재완료인 has lost가 적절
실비아는 정크푸드 먹는 것을 그만둔 후로 살이 많이 빠졌다. 그녀는 더 활력이 넘치고 피부도 더 깨끗해졌다.

8 빌 게이츠가 돈을 기부하는 것(has donated)이 과거부터 현재까지 지속되는 일이고, 그러한 일로 인해 그와 그의 부인이 유명한 박애주의자가 되는 것이므로 결과를 의미 하는 have become이 적절
빌 게이츠는 아프리카의 가난한 사람들에게 많은 돈을 기부해오고 있다. 그와 그의 부인은 세계적으로 유명한 박애주의자가 되었다.

C

1 recently 2 before 3 today
4 since 5 last night 6 how long
7 for 8 since 9 for ages
10 is breaking

해설/해석

1 have written은 과거를 나타내는 부사 last week과 함께 쓸 수 없다. recently는 가까운 과거와 현재를 모두 포함
나는 최근에 대니에게 편지를 썼다.

2 「Have you eaten ~?」은 과거부터 현재까지의 경험을 묻는 것이므로, before(~ 전에)가 적절
너는 전에 이탈리아 음식을 먹어 본 적이 있니?

3 have you been doing은 과거에 시작한 일이 현재에도 진행되고 있음을 나타내므로 오늘 아침(과거)부터 말하는 순간(현재)까지를 포함하는 today가 적절
너는 오늘 무엇을 하며 지냈니?

4 have been living은 과거에 시작한 일이 현재에도 진행되고 있음을 나타내므로, '~한 이래로'라는 뜻을 가진 since가 적절
나는 작년 말부터 여기에서 살고 있다.

5 저녁을 먹었다(had)는 의미이므로 last night가 적절
사실 나는 지난밤에 에이미와 저녁을 먹었다.

6 have had는 과거부터 현재까지 그 시계를 가지고 있음을 나타낸다. '얼마나 오랫동안'이라는 표현은 how long이 적절
내가 얼마나 오랫동안 이 시계를 가지고 있었는지 기억이 나지 않는다.

7 오랫동안 못 봤다는 의미로 haven't seen이 쓰였으므로 기간을 나타내는 for(~동안)가 적절
나는 오랫동안 제리를 못 봤어. 그는 어떠니?

8 과거에 함께 런던에 간 이후로 현재까지 런던에 가본 경험이 없음을 나타내므로, since가 적절
우리가 함께 런던에 갔던 이후로 테리는 런던에 가본 적이 없다.

9 오랫동안 노력해 왔다는 의미로 have been trying이 쓰였으므로, for ages(오랫동안)가 적절
나는 데이비드와 연락을 하면서 지내려고 오랫동안 노력해 왔다.

10 누군가 침입하고 있는 순간을 목격하고 말한 것이므로, 현재진행이 적절
봐! 누군가 저 아파트에 침입하고 있어. 빨리 경찰에 전화해.

D

1 Have you ever traveled
2 have you been studying
3 'm separating
4 has worked
5 haven't seen
6 Have you visited
7 have never seen

해설/해석

1 전에 밴디 버스를 타고 여행한 적이 있는지 묻는 것으로, 현재완료 Have you ever traveled가 적절
A: 너는 밴디(두 대가 연결된) 버스를 타본 적 있니?
B: 아니, 없는 것 같아. 이번이 처음이 될 거야.

2 A에서 How long은 얼마나 오랫동안 공부를 해온 것인지 묻는 것이므로 have you been studying이 적절
A: 여기 UCLA에서 얼마나 오래 공부했니?
B: 2014년부터 여기서 공부하고 있어.

3 B에서 노른자와 흰자를 분리하고 있다는 의미이므로 'm separating이 적절
A: 너 지금 그 계란을 가지고 무엇을 하고 있니?
B: 노른자와 흰자를 분리하고 있어. 노른자에 지방이 모두 들어 있거든.

4 A에서 How long은 얼마나 오랫동안 은행에서 일해 왔는지 묻는 것이므로 A에 대한 대답으로 has worked가 적절
A: 너희 아버지는 그레이트 은행에서 얼마나 오래 일하셨니?
B: 아버지는 재정 분석가로 15년 넘게 그곳에서 일해 오셨어.

5 B에서 어젯밤(과거)부터 현재까지 그를 못 봤으므로 haven't seen이 적절
A: 한 시간 넘게 제이슨과 연락을 시도하고 있어. 그가 어디 있는지 아니?
B: 어젯밤부터 그를 못 봤어.

6 A에서 최근에 그를 만난 적이 있는지 묻고 있는 것이므로 Have

you visited가 적절

A: 윌리엄은 한동안 아팠어. 최근에 그에게 찾아가본 적 있니?

B: 어젯밤에 그를 보러 들렀지만 이미 잠자리에 든 상태였어.

7 현재를 기준으로 이전에 기린을 본 적이 없다는 의미이므로 현재완료인 have never seen이 적절

A: 나는 오늘 동물원에 우리 학생들을 데리고 갔어. 놀랍게도, 그들 중 일부는 전에 기린을 본 적이 없었어.

B: 그건 놀랍지 않은 걸. 나도 전에 기린을 본 적이 없어.

REVIEW PLUS

p. 80

1 had already left
2 has eaten
3 have started, have often dreamed
4 has been crying, haven't been

해설/해석

1 도착한 시점(과거)보다 더 이전에 경찰이 떠났다는 의미가 되어야 하므로 had already left가 적절

A: 네가 도착했을 때 경찰이 여전히 그 사건을 조사하고 있었니?

B: 아니, 그들은 이미 그 현장을 떠났었어.

2 아이스크림을 먹은 과거의 행동으로 인해 현재 아이스크림이 없음을 강조하는 의미가 되어야 하므로 has eaten이 적절

A: 누가 내 아이스크림을 먹었지? 영화 볼 때를 위해 아껴 두고 있었는데!

B: 재민아, 미안해. 네가 먹으려던 건지 몰랐어.

3 A에서 최근에 비행 수업을 듣기 시작하여 현재도 하고 있다는 의미가 되어야 하므로 have started가 적절, B에서 비행하는 법을 배우는 것을 과거부터 현재까지 종종 꿈꿔 왔다는 의미가 되어야 하므로 have often dreamed가 적절

A: 비행 수업을 듣기 시작했어. 얼마나 재미있는지 몰라!

B: 정말? 나도 비행하는 것을 배우기를 종종 꿈꿔 왔어. 어떻게 되어 가고 있는지 내게도 알려줘.

4 A에서 30분 전(과거)부터 말하는 순간(현재)까지 계속 울고 있다는 의미가 되어야 하므로 has been crying이 적절, B에서 울기 시작했을 때(과거)부터 현재까지 우는 이유를 알아낼 수 없었으므로 haven't been이 적절

A: 지수는 지금 30분도 넘게 방에서 울고 있어. 뭐가 잘못된 거니?

B: 내가 문을 두드렸지만, 그녀는 문을 열어 주지 않아. 솔직히 무슨 일인지 알아낼 수가 없어.

③

해설/해석

③ 스쿠버 다이빙을 한 시점이 이미 과거이고, 그 이전에 그렇게 아름다운 해변을 본 적이 없는 것이므로 과거완료 had ever seen이 적절

샘과 그의 친구 제임스는 진정한 모험 여행가다. 그들은 함께 지난 세월 동안 몇몇 놀라운 것들을 경험하고 봐왔다. 예를 들어, 3개월 전에 그들은 두바이를 여행하며 중동 최초의 실내 스키 휴양지인 스키 두바이에서 처음으로 스노보드를 타봤다. 그 후로 그들은 호주의 그레이트 배리어 리프에서 심해 스쿠버 다이빙을 했다. 둘 중 누구도 전에 그렇게 아름다운 해변을 본 적이 없었다. 그들이 호주에 있는 동안 샘은 꼭 해 봐야 할 활동인 황소몰이를 배웠다. 이것은 그들이 찾아왔던 바로 그 신나는 활동이었다! 그래서 지난달에 그들은 산 페르민 축제에서 황소와 경주하기 위해 스페인 팜플로나로 갔다. 통틀어 보면 그들은 지금 10개월간 여행을 하고 있다.

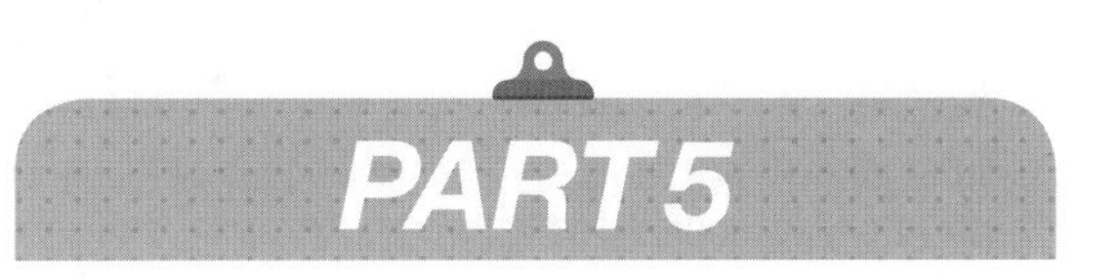

REPLAY

p. 84~85

1 CHECK-UP

1 uncle, kitten, puppies
2 classmate, Linda, Canada, family
3 Peter, bakery, Saturday, bread, cake

2 CHECK-UP

1 deer	2 benches	3 tomatoes	4 boxes
5 cities	6 children	7 photos	8 wolves

3 CHECK-UP

1 C	2 C	3 UC	4 C	5 C
6 UC	7 UC	8 UC	9 UC	10 C
11 UC	12 UC	13 UC	14 UC	15 UC

1 dollars	2 furniture	3 homework
4 information	5 teeth	

4 CHECK-UP

1 주격	2 소유격	3 목적격
4 주격, 소유격	5 주격, 소유격, 목적격	

Unit 15 EXERCISES

p. 88~89

1 matches	2 neckties	3 chimneys	4 chores
5 thieves	6 teeth	7 children	8 feet

해석

1 나는 촛불을 켜려고 항상 성냥을 가지고 다닌다.
2 당신은 여기에 상당히 많은 넥타이를 모아 두었군요!
3 검은 연기가 굴뚝 밖으로 나오고 있었다.
4 너는 네가 해야 할 집안일을 마친 후에 TV를 볼 수 있다.
5 도둑이 사무실에 침입해서 중요한 서류를 훔쳤다.
6 그녀는 앞니 두 개가 빠졌다. 그녀가 웃을 때 귀엽다.
7 박물관 앞에 많은 아이들이 줄을 서서 기다리고 있다.
8 마크에 대해 뭔가 이상한 점을 발견했어. 그는 발에 신발을 신고 있지 않았어.

B

1 block, blocks
2 woman, women
3 mosquito, mosquito(e)s
4 Ferries, ferry
5 sandbox, sandboxes
6 wives, wife
7 Oxen, ox
8 year, years

해석

1 나는 경기장에서 한 블록 떨어진 곳에 산다.
박물관은 여섯 블록이 넘게 떨어져 있다.
2 그녀는 정말로 상냥한 여자이다.
현재 더 많은 여성들이 공학을 공부한다.
3 텐트 안에 모기 한 마리가 있다.
몇몇 종류의 모기들은 인간에게 말라리아를 옮긴다.
4 본토로 가는 페리는 매시간 정시에 떠난다.
우리가 탈 페리가 날씨 때문에 두 시간 늦었다.
5 내가 어렸을 때 우리 아버지가 나에게 모래 상자 놀이터를 만들어 주셨다.
그 공원은 아이들이 놀 수 있는 여러 개의 모래 상자 놀이터를 갖추고 있다.
6 몇몇 나라에서는 남성이 여러 명의 부인을 갖는 것이 허용된다.
나는 어제 처음으로 그의 부인을 만났다. 그녀는 친절했다.
7 한 때 소는 농장에서 쟁기를 끄는 데 사용되었다.
중국의 12지에 따르면 2021년은 소의 해이다.
8 1년은 365일 또는 12개의 달로 이루어져 있다.
제임스는 사고 후 여러 해 동안 악몽에 시달렸다.

1 phenomena
2 glasses
3 tooth
4 salmon
5 shorts
6 series
7 people
8 countries

해석

1 그 작가는 당대의 다양한 사회적 현상을 묘사했다.
2 나는 집에 안경을 두고 와서 수업 중에 필기를 할 수 없었다.
3 지속적인 통증을 유발하는 치아는 심각한 문제의 징조일 수 있다.
4 연어를 요리하는 여러 가지 방법이 있지만, 가장 좋은 방법은 굽는 것이다.
5 그녀는 이웃의 수영장 파티에 낡은 반바지와 티셔츠를 입고 갔다.
6 나는 그 시리즈의 두 번째 편을 놓쳐서 지금 무슨 일이 진행되는지 모르겠다.
7 복권 결과가 발표된 후로 수백 명의 사람이 갑자기 백만장자가 되었다.
8 통계에 의하면 한국인들은 대부분의 다른 산업화된 나라의 근로자들보다 더 오래 일을 한다.

1 are
2 are
3 is
4 have
5 don't
6 is
7 was
8 were
9 is
10 allow
11 is
12 loves

해석

1 시장과 그의 형제들은 교도소에 가게 될 것이다.
2 삽화가 있는 만화책은 내가 읽기 좋아하는 책이다.
3 길 위의 얼음이 10중 추돌 사고의 원인이었다.
4 이번 달에 우리 웹사이트의 방문자 수가 많이 증가했다.
5 나는 채소를 좋아하지 않는 사람들을 이해할 수 없다.
6 고급 물리학은 2학기에만 개설됩니다.
7 우리가 어제 본 그 영화는 이탈리아 감독이 만든 것이다.
8 내 새 선글라스가 내 가방의 무게로 찌그러졌다.
9 경제학은 무역과 자금이 관리되는 방법에 관한 학문이다.
10 헤드폰은 다른 사람을 방해하지 않고 음악을 들을 수 있게 해준다.
11 통계학은 매우 어려운 과목이지만 나는 공부할 가치가 있다고 생각해.
12 아이들은 대개 야채를 먹는 것을 즐겨 하지 않지만 나의 아들 애런은 브로컬리를 좋아한다.

Unit 16 EXERCISES

p. 92~93

1 smells
2 are
3 is
4 is
5 don't[do not] suit
6 is
7 is
8 is
9 is
10 are

해석

1 이 치즈에서 약간 이상한 냄새가 나는 것 같다.
2 이 소포는 파란 끈으로 묶여 있다.
3 매우 미세한 모래가 모래시계를 채우는 데 사용된다.
4 끓고 있는 스튜에서 김이 올라오고 있다.
5 그가 산 그 바지는 그에게 맞지 않는다.
6 대개 금이 은보다 훨씬 더 비싸다.
7 그녀의 영어 문법에 관한 지식은 인상적이다.
8 경제학은 내가 제일 싫어하는 과목이다. 너무 지루하다.
9 김 선생님의 인내심이 바닥이 나려고 하고 있어. 빨리 자리에 앉자!
10 사무실의 모든 불이 꺼져 있다. 모두 사무실을 나간 것이 틀림없다.

B

1 ① an iron ② iron
2 ① papers ② paper
3 ① a glass ② glass
4 ① room ② a room
5 ① a light ② light
6 ① a coffee ② coffee
7 ① business ② businesses

해석

1 ① 그의 주름진 셔츠가 다리미로 다려졌다.
② 의사가 그녀의 식이요법에 더 많은 철분이 필요하다고 말했다.
2 ① 그 사진은 모든 신문의 1면에 실렸다.
② 네 선물을 포장하고 싶었는데 종이가 다 떨어졌어.
3 ① 유리잔을 하나 가져오면, 내가 너에게 마실 것을 따라 줄게.
② 창문 전체가 판유리 한 장으로 되어 있다.
4 ① 공간이 없어요. 다음 엘리베이터를 타세요.
② 우리 형과 나는 어렸을 때 방을 같이 썼었다.
5 ① 누군가 집에 있는 게 틀림없어. 안에 불빛이 있어.
② 불행히도 이 방은 아침에 빛이 충분히 들지 않는다.
6 ① 커피 사러 갈 건데, 너도 원하니?
② 세계에서 가장 좋은 커피 중 일부는 인도네시아산이다.

7 ① 우리 아버지는 수출입 사업 분야에서 일하신다.
② 몇몇 회사들은 불경기로 인해 문을 닫을 수밖에 없었다.

1 tomatoes, food, money, dollars, meat
2 luggage, clothes, jeans, sweater, shirts, pants

해석

1 〈슈퍼마켓에서〉
잭: 파스타, 양상추, 토마토, 스테이크 ……. 저녁으로 먹을 음식은 충분한 것 같아. 계산대로 가자.
에이미: 아, 이런! 너 돈이 좀 있니? 나는 현금이 하나도 없어.
잭: 어디 보자. 20달러 있어. 이거면 충분할 것 같니?
에이미: 안 될 것 같아. 이 고기 중 일부를 도로 가져다 놓자. 어쨌든 약간 비싼 편이잖아.
2 〈공항에서〉
알렉스: 항공사가 내 짐을 분실했다니 믿을 수가 없어. 나는 입을 수 있는 여분의 옷이 없어.
존: 걱정하지 마. 며칠 후에 호텔로 네 짐을 돌려보내 줄 거야.
알렉스: 하지만 내일 회의에 무엇을 입어야 하지? 이 낡은 청바지와 스웨터 차림으로 거기에 갈 수는 없어.
존: 우리는 거의 같은 치수니까 내가 너에게 옷을 좀 빌려줄게. 만일을 대비하여 몇 벌의 셔츠와 바지를 여분으로 가져왔어.

D

1 slice 2 spoonful 3 bottles
4 advice 5 chocolate 6 loaves
7 carton, meat

해석

1 제 샌드위치에 치즈 한 장을 넣어주세요.
2 약간의 버터와 설탕 한 숟가락을 함께 섞어주세요.
3 도둑은 12병의 진귀한 포도주를 훔쳐 달아났다.
4 그녀는 내가 결코 잊지 못할 충고를 한마디 해주었다.
5 내가 가방에 초콜릿 두 개를 넣어놨는데 지금 녹아서 모든 책에 묻었다.
6 우리는 빵이 좀 필요해. 쇼핑하러 나가면 빵 두 덩이만 사다 줄래?
7 오늘 집에 오는 길에 우유 한 팩과 고기 1파운드만 사다 줄래?

Unit 17 EXERCISES p. 96~97

1 much 2 many 3 few 4 member
5 many 6 bottle 7 a few 8 a little

해석

1 이 병에 얼마나 많은 액체가 들어갑니까?
2 그 갯벌은 많은 철새를 유인한다.
3 그는 매우 인기 있다. 그를 적대시하는 사람이 거의 없다.
4 이 집단의 각각의 구성원은 독특한 스타일을 가지고 있다.
5 블랙 씨는 여러 해 동안 이곳의 선생님이었다.
6 판매되는 모든 병마다 10센트씩 자선 단체에 기부된다.
7 나는 새 컴퓨터 때문에 약간의 문제를 겪고 있다.
8 이 소스에 소금을 조금 넣어야겠어요. 소금 병 좀 건네주시겠어요?

B

1 many people 2 much water 3 much sleep
4 many keys 5 much sugar 6 much time

해석

1 그 행성에는 사람이 얼마나 사나요?
2 너는 하루에 물을 얼마나 마시니?
3 너는 어젯밤에 잠을 얼마나 잤니?
4 네 열쇠고리에 열쇠가 몇 개 있니?
5 샐리는 커피에 설탕을 얼마나 넣니?
6 너는 취미에 얼마나 많은 시간을 쓰니?

C

1 a few 2 a little[some] 3 any
4 a little[some] 5 any

해석

1 A: 우리 참치가 다 떨어졌니?
B: 아니, 몇 캔 남았어.
2 A: 머리를 맑게 하려고 신선한 공기를 좀 쐬어야겠어.
B: 왜? 무슨 일인데?
3 A: 지하철역에 어떻게 가는지 아니?
B: 전혀 몰라. 저기 경찰관에게 가서 물어보고 올게.
4 A: 올해 레베카는 학교에서 어떻게 지내요?
B: 잘 지내고 있지만 조금 더 격려를 해준다면 그녀는 훨씬 더 잘할 거예요.
5 A: 질문이 더 없으면 오늘 수업은 마치겠습니다.
B: 잠깐만요, 선생님. 중간고사 시험범위는 몇 챕터나 되나요?

D

1 are 2 has 3 effort
4 is 5 are 6 want, is

해석

1 그 아이디어에 반대하는 사람은 거의 없다.
2 이 책들의 각 페이지는 본문이 3단으로 되어 있다.
3 약간의 노력으로 너는 중요한 정보를 찾을 수 있을 것이다.
4 냉장고에 우유가 조금밖에 남아있지 않다.
5 많은 기회가 너를 기다리고 있어. 그러니 포기하지 마.
6 해외에서 공부하고 싶어 하는 학생들의 숫자가 증가하고 있다.

E

1 a number of reasons
2 The number of newborn babies
3 The number of people
4 a number of questions
5 The number of participants
6 A number of fans

해석

1 그는 많은 이유로 내 제안을 거절했다.
2 매년 신생아의 수가 줄어들고 있다.
3 요즘 애완동물을 키우는 사람들의 숫자가 늘고 있다.

4 나는 발표 후에 많은 질문을 받았다.
5 참가자 수가 100명을 초과해서 우리는 자리가 더 필요하다.
6 한국의 팝 스타들을 보기 위해 외국의 많은 팬들이 서울로 오고 있다.

1 any, a little　　2 much
3 None of　　4 Many
5 few

해석

1 A: 오렌지 주스 있어요?
B: 네, 조금 있어요. 드릴까요?
2 A: 두 그림 사이에 차이점이 많은 것 같지 않아.
B: 나도 그래. 사실, 거의 똑같아 보여.
3 A: 우리 여행이 걱정 돼. 우리 둘 다 영어를 못하잖아.
B: 걱정하지 마. 바디랭귀지로 의사소통을 할 수 있어.
4 A: 봐! 많은 사람들이 쇼핑몰에서 줄을 서서 기다리고 있어!
B: 오늘 유명한 가수가 팬들을 위해 사인회를 할 거야.
5 A: 강연장에 남은 좌석이 거의 없었어.
B: 강연이 매우 인기 있었구나.

Unit 18 EXERCISES

p. 99

1 Jerry's computer
2 the edge of the box
3 the title of the movie
4 his sisters' coats
5 Charles'(s) wallet
6 the curtain of the changing room

1 My father's birthday
2 The beginning of the movie
3 The cost of traveling overseas
4 The owner of the restaurant
5 The new children's center
6 James'(s) graduation ceremony

해석

1 우리 아빠의 생신은 다음 달이야.
2 영화의 시작 부분이 나를 몹시 겁나게 했다.
3 해외여행 비용은 요즘에는 꽤 싼 편이다.
4 그 레스토랑의 주인은 대학 때부터 나의 오랜 친구이다.
5 최근 시내에 새로운 어린이 센터가 문을 열었다.
6 나는 제임스의 졸업식에 참석할 수 없을 거야.

1 tomorrow's　　2 thirty minutes'
3 one day's　　4 evening's

해석

1 나는 내일 시험이 있다. 그래서 시험공부를 하고 있다. → 나는 내일의 시험을 위해 공부를 하고 있다.
2 나는 오늘 오후에 휴식을 취했다. 삼십 분간 휴식이 지속되었다.
→ 나는 오늘 오후에 삼십 분의 휴식을 취했다.
3 캠핑 참가자들의 음식이 바닥나고 있었다. 그들은 고작 하루를 더 버틸 수 있었다. → 캠핑 참가자들에게 단 하루의 음식 분량만이 남아 있었다.
4 저녁에 공연이 있다. 그것은 미뤄질 것이다. → 오늘 저녁의 공연 시간이 미뤄질 것을 알려드리게 되어 죄송합니다.

REVIEW

p. 100~101

1 A dime　　2 a wonderful time
3 apples　　4 a paper
5 time　　6 paper
7 a package　　8 oranges
9 clothing　　10 furniture
11 glass　　12 bottles

해설/해석

1 money는 셀 수 없지만 money를 구성하고 있는 돈의 단위(dime)는 셀 수 있다. 동사가 is이므로 A dime이 적절
1다임은 10센트와 같다.

2 일반적인 '시간'의 개념일 경우 time은 셀 수 없지만, 특정한 시간을 나타낼 때는 셀 수 있다. '좋은 시간'이라는 특정한 기간을 나타내므로 a wonderful time이 적절
좋은 시간 보내!

3 apple은 셀 수 있으므로, 단수나 복수가 가능하다. 단수일 경우 apple 앞에 관사 an이 와야 하므로 apples가 적절
나는 빅토리아 시장에서 사과를 샀다.

4 paper가 '종이'의 뜻일 경우 셀 수 없지만, '신문'을 나타낼 때는 셀 수 있다. 지하철에서 읽을 신문을 발견했다는 의미이므로 a paper가 적절
나는 지하철에서 읽을 신문을 발견했다.

5 기다릴 시간이 없다는 일반적인 시간의 개념일 경우 time은 셀 수 없음
우리는 그를 기다릴 시간이 없다.

6 paper가 '종이'의 뜻일 경우 셀 수 없다. 미술 시간에 쓸 종이가 필요하다는 의미이므로 paper가 적절
미술 시간에 쓸 판지가 필요해.

7 mail의 경우 셀 수 없지만 package의 경우 셀 수 있다. 소포 꾸러미 하나를 받았다는 의미이므로 a package가 적절
나는 친척에게 소포를 받았다.

8 orange는 셀 수 있으므로 단수나 복수가 가능하다. 단수일 경우 orange 앞에 관사 an이 와야 하므로 oranges가 적절
비타민 C는 오렌지와 다른 감귤류에 있다.

9 옷 전체를 나타내는 clothing은 셀 수 없음
체육 시간에 편안한 옷을 입으세요.

10 가구 전체를 나타내는 furniture는 셀 수 없음
우리 언니는 새집에 들여놓을 가구가 필요하다.

11 glass는 '유리'라는 의미로 쓰일 때는 셀 수 없고 '유리컵'이라는 의미로 쓰일 때는 셀 수 있다. 여기서는 자동차의 유리를 의미하

는 것이므로 glass가 적절
부서진 자동차의 깨진 유리가 도로 여기저기에 있었다.

12 bottle은 셀 수 있으므로 단수나 복수가 가능하다. '천백만 개의 병'이라는 의미이므로 bottles가 적절
매년 천백만 개 이상의 빈 플라스틱 물병이 결국 쓰레기가 된다.

B

1	vegetables	2	trousers
3	photos	4	Fur coats
5	bed	6	tubes
7	text messages	8	milk
9	gas	10	dollars
11	mail	12	chairs

해설/해석

1 채소(vegetable)는 셀 수 있음
우리는 신선한 채소를 많이 먹어야만 한다.

2 쌍을 이루는 trousers는 항상 복수형으로 써야 함
이 바지들은 이번 주에 할인 판매 중이다.

3 photo는 셀 수 있으므로 단수나 복수 가능, several 뒤에는 복수명사가 와야 하므로 photos가 적절
나는 블로그에 여러 장의 사진을 업로드했다.

4 coat는 의류 안에 포함되는 개별적인 품목으로 셀 수 있다. 뒤에 나온 동사가 복수동사 have이므로 주어도 복수인 Fur coats가 적절
털 코트가 다시 유행하기 시작했다.

5 bed는 가구를 구성하는 개별적인 품목으로 셀 수 있다. '내 침대'라는 의미이므로 bed가 적절
나는 마침내 내 침대 밑에서 스웨터를 발견했다.

6 tube는 치약을 담고 있는 용기로 셀 수 있다. a few(몇몇의) 뒤에는 복수명사를 써야 하므로 tubes가 적절
우리는 치약을 몇 개 사야 한다.

7 text message는 셀 수 있으며 several(몇몇의) 뒤에는 복수명사가 와야 하므로 text messages가 적절
샐리가 오늘 나에게 여러 개의 문자 메시지를 보냈다.

8 milk는 액체로 셀 수 없음
냉장고에 우유를 다시 넣어 두는 거 잊지 마.

9 gas는 기본적으로 셀 수 없지만, 일산화탄소라는 하나의 종류를 나타내므로 앞에 a가 붙어서 단수형 gas가 들어가야 함
일산화탄소는 무색, 무취의 기체이다.

10 dollar는 money 안에 포함되는 구성 요소로 셀 수 있음
나는 한국 원화를 미국 달러로 바꿔야 한다.

11 mail은 우편과 관련된 모든 것을 포함하는 광범위한 개념으로 셀 수 없음
편지를 읽고 답장을 쓰는 데 아침을 다 보내 버렸다.

12 chair는 가구를 구성하는 여러 품목 중 하나로 셀 수 있다. '여러 학생들의 의자'라는 의미이므로 chairs가 적절
어떤 학생들이 의자 등받이를 뒤로 기울이다가 넘어졌다.

1	money	2	carton	3	handkerchief
4	room	5	men	6	glasses
7	information	8	hairs		

해설/해석

1 How much 뒤에는 셀 수 없는 명사가 와야 하며, 돈이 얼마가 있는지 물어보는 의미이므로 money가 적절
너는 돈이 얼마나 있니?

2 orange juice는 carton을 사용해서 수량을 표현하고, 앞에 a가 왔으므로 carton이 적절
나는 바닥에 오렌지 주스 한 통을 엎질렀다.

3 코를 풀기 위해 필요한 것은 handkerchief(손수건)이며 셀 수 있다. 앞에 a가 왔으므로 handkerchief가 적절
제이슨은 손수건을 꺼내서 코를 크게 풀었다.

4 room이 '방'을 의미할 때는 셀 수 있으나 '공간'을 의미하는 경우에는 셀 수 없음
여기 너무 혼잡하군요. 우리가 지나갈 수 있게 공간을 만들어 주시겠어요?

5 강도 사건 다음 날 체포된 사람이고, two 뒤에는 복수명사가 와야 하므로 men이 적절
한 여자와 두 남자가 강도 사건 다음 날 체포되었다.

6 안경과 같이 쌍으로 된 것은 항상 복수로 쓰고 복수 취급
그녀는 시력이 나쁘다. 그녀는 어렸을 때부터 안경을 썼다.

7 information은 셀 수 없음
스페인의 마드리드에 도착하면, 더 많은 정보를 위해 우리의 직원들 중 한 명에게 연락하세요.

8 hair는 셀 수 없는 명사이지만, 머리카락 한 가닥을 의미할 때는 셀 수 있는 명사가 됨
내 머리를 자른 뒤, 미용사는 스펀지로 내 얼굴에 묻은 머리카락들을 털어주었다.

1 two pieces of chalk
2 St. Michael's Church
3 reading glasses
4 floor
5 the back of the church
6 bread[some pieces of bread 등]
7 is
8 a letter / some letters
9 The neighbor's dog
10 economic advisers
11 The bottom of the bottle
12 thieves
13 half a dozen watermelons
14 three bedrooms
15 A bouquet of flowers

해설/해석

1 chalk는 셀 수 없으므로 piece를 사용해서 수량을 표현
나에게 분필 두 개를 가져다 주실래요?

2 '성 미카엘의 성당'이라는 의미로 생물의 소유격에는 's를 붙이므로 St. Michael's Church가 적절
성 미카엘 성당에 가는 길을 아니?

3 안경은 알이 두 개이므로 reading glasses가 적절
스미스 씨는 앉다가 새로 산 독서용 안경을 깨뜨렸다.

4 floor는 셀 수 있는 명사로 앞에 기수(two)가 아닌 서수(second)가 있으므로 여러 층이 아니라 한 층을 의미한다. 따라서 floor가 적절
2층에 빈 방이 세 개 있다.

5 뒤(back)는 교회(church)의 일부분이므로 the back of the church가 적절
우리는 마침내 교회 뒤에서 마크의 강아지를 발견했다.

6 bread는 셀 수 없는 명사이므로 복수형 s를 붙이지 않고 a piece of, a slice of등의 단위를 이용하여 표현
그는 일어나자마자 빵과 커피 한 잔을 마신다.

7 of these buildings는 The modern design을 수식하는 것이고, 주어는 The modern design이다. The modern design은 단수이므로 is가 적절
이 건물들의 현대적인 디자인은 꽤 주목할 만하다.

8 letter는 셀 수 있는 명사이므로 관사를 붙이거나 복수형으로 써야 한다. 문맥상 편지가 한 장인지 여러 장인지 알 수 없으므로 a letter 또는 some letters가 적절
우편함을 열었을 때, 나는 모르는 사람에게서 온 편지를 발견했다.

9 '이웃집 개'라는 의미로 생물의 소유격에는 's를 써야 하므로 The neighbor's dog이 적절
엄마! 이웃집 개가 장미 정원을 또 엉망으로 만들고 있어요.

10 a new team of로 미루어 보아 한 팀을 구성한 것으로 볼 수 있고, team 안에는 여러 명의 구성원이 있으므로 economic advisers가 적절
대통령은 새로운 경제 고문 팀을 임명했다.

11 무생물의 소유격은 A of B의 형태로 쓰므로 The bottom of the bottle이 적절
병의 바닥에 금이 갔네. 다른 것으로 바꾸는 게 좋겠어.

12 thief의 복수형은 thieves
경찰은 그 남자들이 도둑이라고 믿었지만 그것을 증명할 수는 없었다.

13 half a dozen은 여섯 개이므로 뒤에 복수명사가 와야 한다. half a dozen watermelons가 적절
여섯 개의 수박을 사서, 반으로 자른 후 그것들을 그릇으로 쓰자.

14 bedroom은 셀 수 있고, three 뒤에는 복수형을 써야 하므로 three bedrooms가 적절
이 아파트에는 부부용 침실과 두 개의 작은 침실, 이렇게 세 개의 침실이 있다.

15 a bouquet에는 여러 송이의 꽃이 들어 있다. flower는 셀 수 있으므로 a bouquet of flowers가 적절
신부는 결혼식이 끝날 무렵 들러리에게 부케를 던졌다.

REVIEW PLUS

p. 102

해설/해석

① water는 셀 수 없으므로 waters가 아니라 water가 적절, ② much는 셀 수 없는 명사 앞에, many는 셀 수 있는 명사 앞에 사용되는 수량 형용사, 복수명사 cups가 왔으므로 much가 아니라 many가 적절, ③ Time(시간)은 셀 수 없으므로 항상 단수 취급, fly가 아니라 단수동사 flies가 적절, ④ piece를 이용해서 수량을 표현할 때는 a piece 또는 two pieces 등 수량을 알 수 있어야 하므로 piece가 아니라 a piece가 적절
① 나는 물이 하나도 없다.
② 우리는 남은 컵이 많지 않다.
③ 재미있게 놀 때 시간은 빨리 간다.
④ 내 신발에 껌 한 개가 달라붙었다.
⑤ 메리와 존은 저녁을 먹으면서 포도주 한 병을 나눠 마셨다.

해설/해석

(A) ice는 셀 수 없음, (B) vegetable은 셀 수 있으므로 a vegetable이나 vegetables가 가능, (C) clothing(의복)은 집합 전체를 나타내는 말로 셀 수 없음
• 나는 얼음에서 미끄러져서 다른 차와 충돌했다.
• 무게를 잴 과일과 채소를 저쪽으로 가져가세요.
• 옷 몇 벌이 경매에서 팔렸다.

해설/해석

(A) lots of(많은) 뒤에는 셀 수 있는 명사의 복수형과 셀 수 없는 명사가 모두 올 수 있다. box는 셀 수 있으므로 boxes가 적절, (B) 「a number of+셀 수 있는 명사 복수형」과 「a great deal of+셀 수 없는 명사」의 형태인데, 뒤에 products가 왔으므로 a number of가 적절 , (C) 주어 advertisements가 복수이므로 복수동사 influence가 적절
한 여자가 많은 샴푸 상자 앞에 서 있다. 그녀는 하나의 상표를 선택한다. 그것이 다른 것보다 훨씬 더 좋을까? 아마 그렇지 않을지도 모른다. 요즘에는 많은 상품이 품질과 가격에서 서로 꽤 비슷하다. 상품이 거의 똑같다면 무엇이 소비자로 하여금 다른 것 대신에 특정 상표를 선택하게 하는가? 아마 당신은 TV 광고가 분명히 영향을 미치고 있다는 것을 느낄 수 있을 것이다.

PART 6

Unit 19 EXERCISES

p. 106~107

1 An	2 ×	3 A	4 an	5 ×
6 a	7 a	8 a	9 a	10 ×
11 a, a	12 a	13 a	14 a	15 an

해석

1 오렌지는 과일이다.
2 토마토는 채소인가요?
3 인간은 생존하기 위해서 물이 필요하다.
4 알렉스는 내년에 SUV를 살 예정이다.
5 나는 숙제로 세 챕터를 읽어야 한다.
6 계산대에 있는 그 남자는 신문을 읽고 있었다.
7 동물원 사육사가 원숭이들에게 바나나 한 뭉치를 주었다.
8 제이콥과 그의 가족은 최소한 한 달에 두 번 외식을 한다.
9 내 남동생은 오늘 아침부터 컴퓨터 게임을 계속하고 있다.
10 고래가 멸종의 위기에 처해 있다. 우리는 고래를 보호해야 한다.
11 내 친구 수는 요리사이다. 그녀는 프랑스 식당에서 일한다.
12 내가 너에게 준 책들을 읽었니? 너는 정말로 열렬한 독서가구나!
13 줄리아가 차를 살 것이다. 그녀는 도시 외곽의 새 직장에 가려면 차가 필요하다.
14 크리스마스는 일 년에 한 번 오잖아. 그러니까 최대한 이용해서 재미있게 놀자.
15 존스 씨는 결혼기념일에 부인에게 값비싼 향수를 주었다.

1 gold
2 twice a month
3 an honest man
4 so terrible a mistake[such a terrible mistake]
5 lovely sunshine
6 a European
7 such a diligent student

해석

1 이 목걸이는 금으로 만들어졌다.
2 부모님과 나는 한 달에 두 번 도보 여행을 간다.
3 그 방의 모든 사람들은 그가 정직한 사람이라고 믿었다.
4 그녀가 그렇게 엄청난 실수를 하다니 믿을 수 없어.
5 햇살이 아름다워! 소풍 가는 거 어때?
6 라트비아는 유럽에 속하고 수도는 리가이다.
7 그녀는 항상 학교에 일찍 온다. 그녀는 아주 부지런한 학생이다.

1 such a boring speech	2 such a handsome man
3 quite an interesting party	4 such a cute boy
5 so beautiful a scene	6 quite a long time
7 quite a good impression	

해석

1 모든 사람이 잠이 들었다. 그것은 굉장히 지루한 연설이었다.
2 그는 상당히 잘생긴 사람이다. 그는 또한 정중하게 행동한다.
3 저를 초대해 주셔서 감사해요. 상당히 재미있는 파티였어요.
4 그 아이는 너무 귀여워서 눈을 뗄 수가 없다.
5 경치가 장관이에요. 이렇게 아름다운 풍경을 본 적이 없어요.
6 공연이 정시에 시작하지 않았다. 우리는 꽤 오래 기다려야 했다.
7 그녀는 등교 첫 날 선생님께 좋은 인상을 심어주었다.

1 quite, a, popular, singer
2 A, Smith
3 Cheese, is, made, from
4 is, going, to, university[college]
5 A[The], cell, phone, is
6 four, times, a, year
7 the, tree, such, a, big, tree

Unit 20 EXERCISES

p. 110~111

1 the	2 The	3 a	4 The	5 the
6 The	7 ×	8 a	9 ×	10 ×, ×

해석

1 소파 위에 있는 그 셔츠는 내 것이다.
2 오늘의 주요 토론 주제는 '복제'입니다.
3 나는 오늘 집에 오는 길에 10달러짜리 지폐를 발견했다.
4 가난한 사람들은 그 어느 때보다 더 우리의 도움을 필요로 한다.
5 그는 고등학교 밴드에서 기타를 연주했다.
6 몬트리올 은행은 캐나다에서 가장 큰 은행 중 하나다.
7 우리 아이들은 햄버거와 감자튀김만 먹으면서 계속 살아가는 것 같다.
8 태희는 일주일에 한 번씩 친구들과 에어로빅 수업을 들으러 간다.
9 수은은 온도계에 사용하는 액체 금속 성분이다.
10 계곡은 언덕이나 산의 두 경계 사이에 있는 낮은 땅이다.

1 The, an	2 the	3 the	4 the
5 The	6 a	7 the, the	8 ×, the
9 ×, the	10 the, a		

해석

1 자유의 여신상은 사람의 마음을 끌어당기는 자유를 향한 기념비이다.
2 이분이 내가 전에 너에게 말했던 영국에서 온 다니엘 선생님이시다.
3 사라가 이 어려운 퍼즐을 풀 수 있는 유일한 사람이다.
4 내 여동생은 나의 비밀을 공유할 수 있는 유일한 사람이다.
5 의자 뒤 상자에 있던 옷 가방은 자선 단체에 기부되었다.
6 모든 사람이 매우 놀랍게도, 그는 광대 의상을 입고 있었다.
7 네가 지금 읽는 신문의 스포츠 면을 나에게 건네줘.
8 나는 예전에 뉴욕에 살았었는데, 뉴욕은 세계에서 가장 분주한 도시 가

운데 하나다.

9 호주의 계절은 미국과 유럽의 계절과는 반대이다.

10 존은 내가 아는 가장 똑똑한 사람 중 한 명이다. 그는 모든 방면에 재능이 있다.

C

1 the gram　　2 the guitar
3 the dishes　　4 The young
5 the last day　　6 the laptop computer
7 a wallet, the same

해석

1 체리는 그램 단위로 팔린다.
2 테디는 시간이 나면 기타 치는 것을 즐긴다.
3 내가 설거지하는 동안 거실 좀 진공청소기로 청소해 줄래?
4 젊은이들은 도전에 맞서서 경험으로 배울 필요가 있다.
5 여행 마지막 날 우리는 이메일 주소를 교환했다.
6 내가 지난주에 네게 빌려주었던 노트북 컴퓨터를 돌려줄래?
7 나는 어제 지갑을 하나 발견했다. 놀랍게도, 그 지갑은 내 것과 똑같이 생겼다.

D

1 see, you, at, church
2 The, Bradleys
3 The, earth, is
4 travel, to, the, United, States, this, summer
5 The, only, way, finish, the, work
6 from, the, north, to, the, south
7 the, physically, challenged, the, elderly

Unit 21 EXERCISES

p. 114~115

1 the　　2 the　　3 ×　　4 ×
5 the　　6 The　　7 ×

해석

1 너는 아직도 플루트를 배우고 있니?
2 그는 자신의 부인을 처음 봤을 때 사랑에 빠졌다.
3 나는 기차로 여행할 때마다 일등석을 탄다.
4 운 좋게도 그는 교도소에 가는 것을 피할 수 있었다.
5 그것이 내가 그 상황에서 할 수 있었던 유일한 일이었다.
6 경력자들은 항상 일자리를 쉽게 찾는다.
7 나는 네가 하키를 했는지 몰랐어. 너는 어떤 위치를 맡고 있니?

B

1 the　　2 ×　　3 a　　4 ×
5 the　　6 ×, the　　7 ×

해석

1 창문 좀 열어 주시겠어요? 여기 너무 답답해요.
2 세계의 큰 호텔들은 거의 비슷하다.
3 나는 학교에 가는 길에 한 소녀를 만났다. 그녀는 제인의 쌍둥이 동생이었다.
4 몇몇 운 좋은 어린이들이 김연아와 함께 점심을 먹는 데 뽑혔다.
5 나는 다음 달에 워싱턴을 방문하면 백악관을 보고 싶다.
6 우리는 몇 년 만에 처음으로 오늘 아침을 함께 먹었다.
7 내가 물리학 101을 성공적으로 끝마치기만 하면 올해 졸업할 수 있다.

1 the　　2 the　　3 ×　　4 an, ×　　5 ×, ×

해석

1 A: 올해 학교에서 가장 인기 있는 선생님이 누구니?
B: 최 선생님이 단연 가장 인기 있는 선생님이셔.
2 A: 나는 항상 시험 볼 때 처음 몇 분은 너무 떨려.
B: 무슨 말인지 알아. 그 첫 몇 분이 고통스럽지.
3 A: 너는 한국어를 제외하고 다른 언어를 할 수 있니?
B: 응, 스페인어를 할 수 있어. 스페인에서 태어나고 자랐어.
4 A: 오늘 아침에 우산을 가져갔니?
B: 아니. 출근하는 길에 하나 샀어.
5 A: 너는 서양 음식을 좋아하니? 네가 가장 좋아하는 음식은 뭐니?
B: 사실 난 서양 음식 별로 안 좋아해. 내가 가장 좋아하는 건 중국 음식이야.

1 The English → English
2 an India → India
3 by the train → by train
4 the two blocks → two blocks
5 the French and the English → French and English
6 the basketball → basketball
7 ham → a ham

해석

1 영어는 세계에서 가장 많이 쓰이는 언어이다.
2 인도에서 온 내 사촌이 내게 크리켓 하는 법을 가르쳐주었다.
3 리사는 다음 주말에 기차를 타고 할머니네 집에 갈 것이다.
4 여기서 약 두 블록 떨어진 곳에 공공 도서관이 있다.
5 캐나다의 두 공식 언어는 프랑스어와 영어이다.
6 내 친구들과 나는 이번 일요일 아침에 농구를 할 것이다.
7 로버트는 점심으로 햄과 치즈를 넣은 샌드위치 하나, 사과 두 개, 그리고 우유 작은 팩 하나를 먹었다.

E

1 under, the, bed
2 My, cell, phone, battery
3 have, breakfast, dinner
4 a, nice, lunch
5 in, front, of, the, church
6 by, car, by, bus
7 goes, to, college, goes, to, middle, school

REVIEW

p. 116~117

1 ×　　2 a, the
3 ×, the, the　　4 ×, a, the
5 The, The, ×

해설/해석

1 「by+교통수단」으로 by 뒤에 아무런 관사를 붙이지 않는다. 자동차 행렬을 의미하는 motorcade도 교통수단으로 볼 수 있으므로 by motorcade가 적절
대통령은 자동차 행렬로 오전 10시에 도착할 것이다. 그는 오후에 국회 앞에서 연설할 것이다.

2 beaver는 셀 수 있다. 아이가 비버를 발견해서 처음 언급하는 경우에는 a, 이미 언급한 것을 다시 언급하는 경우 정관사 the가 적절
갑자기 연못에 떨어진 아이가 "여기 보세요! 비버가 있어요!"라고 소리쳤다. 물론 비버도 놀랐다.

3 국가 이름 앞에는 아무런 관사가 붙지 않음. 최상급 앞에는 the가 붙음. 우리 주변의 환경을 나타내는 world 앞에도 the가 붙음
우리는 인도를 여행하는 동안 타지마할을 방문했다. 그것은 세상에서 가장 정교한 무굴 양식의 건축물이다.

4 high school은 공부하는 곳으로서의 본래의 목적으로 쓰였으므로 관사를 붙이지 않음. college는 셀 수 있고, 특정한 곳이 아닌 여러 좋은 대학 중 한 곳을 말하는 것이므로 a를 붙임. most는 최상급이므로 the를 붙임
우리는 좋은 대학에 들어가려고 고등학교에서 열심히 공부한다. 아이비리그 학교인 하버드, 프린스턴, 예일대가 가장 인기 있는 대학이다.

5 Olympic games 앞에는 항상 관사 the가 붙음. athletes는 관계대명사절 who participate in the games의 수식을 받아 올림픽에 참가하는 특정 운동선수들을 의미하므로 the를 붙임. competitors는 셀 수 있는 명사로, 특정한 경쟁자가 아닌 일반적인 경쟁자 전체를 나타내는 경우 관사를 붙이지 않음
하계 올림픽은 4년마다 열린다. 올림픽에 참가하는 운동선수들은 경쟁자로 불린다. 2008년 베이징 올림픽에서는 10,500명의 운동선수가 28종목 302개의 시합에서 경쟁했다.

1 a, the, The　　2 The, a, the
3 ×, a, ×, The, the　　4 A, a, an, The
5 the, ×, ×, ×, ×

해설/해석

1 driver는 셀 수 있고, 처음 언급하는 것이므로 a를 붙임. worst는 bad의 최상급이며, 최상급 앞에는 the를 붙임. car는 she was driving의 수식을 받아 그녀가 운전하고 있던 특정한 차를 가리키는 것이므로 The가 적절
평소에 우리 어머니는 운전을 조심스럽게 하지만 어제 어머니가 살아오면서 가장 심각한 사고가 났다. 어머니가 운전하던 차는 완전히 부서졌지만, 어머니는 작은 상처만 입으시고 살아 남으셨다.

2 instrument는 관계대명사절 that most people use to tell the time의 수식을 받아, 시간을 말할 때 사용되는 특정한 도구를 뜻하므로 The가 적절. 하나의 명사 전체를 대표할 때, 「a(n)+단수명사」, 「무관사+복수명사」, 「무관사+셀 수 없는 명사」 형식을 취하므로 wristwatch 앞에는 a가 적절
대부분의 사람이 시간을 말할 때 사용하는 도구는 손목시계이다. 현대식 시계는 시간뿐만 아니라 종종 요일, 날짜, 달, 년도까지도 보여 준다.

3 advice는 셀 수 없고, 일반적이고 막연한 충고를 나타낼 때는 관사를 붙이지 않음. 가구의 세부 품목을 이루는 sofa는 셀 수 있는 명사로, 처음 언급되었을 때는 a를 붙임. two chairs는 수량 형용사(two)가 붙어 있으므로 아무 관사도 붙이지 않음. sofa가 두 번째로 언급될 때부터는 the를 붙임. chairs 또한 앞에서 이미 언급된 two chairs이므로 the를 붙임
나는 새 가구를 사는 것에 대해 많은 충고를 받았다. 나는 소파 하나와 의자 두 개를 사기로 했다. 소파는 할인판매 중이었지만, 의자는 정가대로 지불해야 했다.

4 허리케인은 셀 수 있고, 허리케인에 대한 일반적인 정의를 내리는 것이므로 A를 붙임. storm은 셀 수 있는 명사이므로 a를 붙임. hour 앞에는 '1시간마다(per)'의 의미를 갖기 위해 a(n)이 필요한데, hour의 h는 발음이 되지 않아 모음 발음으로 시작되는 단어이므로 an을 붙임. strongest는 최상급이므로 앞에 the를 붙임
허리케인은 시속 74마일 또는 그 이상의 속도에 달하는 강풍을 동반한 열대성 폭풍이다. 기록된 가장 강력한 허리케인은 1935년 플로리다 키 폭풍이며, 이 5등급으로 분류된 폭풍으로 총 500명의 사람이 사망했다.

5 second(서수)와 largest(최상급) 앞에는 the를 붙임. French와 English 같이 언어를 나타내는 경우 관사를 붙이지 않음. 운동경기 이름 앞에도 관사를 붙이지 않음
캐나다는 세계에서 면적이 두 번째로 큰 나라이다. 캐나다의 두 가지 공식 언어는 프랑스어와 영어이다. 아이스하키와 라크로스는 캐나다에서 매우 인기 있는 스포츠이다.

1 the, the, the　　2 ×, ×
3 The, a, a　　4 a, the, ×, the

해설/해석

1 집안의 불(light)은 특정 장소의 한정된 light이므로 the를 붙임. switch는 지정된 곳에 있는 것이므로 the를 붙임. fridge는 화자와 청자가 서로 알고 있는 특정한 대상이므로 the를 붙임
A: 어두워지고 있네. 불을 켜는 게 어때?
B: 스위치가 어디 있지? 못 찾겠는데?
A: 냉장고 옆 벽에 있어.

2 일반적인 재료를 나타내는 sugar는 셀 수 없으며, 관사를 붙이지 않음. 소유격(my)이 붙은 명사 앞에는 관사를 붙일 수 없음
A: 내 커피에 설탕을 넣어야겠어. 설탕 좀 있니?
B: 응, 여기 있어.
A: 고마워. 그런데 숟가락은 어디에 있니?

3 of the rice cooker의 수식을 받는 lid는 특정한 뚜껑이므로 the를 붙임. 새로운 것(new one)은 아직 정해지지 않은 물건이므로 a를 붙임. long time은 정해지지 않은 막연히 긴 기간을 나타내므로 a를 붙임
A: 저 좀 도와줄래요? 밥통 뚜껑이 닫히지 않아요.
B: 음. 부서졌네. 가게에 가서 새것을 하나 사야겠어요.
A: 유감이네요! 무척 오랫동안 잘 썼는데.

4 tour는 셀 수 있고, 여행에 대해 처음 언급하는 것이므로 a를 붙임, city는 화자와 청자가 서로 알고 있는 도시를 언급하는 것이므로 the를 붙임, 도시 이름인 New York City 앞에는 아무런 관사도 붙이지 않음, 마지막 문장의 city는 앞서 언급된 New York City를 지칭하는 것이므로 the를 붙임
A: 정말 흥미로운 여행이었어. 나는 그 도시에 대해 많은 것을 배웠어.
B: 나도 그래. 나는 뉴욕이 원래 '뉴암스테르담'이라고 불렸다는 것을 몰랐어.
A: 또, 그 도시를 만든 사람이 네덜란드 사람이었어.

D

1 ×, the　　2 ×, an, a, a
3 a, the　　4 a, the
5 the, a, the

해설/해석

1 소유격 앞에는 the가 붙지 않음, next 앞에는 the를 붙임
A: 내가 어제 본 시험에서 떨어졌다니 믿을 수 없어! 정말 창피해.
B: 걱정하지 마. 다음번에 잘할 거라고 믿어.

2 money는 셀 수 없고, 특정한 돈을 가리키는 것이 아니므로 관사를 붙이지 않음, ATM(현금 자동 입출금기)은 셀 수 있는 명사이고, 모음으로 시작하므로 an을 붙임, B의 응답에서 bank가 처음으로 언급되었으므로 a를 붙임, 거리의 단위로 한 블록을 나타내므로 a가 붙음
A: 돈이 다 떨어졌어. 근처에 현금자동입출금기가 있니?
B: 한 블록쯤 내려가서 은행을 본 것 같아.

3 glass(유리잔)는 셀 수 있고, 처음 언급되었기 때문에 a를 붙임, 설거지를 한다는 말은 wash the dishes라는 관용표현
A: 죄송하지만 제가 설거지를 하다가 유리잔을 하나 깨뜨렸어요.
B: 아, 괜찮아. 다치진 않았지, 응?

4 dictionary는 셀 수 있는 명사이고, 처음 언급되는 것이므로 a를 붙임, B가 말하는 teacher는 화자와 청자가 모두 알고 있는 특정한 선생님을 칭하는 것이므로 the를 붙임
A: 나는 이 단어가 무슨 뜻인지 모르겠어. 사전이 있니?
B: 미안하지만, 없어. 선생님께 여쭤 보는 게 어때? 손을 들어서 주의를 끌어 봐.

5 National Gallery는 하나밖에 없는 특정한 곳이므로 the를 붙임, tourist는 셀 수 있는 명사이고, 많은 관광객 중 특정하지 않은 한 명을 말하는 것이므로 a를 붙임, taxi driver는 화자와 청자가 모두 알고 있는 특정 사람이므로 the를 붙임
A: 실례합니다만, 여기에서 국립 미술관에 가는 법 좀 알려주시겠어요?
B: 사실 저도 관광객이에요. 저쪽에 있는 택시 운전사에게 물어보는 게 어때요?

REVIEW PLUS

p. 118

A

④

해설/해석

① experience는 셀 수 있고, 모음 발음으로 시작되는 형용사 unpleasant의 수식을 받고 있으므로 a unpleasant가 아니라 an unpleasant가 적절
② English(영어)는 관사를 붙이지 않으므로 the English가 아니라 English가 적절
③ kangaroo는 셀 수 있고, 특정 캥거루가 아닌 막연한 한 마리를 의미하는 것이므로 kangaroo가 아니라 a kangaroo가 적절
⑤ taxi는 셀 수 있고, 특정하지 않은 택시 한 대를 나타낼 때는 taxi, Taxi가 아니라 a taxi, A taxi가 적절
① A: 오늘 쇼핑몰에서 아주 언짢은 일이 있었어.
B: 가게 매니저에게 항의해도 돼.
② A: 너는 집에서 어떤 언어로 말하니?
B: 형과 나는 영어로 대화해.
③ A: 캥거루를 본 적 있니?
B: 응. 나는 서커스에서 캥거루를 한 번 본 적 있어.
④ A: 당신의 건물에는 엘리베이터가 있나요?
B: 아니요. 나는 매일 계단을 오르락내리락 해야 해요.
⑤ A: 좀 늦은 것 같은데, 택시를 타야 할 것 같아.
B: 택시? 하지만 지금은 차가 많이 막힐 거야. 대신 지하철을 타자.

B

④

해설/해석

physics와 같은 과목 이름 앞에는 관사를 붙이지 않음, USA는 United States of America로 복수형으로 된 나라 이름 앞에는 the를 붙임, relativity는 추상명사로 셀 수 없는 명사이기 때문에 a를 붙이지 않음
아인슈타인은 1879년에 독일에서 태어났다. 그는 1921년에 노벨 물리학상을 탔다. 아인슈타인은 조국을 떠나서 1955년 사망할 때까지 미국에서 살았다. 아인슈타인은 상대성 이론으로 잘 알려져 있다.

C

②

해설/해석

② college가 '공부하는 장소'라는 본래의 목적으로 사용되었기 때문에 관사를 붙이지 않음, to the college가 아니라 to college가 적절
A: 쇼핑몰에 가서 마이크에게 줄 가구를 좀 찾아보자. 가을에 대학에 가려면 조금은 필요할 거야.
B: 그는 어떤 종류의 가구가 필요하니?
A: 글쎄, 그는 이미 침대와 책상이 있어. 그러니까 우리는 편안한 안락의자와 탁상램프를 찾아볼 수 있겠네. 접시 몇 개와 컵, 그리고 약간의 식기류도 필요할 거야.
B: 좋아. 만약에 상점이 할인 판매 중이면, 좀 저렴한 소파도 사줄 수 있을 거야.

REPLAY

p. 120~121

2 CHECK-UP

1 It　　2 mine, Yours　　3 your

3 CHECK-UP

1 These, those　　2 This, that

4 CHECK-UP

1 another　　2 Others
3 One, the other　　4 One, another, the others

5 CHECK-UP

1 ③　　2 ④

Unit 22 EXERCISES

p. 124~125

A

1 yours　　2 Their
3 its, it　　4 me, mine
5 hers　　6 our, they
7 his, mine　　8 He, His
9 She　　10 my, her

해석

1 저쪽에 있는 저 소녀는 네 친구 아니니?
2 그들의 집은 여기에서 약 두 블록 떨어져 있다.
3 우리 개는 나를 볼 때마다 꼬리를 흔든다.
4 그 휴대 전화를 제게 돌려주세요. 제 거예요.
5 나는 그녀에게 내 전화번호를 알려주었지만, 그녀는 나에게 자신의 전화번호를 알려주지 않았다.
6 우리 방은 작지만 쾌적하다.
7 짐은 벌써 점심을 먹었지만, 나는 나중을 위해 내 것을 남겨놓고 있다.
8 그는 뛰어난 음악가이다. 그의 음악은 꽤 인기 있다.
9 나의 어머니께서는 올해에 50세가 되셨다. 그녀는 흰머리가 몇 가닥씩 나기 시작한다.
10 이 선생님은 나의 담임선생님이시다. 나는 며칠 전 쇼핑몰에서 그녀를 우연히 만났다.

B

1 yours　　2 mine
3 mine　　4 It
5 his or her　　6 its
7 He　　8 Our
9 them　　10 She

해석

1 나는 한국 사람입니다. 제 이름은 지훈입니다. 당신의 이름은 무엇인가요?
2 너는 내 아이스크림을 하나도 먹을 수 없어. 모두 내 거야!
3 네 카메라는 내 것보다 더 유용한 기능들을 갖추고 있다.
4 존의 차가 시동이 걸리지 않았다. 그것은 수리할 수 없을 정도로 고장이 났다.
5 각각의 학생들은 교실에 개인 사물함이 있다.
6 우리 개는 내가 집에 오자 꼬리를 앞뒤로 흔들었다.
7 로버트는 모든 종류의 극한 스포츠에 빠져 있다. 그는 모험가이다.
8 우리 아이스하키 팀이 결승전에 올랐다. 우리는 모두 신이 나 있다.
9 부모님의 결혼기념일이 다가온다. 나는 부모님께 온천 상품권을 드릴 것이다.
10 나는 워크숍에서 켈리를 처음 만났다. 그 후로 그녀와 나는 가장 친한 친구가 되었다.

C

1 his　　2 his　　3 ours　　4 mine
5 theirs　　6 hers　　7 mine　　8 ours
9 yours　　10 yours

해석

1 우리 집 앞에 주차되어 있는 그 차는 그의 차이다.
2 너의 프로젝트가 그의 프로젝트보다 더 독창적이었다.
3 우리는 예약을 했어요. 어떤 방이 우리 방인가요?
4 저쪽에 저것이 당신의 의자입니다. 이것은 제 의자예요.
5 그들은 우리 자리가 자기네 자리라고 계속 우겼다.
6 나는 벽에 있는 저 그림이 그녀의 그림 중 하나라고 생각한다.
7 정말 재미있네요! 당신의 아들과 우리 아들이 동갑이네요.
8 마침내 우리는 이 집을 샀다. 이 집은 이제 우리 것이다!
9 너는 스스로 네 과제를 해야 해. 그것은 네 과제잖아.
10 나는 공책을 잃어버린 것 같아. 기말고사를 위해 네 것을 빌려도 될까?

his, you, She, her

해석

A: 안녕, 수. 이번 주말에 마크의 파티에 가니?
B: 아직 결정하지 못했어. 지금 마크의 누나랑 말하지 않고 있거든.
A: 왜? 무슨 일이 있었어? 제니랑 싸웠니? 약간 놀라운 걸. 너와 제니는 가장 친한 친구인 줄 알았는데.
B: 못 들었어? 제니가 내게 거짓말을 해서 내 믿음을 완전히 배신했어.
A: 정말? 전혀 제니 같지 않은데. 무슨 일이 있었는지 말해 줄 수 있니?
B: 그러고 싶지만 나는 지금 급히 가야 해. 오늘 밤에 전화해서 무슨 일이 있었는지 설명해 줄게.

① its　　② It's　　③ its　　④ it's

해석

산이 있는 대부분의 나라에서 사람들은 스키의 독특한 매력을 느낀다. 가장 간단한 형태 면에서 보면, 스키는 스키라고 불리는 한 쌍의 길고 가느다란 판을 신고 눈 덮인 슬로프를 미끄러져 내려오는 것이다. 그것은 동력 발생 장치 없이 고속으로 움직이게 해주는 몇 안 되는 스포츠 중의 하나이다. 그것의 가장 진보된 형태 면에서 보면, 스키는 전문가들이 산길을 시속 60마일 이상으로 미끄러지거나, 하늘로 수백 피트 올라가거나, 또는 장애물 코스를 통과하는 빠른 턴을 하는 매우 기술적인 운동이다.

Unit 23 EXERCISES

p. 128~129

1 myself　　2 him, himself　　3 ourselves
4 yourself　　5 yourself　　6 ourselves
7 herself

해석

1 나는 그 거대한 조각상을 직접 보았다.
2 그는 그에게 커피 한 잔을 만들어 주었다. / 그는 자신이 마실 커피 한 잔을 만들었다.
3 우리는 이 바위를 직접 옮길 수 없다.
4 다른 사람을 사랑하려면 너 자신을 사랑해야 한다.
5 쉽지 않더라도 너는 네 자신을 용서해야 한다.
6 우리가 그러한 야단법석을 일으킨 데 대해 우리 스스로 부끄러워해야 한다.
7 그녀는 머리를 말리면서 거울에 비친 자신의 모습을 보았다.

B

1 herself	2 ourselves	3 himself
4 themselves	5 herself	6 himself

해석

1 그녀는 스스로 그것을 할 수 있다.
2 우리는 서로에게 스스로를 소개했다.
3 다니엘은 새 디지털 카메라를 직접 샀다.
4 그들은 직접 자신들의 컴퓨터를 업데이트하는 법을 배워야 한다.
5 그 여자는 아들의 나쁜 행동에 대해 스스로를 탓했다.
6 데이비드는 연습실 거울에 비친 자신을 감탄하며 쳐다보았다.

C

1 ⓒ	2 ⓒ	3 ⓑ	4 ⓑ
5 ⓐ	6 ⓐ	7 ⓐ	8 ⓑ

해석

1 나는 신선한 유기농 채소를 선호한다.
2 나는 네가 그 선물을 마음에 들어 하길 바라. 내가 직접 골랐거든.
3 혼자서 휴가를 가는 게 어때?
4 "릴리는 어디 있는 거지?"라고 그녀는 혼잣말을 했다.
5 캐시는 좀 더 자주 쉬지 않으면 병이 날 것이다.
6 그들은 시드니에서 정말로 즐겁게 지냈다.
7 어서 들어오세요. 저희 집에 오신 걸 환영해요. 편히 계세요.
8 그녀는 자신에 대해 좀 더 자신감을 가질 필요가 있다.

D

1 yourself	2 ourselves
3 myself	4 myself
5 yourselves	6 myself
7 herself	8 yourself

해석

1 A: 네 스스로 해볼 만한 목표를 몇 개 정할 필요가 있어.
B: 맞아. 몇 개의 단기간 목표를 갖는 것은 내가 집중하는 데 도움이 될 거야.
2 A: 너와 제스가 휴가 때 몰디브에 간다고 들었어.
B: 응. 우리는 올해 좋은 휴가를 보내기로 약속했거든.
3 A: 방금 니콜라스 씨로부터 전화를 받았습니다. 그에게 계약서를 팩스로 보냈습니까?
B: 네. 오늘 아침에 제가 직접 그에게 계약서를 팩스로 보냈습니다.
4 A: 내가 신을 새 부츠를 샀어. 어때?
B: 응! 정말 너에게 잘 어울린다.
5 A: 오늘 너희들 모두 왜 이렇게 늦었니? 설명 좀 해줄래?
B: 정말 죄송해요. 최 선생님의 수업이 10분 늦게 끝났어요.
6 A: 무슨 일이니?
B: 어젯밤에 욕조에서 나오다가 다쳤어. 정말 창피했어.
7 A: 반창고 있니? 엄마가 고기를 다지다가 손을 베었어.
B: 잠깐만. 내 방에 있을 거야.
8 A: 이 시점에 네가 할 수 있는 건 없어. 스스로를 너무 힘들게 하지 마.
B: 알아. 하지만 그게 다 내 잘못인 것 같아.

E

① her → herself

해석

루이스 윌킨슨은 낮에는 도서관 사서로 일한다. 해가 지고 나면, 그녀는 흡혈귀로 변신을 한다. 루이스는 심지어 흡혈귀 이도 가지고 있다. 흡혈귀로서 지난 10년 동안 그녀는 공포 영화 비디오와 해골, 박쥐를 집안 가득 수집해 왔다. 비록 장난이기는 하지만 그녀는 사람들을 놀라게 하는 것을 즐긴다. 110명의 회원을 가진 드라큘라 모임의 간사로서 루이스는 드라큘라의 출생지에도 다녀왔다. 그녀는 '어둠의 여왕'으로 분장하고 파티에 가기를 즐기며, 그곳에서 다른 손님들의 목을 무는 시늉을 한다. 가끔 그녀는 드라큘라 피해자 중 하나로 분장을 하고 가짜 피가 잔뜩 묻은 하얀색 드레스를 입는다.

Unit 24 EXERCISES

p. 131

A

1 this	2 this	3 that
4 that	5 Those	6 this

해석

1 저를 위해서 이 양식에 서명해 주시겠어요?
2 죄송하지만, 이 코트는 제 것인 것 같네요.
3 저 정신 나간 운전자 봤니? 그가 나를 거의 칠 뻔했어!
4 저거 봤어? 뭔가 번개처럼 반짝였는데.
5 저것들은 도서관에 반납되어야 하는 책들이다.
6 이리 와서 이것 좀 봐! 우리 팀이 지금 이기고 있어!

B

1 They	2 they, they	3 It, it
4 It	5 He	

해석

1 A: 이 사람들이 네가 한 달 동안 팀을 이룰 사람들이야.
B: 와. 그들 모두 좋은 사람들 같아.
2 A: 이거 좋아 보인다. 그렇지 않니? 조금 주문하는 게 어때?
B: 진심이니? 너는 그것들이 뭔지도 모르잖아.
3 A: 이 개가 너의 개니? 정말 귀엽다!
B: 아니, 그 개는 우리 언니 개인데 그녀가 이번 주에 다른 곳에 갔어.
4 A: 이것은 너무 작아요. 저것이 내가 원하는 종류의 나무예요.
B: 저것들은 단풍나무예요. 20미터 정도 높이까지 자라죠.
5 A: 저 소년은 누구니? 그를 알아볼 순 없지만, 전에 어디선가 본 적이 있어.
B: 그는 멜버른에서 온 나의 사촌이야. 너는 그를 몇 년 전에 만났어.

C

1 that	2 those	3 those
4 that	5 that	6 those

해석

1 중국의 고층 건물의 수가 호주의 고층 건물 수보다 더 많다.
2 내 운동화의 밑창이 네 운동화의 밑창보다 더 튼튼하다.
3 오늘날의 어린이들은 일반적으로 바로 한 세대 전의 어린이들보다 몸무게가 더 많이 나간다.
4 해리스의 성적은 학급 친구들보다 훨씬 더 많이 향상되었다.
5 초판의 레이아웃과 두 번째 판의 레이아웃이 완전히 다르다.
6 그 회사의 모니터들이 다른 회사의 모니터들보다 훨씬 더 비싸다.

Unit 25 EXERCISES

p. 134~135

1 one	2 ones	3 one	4 ones
5 ones	6 it	7 it	8 it
9 them	10 one	11 them	

해석

1 이 지하철은 꽉 찼어. 다음 지하철을 기다리자.
2 빨간 사과가 녹색 사과보다 종종 더 맛있다.
3 격자무늬 치마와 주름치마 중에서 어떤 것이 더 좋니?
4 이 신발은 너무 꽉 끼네요. 좀 더 큰 거 있나요?
5 이 양말은 너무 얇아. 더 두꺼운 것 있니?
6 너의 재킷이 약간 해졌구나. 다른 재킷으로 바꾸는 게 어때?
7 이거 네 사전이니? 내가 잠깐 그걸 써도 되겠니?
8 책상 위에 있는 빨간 책 보이니? 그것 좀 건네줘.
9 너 새 선글라스 샀구나. 나에게 보여 줄 수 있니?
10 한국에 관한 책이 몇 권 있어. 원한다면 그 중에 한 권을 빌려가도 돼.
11 이 반바지가 마음에 드시면 한 번 입어보실래요? 탈의실은 저쪽에 있어요.

B

1 another	2 others	3 others	4 other
5 another	6 another	7 another	8 other
9 another	10 others	11 another	12 others

해석

1 이 마커는 다 썼어. 너 다른 마커 있니?
2 어떤 사람들은 생선을 좋아하지만 다른 사람들은 고기를 좋아한다.
3 부모는 아이들에게 다른 사람을 존중하도록 가르쳐야 한다.
4 다른 사람들이 하는 것에 대해 신경 쓰지 마.
5 나는 커피 한 잔 더 마실 거야. 너도 한 잔 갖다 줄까?
6 방금 모기를 한 마리 더 발견했어요. 창문 좀 닫아 주세요!
7 네 형에게 가서 너에게 5달러를 더 빌려 줄 수 있는지 물어봐.
8 개리는 같은 취미를 가진 다른 사람들을 만나고 싶다.
9 불경기 때문에 잭은 올해 외국으로 또다시 여행을 갈 여유가 없다.
10 오만한 사람들은 자신들이 다른 사람들보다 낫다고 믿는 사람들이다.
11 죄송합니다, 손님. 손님의 신용 카드가 안 되네요. 다른 것이 있으신가요?
12 어떤 사람들은 영화 보러 가는 것을 좋아하지만 또 다른 사람들은 집에서 보는 것을 선호한다.

1 one	2 the others
3 others	4 One, The other
5 One, the other	6 One, The others
7 One, the other	8 One, Another, The other
9 One, another, the other	
10 One, another, the other	

해석

1 물을 세 병 샀어. 한 병 줄까?
2 내 열대어 중 한 마리가 죽었어. 하지만 다른 것들은 아직 살아있어.
3 어떤 사람들은 적포도주를 원하고 다른 사람들은 백포도주를 원한다.
4 나는 언니가 두 명 있다. 한 명은 서울에 산다. 다른 한 명은 부산에 산다.
5 우리는 두 개의 다른 피자를 시켰다. 하나는 마르게리타이고, 다른 하나는 나폴리이다.
6 그는 고양이를 몇 마리 기르고 있다. 하나는 갈색 얼룩 고양이고, 다른 것들은 순백색 페르시안 고양이다.
7 그 CEO는 휴대 전화를 두 개 쓴다. 하나는 개인적인 용도이고, 다른 하나는 업무용이다.
8 그에게는 세 명의 딸이 있다. 한 명은 선생님이고, 다른 한 명은 변호사이며, 나머지 한 명은 바이올리니스트이다.
9 그녀는 세 가지 언어를 할 수 있다. 하나는 한국어, 다른 하나는 영어, 그리고 나머지 하나는 스페인어이다.
10 나는 크리스마스카드를 세 개 받았다. 하나는 부모님께, 다른 하나는 선생님께, 그리고 나머지 하나는 가장 친한 친구에게 받은 것이다.

1 anybody	2 everybody
3 nothing	4 everyone
5 nobody	6 no one
7 Something	8 anyone
9 Someone	10 something

해석

1 메리는 온종일 누구에게도 말을 하지 않고 있다.
2 당신은 다른 모든 사람처럼 줄 서서 기다릴 수 없나요?
3 약간 지루하다. 할 일이 많지 않다.
4 나는 모든 사람이 동등하게 기여해야 한다고 생각한다.
5 그가 여러 번 벨을 울렸지만 아무도 대답하지 않았다.
6 아무도 나에게 도움을 주지 않아서 나는 약간 화가 났다.
7 냉장고에 있는 무언가가 상한 냄새가 나. 그것을 꺼내버리는 게 좋겠다.
8 누가 왜 방어할 수 없는 상태의 동물을 해치길 원하겠는가?
9 누군가가 너에게 전화하고 있어. 내가 메시지를 받아 줄까?
10 흥미롭군요. 제 생각에 당신 말에 일리가 있는 것 같아요.

Unit 26 EXERCISES

p. 138~139

A

1 of	2 (of)	3 ×	4 (of)

5 of	6 ×	7 of	8 of
9 of	10 of	11 ×	12 (of)

해석

1 나에게는 두 명의 누나가 있다. 그들은 둘 다 간호사다.
2 너 혼자서 그 팝콘을 모두 먹었니?
3 각각의 문제는 그것만의 독특한 해결책이 필요하다.
4 새 가구가 모두 도착했어. 이제 풀어 보자.
5 회의실의 어느 누구도 그의 아이디어에 찬성하지 않는다.
6 각각의 학생들은 이번주 금요일에 교복을 지급받을 것이다.
7 나는 이번 주에 시험이 세 개 있다. 그리고 각각의 시험들은 어려울 것이다.
8 여기 우리 ABC회사에게는 고객 한 분 한 분이 중요합니다.
9 존스 씨에게는 세 명의 아들이 있다. 그들은 모두 공군에 입대했다.
10 우리 둘 다 그 여행을 정말로 즐겼고, 그 여행은 영원히 기억될 것이다.
11 모든 새로운 운전자들은 면허를 받기 전에 청력 테스트를 통과해야 한다.
12 그녀의 개들은 모두 주인에 의해 버려진 유기견들이었다.

1 recipes	2 wants	3 has	4 learns
5 is	6 have	7 candidate	8 is
9 All	10 is	11 were	

해석

1 그 요리법들 중 어느 것도 그다지 좋지 않다.
2 각각의 아이들은 상을 타기를 원한다.
3 우리 학교의 모든 아이들은 자신만의 사물함을 가지고 있다.
4 모든 작가는 매일 연습함으로써 글 쓰는 것을 배운다.
5 각각의 지원자들은 지원서를 작성해야 한다.
6 학생들은 둘 다 숙제를 끝마쳤다.
7 나는 두 후보자 중 누가되든 그 일에 적합하다고 생각한다.
8 각각의 양탄자는 우리 직조공 중 한 명에 의해 일일이 손으로 만들어진 것이다.
9 아프리카에 있는 모든 야생 동물들은 시행착오를 겪으며 사냥하는 것을 배운다.
10 그 토론 팀의 모든 구성원은 장학금을 받을 것이다.
11 휴일이어서 모든 공공 도서관이 지난 월요일에 문을 닫았다.

1 has	2 the team members
3 Most of	4 student gets
5 either one	6 most
7 no	8 has
9 both of them	

해석

1 베키도 톰도 아직 스마트폰이 없다.
2 모든 팀원들은 매일 훈련을 받는다.
3 제이크는 매우 인기가 많다. 대부분의 반 친구들이 그를 좋아한다.
4 모든 학생들은 일 년에 한 번 건강검진을 받아야 한다.
5 501번 버스와 511번 버스가 여기서 서. 너는 둘 중 어느 것이든 타도 돼.
6 래리는 거의 모든 채소를 싫어하지만 토마토는 좋아한다.
7 아이스크림과 같은 맛이 나는 얼린 요구르트는 지방이 없다.
8 우리 반 친구들은 저마다 성격이 다르고 다양한 재능을 지니고 있다.
9 나는 두 가지 선택권이 있지만 둘 다 마음에 들기 때문에 하나만 선택할 수가 없다.

D

1 was	2 was	3 were
4 were	5 was	6 was

해석

1 직원들 중 누구도 행사에 늦지 않았다.
2 그는 주디네 집에 전화를 했으나 거기에는 아무도 없었다.
3 국경일이었기 때문에 대부분의 가게들은 문을 닫았다.
4 그들 둘 다 파티에 초대를 받았으나 지난밤에 아무도 나타나지 않았다.
5 아빠나 엄마가 나를 6시에 데리러 올 것이다.
6 피자가 거의 다 식고 딱딱해져서 나는 매우 실망했다.

E

1 drops by	2 seems	3 is
4 has	5 is	6 are

해석

1 그들 중 한 명이 들르면, 이것을 그에게 전해주세요.
2 두 지원자들 중 어느 한쪽도 자신 있어 보이지는 않는다.
3 각각의 참가자들은 총 세 번의 기회가 주어진다.
4 내가 저축한 돈은 모두 노트북 컴퓨터를 사는데 쓰였다.
5 이 도서관의 모든 책은 시민들과 기업들에게 기증받은 것이다.
6 코치나 그녀의 조수들 중 한쪽이 이번 시즌 말에 승진할 것이다.

REVIEW

p. 140~141

1 her	2 mine
3 yours	4 he
5 He	6 you, his
7 her, her	8 him, his

해설/해석

1 전치사(to) 뒤에 대명사가 단독으로 오면 목적격을 써야 하므로 her가 적절
나는 저 머그컵이 그녀의 것이라고 생각한다.

2 '내 아파트'라는 의미가 되어야 하므로 '나의 것'을 의미하는 mine이 적절
이 아파트는 내 것보다 훨씬 더 크다.

3 '내 교과서를 안 가져왔으므로 상대방의 교과서를 같이 보자'는 의미가 되어야 하므로 your textbook을 가리키는 yours가 적절
교과서를 가져오는 걸 잊어버렸어. 네 교과서를 같이 봐도 될까?

4 '그가 할 수 있다'는 의미가 되어야 하므로 동사(can) 앞에 주어 he가 적절
피터가 할 수 있는 한 온 힘을 다해 일하고 있다는 것에 우리 모두 동의한다.

5 동사(is) 앞에는 주어가 와야 하므로 He가 적절
나는 마이크를 중학교 때부터 알아왔다. 그는 아주 재치 있는 사람이다.

6 '너에게 그의 계획에 대해 말하다'라는 의미가 되어야 하므로 동사 told의 목적어 you가 적절, 「전치사(about)+소유격+명사」이므로 his가 적절
팀이 너에게 앤과 결혼하겠다는 그의 계획에 대해 말했니?

7 '그녀의 동료'라는 의미가 되어야 하므로 her가 적절, 동사 treat의 목적어가 필요하므로 her가 적절
사라는 그녀의 동료가 자신을 동등하게 대우해 주기를 원한다.

8 '그에게 말을 하다'는 의미로 동사(tell)의 목적어 him이 적절, '그의 자존심'이라는 의미가 되어야 하므로 소유격 his가 적절
네가 그에게 잘생겼다고 말하면 그의 자존심을 훨씬 더 부추기게 될 거야.

1 us, It　2 myself, They　3 you, it, the others

해설/해석

1 전치사(to) 뒤에 대명사가 단독으로 오면 목적격을 써야 하므로 us가 적절, 앞에 이미 언급된 것(Kung fu)을 다시 언급하는 경우 대명사 It이 적절
〈'쿵푸 판다'의 스타, 포와 함께한 인터뷰〉
기자: 우리에게 쿵푸가 무엇인지 설명해 주세요.
포: 물론이죠. 기꺼이 그러겠어요. 쿵푸는 힘든 노력, 훈련과 자기 제어를 통해 본질적으로 자신의 장점을 추구하는 것입니다. 그것은 단순히 싸움에 관한 것이 아닙니다. 사람은 삶의 많은 범위, 예를 들어 요리하거나, 노래를 하거나 정원 일을 하는 것, 즉 어느 정도의 기술을 요구하는 어떤 것에서나 훌륭한 쿵푸 권법을 지닐 수 있습니다.

2 '제가 입을 몇 벌의 와이셔츠'라는 의미로 자신을 나타내므로 myself가 적절, 앞서 언급된 these shirts는 복수명사이므로 이를 대신하는 대명사 또한 복수형 They가 적절
〈백화점 남성복 코너에서〉
A: 안녕하세요. 뭘 도와드릴까요?
B: 제가 입을 몇 벌의 와이셔츠와 아버지께 드릴 생신 선물을 찾고 있어요.
A: 이 셔츠들은 봄 상품으로 막 도착한 것인데요. 다양한 색상과 무늬가 있어요.

3 전치사 뒤에 대명사가 단독으로 오는 경우 목적격을 써야 하므로 you가 적절, 구매한 바로 그 벨트인 특정한 사물을 지칭할 때는 대명사 it이 적절, 벨트를 제외한 나머지 물건들(셔츠 세 개, 넥타이) 모두를 나타낼 때는 the others로 받음
〈계산대에서〉
A: 이 와이셔츠 세 개와, 넥타이, 벨트로 할게요.
B: 네. 포장해 드릴까요?
A: 벨트만 포장해 주세요. 그건 선물이거든요. 다른 것들은 일반 가방에 넣어 주시면 돼요.

1 ourselves	2 yourself	3 herself
4 yourself	5 himself	6 myself
7 yourself	8 themselves	9 himself
10 myself	11 yourself	12 themselves

해설/해석

1 '우리 스스로 해결해야 한다'는 의미이므로 ourselves가 적절
우리 스스로 이 문제들을 풀어야만 한다.

2 '직접 물어봐'라는 의미가 되어야 하므로 yourself가 적절
그렇게 궁금하면 가서 토니에게 직접 물어봐.

3 '너의 언니가 직접 만들었다'는 의미가 되어야 하므로 herself가 적절
너의 언니가 직접 이브닝 가운을 만들었니?

4 '당신 자신을 소개하다'는 의미가 되어야 하므로 yourself가 적절
그룹에게 자기소개를 해주시겠어요?

5 '혼잣말을 하다'라는 뜻의 talk to oneself는 관용적 표현
그는 뭔가를 쓰면서 혼잣말을 했다.

6 '나 혼자서 먹고 싶지 않다'는 의미가 되어야 하므로 myself가 적절, by oneself는 '홀로, 혼자서'라는 뜻
와서 나랑 저녁 먹자. 혼자 먹고 싶지 않아.

7 네가 전화를 받아 줄 수 있는지 물어보는 것이므로 yourself가 적절
나는 욕실에 있어요. 전화 좀 받아줄래요?

8 enjoy oneself는 '즐기다'라는 의미의 관용 표현
학생들은 놀이공원에서 정말 신나게 즐겼다.

9 '혼자 살다'라는 의미가 되어야 하므로 himself가 적절
그는 고등학교를 졸업한 이후로 혼자 살았다.

10 teach oneself는 '독학하다'라는 의미의 관용 표현
나는 프랑스어를 독학했다. 어느 누구에게도 배운 적이 없다.

11 make oneself at home은 '편히 지내다'라는 의미의 관용 표현
여기 계시는 동안 편히 지내시길 바랍니다.

12 consider의 목적어로서 문장의 주어를 받는 것이므로 women을 가리키는 themselves가 적절
조사에 따르면, 많은 여성들이 자신들을 과체중이라고 여긴다.

1 anyone	2 our companies	3 his
4 that	5 its	6 All
7 he	8 me	9 we
10 his	11 those	12 his
13 that		

해설/해석

1 some으로 시작하는 부정대명사는 주로 긍정문과 권유문에 쓰이고, any로 시작하는 부정대명사는 주로 부정문, 의문문, 조건문에 사용되므로 여기서는 someone이 아닌 anyone이 더 적절
제레미라는 이름을 가진 사람이 여기 있나요?

2 「Each of+소유격+복수명사」가 되야 하므로 companies가 적절
우리 회사들은 각각 적어도 하나의 지역 자선 단체를 지원한다.

3 own textile business를 수식해 주어야 하므로 소유격인 his가 적절
우리 아버지는 퇴직하기 전에 섬유 사업체를 운영했었다.

4 비교 구문에서 앞서 언급된 명사를 받을 때 that이나 those를 사용, 비교 대상인 The economic crisis는 단수이므로 that이 적절

2008년의 경제 위기는 1971년의 경제 위기보다 더 심각했다.

5 it's는 it is 또는 it has를 줄인 말이다. 이 문장에서는 '그것(사자)의 시간'에 해당하는 소유격이 필요하므로 its가 적절
사자는 자신의 시간의 대부분을 잠을 자면서 보낸다. 매일 20시간까지 잠을 잔다.

6 Every 뒤에는 「of+복수명사」를 쓸 수 없다. 뒤에 their thanks라는 표현으로 보아, 주어를 복수 취급하는 형태가 필요하므로 All이 적절
모든 방문객이 폐막식 후에 감사를 표현했다.

7 the man을 받는 대명사로 he가 적절
그 남자가 호텔에 들어갔을 때, 그는 매니저와 말하고 싶다고 했다.

8 올바른 방향을 내게 알려주겠느냐고 물어보는 의미가 되어야 하므로 목적격 me가 적절
나는 약국을 찾고 있어요. 올바른 방향을 알려주시겠어요?

9 My friend and I를 받는 대명사로 we가 적절
내 친구와 나는 정시에 기차를 탈 수 있도록 일찍 떠나야 했다.

10 his driver's license를 대신할 수 있는 말로 소유대명사가 와야 하므로 his(그의 것)가 적절
나는 지난달에 운전면허증을 받았어. 하지만 우리 형은 그의 것을 1년도 더 전에 받았다.

11 비교 문장에서 앞에 언급된 명사를 다시 언급할 때는 that이나 those를 사용한다. 비교 대상인 이전 세대의 the freedoms를 대신하는 말이므로 복수형 those가 적절
우리가 오늘날 즐기는 자유와 이전 세대의 자유를 비교해 봐라.

12 제임스가 공책을 빌리고 싶어 한 이유는 그의 공책이 완전하지 않기 때문이므로 his가 적절
제임스가 내 공책을 빌려 달라고 부탁했다. 왜냐하면 그의 것은 완전하지 않았기 때문이었다.

13 over there로 미루어보아 가까이 있는 음식이 아닌 멀리 있는 음식을 가리키는 것이므로 that이 적절
저쪽에 있는 아가씨가 먹고 있는 저 요리는 무엇인가요? 저도 그걸로 할게요.

REVIEW PLUS p. 142

⑤

해설/해석

(A) '내가 직접 무슨 일이 있었는지 보았다'는 의미이므로 myself가 적절, (B) '그녀 스스로 해야 할 것이다'라는 의미이므로 herself가 적절, (C) were의 주어는 복수가 되어야 하므로 All이 적절

- 나는 직접 무슨 일이 있었는지 보았다.
- 그녀 스스로 그 일을 해야 할 것이다.
- 지진 후에 찬장의 모든 접시가 깨졌다.

①

해설/해석

① 부정문이므로 something을 anything으로 고친다.

① A: 이 벽을 최근에 칠했나요?
B: 아니요, 하지만 이 가구는 최근에 칠했어요. 아무것도 만지지 마세요.

② A: 다른 만화책을 빌리고 싶니?
B: 응. 네가 빌려 줬던 것들은 정말 재미있었어.

③ A: 나에게 너의 가족 중 누군가에 대해 무언가를 말해 줄 수 있니?
B: 글쎄, 내 사촌 제인은 아주 똑똑해. 그녀는 전기 공학 학위를 가지고 있어.

④ A: 나는 항상 너와 질이 함께 있는 걸 보게 되는구나. 너희는 가장 친한 친구들인 게 틀림없어.
B: 우리는 많은 관심사를 공유해서 함께 시간을 보내는 걸 좋아해.

⑤ A: 이 문은 잠겼어. 열 수 없어.
B: 다른 쪽을 시도해 봐. 그곳으로 들어갈 수 있을 거야.

④

해설/해석

④ 뒤에 and가 왔고, 동사가 want이므로 Both가 적절

영국에서 연구원들은 휴대 전화로 통화를 하면서 운전을 하는 것이 위험한지 아닌지 알아내려고 자료를 모으기 시작했다. 이제 교통사고가 있을 때마다 경찰관들은 운전자 중 누구라도 휴대 전화를 사용하고 있었는지 알아내도록 요청받고 있다. 그들은 이 정보를 그들의 교통사고 기록에 적을 것이다. 그러면 연구원들은 반복성을 찾으며 이 기록들을 연구할 것이다. 연구원들이나 경찰 당국 둘 다 도로가 누구에게나 안전하기를 바란다.

Unit 27 EXERCISES p. 146~147

1 to read, 주격보어
2 to enter, 목적격보어
3 to find, 진주어
4 to win, 목적격보어
5 to go, 목적어
6 to cut, 진주어

해석

1 내가 가장 좋아하는 취미는 추리 소설을 읽는 것이다.
2 나는 그가 경기에 참가하리라 예상하지 못했다.
3 나의 예전 공책에서 돈을 발견한 것은 행운이었다.
4 사람들 대부분 미셸이 그 경기에서 승리할 것이라고 예상했다.
5 우리 반은 다음 달에 경주에 가려고 계획하고 있다.
6 새치기를 하는 것은 잘못된 거야. 이 모든 사람들을 좀 봐.

1 to take
2 not to sleep
3 to play
4 not to punish
5 not to run

해석

1 우리는 샐리가 우리와 함께 사진을 찍는 것을 승낙해서 매우 좋았다.
2 우리 선생님은 늘 우리에게 수업 중에 자지 말라고 말한다.
3 에반은 축구 선수가 되고 싶어 한다. 그의 꿈은 유럽에서 축구를 하는 것이다.

4 전문가들은 아이들의 자존감을 위해 다른 사람들 앞에서 아이들을 혼내지 않는 것이 중요하다고 말한다.
5 우리 이모 마거릿은 아래층에 산다. 그녀는 우리가 너무 시끄럽다고 말하면서 뛰어다니지 말라고 부탁했다.

C

1 to use	2 to finish	3 to be
4 to ski	5 to help	6 to forget, to make

해석

1 나는 이 복사기를 사용하고 싶어요.
2 나는 11시까지 이 기말 보고서 쓰는 것을 끝냈으면 좋겠다.
3 선생님은 학생들에게 시험에 늦지 말라고 말했다.
4 영진이와 세리는 겨울 방학 때마다 콜로라도에서 스키 타는 것을 좋아한다.
5 엄마는 손님들이 오시기 전에 집 청소하는 것을 도와달라고 내게 부탁했다.
6 제임스는 같은 실수를 반복하고 싶지 않았기 때문에 그 문제를 잊고 싶지 않았다.

D

1 It is very interesting to design and build a model robot.
2 It is difficult to organize all the books on this shelf.
3 It is sometimes difficult to please our parents.
4 It is not good for your health to study in the library all day.
5 It is very thrilling to watch the World Cup final match at the stadium.
6 It is dangerous to let children swim in the sea by themselves.
7 It is not easy to become fluent in foreign languages in a short time.

해석

1 모형 로봇을 디자인하고 만드는 것은 매우 흥미롭다.
2 이 선반에 있는 모든 책을 정리하는 것은 어렵다.
3 우리 부모님을 즐겁게 하는 것은 때때로 어렵다.
4 온종일 도서관에서 공부하는 것은 건강에 좋지 않다.
5 경기장에서 월드컵 결승전을 관람하는 것은 매우 흥미진진하다.
6 아이들을 바다에서 혼자 수영하게 두는 것은 위험하다.
7 외국어를 짧은 시간에 능숙하게 하는 것은 쉽지 않다.

E

1 where to	2 how to
3 what to	4 whether to

해석

1 A: 실례합니다. 공항으로 가는 버스를 어디서 타야 하는지 말해 주시겠어요?
B: 물론이죠. 공항버스 정류장은 바로 이 블록 끝에 있어요.
2 A: 너는 김치를 어떻게 만드는지 아니? 매우 어렵다고 들었어.
B: 사실, 나도 직접 만들어 본 적이 없어. 하지만 우리 어머니가 너에게 알려주는 걸 좋아하실 거라고 확신해.
3 A: 나는 미술 숙제를 어떻게 해야 할지 모르겠어. 내일이 마감인데 심지어 아직 시작도 안 했어.
B: 당장 시작해야겠네. 다음번에는 마지막까지 미루지 마.
4 A: 휴가 때 밴쿠버로 갈지 토론토로 갈지 결정하려고 해.
B: 나는 네가 밴쿠버에 가야 한다고 생각해. 왜냐하면 거기에서는 산과 바다를 즐길 수 있거든.

Unit 28 EXERCISES p. 149

A

1 to put	2 to relax	3 to spend
4 to paint	5 to please	6 to lend

해석

1 저에게 이 꽃들을 꽂을 꽃병을 주세요.
2 많은 서울 사람들이 휴식을 취할 수 있는 더 많은 공원을 원한다.
3 멜리사는 함께 시간을 보낼 친구를 찾고 있었다.
4 나는 파란색이 침실을 칠할 완벽한 색이라고 생각한다.
5 제니퍼는 어머니를 기쁘게 해 드릴 선물을 찾고 있었다.
6 미안하지만 지금 당장은 네게 빌려줄 돈이 하나도 없어.

B

1 to listen to	2 to eat
3 to play in	4 to read
5 to put those books in	6 to have
7 to play with	8 to take pictures of

해석

1 지니가 나에게 들을 CD를 주었다.
2 상어는 먹이를 먹지 않고 며칠을 지낼 수 있다.
3 LA 다저스는 경기할 새 경기장이 필요하다.
4 공항에서 모니카가 읽을 소설을 한 권 샀다.
5 나는 그 책들을 넣을 상자가 좀 더 필요하다.
6 사무엘은 종종 저녁 식사 후에 먹을 딸기를 딴다.
7 그 소년은 같이 놀 친구가 없어서 외로웠다.
8 나는 사진 찍을 만한 아름다운 건물이 없어서 실망했다.

1 ⓑ	2 ⓔ	3 ⓐ	4 ⓒ	5 ⓓ

해석

1 학교 복도에서 뛰어서는 안 된다.
2 빌 게이츠는 미국에서 가장 부유한 사람이 될 운명이었다.
3 샌프란시스코행 다음 비행기는 오전 8시에 이륙할 예정입니다.
4 그녀는 사방을 다 찾아봤지만 그녀의 사물함 열쇠는 찾을 수 없었다.
5 앞자리에 앉을 작정이라면, 아주 일찍 일어나야 할 거야.

Unit 29 EXERCISES p. 152~153

A

1 ⓑ	2 ⓐ	3 ⓓ	4 ⓒ	5 ⓐ
6 ⓒ	7 ⓑ	8 ⓒ	9 ⓑ	10 ⓓ

해석

1 내가 다시 너를 믿다니 정말 어리석었다.
2 그녀는 날씬해 보이려고 항상 검은색 청바지를 입는다.
3 그는 잠에서 깨어나 집에 혼자 있음을 알게 되었다.
4 나는 11월에 서울에 돌아가게 되어 정말 기쁘다.
5 실비아의 부모님이 그녀를 데리러 도서관에 왔다.
6 조이스는 대학에 가기 위해 자신의 가족을 떠나게 되어 슬프다.
7 가난한 사람들을 돕고 있었다니 그녀는 천사임이 틀림없다.
8 교통사고에서 아무도 다치지 않았다는 것을 알고 우리는 매우 안도했다.
9 토비 맥과이어가 그렇게 성공적인 영화를 만들다니 매우 재능이 있음이 틀림없다.
10 저스틴 팀버레이크는 자라서 가장 인기 있는 남자 가수 중 한 명이 되었다.

B

1 to pass 2 to make 3 to get
4 to hear 5 to understand 6 to sing
7 to remind 8 to learn 9 to keep
10 to read

해석

1 보니는 시험에 통과해서 행복했다.
2 의사 선생님과 약속을 잡으려고 전화했어요.
3 나는 정밀 검사를 받기 위해 병원으로 갔다.
4 중간고사가 연기되었다는 이야기를 들으니 기쁘다.
5 동화는 이해하기 쉬워서 모든 문화에서 매우 인기가 있다.
6 이 노래는 음이 너무 높아서 부르기 어렵다.
7 그녀는 내게 그 약속에 대해 상기시켜주려고 전화했다.
8 우리 부모님은 내가 거짓말을 했다는 사실을 알고는 매우 실망하셨다.
9 매일 아침 우리 어머니는 건강을 유지하기 위해 열심히 수영한다.
10 이 책은 한자가 너무 많아서 읽기가 어렵다.

C

1 되었다 2 보아서 3 않기 위해
4 타기 위해 5 사과하기 위해 6 끝내다니

D

1 to, lose, weight
2 to, catch, up, on, my, classes
3 it, pleasant, to, hear
4 were, delighted, to, see
5 to, find, an, empty, bottle
6 must, be, smart, to, solve, the, puzzle

Unit 30 EXERCISES

p. 156~157

A

1 me 2 Peter 3 me
4 me 5 many students 6 you

해석

1 이 퍼즐은 내가 풀기에 어렵다.
2 미국 사람들은 피터가 금메달을 따기를 바란다.
3 선생님이 나에게 교실 청소를 부탁했다.
4 나는 커피 없이 밤늦게까지 깨어 있는 것이 어렵다.
5 요즘 많은 학생들에게 있어 유학 가는 것은 비싸다.
6 그 프로젝트에 대해 내게 질문하는 것을 주저하지 말아라.

B

1 for 2 of 3 of 4 of
5 of 6 of 7 for 8 for

해석

1 매튜의 경기는 우리가 보기에 흥미진진했다.
2 우리의 학교 연극을 도와주다니 너는 참 친절했다.
3 이 어려운 시기에 나를 도와주다니 너는 참 자상하다.
4 결정을 내리기 전에 신중하게 생각하다니 너는 현명하다.
5 병원에 계신 할머니께 병문안을 가다니 너는 참 사려가 깊다.
6 네 방을 삼촌과 함께 사용하다니 너는 착하구나.
7 그 나라는 여자들이 혼자 여행하기에 위험할 수도 있다.
8 톰은 자신의 인기 덕분에 광고에 등장하기가 쉽다.

C

1 to leave 2 to be accepted
3 to sign 4 to see
5 to be finished 6 to win
7 to be painted 8 to be set

해석

1 크리스는 친구들을 떠나게 되어 슬프다.
2 그는 자신의 사과가 받아들여질 것으로 예상한다.
3 리사는 자신의 이름을 서명할 펜이 필요하다.
4 우리는 당분간 서로 만나지 않기로 했다.
5 내 상사는 보고서가 이번 주 금요일까지 마무리되기를 원한다.
6 그는 올림픽에서 두 개의 금메달을 따는 데 실패했다.
7 아버지는 지난 주말까지 우리 집이 페인트칠 되기를 원했었다.
8 한 사람에 의해 네 개의 세계 기록이 수립된 것은 매우 이례적인 일이다.

D

1 It seems that Kate finished[has finished] her homework early.
2 It seems that my father is tired after a long day at work.
3 It seems that we have everything we need for our school trip.
4 It seemed that no one listened to the teacher because of the beautiful weather.
5 Because of his tan, it seems that David has been to the seaside.
6 It seems that he did[has done] terribly on the test because he looks unhappy.

해석

1 케이트는 숙제를 일찍 끝낸 것 같다.
2 아버지는 직장에서 긴 하루를 보내고 피곤한 것처럼 보인다.
3 우리는 수학여행에 필요한 모든 것을 다 가진 것 같다.
4 좋은 날씨 때문에 아무도 선생님의 말씀을 듣지 않는 것처럼 보였다.
5 햇볕에 탄 것 때문에 데이비드는 바닷가에 갔던 것처럼 보인다.
6 그가 기분이 안 좋아 보이는 것을 보니 시험을 망친 것 같다.

E

1 I hope that I will make a lot of friends in the new school.
2 Minsu is hoping that he will get an invitation to the party.
3 We expect that Beyonce will win a Grammy for her new song.
4 Everyone expects that William will do well at the Olympics.
5 Many people expect that Black Hole will be the most popular band of the year.
6 Most experts expect that Korea will dominate Olympic archery for many years.

해석

1 나는 새로운 학교에서 많은 친구들을 사귀기를 바란다.
2 민수는 그 파티에 초대받기를 바라고 있다.
3 우리는 비욘세가 새로운 노래로 그래미상을 수상할 거라고 기대한다.
4 모든 사람이 윌리엄이 올림픽에서 잘할 거라고 기대한다.
5 많은 사람이 블랙홀이 올해의 가장 인기 있는 밴드가 될 거라고 기대한다.
6 대부분의 전문가들은 한국이 오랫동안 올림픽 양궁에서 우위를 차지할 거라고 기대한다.

Unit 31 EXERCISES p. 161~163

A

1	sing, singing	2	take, to take
3	to finish	4	think
5	know	6	practice, practicing
7	laugh	8	to study
9	crawl, crawling	10	to help

해석

1 메리는 밤에 새들이 노래하는 것을 듣는다.
2 정현이는 언제나 내가 개들을 돌보는 것을 도와준다.
3 우리는 모두 마감 전에 그 프로젝트를 간신히 끝냈다.
4 구운 칠면조는 언제나 내게 추수 감사절을 생각나게 한다.
5 코엑스에 가려면 어떤 버스를 타야 하는지 저에게 알려주실래요?
6 조이스는 그 소녀들이 배구 연습하는 것을 보았다.
7 나는 만화책이 나를 웃게 하기 때문에 그것을 정말 좋아한다.
8 제시카는 가을 학기를 시작하면서 공학을 공부하기로 했다.
9 내가 아이였을 때 우리 어머니는 내가 벽장 안으로 기어들어가는 것을 바라보곤 하셨다.
10 부모님이 내게 집안일 하는 것을 도와달라고 하셔서 이번 주말은 너무 바빴다.

B

1 too fast, to catch up
2 foolish enough to believe
3 too tall to fit
4 enough time to accomplish
5 too small to go around
6 enough money to have

해석

1 토미는 너무 빨리 달려서 내가 따라잡을 수 없었다.
2 그를 믿을 만큼 어리석은 사람은 없다.
3 레이첼은 그 바지를 입기에는 너무 키가 크다.
4 우리가 원하는 모든 것을 완수할 시간이 충분히 있다.
5 피자 크기가 너무 작아서 모두에게 돌릴 수가 없다.
6 그는 그런 화려한 결혼식을 할 만큼 충분한 돈이 없다고 그녀에게 말했다.

C

1	jaywalk[jaywalking]	2	(to) do
3	learn	4	stare[staring]
5	to share	6	to compete

해석

1 나는 한 남자가 도로에서 무단 횡단을 하는 것을 보았다.
2 나는 우리 엄마가 집안일 하는 것을 도왔다.
3 우리 엄마는 내가 피아노 치는 법을 배우게 했다.
4 나는 낯선 사람이 우리 이웃집 창문을 들여다보고 있는 것을 발견했다.
5 우리는 나눠 먹을 케이크가 충분한지 확실히 해야 한다.
6 국내 자동차 산업은 외국의 자동차 제품과 경쟁할 만큼 충분히 빠르게 성장하고 있다.

D

1 You are so short that you can't ride this roller coaster.
2 My little brother is too young to watch that scary movie.
3 David is so talented that he can be a professional boxer.
4 My friend Jiho is smart enough to study physics.
5 She stayed up late so as to study for the final exam.
She stayed up late in order to study for the final exam.
She stayed up late so that she could study for the final exam.
She stayed up late in order that she could study for the final exam.
6 I ran to school so as to be in time for the first class.
I ran to school in order to be in time for the first class.
I ran to school so that I could be in time for the first class.
I ran to school in order that I could be in time for the first class.
7 She had enough sleep so as not to doze off in class.
She had enough sleep in order not to doze off in class.

She had enough sleep so that she wouldn't doze off in class.
She had enough sleep in order that she wouldn't doze off in class.

해석

1 너는 키가 너무 작아서 이 롤러코스터를 탈 수 없다.
2 내 남동생은 너무 어려서 그렇게 무서운 영화를 볼 수 없다.
3 데이비드는 재능이 충분히 많아서 프로 권투선수가 될 수 있다.
4 내 친구 지호는 물리학을 공부할 만큼 충분히 똑똑하다.
5 그녀는 기말고사 공부를 하려고 밤늦게까지 깨어 있었다.
6 나는 1교시 시간에 맞추려고 학교를 향해 달렸다.
7 그녀는 수업 중에 졸지 않으려고 잠을 충분히 잤다.

1 To, start, with
2 Strange, to, say
3 to, say, nothing, of
4 were, supposed, to, meet
5 To, begin, with
6 To, be, frank, with, you
7 not, to, mention
8 are, likely, to, fall, off
9 To, tell, the, truth
10 to, be, honest, with, you
11 To, make, matters, worse

REVIEW

p. 164~165

A

1 ⓑ	2 ⓐ	3 ⓐ	4 ⓒ	5 ⓑ
6 ⓐ	7 ⓑ	8 ⓒ	9 ⓒ	10 ⓒ

해설/해석

1 to write on이 some paper를 수식, '쓸 종이'라는 의미의 형용사적 역할
저에게 쓸 종이 좀 주세요.

2 to enter는 hope의 목적어로 '들어가기를 기대한다'라는 의미로 사용되어 명사적 역할
우리 형은 좋은 대학에 들어가고 싶어 한다.

3 to exercise는 wish의 목적어로 명사적 역할
그녀는 최소한 일주일에 3번은 운동하고 싶어 한다.

4 to persuade는 '설득하기 위하여'라는 의미로 사용, 목적을 나타내는 부사적 역할
그는 자신의 제안을 받아들이도록 설득하려고 내게 편지를 보냈다.

5 to read가 a fashion magazine을 수식, '읽을 잡지'라는 뜻으로 형용사적 역할
읽을 만한 패션 잡지를 좀 주시겠어요?

6 to go and see가 동사 want의 목적어로 사용되어 '보러 가기를 원하다'라는 의미로 명사적 역할
우리 반의 남자 아이들은 새 액션 영화를 보러 가기를 정말로 원한다.

7 to use가 olive oil을 수식하여 '사용할 올리브 오일'이라는 의미가 되어 형용사적 역할
요리에 사용할 올리브 오일이 없다면 대신 버터를 사용하세요.

8 to have가 감정을 나타내는 형용사 pleased(기쁜)를 수식하여 '갖게 되어 기쁜'이라는 의미로 부사적 역할
아프리카계 미국인들은 버락 오바마가 대통령이 되어 기뻤다.

9 to see가 감정을 나타내는 형용사 amazed(놀란)를 수식하여 '보게 되어 놀란'이라는 의미로 부사적 역할
모든 아이들은 판다를 처음 봐서 몹시 놀랐다.

10 to survive는 '살아남기 위해'라는 의미로 목적을 나타내는 부사적 역할
북극곰은 혹독한 북극의 겨울 동안 살아남기 위해 봄과 여름에 많이 먹어야 한다.

B

1 to speak
2 of her
3 dye
4 skating
5 to stay at
6 to live in
7 to say
8 to play soccer with
9 to receive
10 for me
11 to visit
12 to be left

해설/해석

1 It은 가주어, 동사 speak가 진주어 역할을 하기 위해서 to부정사가 와야 하므로 to speak가 적절
영어를 유창하게 하는 것이 내 꿈이다.

2 사람의 성질이나 태도를 나타내는 형용사 gracious(인자한, 상냥한) 뒤에 의미상 주어를 나타낼 때는 「of+목적격」이 오므로 of her가 적절
나의 사과를 받아주다니 그녀는 참 상냥하다.

3 사역동사 have는 목적어(me)의 행동을 나타내는 목적격보어로 to부정사를 취할 수 없으므로 dye가 적절
어제 우리 오빠가 나에게 자신의 머리를 금발로 염색하게 했다.

4 지각동사 see는 목적어(her)의 행동을 나타내는 목적격보어로 to부정사를 취할 수 없으므로 skate 또는 skating이 적절
제이슨은 그녀가 얼음을 가로지르면서 우아하게 스케이트 타는 것을 보았다.

5 to stay at이 the best hotel을 수식하여 '머무르기 좋은 호텔'이라는 의미로 사용되어 형용사적 역할을 한다. the best hotel을 부정사 뒤에 놓아보면 stay at the best hotel이 되므로 전치사를 꼭 수반해야 함
이곳은 여름휴가 때 머무르기 가장 좋은 호텔이다.

6 형용사적 쓰임으로 전치사의 수반 여부는 수식받는 명사(an apartment)를 부정사 뒤에 목적어로 놓아 보면 알 수 있다. '아파트에 살다'라는 의미로 live in an apartment가 되므로 to live in이 적절
그들은 거주할 아파트를 사려고 돈을 모으고 있다.

7 It은 가주어, 동사 say가 진주어 역할을 하기 위해서 to부정사가 되어야 하므로 to say가 적절
다른 사람들이 '네'라고 말할 때 '아니요'라고 말하는 것은 매우 어렵다.

8 형용사적 쓰임으로 전치사의 수반 여부는 수식받는 명사(some new friends)를 부정사 뒤에 목적어로 놓아 보면 알 수 있다. '새로운 친구들과 함께 축구하다'라는 의미로 play soccer with some new friends가 되므로 to play soccer with가 적절

나와 함께 축구를 할 새로운 친구들을 만나고 싶다.

9 me가 용돈을 받는 것이므로 to receive가 적절
우리 어머니는 내가 용돈을 미리 받는 것을 좋아하지 않는다.

10 「It+형용사+to부정사」에서 사람의 성질이나 태도를 나타내는 형용사를 제외하고 의미상의 주어는 to부정사 앞에 「for+목적격」을 쓰므로 for me가 적절
우리 형을 위해 어떤 게임을 사야 할지 결정하는 것은 나에게 어려운 일이다.

11 형용사적 쓰임으로 수식받는 명사를 목적어 자리에 두었을 때 '아름다운 나라를 방문하다(visit a beautiful country)'라는 의미로 전치사가 필요 없으므로 to visit가 적절
핀란드는 백야가 있어서 여름에 방문하기에 아름다운 도시이다.

12 우리가 남들을 뒤처지게 하는 것이 아니라 남들에 의해 뒤쳐짐을 당하는 것이므로 to be left가 적절
우리는 뒤처지고 싶지 않으면 자기 계발에 많은 시간을 써야만 한다.

1	to study	2	to take
3	to be disturbed	4	to rely on
5	to send	6	(to) move
7	climb[climbing]	8	walk[walking]
9	to live in	10	to get

해설/해석

1 to study는 '공부하기 위해'라는 의미로서 to부정사의 목적을 나타내는 부사적 역할
제인은 졸업 후에 유학을 가기 위해 돈을 모았다.

2 목적어 me의 행동을 설명하는 목적격보어가 필요. 따라서 to take가 적절
우리 부모님은 내가 혼자 여행을 가는 것을 결코 허락하지 않으신다.

3 내가 방해를 하는 것이 아니라 방해를 받는 것이므로 수동태를 써야 하고, 동사 want의 목적어이므로 to be disturbed가 적절
나는 방해받고 싶지 않아서 조용한 장소를 찾고 있었다.

4 명사 three friends를 동사 rely on이 뒤에서 수식해 주기 위해서는 to부정사의 형태가 되어야 한다. 따라서 three friends to rely on의 형태가 되는 것이 적절
최소한 의지할 수 있는 세 명의 친구가 있다면 너는 운이 좋은 것이다.

5 동사 promise의 목적어로 동사 send를 쓰기 위해서는 to부정사의 형태가 되어야 하므로 to send가 적절
그는 내가 주문한 상품을 가능한 한 빨리 보내준다고 약속했다.

6 help는 목적어로 동사원형과 to부정사를 모두 취하므로 move 또는 to move 둘 다 가능
그는 내게 자신의 물건을 옮기는 것을 도와달라고 부탁했다.

7 지각동사 see는 목적격보어로 동사원형 또는 분사를 취하므로 climb 또는 climbing이 적절
나는 누군가 건물의 창문으로 기어 올라가는 것을 보았다.

8 사역동사 have는 목적격보어로 동사원형 또는 분사를 취하므로 walk 또는 walking이 적절
우리 엄마는 저녁 후에 나에게 개를 공원에서 산책시키도록 하였다.

9 동사 live in이 명사 place를 꾸며주기 위해서는 to부정사의 형태가 되어야 하므로 to live in이 적절
누군가 살 곳이 없다면 우리는 그들을 노숙자라고 부른다.

10 disappointed는 '실망한'이라는 의미로 to부정사를 취하여 '~해서 실망한'이라는 의미가 되므로 to get이 적절
나는 기말 시험에서 최하위 점수를 받아 실망했다.

1	to enjoy	2	to read	3	to eat
4	to win	5	to get	6	to be fixed

해설/해석

1 It은 가주어, '즐기는 것'이라는 의미의 to enjoy가 진주어로 명사적 역할
A: 브라이언은 자신의 일을 좋아해. 그는 정말 운이 좋아.
B: 잘됐다. 하는 일을 즐긴다는 게 중요해.

2 '일본 만화책을 읽기 위해'라는 의미로 목적을 나타내는 부사적 역할
A: 미수는 일본 만화책을 읽으려고 일본어를 공부하고 있어.
B: 음, 그녀가 일본 만화책이 재미있다는 것을 알게 되면 더 빨리 배우게 될 거야.

3 '우리에게 먹을 것을'이라는 의미로 목적어(us)의 행동을 보충 설명하는 목적격보어
A: 선생님께서 우리에게 매일 건강한 아침 식사를 하라고 말씀하셨어.
B: 맞아. 아침 식사가 하루 중 가장 중요한 식사야.

4 to win은 '이기기 위해'라는 의미로 to부정사의 부사적 역할
A: 닉은 그 경기에서 이기기 위해 하루에 6시간 이상 훈련하고 있어.
B: 알고 있어. 하지만 그가 너무 자신을 혹독하게 몰아붙이는 것 같아서 너무 걱정돼.

5 '공항까지 가는 가장 빠른 방법'이라는 의미로 명사 way를 수식하는 형용사적 쓰임
A: 비행기 시간에 늦었어요. 여기에서 공항까지 가는 가장 빠른 방법이 뭐죠?
B: 내 생각에 가장 빠른 방법은 지하철을 타는 거예요. 이 시간대에는 교통 상황이 좋지 않거든요.

6 TV와 fix는 수동의 관계이므로 to be fixed가 되어야 함
A: 수, 우리 TV는 수리를 받아야 해. 수리 기사에게 전화를 해 주겠니?
B: 걱정 마. 내가 할게.

REVIEW PLUS

p. 166

1 ①　　2 ⑤

해설/해석

1 (A) 형용사 fun 뒤의 to부정사의 의미상 주어는 「for+목적격」 형태, (B) 사역동사 make는 목적어(me)가 하는 행동인 목적격보어로 to부정사를 취할 수 없으므로 brush가 적절, (C) 서류를 확인할 의무가 있다는 의미가 되어야 하므로 '~하기로 되어 있다'라는 의미를 지닌 are supposed to가 적절, be likely to는 '~할 것 같다'라는 의미
• 컴퓨터 게임을 하는 것이 나는 매우 재미있다.
• 우리 어머니는 항상 잠자기 전에 나에게 이를 닦도록 시키신다.
• 당신은 팩스를 보내기 전에 서류를 확인할 의무가 있다.

2 (A) decide는 to부정사를 목적어로 취하는 동사, (B) 사역동사 have는 목적어(you)가 하는 행동인 목적격보어로 to부정사를 취할 수 없으므로 finish가 적절, (C) 전에 젓가락을 사용해 보지 않은 것은 현재보다 더 이전에 일어난 일이므로 완료형 부정사인 to have used가 적절
- 케빈은 공부를 계속하려고 저녁을 일찍 먹기로 결정했다.
- 도널드가 너에게 점심 먹기 전에 잔디 깎는 것을 끝내도록 시켰니?
- 테리는 전에 젓가락을 한 번도 사용해 본 적이 없는 것 같다.

④

해설/해석

④ 사역동사 let은 목적어(children)의 행동을 설명하는 목적격보어로 to부정사를 취할 수 없으므로 listen이 적절

수년간 많은 나라의 젊은이들은 미국과 영국 같은 나라의 음악만을 듣기 원했다. 하지만 요즘은 다른 나라의 가수들도 무시할 수 없을 만큼 인기가 있다. 중국과 태국 같은 동아시아 나라에서 몇몇 한국 밴드는 신문에 크게 보도될 정도로 충분히 인기가 있다. 그들의 귀여운 이미지와 순수한 가사 때문에 심지어 부모들도 아이들이 미국의 팝 음악 대신에 그들의 음악을 듣게 하는 것을 선호한다. 이것이 아시아 전역에 전파되며 성장하는 한류를 설명하는 데 도움이 될 것이다.

Unit 32 EXERCISES

p. 170~171

1 ⓒ 2 ⓒ 3 ⓐ 4 ⓓ 5 ⓓ 6 ⓑ

해석

1 태현이의 취미는 웨이크 보드이다.
2 내가 가장 무서워하는 것은 많은 관중 앞에서 말하는 것이다.
3 문자 메시지를 보내는 것은 젊은이들의 문화에서 중요한 부분이다.
4 혹등고래는 장거리 수영을 하는 것으로 잘 알려져 있다.
5 애완동물을 기르는 것은 스트레스를 줄이고 건강하게 지낼 수 있는 좋은 방법이다.
6 젊은 사람들은 여름 내내 유럽을 배낭여행하는 것을 즐긴다.

B

1 raining[to rain] 2 exercising
3 helping 4 Starting[To start]
5 playing 6 working
7 Taking 8 being[to be]

해석

1 비가 짧게 그쳤다가 다시 오기 시작했다.
2 그녀는 살을 빼기 위해 매일 운동하는 것을 그냥 포기해 버렸다.
3 내가 발표 준비하는 것을 도와주어서 고마워.
4 아무 도움 없이 우리의 식당을 여는 것은 쉬운 일이 아니었다.
5 지선이는 한가한 시간에 햄스터와 함께 노는 것을 정말 즐긴다.
6 민희는 자신의 목표를 성취하기 위해 매우 열심히 일하는 것으로 유명하다.
7 교통 혼잡 시간에는 차를 가져가는 것보다 지하철을 타는 것이 훨씬 빠르다.
8 내 여동생은 관심의 중심에 서는 것을 좋아하지 않는다.

C

1 traveling 2 remaining 3 painting
4 Eating 5 Getting 6 Taking

해석

1 존은 종종 여행에 관한 책을 읽는다.
2 어려운 것은 위기 속에서 냉정함을 유지하는 것이다.
3 질과 톰은 거실을 페인트칠하기 시작했다.
4 건강한 아침 식사를 하는 것은 온종일 네게 힘을 줄 것이다.
5 새로운 학교생활에 적응하는 것은 많은 학생에게 어려운 일일 수도 있다.
6 쌍둥이를 동시에 돌보는 것은 내가 생각한 것보다 더 어려웠다.

1 eating bagels for breakfast
2 working in the stock market
3 Preserving languages and cultures
4 speaking English
5 eating a late-night snack
6 getting poor service
7 making such a big mistake

해석

1 그는 아침 식사로 베이글을 좋아한다. → 그는 아침 식사로 베이글을 먹는 것을 좋아한다.
2 내 친구 수잔은 증권 시장에 관심이 있다. → 내 친구 수잔은 증권 시장에서 일하는 것에 관심이 있다.
3 언어와 문화는 모든 나라에서 중요하다. → 언어와 문화를 보존하는 것은 모든 나라에서 중요하다.
4 그는 캐나다에 1년째 살고 있지만, 여전히 영어를 못한다. → 그는 캐나다에 1년째 살고 있지만, 여전히 영어를 말하는 데 서투르다.
5 살을 빼려면 야식을 끊어야 한다. → 살을 빼려면 야식 먹는 것을 끊어야 한다.
6 그는 식당의 형편없는 서비스에 대해 불평했다. → 그는 식당에서 형편없는 서비스를 받은 것에 대해 불평했다.
7 나는 그런 큰 실수에 대해 부끄러웠다. → 나는 그런 큰 실수를 한 것에 대해 부끄러웠다.

1 PP 2 G 3 PP 4 PP 5 G
6 PP 7 PP 8 G 9 G 10 G

해석

1 나는 쇼핑몰에서 춤추는 새를 보았다.
2 우리 아버지의 취미는 바다에서 낚시하는 것이다.
3 우리는 몇 시간 동안이나 여행을 해왔지만 나는 아직 피곤하지 않다.
4 제프리는 수업에 있을 발표를 준비하고 있다.
5 우리 어머니는 요리하면서 텔레비전 보는 것을 좋아한다.

6 이 소설은 전국에서 수천 명에 의해 읽히고 있다.
7 나는 소희가 아리랑을 부르는 것을 처음 듣고 매우 감동했다.
8 북경까지는 긴 여행이 될 거야. 그러니까 침대 칸에 자리를 잡도록 하자.
9 탈의실은 옷을 사기 전에 입어 볼 수 있는 장소이다.
10 앤은 자유 시간이 있을 때 비디오 게임을 하는 것보다 자전거 타는 것을 더 좋아한다.

Unit 33 EXERCISES p. 174~175

1 his	2 him	3 her	4 her
5 our	6 you	7 Brandon's	8 my

해석

1 나는 그가 이곳을 떠나기를 원한다는 것을 이해할 수 없다.
2 너는 그가 너를 그렇게 많이 곤란하게 한 것을 용서해야 한다.
3 사실 나는 그녀가 자전거 여행을 간다는 생각이 마음에 들지 않는다.
4 그는 그녀가 그 대학에 입학하게 된 것이 기뻤다.
5 우리 할머니는 우리가 집안일을 돕는 것을 정말로 고마워하신다.
6 오늘 밤 우리 아이를 돌봐 주셔서 정말로 고맙습니다.
7 미국인들은 브랜든이 수영에서 금메달을 딴 것을 자랑스러워한다.
8 우리 아빠는 언어학이 실용적이라고 생각하지 않았기 때문에 내가 언어학을 공부하는 것에 반대했다.

1 helping	2 having developed
3 having robbed	4 having received
5 having promised	6 working
7 practicing	

해석

1 크리스는 친구가 시험에서 부정행위를 하는 것을 도왔다고 인정했다.
2 그들은 사업을 무척 빨리 성장시킨 것을 매우 자랑스러워한다.
3 그는 경찰 조사에서 은행을 턴 것을 인정했다.
4 그는 이번 학기에 전 과목 A를 받은 것을 자랑스러워했다.
5 나는 내가 오늘 밤 너와 영화보기로 약속했던 것을 기억하지 못한다.
6 나는 그와 같은 팀에서 일하게 되어 정말 신이 난다.
7 나는 연습을 많이하는 것이 내 미래의 성공으로 이끌 것이기 때문에 개의치 않는다.

1 your relaxing on the beach
2 her husband's working until late at night
3 Tom's having won the marathon
4 my staying at her house
5 his playing a mean trick
6 his son's attending college

해석

1 네가 해변에서 휴식을 취하고 있다고 상상해 봐.
2 앨리슨은 남편이 밤늦게까지 일 하는 것을 싫어한다.
3 나는 톰이 마라톤에서 승리한 것을 기억한다.
4 그녀는 내가 파리에 있는 동안 그녀의 집에서 머무르기를 고집했다.
5 켈리는 그가 자신에게 짓궂은 장난을 한 것에 화가 났다.
6 에릭은 아들이 전액 장학금을 받고 대학에 다니는 것을 자랑스러워한다.

1 she was a musician
2 she was unable to read
3 he was employed at a world-renowned company
4 her son played computer games too much
5 he felt jealous of Garry's looks and popularity
6 he had used inappropriate language before
7 he had copied someone else's writing from the Internet

해석

1 그는 그녀가 음악가임을 확신했다.
2 그녀는 읽지 못한다는 것이 부끄러웠다.
3 그는 세계적으로 유명한 회사에 취업해서 기뻤다.
4 그녀는 아들이 컴퓨터 게임을 너무 많이 하는 것이 걱정스러웠다.
5 제이크는 개리의 외모와 인기에 질투를 느낌을 인정했다.
6 그는 전에 부적절한 언어를 사용했음을 인정했다.
7 그는 인터넷에서 다른 사람의 글을 베낀 것을 부인했다.

Unit 34 EXERCISES p. 178~179

1 talking, to talk	2 wasting, to waste
3 holding	4 to spend
5 to live	6 playing
7 to appreciate	8 pouring, to pour
9 crying	

해석

1 그녀는 잠시 후에 말도 안 되는 소리를 하기 시작했다.
2 나는 쓸데없는 것에 시간과 돈을 낭비하는 것을 싫어한다.
3 패리스 힐튼은 서울에서 콘서트를 개최하려고 생각했다.
4 시빌과 제이슨은 신혼여행을 하와이에서 보내기로 계획을 세웠다.
5 코끼리 거북이는 음식이나 물 없이도 매우 오랜 시간을 살 수 있는 것처럼 보인다.
6 나탈리는 키가 너무 작아서 농구를 하는 것을 포기해야 했다.
7 가족에게 감사하는 것을 배우는 것은 우리 모두가 배워야 할 교훈이다.
8 아침 일찍부터 비가 내리기 시작해서 오후 내내 퍼부었다.
9 임 선생님, 오늘 우리 아기를 선생님께 데려가도 될까요? 계속 울기만 하는데 왜 그런지 모르겠어요.

1 to help	2 writing	3 getting
4 brushing	5 to install	6 to be
7 to move	8 changing	9 having

해석

1 딘이 우리가 시험 공부하는 것을 도와주겠다고 제안했다.
2 내가 열대 우림에 관한 작문을 끝내려면 너의 도움이 필요하다.
3 그녀와 나는 가능한 오랫동안 승차하는 것을 미루었다.

4 치과 의사는 내게 식사 후에 매번 이를 닦아야 한다고 강조했다.
5 그들은 사고 후에 안전장치를 설치하겠다고 약속했다.
6 그녀는 자신이 주문한 음식이 별로였지만 즐기는 척을 했다.
7 미오는 유명한 코치와 함께 일하려고 미국으로 가기로 결정했다.
8 채널을 좀 돌려줄 수 있겠니? 내가 가장 좋아하는 드라마가 8시에 하거든.
9 그는 지금까지 휴대 전화를 훔친 것을 부인했지만 경찰은 이미 그의 유죄를 입증할 증거를 가지고 있었다.

C

1 to play	2 going	3 eating
4 to do	5 to move	6 reducing
7 to rescue		

해석

1 그녀는 어렸을 때 피아노 치는 법을 배웠다.
2 그들은 악천후로 캠핑 가는 것을 연기했다.
3 켈리는 건강을 유지하려고 너무 많은 고기를 먹는 것을 피한다.
4 제이슨은 실제로는 인터넷 서핑을 하면서 숙제를 하는 척했다.
5 우리 선생님은 그렇게 화창한 날이었는데도 야외에서 수업하는 것을 거절했다.
6 정부는 지구 온난화를 막기 위해 탄소 배출을 줄이는 것을 고려해야 한다.
7 소방관들은 화재가 난 아파트 건물에서 주민들을 겨우 구해냈다.

D

1	① taking	② to reduce
2	① buying	② to take
3	① to buy	② eating
4	① to buy	② leaving
5	① becoming	② to inform

해석

1 ① 나는 찬물로 샤워해 보았지만, 여전히 너무 더웠다.
② 우리는 소음 공해를 감소시키려고 노력해야 한다.
2 ① 나는 파티에 쓸 풍선을 산 것은 기억하는데, 지금 어디에 있는지 찾을 수가 없다.
② 오븐에서 로스트(구운 고기)를 꺼내야 한다는 걸 기억해. 만약 꺼내지 않으면 로스트가 타버릴 거야.
3 ① 그녀는 늦었지만, 커피를 사려고 멈췄다.
② 의사는 튀긴 음식이 나에게 좋지 않기 때문에 그것을 먹지 말아야 한다고 말했다.
4 ① 우리 아버지가 내 생일 선물로 자전거 사 주기로 한 것을 잊어버렸다. 그래서 내년에 사 주겠다고 약속했다.
② 내 여동생은 휴대 전화를 집에 놓고 왔다는 걸 잊어버렸다. 그래서 그녀는 모든 곳을 찾아보고 있다.
5 ① 릭은 반장이 되는 걸 몹시 기대했었지만, 지금은 반장이 된 걸 후회하고 있다.
② 윌은 예일 대학에서 편지를 받았다. 편지에는 '당신의 입학이 허가되지 않았다는 소식을 알리게 되어 유감입니다.'라고 쓰여 있었다.

Unit 35 EXERCISES

p. 181

1 to paying	2 mowing	3 watching
4 to reading	5 to spending	

해석

1 많은 사람이 더 많은 세금을 내는 데 반대한다.
2 마이클은 정원에서 잔디를 깎느라 바쁘다.
3 나는 그 영화가 볼만한 가치가 있다고 생각한다. 그것은 대공황 시절의 삶을 생생하게 묘사한다.
4 톰은 여행하면서 음악을 듣는 데 휴대 전화를 사용한다. 아마 그 대신 책을 읽으면서 시간을 보내는 데 익숙해진다면 더 좋을 것이다.
5 우리 가족 모두 7월에 해변에서 일주일을 보낼 것을 고대한다. 특히 올해는 우리 아빠가 휴가 동안 쉬는 것을 간절히 바라신다.

B

1 preparing	2 building	3 wearing
4 receiving	5 staying, hiking	

해석

1 우리 엄마는 저녁 식사를 준비하느라 바쁘셨다. 나는 상 차리는 것을 도와드렸다.
2 비버는 큰 나무를 베어 넘겨서 그것으로 댐을 만드는 것을 잘한다.
3 수는 안경을 쓰는 데 익숙하지 않다. 그녀는 때때로 안경을 잃어버린다.
4 많은 유명 인사들이 많은 관심을 받는 것에 익숙해지는 데 어려움을 겪고 있다.
5 나는 날씨가 이렇게 좋을 때 집안에 있고 싶지 않아. 하이킹하러 가는 게 어때?

C

1 spend, much, time, reading
2 don't, feel, like, having
3 couldn't, help, laughing
4 looking, forward, to, hearing

REVIEW

p. 182~183

1 playing	2 skipping	3 to buy
4 starting	5 to notice	6 playing
7 living	8 put, to put	9 going
10 watching	11 thinking	12 to renegotiate

해설/해석

1 prefer는 동명사와 to부정사 모두 목적어로 취하지만, prefer A to B(B보다 A를 선호하다)의 구문에서는 A와 B의 형태를 일치시켜야 하므로 playing이 적절
은지는 테니스를 치는 것보다 요가하는 것을 선호한다.
2 keep은 동명사를 목적어로 취하는 동사
나는 왜 클레어가 계속 수업을 빠지는지 궁금하다.

3 hope는 to부정사를 목적어로 취하는 동사
사만다는 곧 새 아파트를 사기를 바란다.

4 admit는 동명사를 목적어로 취하는 동사
소년들 중 한 명이 결국 불을 냈다는 것을 인정했다.

5 pretend는 to부정사를 목적어로 취하는 동사
웬디는 '주차 금지' 표지판을 보지 못한 척했다.

6 give up은 동명사를 목적어로 취하는 동사
마크는 무릎을 다쳤을 때 농구 경기하는 것을 포기했다.

7 go on은 동명사를 목적어로 취하는 동사
재민이는 미란다에게 그녀 없이는 계속 살아갈 수 없다고 말했다.

8 help는 to부정사와 동사원형을 목적어로 취하는 동사
우리 형은 내가 모형 배를 조립하는 것을 도와주겠다고 약속했다.

9 suggest는 동명사를 목적어로 취하는 동사
재훈이는 수학 시험공부를 하러 도서관에 가자고 제안했다.

10 enjoy는 동명사를 목적어로 취하는 동사
피터는 텔레비전으로 영국 프리미어 리그 축구를 보는 것을 즐긴다.

11 can't help -ing는 '~하지 않을 수 없다'는 의미의 관용표현
나는 월드컵 시즌 동안 축구에 대해 생각하지 않을 수 없었다.

12 agree는 to부정사를 목적어로 취하는 동사
대통령은 며칠간의 항의 끝에 그 조약을 재협상하는 데 동의했다.

B

1	having	2	to reduce
3	to expand	4	volunteering
5	to eating	6	growing[to grow]
7	to seeing	8	behaving
9	taking	10	going
11	is	12	to search

해설/해석

1 '~로 유명하다'는 be well known for, 전치사(for) 뒤에는 명사나 동명사가 와야 하므로 having이 적절
유튜브는 재미있는 비디오를 보유한 것으로 잘 알려져 있다.

2 need는 to부정사를 목적어로 취하므로 to reduce가 적절
우리는 화석 연료에 대한 의존도를 줄일 필요가 있다.

3 hope는 to부정사를 목적어로 취하는 동사이므로 to expand가 적절
미국 IT 회사는 한국으로 진출하기를 희망한다.

4 「be worth+-ing」 ~할 가치가 있다
여가 시간에 친구들과 자원봉사를 하는 것은 가치가 있다.

5 get used to(~하는 데 익숙해지다)에서 to는 전치사로 뒤에 명사나 동명사가 와야 함
바바라는 처음에 김치를 좋아하지 않았지만 그것을 먹는 데 익숙해졌다.

6 start는 to부정사와 동명사 둘 다 목적어로 취하는 동사
그 한국 가수는 중국에서 인기가 높아지기 시작했다.

7 「look forward to+-ing」 ~하기를 고대하다
그녀는 부산에서 브라이언의 다음 콘서트를 관람할 것을 고대하고 있다.

8 「regret+to부정사」 ~하게 되어 유감이다, 「regret+-ing」 ~한 것을 후회하다
스미스 씨는 어렸을 때 불량스럽게 행동했던 것을 후회한다.

9 「try+to부정사」는 '~하려고 노력하다', 「try+-ing」는 '~을 해보다'라는 의미이다. 머리가 아프니 아스피린을 한번 먹어 보는 것이 어떤지 제안하고 있으므로 taking이 적절
두통이 있으면 아스피린을 먹어 보는 게 어때?

10 「remember+-ing」는 '~한 것을 기억하다'라는 의미이며, 「remember+to부정사」는 '(앞으로) ~해야 하는 것을 기억하다'라는 의미로 going이 적절
엘리자베스는 어렸을 때 디즈니랜드에 갔던 것을 기억했다.

11 동명사 주어는 단수 취급
약속을 지키는 것은 친구가 되는 데 매우 중요한 부분이다.

12 allow는 목적어(people)가 하는 행동인 목적격보어로 to부정사를 취하는 동사
인터넷 검색 엔진은 사람들이 흥미 있는 정보를 찾도록 해준다.

C

1	to go	2	eating out	3	drinking
4	to drop by	5	eating	6	to go
7	promising				

해설/해석

1 intend는 목적어로 to부정사를 취하는 동사
A: 휴가 때 어디에 가고 싶니?
B: 나는 라스베이거스에 갈 생각이었어.

2 「feel like -ing」 ~하고 싶다
A: 오늘 나는 외식하고 싶지 않아.
B: 그렇다면, 음식을 배달시키는 게 어때?

3 「give up -ing」 ~하는 것을 포기하다
A: 나는 살을 빼기 위해 탄산음료 마시는 것을 끊었어.
B: 정말? 그게 얼마나 갈지 궁금하다.

4 「forget+to+동사원형」은 '~해야 할 것을 잊다', 「forget+-ing」는 '~했던 것을 잊다'라는 의미, 집에 오는 길에 식료품 가게에 들러야 하는 것을 잊었으므로 to drop by가 적절
A: 엄마, 시리얼하고 우유 좀 사왔어요?
B: 미안해, 집에 오는 길에 식료품점에 들르는 것을 깜빡했어.

5 「stop+-ing」는 '~하는 것을 그만두다'라는 의미, 「stop+to부정사」는 '~하기 위해 멈추다'라는 의미, 여기서는 '단 것을 그만 먹다'라는 의미이므로 eating이 적절
A: 너는 단 것을 그만 먹어야 해. 건강에 안 좋아.
B: 알아, 하지만 나도 어쩔 수 없어.

6 plan은 to부정사를 목적어로 취하는 동사
A: 왜 이렇게 일찍 일어났어?
B: 제프와 내가 오늘 낚시를 가기로 했거든. 7시에 그를 만날 거야.

7 「remember+to부정사」는 '~할 것을 기억하다'라는 의미, 「remember+-ing」는 '~했던 것을 기억하다'라는 의미, 이미 약속했던 사실을 기억하느냐는 의미이므로 promising이 적절
A: 제시카, 설거지하는 것을 도와주겠다고 약속한 것 기억 안 나니?
B: 하지만 아빠, 저는 그냥 나가서 자전거를 타고 싶어요.

1 loves, to, cook

2 is, famous, for, developing
3 continue, to, work
4 regretted, watching, TV
5 is, accustomed, to, doing
6 decided, to, go, started, to, save

REVIEW PLUS

p. 184

1 ② 2 ①

해설/해석

1 ② look forward to(~하기를 고대하다)에서 to는 전치사로 뒤에 명사나 동명사가 와야 하므로 visiting이 적절
① 베티는 이번 주말에 외출하는 것을 기대하고 있다.
② 수진이는 할머니를 방문하기를 고대한다.
③ 데비가 그의 결혼식에 그 파란색 드레스를 입겠다고 고집을 부린다.
④ 윤지가 휴가 동안 해변에 갈 것을 제안한다.
⑤ 현진이는 군대에 가는 것을 졸업 후로 미루었다.

2 ① deny는 동명사를 목적어로 취하는 동사. 시험에서 부정행위를 한 것이 그것을 부인하는 시점보다 먼저 있었던 일이므로 완료형 동명사인 having cheated가 적절
① 그는 시험에서 부정행위를 한 것을 부인한다.
② 질은 남자 친구와 영화를 볼 것을 기대한다.
③ 재민이는 화장실에 갈 수 있게 교실에서 나가게 해달라고 부탁했다.
④ 윌리엄은 학교 팀을 위해 농구 경기하는 것을 의논했다.
⑤ 해리는 아버지가 집에 도착하시기 전에 세차하는 것을 끝냈다.

②

해설/해석

② '숙제를 도와주겠다고 약속했다'는 의미가 되어야 하므로 「help(+to)+동사원형」이 된다. 그러므로 (to) do가 적절
① A: 발레 보러 가는 것을 즐기는 편이니?
B: 응. 그리고 이번 주말에 '호두까기 인형' 공연이 있다고 들었어.
② A: 엄마, 토요일에 샐리와 쇼핑몰에 가도 되나요?
B: 미안하지만, 너는 네 동생이 과학 숙제하는 것을 도와주겠다고 약속했잖니.
③ A: 이번 주말에 나와 '스파이더맨' 보러 갈래?
B: 나는 로맨틱 코미디 보는 걸 더 좋아해. '러브 액추얼리'를 보러 가는 건 어때?
④ A: 이번 주말에 무엇을 할 계획이니?
B: 나와 함께 경기할 사람이 있으면 테니스 치기를 원해.
⑤ A: 오늘은 아름답고 화창한 날이 될 거야. 무엇을 하고 싶니?
B: 나는 리버사이드 파크에 가고 싶어.

⑤

해설/해석

⑤ suggest는 동명사를 목적어로 취하는 동사이므로 trying이 적절
스키와 같은 겨울 스포츠는 현대 생활의 스트레스를 줄이는 데 좋다. 위슬러는 캐나다 브리티시 컬럼비아의 서해안에 있는 곳이고, 놀랄만한 풍경을 지녔다. 많은 방문객이 모든 형태의 겨울 스포츠를 즐기려고 거기에 온다. 도보 여행이든, 스키든, 자연의 소리에 귀를 기울이든, 단순히 휴식을 취하든지 간에, 모든 사람을 위한 특별한 것이 있다. 따뜻하게 있는 것을 선호하는 방문객을 위해 멋진 쇼핑 구역과 멋진 식당 같은 실내 활동을 할 수 있는 장소도 있다. 겨울 휴가를 가질 생각이라면 북미에서 최고의 스키 휴양지인 위슬러에서 보내기를 제안한다.

PART 10

Unit 36 EXERCISES

p. 188~189

1 is written
2 painted
3 was not invented
4 taught
5 were served
6 be cleaned up
7 was designed
8 organized

해석

1 주소가 봉투 뒷면에 쓰여 있다.
2 파블로 피카소는 1951년에 '한국에서의 학살'을 그렸다.
3 현대식 칫솔은 1938년이 되어서야 발명되었다.
4 이 선생님은 2014년에 그 지역 고등학교에서 과학을 가르치셨다.
5 환영회에서 여러 가지 많은 종류의 이국적인 음식이 제공되었다.
6 엄마가 집에 와서 보기 전에 이 난장판은 치워져야 한다.
7 그 회사의 광고 캠페인은 한 대학교 1학년생에 의해 고안되었다.
8 교수님이 실력에 따라 영어 말하기 수업을 편성했다.

1 The package wasn't mailed by Junsu.
2 A lot of money for charity was raised by Brian.
3 Egypt was conquered by the Ottoman Empire
4 Minji is tutored by Jenny's sister
5 Was Julia invited to the housewarming party by Ryan?
6 The Gulf Coast of the USA was devastated by Hurricane Katrina
7 Many of the world's most beloved symphonies were composed by Mozart.
8 Was the product I ordered last night delivered (by them)?

해석

1 준수는 소포를 부치지 않았다.
2 브라이언은 자선 단체를 위해 많은 돈을 모았다.
3 오스만 제국은 1517년에 이집트를 정복했다.
4 제니의 언니가 민지에게 수학과 과학 개인 교습을 해준다.
5 라이언이 줄리아를 집들이에 초대했니?
6 허리케인 카트리나가 2005년에 미국의 걸프 만을 황폐화시켰다.
7 모차르트는 세계적으로 가장 사랑받는 교향곡 중 다수를 작곡했다.
8 그들이 내가 지난밤에 주문한 상품을 배달했니?

1 was, invited　　2 be, delayed
3 was, discovered　　4 has, exhibited
5 be, sent　　6 have, attended

해석

1 나는 지난 토요일에 브렌다의 생일 파티에 초대받았다.
2 그날 비가 오지 않는다면 그 행사는 연기되지 않을 것이다.
3 페니실린은 1920년대에 알렉산더 플레밍에 의해 발견되었다.
4 그 박물관은 5월 1일부터 피카소의 스케치들을 전시해왔다.
5 그 소포는 가능한 한 빨리 그에게 보내져야 한다.
6 지금까지 수백 명의 사람들이 그 영화배우의 장례식에 참석했다.

D

1 was, found
2 is, being, repaired, by
3 are, going, to, be, taught
4 must, be, completed

1 is being treated　　2 was bitten, separated
3 was independently discovered, published

해석

1 나의 가장 친한 친구 레오가 병원에 입원해 있다. 그는 희귀하지만 치료가 가능한 심장병으로 치료받고 있다.
2 2003년 10월 3일에 로이 혼은 자신이 훈련하던 호랑이에 의해 목을 물렸다. 하지만 다행히도 팀원들이 혼을 호랑이로부터 떼어냈고 그를 병원으로 급히 데려갔다.
3 미적분학은 동시대의 두 명의 뛰어난 수학자인 아이작 뉴턴과 고트프리트 라이프니츠에 의해 독자적으로 발견되었다. 하지만 그 발견을 처음으로 발표한 사람은 라이프니츠였다.

Unit 37 EXERCISES

p. 192~193

1 My trip to Jejudo was spoiled by bad weather.
2 ×
3 ×
4 All of the windows in my room were closed (by someone).
5 ×
6 Toyota Motor Corporation was established in 1937 by Kiichiro Toyoda.
7 The meeting has been rescheduled for tomorrow afternoon by the manager.

해석

1 악천후가 내 제주도 여행을 망쳤다.
2 그 남자는 재빨리 군중 속으로 사라졌다.
3 관광 산업이 말레이시아에서 호황을 이루고 있다.
4 누군가 내 방 창문을 모두 닫았다.
5 그 회사는 복잡한 경영 구조를 가지고 있다.
6 키치로 도요타는 1937년에 도요타 자동차 회사를 설립했다.
7 부장이 내일 오후 회의 일정을 변경했다.

1 was told the good news by Jake, was told to me by Jake
2 was bought for me by my tutor
3 was sent to Inhye by Sally
4 was given some advice about dating by Rachel, was given to Mark by Rachel
5 were shown the way to the ancient ruins by the tour guide, was shown to us by the tour guide

해석

1 제이크가 나에게 좋은 소식을 말해 주었다.
2 과외 선생님이 나에게 공책을 사 주었다.
3 샐리가 인혜에게 바티칸에서 엽서를 보냈다.
4 레이첼이 마크에게 데이트에 관한 몇 가지 조언을 해주었다.
5 관광가이드는 우리에게 고대 유적으로 가는 길을 알려주었다.

1 Diana was seen playing basketball by her father.
2 The new invention was called a miracle (by everyone).
3 William was elected the new chairman through the vote (by them).
4 I was told to have breakfast (by my mother) before I went to school.
5 Rebecca's hair was washed clean in the shower (by Rebecca) after the food fight.
6 Eunhye was heard to recite a touching poem at her sister's wedding (by us).

해석

1 다이애나의 아버지는 그녀가 농구하는 것을 보았다.
2 모든 사람이 그 새로운 발명을 기적이라 불렀다.
3 그들은 투표를 통해 윌리엄을 새로운 의장으로 선출했다.
4 우리 어머니는 내게 학교에 가기 전에 아침을 먹으라고 말했다.
5 레베카는 음식 던지는 놀이를 한 후에 샤워하면서 머리를 깨끗하게 감았다.
6 우리는 은혜가 언니의 결혼식에서 감동적인 시를 암송하는 것을 들었다.

1 ① cry　　② to cry
2 ① to explain　　② to explain
3 ① shooting　　② shooting
4 ① wear　　② to wear
5 ① to leave　　② to leave
6 ① breaking　　② breaking
7 ① play　　② to play

해석

1 ① 나는 아기가 밤새 우는 소리를 들었다.
② 밤새 아기의 우는 소리가 들렸다.
2 ① 그들은 교수님에게 그 이론을 설명해 달라고 부탁했다.

② 교수는 그 이론을 설명해 달라고 요청받았다.
3 ① 우리 모두 밤하늘을 가로질러 별이 떨어지는 것을 보았다.
② 별이 밤하늘을 가로질러 떨어지는 것이 보였다.
4 ① 그 남학생 사교 클럽은 새 구성원들에게 바보 같은 의상을 입도록 했다.
② 새 멤버들은 남학생 사교 클럽에 의해서 바보 같은 의상을 입게 되었다.
5 ① 우리 선생님은 내가 아파서 집에 가도록 허락해 주었다.
② 나는 아파서 집에 가도록 허락받았다.
6 ① 누군가 마스크를 쓴 두 남자가 집에 침입하는 것을 목격했다.
② 마스크를 쓴 두 남자가 집에 침입하는 것이 목격되었다.
7 ① 선생님은 학생들이 운동장에서 축구하는 것을 보았다.
② 학생들이 운동장에서 축구를 하는 것이 선생님에게 목격되었다.

Unit 38 EXERCISES

p. 196~197

1 to	2 off	3 for	4 with
5 at	6 with	7 to	8 with
9 at	10 with	11 from	12 out

해석

1 존의 암은 흡연과 관계가 있다.
2 회의는 CEO가 돌아올 때까지 연기될 것이다.
3 너는 다가오는 허리케인을 위해 준비가 되어 있어야 한다.
4 우리는 괌의 호텔방에 매우 만족했다.
5 나는 런던에 있는 짐의 아파트 규모에 놀랐다.
6 네가 가진 것에 만족한다면 너는 행복할 것이다.
7 그녀는 조슈아라는 호주 남자와 결혼했다.
8 나는 B+를 받고 약간 실망했다. 나는 A를 기대하고 있었다.
9 수희의 친구들은 그녀가 약혼을 했다는 소식을 듣고 놀랐다.
10 내가 오늘 아침 일어났을 때 거리는 눈으로 덮여 있었다.
11 잠을 좀 자는 게 어때? 장시간 비행에 피곤할 텐데.
12 쇼핑몰의 전단지가 행인에게 배포되고 있다.

1 will be taken care of by me
2 were passed out silently by the teacher
3 cannot be put off forever (by us)
4 was almost run over by a bicycle courier
5 is going to be dealt with in the documentary (by them)
6 will be carried out for two hours through computers (by them)
7 was taken away by his mother

해석

1 내가 오늘 밤 너의 개를 돌봐줄 것이다.
2 선생님은 조용히 시험지를 나눠주셨다.
3 불행히도, 우리는 집안일을 영원히 미룰 수 없다.
4 자전거 배달원은 오늘 시내에서 내 애완동물을 거의 칠 뻔했다.
5 그들은 다큐멘터리에서 아이작 뉴턴의 삶을 다룰 것이다.
6 그들은 컴퓨터로 두 시간 동안 말하기 시험을 실시할 것이다.
7 그의 엄마는 그가 헬멧을 쓰지 않고 오토바이를 타는 것을 본 뒤에 그의 오토바이를 치워버렸다.

1 with 2 at 3 of 4 to 5 in

해석

1 모든 손님들은 좋은 서비스를 받아야 한다.
흡연은 폐암과 관련이 있다.
2 나는 조카의 지식에 놀랐다.
그녀는 과체중으로 학교에서 웃음거리가 되었다고 말했다.
3 이 반찬통은 유리로 만들어져서 약간 무겁다.
그가 어렸을 때, 그는 할머니에 의해 돌봐졌다.
4 그 감독은 유명해서 그의 영화는 많은 사람들에게 알려져 있다.
그녀는 전공이 그 일자리와 관련이 없어서 그 일을 해야 할지 망설여졌다.
5 그녀는 심각한 논쟁에 휘말렸음을 깨달았다.
나는 두 달 동안 이 프로젝트에 참여했지만 진전이 있는 것 같지 않다.

1 was taken away by
2 were crowded with
3 was filled with
4 were shocked at
5 been put off
6 be passed out
7 be prepared for
8 been involved in, be punished

REVIEW

p. 198~199

1 be cut	2 was eaten
3 is being polished	4 resemble
5 described	6 are collected
7 is preparing	8 be tested
9 organizing	10 being driven
11 to attack	12 will be released

해설/해석

1 머리카락이 그의 어머니에 의해 잘리는 것이므로 수동
그의 머리카락은 어머니에 의해 잘리게 될 거예요.
2 음식이 축구 선수들에 의해 먹히는 것이므로 수동
많은 음식은 축구팀에 의해 섭취되었다.
3 차가 아빠에 의해 닦이는 것이므로 수동
그 차는 아버지에 의해 닦이고 있다.
4 아이들이 그들의 부모를 닮는 것이므로 능동
아이들은 부모를 닮는다.
5 힐튼이 상황을 설명한 것이므로 능동
힐튼이 나에게 상황을 설명해 주었다.
6 우표와 동전이 수집되는 것이므로 수동
희귀한 우표와 동전이 존에 의해 수집된다.
7 엄마가 코코아를 준비하는 것이므로 능동
엄마는 따뜻한 코코아 한 잔을 준비하고 있다.

8 우리의 영어가 테스트되는 것이므로 수동
선생님이 다음 주에 영어 시험을 볼까?

9 그녀가 귀국 행진을 준비하는 것이므로 능동
그녀가 귀국 행진을 준비하고 있나요?

10 차가 운전되는 것이므로 수동
그 차는 사고 당시에 누구에 의해 운전되고 있었나요?

11 지각동사의 경우 목적격보어가 동사원형일 때 수동태 변환 시 to 부정사를 씀
코끼리가 관객 여러 사람을 공격하는 것이 목격되었다.

12 정치범들이 풀려나게 되는 것이므로 수동
며칠 안에 많은 정치범이 석방될 것이다.

Ⓑ

1 Our class, these trees
2 The plate, the boy
3 These clothes, Victoria
4 The house key, Nicole
5 The mixture, Tim
6 Jane, her mother
7 The man, that luxurious ship
8 Candidates, the application form
9 Breakfast, the waiter
10 The money, Nicky
11 Nice meals, our top chefs
12 Paintings by Edgar Degas, the art museum

해설/해석

1 능동태 문장: 심는 행위를 한 주체인 our class가 주어 자리에, these trees는 동사 뒤 목적어 자리에 위치
우리 학급이 이 나무들을 심었다.

2 수동태 문장: 전달되는 것은 접시이므로 the plate가 주어 자리에, to 뒤에 간접목적어(받는 사람)인 the boy가 위치
접시가 그 소년에게 건네졌다.

3 수동태 문장: 입혀지는 것은 옷이므로 these clothes가 주어 자리에, 입는 행동을 한 행위자인 Victoria는 by 뒤에 위치
이 옷은 빅토리아가 입었었다.

4 수동태 문장: 분실 당한 것은 열쇠이므로 the house key가 주어 자리에, 행위자인 Nicole은 by 뒤에 위치
집 열쇠가 니콜에 의해 분실되었다.

5 수동태 문장: 오븐 안에 넣어진 것은 the mixture이므로 주어 자리에 위치하고, 넣은 행동을 한 행위자 Tim은 by 뒤에 위치
그 혼합물은 팀에 의해 오븐에 넣어졌다.

6 수동태 문장: 혼나게 된 사람인 Jane이 주어 자리에, 혼을 낸 행위자인 her mother는 by 뒤에 위치
제인은 엄마에게 혼나고 있었다.

7 능동태 문장: 사지 않은 행위의 주체인 the man이 주어 자리에, that luxurious ship이 목적어 자리에 위치
그 남자는 저 호화스러운 배를 사지 않았다.

8 능동태 문장: 지원서를 작성하는 행동을 하는 주체인 candidates가 주어 자리에, the application form이 목적어 자리에 위치
지원자들은 이 지원서를 작성해야 한다.

9 수동태 문장: 제공되는 것인 breakfast가 주어 자리에, 제공하는 행동을 하는 행위자 the waiter는 by 뒤에 위치
아침 식사는 오전 7시에 웨이터에 의해 제공될 것이다.

10 수동태 문장: 송금되는 것인 the money가 주어 자리에, 송금하는 행동을 하는 행위자 Nicky는 by 뒤에 위치
돈은 니키에 의해 내 은행 계좌로 송금되었다.

11 수동태 문장: 준비되는 것인 Nice meals가 주어 자리에, 준비하는 행위를 하는 행위자인 our top chefs는 by 뒤에 위치
결혼식을 위한 훌륭한 식사가 우리 최고 요리사들에 의해 준비되고 있다.

12 수동태 문장: 전시되는 것인 Paintings by Edgar Degas가 주어 자리에, 전시되는 장소인 the art museum이 in 뒤에 위치
에드가 드가의 그림들이 미술관에 전시될 것이다.

Ⓒ

1 생략할 수 없음　　2 (by the bellhop)
3 (by someone)　　4 (by the police officer)
5 생략할 수 없음　　6 (by people)

해설/해석

1 책을 쓴 무라카미 하루키는 특정한 행위자로 밝힐 필요가 있으므로 생략할 수 없음
그 책은 무라카미 하루키에 의해 쓰였다.

2 호텔에서 짐을 옮기는 것은 누구인지 밝히지 않더라도 호텔 벨보이의 행동인지 알 수 있으므로 생략 가능
우리 짐이 방으로 옮겨지고 있나요?

3 도둑질한 사람이 누구인지 알 수 없으므로 생략 가능
그가 가장 좋아하는 코트는 어젯밤에 도둑맞았다.

4 과속을 단속하는 사람이 경찰임을 짐작할 수 있으므로 생략 가능
그 남자는 과속으로 붙잡혔다.

5 어젯밤의 NBA 결승전을 매우 많은 사람들이 보았다는 것을 밝히는 것이므로 생략할 수 없음
NBA 결승전은 어젯밤 수백만 명의 사람들에 의해 시청되었다.

6 불특정 다수의 일반인이 숲을 파괴하고 있는 것이므로 생략 가능
넓은 숲 지역이 매일 파괴되고 있다.

Ⓓ

1 ① find　　② be found
2 ① are eaten　　② made
3 ① is cleaned　　② clean
4 ① have　　② are mostly pollinated
5 ① was invented　　② contains
6 ① was known　　② know

해설/해석

1 ① 내가 잃어버린 귀걸이를 찾는 것이므로 능동 ② 귀걸이가 찾아지는 것이므로 수동
① 나는 내가 잃어버린 귀걸이를 찾을 수 없을 것 같다.
② 나는 잃어버린 귀걸이가 찾아질지 의문이다.

2 ① 도넛은 (사람들에 의해) 먹히는 것이므로 수동 ② 엄마가 도넛을 만드는 것이므로 능동
① 매일 전 세계에서 수백만 개의 도넛이 소비된다.
② 우리 엄마가 파티를 위해 도넛을 만들었다.

3 ① 환경미화원에 의해 거리가 청소되는 것이므로 수동 ② 아이들이 방을 청소하는 것이므로 능동
① 거리가 매일 환경미화원에 의해 청소된다.
② 아이들이 매일 방을 청소한다.

4 ① 벌이 후각을 가지고 있는 것이므로 능동 ② 곡식이 벌들에 의해 수정되는 것이므로 수동
① 벌은 훌륭한 후각을 가지고 있다.
② 곡식은 대부분 벌들에 의해 수분이 된다.

5 ① 초콜릿이 다니엘 피터에 의해 발명되었으므로 수동 ② 초콜릿이 카페인을 포함하므로 능동
① 밀크 초콜릿은 다니엘 피터에 의해 발명되었다.
② 초콜릿 1온스는 20mg의 카페인을 포함한다.

6 ① 줄리어스 시저가 (다른 사람들에게) 알려진 것이므로 수동 ② 내가 알고 있는 것이므로 능동
① 줄리어스 시저는 수영을 잘한 것으로 알려졌다.
② 나는 줄리어스 시저가 로마의 군사적, 정치적 지도자였다는 것을 안다.

1	to	2	at	3	in	4	with
5	in	6	in	7	with		

해설/해석

1 be related to: ~에 관련되다
우리는 사돈지간이다.

2 be amazed at: ~에 놀라다
짐은 그의 새 학생들의 재능에 놀랐다.

3 be located in: ~에 위치하다
우리의 새 본사는 도시의 중심부에 자리 잡고 있다.

4 be crowded with: ~로 붐비다
시내에 있는 쇼핑몰은 휴일 쇼핑객으로 붐볐다.

5 be interested in: ~에 관심 있다
모든 사람은 그의 인생에 대해 더 많이 아는 데 관심이 있었다.

6 be engaged in: ~에 종사하다
우리 부모님은 평생 동안 농업에 종사해 오셨다.

7 be pleased with: ~에 기뻐하다
나는 A+를 받지는 못했지만 시험 결과에 기쁘다.

REVIEW PLUS

p. 200

③

해설/해석

1 ③ 서류는 인쇄되는 것이므로 printed가 아니라 been printed가 적절
① CD 가게는 문을 닫지 않았다.
② 작은 노란색 물고기들이 빠르게 헤엄쳤다.
③ 당신의 서류가 인쇄되었다.
④ 칠판이 지워졌다.
⑤ 그 강도는 체포되어 재판받을 것이다.

①

해설/해석

② 웨이터가 메뉴를 가져다 준 것이므로 been brought가 아니라 brought가 적절
③ 사람들이 경기장을 방문하는 것이므로 be visited가 아니라 visit이 적절
④ 카펫은 팔리는 것이므로 selling이 아니라 sold가 적절
⑤ 사람들이 사용하는 것이므로 are used가 아니라 use가 적절
① 너는 언제 그 새 규칙에 대해 들었니?
② 그 웨이터가 우리에게 메뉴를 가져다주었다.
③ 수백만 명의 사람들이 새 올림픽 경기장을 방문할 것이다.
④ 죄송합니다만 부인, 이 카펫은 이미 팔렸습니다.
⑤ 천 명 이상의 사람들이 매주 이 수영장을 사용한다.

have been scraped out, should be used, is going to thrill

해설/해석

(A) 씨앗은 등을 만들고 있는 사람에 의해 도려내지는 것이므로 수동 (B) 감자 깎는 칼은 호박 등을 만들고 있는 사람에 의해 사용되는 것이므로 수동 (C) 창작물이 이웃들을 놀라게 만드는 것이므로 능동

호박

등을 직접 만드는 것은 아주 쉬워요. 호박의 윗부분에 구멍을 내고 안의 내용물을 비우는 것으로 시작하세요. 일단 씨를 모두 긁어내고 나서 펠트펜을 이용해서 바깥쪽에 무서운 얼굴을 그리세요. 그런 다음 작은 부엌칼로 조심스럽게 얼굴 모양을 잘라내기 시작하세요. 어려운 부분에는 감자 깎는 칼이 사용됩니다. 마지막으로 안에 초를 넣으면 끝난 것입니다. 당신의 창작물이 과자를 얻으러 온 이웃 사람들을 깜짝 놀라게 할 것입니다.

③

해설/해석

③ 종이가 분리되어지는 것은 수동이므로 is kept가 적절
재활용은 환경을 보호하는 데 도움이 된다. 예를 들어, 재활용된 종이 50kg은 나무 한 그루를 살린다. 어떤 도시들은 시민들이 쓰레기를 분리하도록 훈련시켜 왔다. 사람들은 각각 다른 쓰레기봉투에 캔과 플라스틱 병을 넣어야 한다. 종이도 또한 분리되어진다. 플라스틱, 철, 종이는 재활용을 위해 특별한 재활용 센터로 보내진다.

Workbook

PART 1

UNIT 01

A **1** appeared **2** sets **3** will go **4** works **5** arrive **6** rained **7** was walking

B **1** 이익이 **2** 듣는다 **3** 충분할 **4** 지속된다 **5** 중요하다 **6** 작동하지

C **1** suddenly disappeared **2** is opposite the bank **3** stayed in the school **4** happened on Sunday morning **5** is recovering very quickly **6** live in the quiet countryside **7** will be in the main hall

D **1** Honesty doesn't pay all the time. **2** The remote control doesn't work properly. **3** was watching TV on the couch **4** Newborn babies sleep about 17 hours a day. **5** The sandwich shop opens at 8 every morning. **6** drives to work except on Mondays and Fridays

UNIT 02

A **1** rich **2** president **3** sour **4** empty **5** bitter **6** fresh

B **1** I hope your wish comes true. **2** We've run short of sugar and eggs. **3** She looked beautiful in the blue dress. **4** While I was cooking dinner, she fell asleep. **5** The singer seemed nervous on the stage. **6** Almost half of the tomatoes have gone bad. **7** As soon as she heard the news, she turned pale.

C **1** gets dark **2** appeared, intelligent **3** sounded familiar **4** become available **5** grew angry **6** stay open

D **1** it got very cold **2** appeared very rude **3** the students grew bored **4** fell asleep on the sofa **5** remained silent during the debate **6** are fighting to keep awake **7** became involved in several projects

UNIT 03

A **1** approached me **2** knows that **3** put his coat **4** explain that **5** need to reach **6** regret to say

B **1** steal anything **2** poured some hot coffee **3** laid her eyes **4** put his dirty clothes **5** wanted to know **6** sent a gift with a card

C **1** He didn't mention the problem. **2** She married Michael on Christmas Eve. **3** The houses in this town resemble one another. **4** The phone kept ringing, but she didn't answer it. **5** The salesperson explained how to use the machine. **6** I won't be at home because I have to attend a wedding. **7** Feel free to call me if you want to discuss the matter. **8** Don't forget to knock before you enter the professor's office.

D **1** buried her head in her hands **2** had better clean your room **3** introduced his girlfriend to his parents **4** opened a coffee shop, left school **5** I explained that I couldn't come on time **6** knows how to get there, follow her

UNIT 04

A **1** of **2** to **3** to **4** to **5** to **6** for **7** for **8** to **9** for **10** for

B **1** Will you show the painting to me? **2** She taught me how to cook spaghetti. **3** He needed to ask a few questions of her. **4** Will you get a glass of iced water for me? **5** The artist sold her paintings to an old lady. **6** Maria teaches basic cooking skills to young children. **7** My father makes simple dishes like sandwiches for us on weekends.

C **1** Mike handed some books to me at the station. **2** She made a black and white mobile for her newborn baby. **3** They showed a crew member their tickets at the gate. **4** You'd better tell him the truth before he gets more upset. **5** My grandmother sent gloves and a muffler to me this Christmas. **6** During the class, a few students asked some questions of the teacher.

D **1** order you room service **2** showed us her family photos **3** gave him another chance **4** cooked me a great dinner **5** made his wife a beautiful **6** made a beautiful wedding dress for

UNIT 05

A **1** interesting **2** Peter **3** feel **4** argue **5** to return **6** "Princess" **7** nice and warm-hearted **8** the leader **9** honest, responsible and reliable

B **1** show up **2** (to) adjust **3** to participate **4** to make **5** to take **6** grow

C **1** let you know **2** want you to make **3** kept me awake **4** had me water **5** made my brother help **6** kept the window open **7** want you to finish

D **1** We found the meeting useful. **2** kept him waiting in the coffee shop **3** persuaded him to choose law **4** felt the earth shake for about five minutes **5** call him a walking encyclopedia **6** allow me to sleep over at my friend's place

PART 2

UNIT 06

A **1** come **2** has **3** arrive **4** will like **5** rains **6** gets up **7** have **8** gets

B **1** don't blend **2** departs **3** gives **4** starts **5** buy

C **1** human body consists of water **2** My whole family gets together **3** you wear a life jacket **4** am not comfortable with **5** The train for Daejeon leaves **6** She volunteers at the school library
7 My parents receive medical checkups

D **1** Many people believe in God. **2** He reminds me of a famous actor. **3** after the meeting ends **4** I walk my dog three times a week. **5** if you fix my computer **6** The sun rises in the east and sets in the west. **7** My children are usually back home at 5 p.m.

UNIT 07

A **1** changed **2** scratched **3** became **4** goes, took **5** put, is

B **1** slipped, hurt **2** waited, showed up **3** broke out, was ended
4 was worried, wasn't able to reach **5** lived, moved into **6** fell off, are

C **1** forgot to call you **2** believed, moves **3** began, lasted **4** won the gold medal **5** said sorry, didn't let go **6** got into college, graduated **7** needed to do the shopping, the market closes

D **1** did you go on your summer vacation **2** was cold and snowed a lot last year **3** changed my mind at the last minute **4** many people lost their jobs **5** did too much exercise yesterday **6** composed his first work when he was 5 years old **7** did well in college, got a scholarship

UNIT 08

A **1** Will, buy **2** will give **3** will help **4** am not going to quit **5** will book **6** is going to pick up **7** are going to have

B **1** is going to get promoted **2** Are you coming **3** are you meeting **4** is going to snow

C **1** He is going to retire next year **2** The plane is about to take off **3** you doing tonight **4** The movie starts at 6:30 **5** Her plane arrives at 11 o'clock **6** I am going to watch a baseball game **7** not coming back, anything happens

D **1** It won't happen again. **2** She will be okay soon. **3** is getting married next March **4** Will you lend me some money? **5** I am not going out this weekend **6** I will cancel the meeting **7** is going to her high school reunion this Saturday

PART 3

UNIT 09

A **1** Do, travel **2** is studying **3** hates **4** are taking **5** Are, going **6** are having **7** is pouring **8** takes, feels **9** is staying

B **1** William resembles his father very much.
2 August is the hottest month of the year.
3 Tommy has breakfast at 7 every morning.
4 Where is Mr. Park? Is he meeting a client now? **5** This pizza tastes too greasy. I need some more soda. **6** We belong to a hiking club and meet once a month. **7** I think she knows why they had a fight last Wednesday.
8 I appreciate that you were not badly hurt in the accident. **9** I preter to study in the library

rather than at home.

C 1 sounds funny 2 am having a housewarming party 3 am having dinner 4 am taking an economics class 5 am thinking of changing 6 is, forgetting 7 always has

D 1 am working on the night shift 2 are having hamburgers after school 3 is weighing a piece of meat now 4 envies girls with long blonde hair 5 am taking my first dance sports lesson 6 usually spends most of the time in church 7 are coming to my house tomorrow, am cleaning up

UNIT 10

A 1 was watching 2 was walking 3 was helping 4 was sleeping 5 were arguing 6 was snowboarding

B 1 was taking a shower, made 2 was working, went off 3 was walking, ran into

C 1 had a cramp, she was, swimming 2 was walking, began 3 cut her finger while she was chopping carrots 4 was studying, last night 5 At this time last year, was teaching English 6 was sleeping when I got home late yesterday 7 was listening to, when her mother called her

D 1 was driving when his friend called him 2 was traveling around Europe at this time last year 3 When I was walking down the street 4 was talking to her boss, she couldn't take call 5 was washing the dishes when he arrived home 6 was playing soccer with his friends when the accident happened

UNIT 11

A 1 will be packing 2 will be teaching 3 Will, be using 4 will be visiting 5 will be studying 6 will be working 7 will be attending

B 1 will be fixing my computer 2 will be using a new cell phone 3 will be driving across the country

C 1 will be staying, until next month 2 will be sleeping 3 will be spending Christmas 4 will be waiting, when you arrive 5 will be studying, this summer vacation 6 will be having lunch 7 will be having, this time next year

D 1 will be going to college next spring 2 will be staying with us tonight 3 will be waiting for you over a cup of coffee 4 will be wearing a blue dress 5 tomorrow morning, it will be snowing outside 6 will be carrying more than 800 passengers 7 won't be studying while their teacher isn't

PART 4

UNIT 12

A 1 has lost 2 have used 3 has gone out 4 have lived 5 have had 6 have studied 7 have, put

B 1 I have been to Africa once. 2 He went to Canada two years ago. 3 The shop hasn't opened for business yet. 4 Someone broke a window yesterday. 5 She hasn't eaten anything for eight hours. 6 I had a lobster for the first time yesterday.

C 1 have you been to 2 have lived, since 2008 3 have left my identification card 4 have arrested a 17-year-old boy 5 have had many problems, so far 6 have spent, this month 7 emailed, two days ago, hasn't checked, yet

D 1 has never traveled abroad 2 I have lost mine 3 has just missed the train 4 have already had dinner 5 has had surgery three times since last year 6 have had noodles too many times this month 7 ordered the food, it hasn't come yet

UNIT 13

A 1 has been raining 2 have been receiving 3 have been arguing 4 have been working 5 has been cooking 6 has been watching

B 1 have been reading 2 has stolen 3 have watched 4 has been waiting 5 has been 6 has been doing

C 1 When did you start 2 have you collected so far 3 How long have you been staying 4 has thrown, away 5 has been seeing, since last year 6 has been working out 7 have been trying, for half an hour

D **1** has been putting on her make-up **2** have been helping senior citizens **3** has been working at the same company **4** have been teaching math and science **5** have been preparing the presentation for three hours **6** has been talking about a boring topic

UNIT 14

A **1** had already begun **2** had never been **3** had just had **4** had never had **5** had done **6** got **7** had already passed away **8** couldn't go **9** had never learned **10** had been thinking

B **1** had lost **2** had been cleaning **3** had been washing **4** had forgotten **5** had stopped **6** had worked **7** had been watching

C **1** had been snowing all night long **2** realized, had left **3** had been listening to, all day long **4** had been working well, went out **5** had never eaten, came to **6** had never had, became **7** had already had, didn't want

D **1** It had snowed a lot **2** had never talked to him **3** she had never been late **4** had been studying for three hours **5** had never experienced cold weather like that **6** The phone had been ringing for minutes

PART 5

UNIT 15

A **1** were **2** feet **3** was **4** thieves **5** Statistics **6** fish **7** Salmon

B **1** oases **2** matches **3** Shorts **4** phenomena **5** mice **6** series **7** glasses **8** parents

C **1** glasses **2** women live, men **3** Mathematics was **4** many fish, river **5** cows, goats, sheep **6** scissors, knives, children's **7** accident, accidents

D **1** have lost a pair of black socks **2** My sister always brushes her teeth **3** My uncle raises cows, goats and geese **4** My major is economics, my minor is politics **5** A flock of sheep was grazing peacefully **6** your sunglasses in the case **7** used binoculars to watch the birds at the top of the tree

UNIT 16

A **1** is melting **2** lies **3** valuables **4** doesn't matter **5** is produced **6** spoonfuls of sugar **7** is **8** is **9** is, is **10** is

B **1** furniture **2** shoes **3** arms **4** cocoa **5** mail, letter **6** sunlight, lights **7** clothing, dresses

C **1** meat is **2** English has **3** a cup of tea, coffee **4** courage was **5** Pepper is **6** Gas is, windows **7** women need, iron, babies

D **1** When the water starts to boil **2** realized that my luggage was missing **3** he finished up a glass of juice **4** flies when you have fun **5** I bought a bar of soap and a carton of milk **6** because I found a hair in my soup **7** didn't have much money, had only five dollars

UNIT 17

A **1** a three-year-old boy **2** few **3** shop **4** is **5** furniture **6** has **7** information

B **1** many competitors **2** many races **3** much sunlight **4** much time

C **1** a little sugar **2** little water **3** a few days off **4** few people

D **1** many stops is **2** have little doubt **3** don't have much time **4** in a few minutes **5** a number of celebrities visit **6** a large amount of time **7** Each student has to prepare

E **1** Taking too many drugs is **2** There are a few days left **3** There is plenty of cola in the refrigerator. **4** Each room in the hotel has a closet **5** How much discount, buy a large volume **6** Every child has different talents **7** paid little attention to the social status of women

UNIT 18

A **1** Hines' idea **2** The dog's tail **3** The boy's cap **4** James' behavior **5** the end of the story **6** three months' maternity leave **7** Last year's winner **8** the title of honorary professor **9** My grandparents' house **10** the patients' convenience

B **1** the dog's barking **2** the title of the song

3 Louis' puppy **4** Last Sunday's match **5** the boss' decision **6** Thursday's meeting

C **1** For tomorrow's party **2** the result of the game **3** in yesterday's newspaper **4** pay two months' rent **5** the girls' middle schools **6** paint my daughter's room **7** stay at her sister's house

D **1** apologize to you from the bottom of my heart **2** knows all of her students' names **3** knows the cause of the disease yet **4** two for the price of one at the store **5** My father's car is ten years old **6** A man is giving out next year's calendars **7** by pressing the buttons of the TV remote control

PART 6

UNIT 19

A **1** ×, × **2** a, a **3** a, × **4** an **5** a **6** A, an **7** × **8** an, a **9** a **10** a

B **1** an Einstein **2** so beautiful a dress **3** with dust **4** half an hour **5** an M.A. **6** a university **7** a king, in a big country

C **1** Sheep, horses feed **2** An octopus has **3** twice a month **4** Dolphins are **5** quite an expensive gift **6** Furniture plays an important role **7** needs a Steve Jobs

D **1** I want to build a house **2** The price of gold and oil went up **3** A girl was walking through the forest **4** to brush my teeth three times a day **5** has received a uniform, in the shop **6** a fried egg, a sausage and milk for breakfast

UNIT 20

A **1** the **2** the, the **3** the **4** the **5** the **6** the, the **7** The, the **8** ×, The, the **9** an, the

B **1** The largest ocean **2** the only hobby **3** movies, the movie **4** the guitar, an amateur rock band **5** France, Sweden, the north **6** a girl, The girl **7** the rich, the poor

C **1** The sun is **2** was listening to the radio **3** you finished the book **4** by the gram, by the kilogram **5** take the clothes on the table **6** the garbage, I'm doing the dishes

D **1** if I close the window **2** The injured were taken to the hospital **3** believed that the earth was not round **4** placed the stapler in the third drawer **5** leave their homework until the very last minute **6** traveled around France, the French were very kind

UNIT 21

A **1** × **2** × **3** × **4** × **5** ×, a **6** ×, × **7** ×, × **8** a, × **9** ×, ×, a, × **10** a, ×, an

B **1** Could you show me that skirt? **2** My mother prepared a special dinner for my birthday. **3** I'm meeting my mother in front of the church. **4** My family goes to church by car on Sundays. **5** It is hard for the young to find work these days. **6** He went to prison because he stole jewelry.

C **1** Accidents can happen **2** I like strawberries **3** an upset stomach, she skipped **4** is in bed, a fever with flu **5** a conference room in the hotel **6** Traffic is, to work by subway

D **1** He was playing basketball **2** enjoy having a light breakfast **3** is taking Linguistics 101 this semester **4** get along well, like water and oil **5** he was playing soccer, for a month **6** listening to the radio, like watching TV **7** stays in contact with her friends by email

PART 7

UNIT 22

A **1** Mine **2** yours **3** she **4** She **5** He **6** He **7** mine **8** we **9** They

B **1** yours **2** ours **3** her, her **4** us **5** They ours/mine **6** theirs **7** me, him

C **1** Can I borrow yours **2** change its strategy **3** I can't believe it **4** across from ours **5** wagging its tail **6** her boyfriend comforted her **7** He spent, his life

D **1** he hasn't changed a bit **2** she is on maternity leave **3** they can't ride a roller coaster **4** It will be the biggest in the world **5** I asked him to pick them up **6** it is nothing compared to hers **7** We use a bunk bed, she uses the lower bunk

UNIT 23

A **1** myself **2** herself **3** itself **4** himself **5** yourself **6** herself **7** itself **8** himself **9** themselves **10** ourselves

B **1** Take a seat here. Make yourself at home. **2** My daughter smiled at herself in the mirror. **3** The actress tried to kill herself because of her depression. **4** He devoted himself to taking care of his sick parents. **5** Please leave me alone. I can take care of myself. **6** My sister is on a diet, but she can't control herself around sweets.

C **1** students enjoyed themselves **2** I forced myself **3** he taught himself French **4** get myself a coat for this winter **5** not to hurt yourself **6** we decided to make one ourselves

D **1** Help yourself to the cookies **2** Sit down and make yourself at home **3** My mother burned herself **4** She is talking to herself for half an hour. **5** You should be ashamed of yourself **6** you taught yourself how to play the guitar **7** We can't finish this project by ourselves

UNIT 24

A **1** this **2** This **3** those **4** that **5** that **6** that **7** these

B **1** it **2** she **3** he, He **4** It **5** those **6** it, This

C **1** those in Korea **2** This one, that one **3** that of adults **4** those on the first floor **5** those of other women **6** these are not good **7** that of an amateur

D **1** is more beautiful than this **2** These are Siamese cats **3** Those jackets are my type **4** Who is that man over there **5** faster than those of other companies **6** These animals' intelligence is as high as that of humans. **7** This restaurant is more crowded than that one

UNIT 25

A **1** One, the other **2** another **3** Others **4** ones **5** One, another, the other

B **1** anyone **2** one's **3** it **4** One, the others

C **1** is not anybody **2** want nothing to eat **3** have no one

D **1** was no one upstairs **2** Will you try some **3** the others were, closed **4** eaten anything today **5** exchange it for another **6** nobody was injured **7** larger ones

E **1** you have nobody around you **2** the others were dozing off **3** no one is too old to learn **4** want a black scarf or a white one **5** Can you show me cheaper ones **6** One is an English teacher, the other is a pianist **7** Some people like sunny days, others like rainy days

UNIT 26

A **1** Every **2** either **3** all **4** neither **5** none **6** both **7** each

B **1** either **2** your money/the money **3** Both of them **4** question **5** none/nothing **6** has **7** is **8** liked **9** All **10** all

C **1** every three weeks **2** Either Henry or Brian **3** Neither of them **4** blind in both eyes **5** Each student has to choose **6** each end of a rope **7** thank all of you for coming

D **1** none of my business anymore **2** are parked on each side of the street **3** Every child will have a chance **4** Because neither of us had a car **5** we got nothing from our efforts **6** I walked with both hands in my pockets **7** I didn't like either of them

PART 8

UNIT 27

A **1** to lend **2** to take **3** to work **4** to go **5** to win

B **1** to solve **2** to take **3** to get/getting **4** to major **5** to go

C **1** where to get off **2** where to put **3** how to read **4** when to invite **5** how to cook

D **1** It can be very dangerous to drive on icy roads. **2** It is almost impossible to change his opinion. **3** It is difficult to admit one's mistake in front of others. **4** It is dangerous to walk around in this area at night. **5** whether to go to the party **6** what to do when their babies cry

E **1** how to deal with **2** afford to buy an apartment **3** decided to cram **4** which hotel to stay in **5** intend to make him upset **6** It, to learn a foreign language **7** It, to study abroad, want to send

UNIT 28

A **1** a perfect time to go on a trip **2** something to drink **3** someone to feed **4** a book to read **5** some milk to put **6** some clothes to wear

B **1** are to make a final decision **2** are to follow many rules in school **3** was to become a great artist **4** was to survive in the earthquake **5** are to go to a concert this evening **6** are to succeed in business

C **1** enough money to buy **2** anyone to go **3** any friends to borrow **4** a broom to sweep **5** a hotel to stay at/in **6** a plastic bag to put things in **7** her own room to spend time

D **1** it's time to say goodbye **2** is to be promoted to executive director **3** there's nothing to worry about **4** she didn't have anyone to rely on **5** was to become the president of the country **6** I have lots of heavy bags to carry **7** We don't have anything to eat

UNIT 29

A **1** to get **2** to be **3** to borrow **4** to donate **5** to hear

B **1** She cut down on food in order to lose weight. She cut down on food so as to lose weight. **2** He drove faster in order not to be late for the meeting. He drove faster so as not to be late for the meeting. **3** We took the subway in order not to waste time on the road. We took the subway so as not to waste time on the road. **4** I have to go to bed early in order to get up early tomorrow morning. I have to go to bed early so as to get up early tomorrow morning. **5** She drank some coffee in order to stay awake during the boring class. She drank some coffee so as to stay awake during the boring class.

C **1** were happy to go **2** as not to forget **3** to catch the last bus **4** to make him upset **5** shocked to hear **6** ready to grab the chance **7** tolerant to forgive

D **1** lived to be 90 years old **2** kind of you to help the old lady **3** need to work out regularly to stay healthy **4** careful with the oven so as not to burn yourself **5** lucky to have friends like you **6** My mother was very disappointed to know **7** to go to New York in order to be a world-famous fashion model

UNIT 30

A **1** for me **2** for you **3** of her **4** of you **5** of him

B **1** to be respected **2** to have already decided **3** to be finished **4** for you **5** for Koreans

C **1** It seems that **2** difficult to read **3** to have already gone abroad **4** silly of her not to follow **5** to have agreed with his idea

D **1** necessary for me to take **2** stupid of him to waste **3** easy to train **4** needs to be cleaned **5** brave of you to say no **6** seemed to have known **7** expect to finish

E **1** foolish of you to do **2** seems to have a lot of work to do **3** allowed me to take a trip **4** possible for him to arrive on time **5** seems to have failed his driving test **6** rude of her to have kept me waiting **7** expect him to be involved in

UNIT 31

A **1** washed **2** know **3** play/playing **4** to recharge

B **1** is too short to tie her hair in the back **2** so sick that she couldn't go to work this morning **3** so old that he can't take a long drive with it **4** too young to ride the rides in the amusement park

C **1** He is doing a part-time job so as to make money for tuition. He is doing a part-time job in order to make money for tuition. He is doing a part-time job so that he can make money for tuition. He is doing a part-time job in order that he can make money for tuition. **2** She ran as fast as she could so as not to be late for school. She ran as fast as she could in order not to be late for school. She ran as fast as she could so that she wouldn't be late for school. She ran as fast as she could in order that she wouldn't be late for school.

D 1 To tell the truth 2 To begin with 3 helped her do housework 4 made me take care of my brother 5 to make matters worse 6 saw a man jump over, run away 7 Strange to say

E 1 not to speak of her singing ability 2 not to mention his good looks 3 large enough for us to sleep in 4 To be honest with you 5 too fat to wear this red coat 6 let me know when you are ready to be interviewed

PART 9

UNIT 32

A 1 studying 2 changing 3 replying 4 Eating[To eat] 5 Walking[To walk] 6 attending 7 building[to build] 8 discussing

B 1 painting pictures 2 Eating instant noodles 3 playing mobile games 4 playing tennis with his friend every weekend 5 Working overtime all week long 6 spending time with her friends 7 learning Spanish and French

C 1 waiting room 2 Skipping breakfast, overeating 3 was afraid of saying 4 Drinking lots of water doesn't help 5 Not being stressed out is 6 meeting lots of people 7 are excited about having a picnic

D 1 denied stealing a hat 2 kept banging on the door 3 suggested going for a walk after lunch 4 The thought of traveling around the US made 5 decided to remodel our house instead of moving 6 gave up developing his career

UNIT 33

A 1 him[his] chatting during the group work in class 2 some parents[some parents'] letting their kids run around 3 my son[my son's] winning first prize

B 1 that she had lied to her parents 2 that they had broken up 3 that he had to pay for the dinner that day 4 that he found a new home for the abandoned dog

C 1 not having told you about this earlier 2 me[my] asking you your phone number 3 not having called you back immediately 4 you[your] having taken care of my kids for two days

D 1 like having ice cream 2 insisted on her buying 3 hates my[me] coming home 4 regret spending too much money 5 giving, to work 6 Taking pictures is not allowed 7 remember his[him] saying that

E 1 I'm sorry for not having paid 2 He didn't recall having met me 3 I was embarrassed about having made a big mistake 4 has avoided making eye contact with her mother 5 complain about not being understood by adults 6 I couldn't resist scratching the mosquito bites 7 were afraid of being punished for fighting with each other

UNIT 34

A 1 working 2 spreading 3 to attend 4 to quit 5 becoming 6 to escape 7 to get 8 buying

B 1 joining 2 to have 3 studying 4 smoking 5 to comply 6 to participate 7 hiring 8 getting 9 taking 10 to know

C 1 telling him 2 striking 3 causing great damage to the forest 4 to turn off the TV 5 booking the ticket 6 losing games 7 to study at the library

D 1 tell her to call 2 tried sniffing at 3 remember turning off the gas 4 stopped to send a text message 5 forgot to put 6 regret not apologizing to her 7 avoided mentioning his girlfriend

UNIT 35

A 1 mentioning 2 going 3 spending 4 skiing 5 concentrating 6 wearing 7 decorating 8 conducting 9 grading 10 playing

B 1 is no use regretting 2 is accustomed to staying awake 3 is poor at cooking 4 couldn't but laugh 5 prevents his children from going out

C 1 no use making excuses 2 couldn't help shouting 3 objected to moving 4 had trouble concentrating 5 looking forward to hearing

6 spend the weekend studying **7** didn't feel like going for a walk

D **1** is good at playing the violin **2** They were busy planning their trip. **3** are accustomed to getting up early **4** This project is worth taking part in **5** I got used to cleaning the house **6** never goes to bed without drinking warm milk **7** prevented the stray cat from coming into his home

PART 10

UNIT 36

A **1** was broken (by someone) **2** has been moved back (by them) **3** must be done about the problem (by you) **4** will be built for her in her native place (by them) **5** must be kept in a safe place (by you)

B **1** be protected **2** is included **3** be changed **4** be followed **5** be delayed **6** was unlocked **7** were taken

C **1** was seriously injured **2** was not invited **3** is being repaired **4** was arrested, by the police **5** has been canceled **6** will be discontinued **7** had been broken into

D **1** you have been admitted to university **2** must be replaced for your safety **3** will be announced next Monday **4** All the rooms of the hotel are already filled up. **5** the reference books cannot be checked out **6** The assignment must be finished by this Friday. **7** My grandmother's picture was found in the basement.

UNIT 37

A **1** was raised by my aunt in Daegu **2** hasn't been returned to the library yet (by Mary) **3** were passed to him (by me) **4** was bought for me by my parents **5** was taught English songs by my mother, were taught to me by my mother **6** was given another chance (by them), was given to me (by them)

B **1** was told to lock the door when I went out **2** was advised to study art in college **3** was made to do my homework by myself **4** was allowed to stay in Alicia's house **5** was asked to tell Lisa that he would be back in an hour **6** was helped by the student to go upstairs in the hospital **7** was seen playing with her friends in the playground

C **1** was told to wait **2** occurred, were killed **3** will be given to **4** was made to help **5** was persuaded to have an operation **6** was seen entering the theater **7** appeared around the corner, was, hit by

D **1** How much will it cost me to fix **2** resemble each other like twins **3** has been elected the president of her class **4** The mystery man disappeared into the crowd. **5** was shown to the customers before purchase **6** was brought to him by the TV commercial **7** wasn't allowed to sleep over at my friend's house

UNIT 38

A **1** in **2** from **3** with **4** to **5** at **6** to **7** of **8** with

B **1** must be carried out secretly **2** should be dealt with sincerely by the shop manager **3** was called off because of the rain (by them) **4** are taken care of by her mother while she is at work **5** was called in last night **6** was almost run over by a truck **7** was taken away by a tow truck

C **1** were frightened at **2** were involved in the accident **3** was crowded with people **4** was covered with snow **5** were passed out **6** was laughed at by everyone **7** am satisfied with, be disappointed with

D **1** These boots are made of genuine leather. **2** Test papers will be passed out in ten minutes. **3** he is interested in fine arts **4** Many health problems are associated with obesity. **5** School violence must be dealt with more seriously. **6** Education is closely related to our country's future. **7** are not prepared for global warming

THIS IS GRAMMAR

이것이 진화하는 New This Is Grammar다!

- 판에 박힌 형식적인 표현보다 원어민이 실제 일상 생활에서 바로 쓰는 생활 영문법
- 문어체뿐만 아니라 구어체 문법을 강조한 회화, 독해, 영작을 위한 실용 영문법
- 현지에서 더는 사용하지 않는 낡은 영문법 대신 시대의 흐름에 맞춘 현대 영문법

이 책의 특징

★ 실생활에서 쓰는 문장과 대화, 지문으로 구성된 예문 수록
★ 핵심 문법 포인트를 보기 쉽게 도식화 · 도표화하여 구성
★ 다양하고 유용한 연습문제 및 리뷰, 리뷰 플러스 문제 수록
★ 중 · 고등 내신에 꼭 등장하는 어법 포인트의 철저한 분석 및 총정리
★ 회화 · 독해 · 영작 실력 향상의 토대인 문법 지식의 체계적 설명

This Is Grammar (최신개정판) 시리즈

초급 1, 2 **기초 문법 강화 + 내신 대비**
예비 중학생과 초급자를 위해 영어의 기본적 구조인 형태, 의미, 용법 등을 소개하고, 다양한 연습문제를 제공하고 있다. Key Point에 문법의 핵심 사항을 한눈에 보기 쉽게 도식화·도표화하여 정리하였다.

중급 1, 2 **문법 요(Key Point) + 체계적 설명**
중·고등 내신에 꼭 등장하는 문법 포인트를 철저히 분석하여 이해 및 암기가 쉽도록 예문과 함께 문법을 요약해 놓았다. 중급자들이 체계적으로 영문법을 학습할 수 있도록 충분한 콘텐츠를 제공하고 있다.

고급 1, 2 **핵심 문법 설명 + 각종 수험 대비**
중·고급 영어 학습자들을 대상으로 내신, 토익, 토플, 텝스 등 각종 시험을 완벽 대비할 수 있도록 중요 문법 포인트를 분석, 정리하였다. 다양하고 진정성 있는 지문들을 통해 풍부한 배경지식을 함께 쌓을 수 있다.

www.nexusEDU.kr
넥서스 초·중·고등 사이트

www.nexusbook.com
넥서스 홈페이지

책에 대해 궁금한 사항은 넥서스에듀 홈페이지 1:1 고객상담 게시판을 이용하세요.